MW00415079

AND THEN WE
WORK FOR GOD

AND THEN WE WORK FOR GOD

Rural Sunni Islam in Western Turkey

KIMBERLY HART

STANFORD UNIVERSITY PRESS
STANFORD, CALIFORNIA

Stanford University Press
Stanford, California

©2013 by the Board of Trustees of the Leland Stanford Junior University.
All rights reserved.

This book has been published with the assistance of the Institute for Turkish Studies.

Printed in the United States of America on acid-free, archival-quality paper

Library of Congress Cataloging-in-Publication Data

Hart, Kimberly, 1967- author.
  And then we work for God : rural Sunni Islam in western Turkey / Kimberly Hart.
    pages cm
  Includes bibliographical references and index.
  ISBN 978-0-8047-8330-9 (cloth : alk. paper)--
  ISBN 978-0-8047-8660-7 (pbk. : alk. paper)
  1. Islam--Turkey--Customs and practices. 2. Islam and culture--Turkey. 3. Rural population--Turkey. 4. Turkey--Religious life and customs. I. Title.
  BP63.T8H27 2013
  297.8'109562--dc23   2013013864

  ISBN 978-0-8047-8668-3 (electronic)
Typeset by Bruce Lundquist in 10/14 Minion

For Michele Sutherland Boyle Hart, my mother

CONTENTS

Photographs follow page 140

ACKNOWLEDGMENTS

Many have helped me over the years in conducting research in Turkey, and I thank them all. Above all, I thank villagers in the Yuntdağ and their relatives who invited me into their homes in towns and cities in Turkey and Germany. I invoke the memory of Josephine Powell, who, until her death in 2007, helped me research in the villages of the Yuntdağ. I also thank Harald Böhmer for introducing me to the villagers in Kayalarca in 1998. Among friends and colleagues inside and out academia who specialize on Turkey and the Islamic world and beyond, who have helped and supported me in conversation, through email, and in the occasional shared space of the conference, I thank Bilge Taner, Nathalie Arnold, Şerife Atlıhan, Gracia Clark, Claudia Diehl, Markus Dressler, Can Erimtan, Beril, Murat, Selim, and Üner Eyuboğlu, Didier Fassin, Frances Gage, Michael Herzfeld, Damla Işik, Maureen Jackson, Susan Maguire, the late Murad Megalli, Vasiliki Neofontistos, Leyla Neyzi, Esra Özyürek, Steven Pierce, Deborah Reed-Danahay, Linda Robinson, Nazif Shahrani, Winnifred Sullivan, Anna Sun, Jeremy Walton, Jenny White, and Deniz Yükseker.

Delivering papers helped me focus the work through questions from the audience: in Istanbul at the American Research Institute in Turkey (ARIT); Koç University; and Istanbul Technical University; in Beer Sheva, Israel, at Ben Gurion University; in Trondheim, Norway, at the Norwegian University of Science and Technology; in Buffalo, New York, at SUNY Buffalo State and SUNY University at Buffalo; and in Princeton, New Jersey, at the Institute for Advanced Study. I also thank members of the seminars on secularism, led by Joan Scott; and on morality, led by Didier Fassin, at the Institute for Advanced Study during 2010–11. Funding sources supported research connected to this publication and include a Fulbright-Hays, grants from the Institute for Turkish Studies, the American Research Institute in Turkey, the Research Foundation at Buffalo State, and the Institute for Advanced Study.

Dean Severson at Buffalo State has been supportive of my research leaves, and I thank him for his help. I also thank my colleagues who have been generous in accommodating my work outside the classroom. I thank the editorial support from Stanford University Press for bringing this work to fruition. Finally, I thank my mother, Michele Hart, and grandfather, George Hart, for their continued support in all my academic efforts.

AND THEN WE
WORK FOR GOD

Map of Turkey

INTRODUCTION
Competing Claims to Religious Authority

I climb out from under a load of heavy quilts and pull on my *şalvar*, brightly colored baggy trousers made from cloth I bought in an open market in Manisa, sewn by a friend in the village. I tie my headscarf tightly around my face, knotting it on the top of my head. This way, my hair is protected from the dust and flies but more importantly, I show respect for women's Islamic clothing. I feel in context, ready to spend the day sitting on the floors of village homes, on layers of kilims woven for dowries decades ago or from machine-made textiles bought more recently. I spend my days in conversation with women over glasses of tea. They persuade me to add sugar as they tell me about the discipline of prayer, the cost of a sheep for the sacrifice holiday, their memories of Mecca while on pilgrimage, the rigors of the fast during Ramazan, and their children attending Qur'an schools. *Ezan*, the call to prayer, rings out from the mosque loudspeaker. We can hear the call in the next village faintly echo ours. They pause. Young women turn down the sound on the television. The older ones, who have no TV or simply are not immersed in it, fall silent. They listen. When the call is over, they whisper a prayer, wiping their hands down their faces, sighing deeply.

The mountainous Yuntdağ region in western Turkey is close to the big city of Manisa, only an hour away by bus, but far in spirit from the bustling urban world. In the city, open markets are a draw; students dominate the streets in their uniforms, mothers clothed in urban-style *mantos*,[1] or enveloping raincoats, and polyester headscarves watch over their children in playgrounds; tea gardens are filled with youths who spend hours flirting, playing with their cell phones; and Ottoman mosque complexes punctuate the landscape. Men sit outside the grand mosques, waiting for the call to prayer. Villagers enjoy these sights and activities of the city, which for them is a place to shop for weddings, a place where one attends high school, a destination for migration, and where the doctors are. In contrast, the village is where one is born and buried, wherever one dies. It is one's *memleket*, homeland. But, as villagers remind me, this—all the pleasures, pains, sources of boredom, and consternation—is an illusion, *yalan dünya*, literally, a world of lies. The real life is the next one, where we go after we die. This life is merely a prelude, a world filled with chores and tasks, which must be completed in preparation for that other world, the real one. I'm not sure I understand yalan dünya: "What does it mean?" I ask Çevriye, the woman I live with. She says, "It's like that person who said this or that, the thing I desire, what I want. This life, all our tears and things we find funny, it will all be gone."

What is Islam? For villagers, Islam is a path to the next world. This book is about how villagers in the western Anatolian region of the Yuntdağ prepare for this other world by "working for God" in this one. Though Islam is the path to the next world, the exact route is uncertain. No one knows, because only God can. Meanings are hidden, embedded in the Qur'an, and therefore require study and effort to be understood. As one man pointed out, "All the answers to every question are in the Qur'an, but it is not so easy to read or understand." And for this reason, there are debates about what is orthodox. What is the correct path and the procedures for following that path?

Villagers consider these debates through their practices, deriving from three sources: what I call cultural Islamic traditions, the state version of Islam delivered by the Diyanet İşleri Başkanlığı, the Presidency of Religious Affairs, or the Diyanet (as it will be referred to), and Islamic brotherhoods and communities. The mixture of sources for Sunni Islam shows that Islam itself is in a state of flux, open to interpretation and transformation. The multiple sources for Islamic practice create a contradiction in that people expect there to be one form of Islam. Despite the expectation that Islam should be fixed, religious tradition is living. Furthermore, Sunni Islam is under state control and meant to follow state-mandated rules. This is referred to as laicism. Thus, Islam, which is intended to address eternal questions, is contained within a secular one, a state, which has a temporal beginning and end. The state control of Sunni Islam creates a contradiction because Islam is meant to be the word of God and therefore timeless, perfect, and not tampered with by humans.

While villagers are careful to express their support for the state, they subtly critique state control of Islam by recounting memories of radical secularization policies of the early Republic, which thereby demonstrates how people tampered with Islam. Furthermore, by becoming involved with religious communities and brotherhoods, which work outside the Diyanet's control, they show that there are alternative sources for Islamic leadership, not only that created by the government.

In one regard, then, Islam, as it is considered within the context of worldly power, has multiple sources, is living, and is in a state of constant transformation because people are concerned about locating the true path. But from another perspective, Islam addresses questions which supersede this world. In this regard, men and women strive for a spiritual life, infused with meaning, relating to a temporal trajectory which stretches beyond that of the nation, this world, and addresses eternity. But because one's individual salvation is measured by the deeds one commits in this world, villagers strive to be attentive: caring for others, assisting the poor, guiding children, worrying about the fate of other Muslims, and more generally, showing interest in global humanity. Thus, Islam is both directed toward a reality superseding this life and deeply embedded within it. In managing this intersection between this world and the next, deeds are regarded as both spiritual and political acts because they change the world and affect one's standing in the next. While this orientation toward reality is simultaneously political and spiritual, none of the rural people discussed here is a member of an Islamist association (*dernek*), a brotherhood (*tarikat*), community (*cemaat*), or party. Thus, their interest in the politics of Islam or Islamist movements is different from people who are members of these groups. Due to the fact that villagers combine sources for Islamic practice from the state, cultural memory, and movements—they straddle a line between private piety as mandated by the state, collective traditional spirituality as remembered locally, and public religion, as formulated through the deprivatization of Islam in movements, in communities, and in brotherhoods. Because they do not belong to a distinct political or ideological group, but mix practices from different sources, their reflections on Islam and the competing array of Islamic brotherhoods, communities, and parties are more open-ended and thoughtful than rehearsed ideological statements by those who work to further the goals of their particular constituency.

Though thoughtful, their reflections on state power and the control of Islam, the work of communities and brotherhoods, Islamically based political parties, and the uncertain status of religious tradition are marked by anxiety. This anxiety points to their relationship to state power and their uncertainty about the path to the next world. They are fearful that words or deeds that critique the state will be interpreted as being against the state. Furthermore, because they engage with alternative Islamist groups, they are fearful that this will be regarded as an expression of resistance to state orthodoxy. Finally, because local Islamic traditions are built on imperfect and partial memories, people worry that these practices are not Islamic or are maybe even heretical. In fact, both the state representatives of Sunni Islam locally, that is, their imams, and the leaders of Islamic communities, such as female *hocas* from the Süleymancı community, are critical of traditional Islamic practices.[2] Thus, villagers express uncertainty about whether they are on the correct path and how God will judge them. As one elderly woman explained, "We say our prayers, but who knows what will happen? I am afraid."

I ask, "Afraid of what?"

She replies, "Of going to hell!"

"But," I respond, "you have done everything: prayers, fasting, charity, sacrifice . . ."

"But we will not know until we read the door of our tomb if God will forgive us."

What she is afraid of are her sins, of having committed, perhaps without realizing, heretical acts. Villagers work to increase the numbers of good deeds they perform for others and God so they can outweigh their sins, as these will be assessed on the Judgment Day. The accumulation of good deeds requires constant effort. Though one man said when I asked him what they do during the month of Ramazan, "We work for God," I found that villagers spend most moments paying attention to God's interests. These require not only the five daily prayers, a month of fasting, correct physical comportment, attention to structures of authority, and efforts to read the Qur'an, but innumerable verbal expressions which show that human action is ordered by a framework based on God's will. They thereby cultivate a state of constant attention to God's authority in shaping every imaginable thing. Nothing can be done, for example, without evoking God's will, *inşallah*. While sitting with an elderly man, I mentioned that I would go to Manisa the next day. He quickly corrected me, lifting his finger in instruction, "İnşallah!"

While God wields the ultimate authority in shaping whether one will be able to act, others do as well. Power is structured hierarchically among people in this world: male over female, age over youth, state over the citizen, and God over all. While one invokes God's will when framing the desire for action, one asks for permission, *izin*, from those senior to oneself when seeking the right to do something. That is, the authority to take action on an individual level is not understood as a rational claim. And those who act individualistically are critiqued for their hubris, as I was when I announced my intention to go somewhere on my own without requiring anyone's permission, not even God's will. Even if one conforms to these layers of authority, one is never entirely certain that one will be able to act or if one's actions are undergirded by the "right" (*hak*) to act.

Despite the insistence that Islam is about exact laws governing behavior, structuring authority, making everything possible, as three men urged me to accept and thereby see the peculiar discrepancies in Christianity, there is always some uncertainty about these rules, rights, and authorities who legitimize them. Achieving an understanding of what is correct requires study; ultimately, if one perseveres, knowledge is possible. For this reason, villagers praise individuals who *pek biliyor*, know a lot. But not everyone, as a middle-aged man expressed to me, can take the time or has the patience and resolve to study Arabic and read the texts. A lack of understanding, then, is due to human limitations, the concealed messages in the Qur'an, and the uncertainty about the legitimacy of those who claim authority from God to structure their power controlling others' actions.

As I trace in this book, anxieties about the correctness of practice, orthopraxy, underline the configurations of power, which are used to confine and categorize Islamic practices as correct or incorrect, orthodox or heterodox, religious or irrelevant. As such, the discourses of power and authority which underscore rural anxieties gesture to Asad's insistence that it is "not the mind that moved spontaneously to religious truth, but power that created the conditions for experiencing that truth."[3] The study of orthodoxy and orthopraxy, in other words, has to be ethnographic, not limited to textual analysis of doctrine. Though a heretical statement from the perspective of the people in this book, I argue that orthodoxy is created through dialogue, practice, and engagement with cultural memory, as well as through state power and God's plan.

Villagers and townspeople described here do not experience "religion" as an abstract set of principles that they "believe," but as a complex of practices and activities expressing domains of power in which they engage. I do not pretend to define or explain all aspects of what can be thought of as Islamic, but only a selection of those activities I could observe and that villagers would discuss. Any misunderstandings about the veracity of practice are entirely my own.

Often, rural people such as those in this book are treated by urban Islamists as an underclass of traditionally pious or religiously unconscious, uneducated Muslims. The people in this study are in part traditionally pious, meaning that many of their Islamic practices are deeply rooted locally. Because debates about orthodoxy inform many decisions about local practice, I use the phrase *cultural rituals* to describe practices unconnected to Islam, such as wedding music and dance, while *culturally Islamic rituals* is the phrase used for such practices as the Mevlut, a prayer service commemorating Muhammed's birth and show-ing the hair of the Prophet (Sakal-ı Şerif); these practices are connected to Islam but are contested by purifying movements which eschew veneration of the Prophet's body. Though I employ the idea of tradition, I do not use it with the understanding that it relates to a fixed set of practices from the past, but to local practices, many of which have changed, some of which are relatively new, but all of which are treated as not as serious or important as those which involve the Qur'an as a foundation of doctrinal knowledge and ritual action. Cultural Islamic traditions often are led by women, which tends to further dis-credit their spiritual efficacy in the eyes of others.

Cultural traditions in the sense I just described are visible and public but are not the expression of a re-Islamization of society, or as Jose Casanova describes, a deprivatization of religion.[4] The deprivatization of religion refers to how re-ligion has shifted from being private and personal as ideally shaped through secularization policies, to becoming, once again, public and a meaningful basis for shaping social roles, duties, and action. Though many activists would like religion to return to an (imagined) condition prior to secularization as the lived, collective, legal foundation of the social world, it is now employed po-litically and deliberately, self-conscious of the intrinsic power of its evocation.[5]

Depending on how they are defined, cultural Islamic rituals are not typically regarded as a demonstration of the self-conscious Islamicization of society, but Islamic scholarship and training is. Imams trained by the state or by other re-ligious communities come from this region and become leaders of their own congregations in villages, towns, and cities, in Turkey and abroad. Furthermore, men and women strive to improve their standards of Islamic knowledge by learning to read the Qur'an, often with local imams, official and unofficial. An additional demonstration of the deliberate and self-conscious reconfiguration of Islam locally is in how, since the 1960s, villagers have been making judgments about cultural traditions and replacing them with Islamic cultural practices. These actions are signs of an attempt to purify practices, and they come from local religious authorities, rather than from a group, as Kristen Ghodsee describes for a town in Bulgaria.[6] Thus villagers are part of the purifying movements that have reshaped Sunni Islam into a more standardized global practice.

A number of ethnographers explore the implications and effects of Islamist movements in different parts of the world—Ghodsee in Bulgaria; Samuli Schielke,[7] Saba Mahmood,[8] and Amira Mittermaier in Egypt;[9] Mandana Limbert in Oman;[10] and Dorothea Schultz in Mali.[11] In this book, I focus on the transnational connections between Turkey and Germany because this is where my research took me. In this regard Berna Turam,[12] as well as Ahmet Yükleyen,[13] demonstrate the importance of further international connections between pious Sunni Turks in central Asia and western Europe.

In addition to involvement with the state formulation of Sunni Islam and local cultural Islamic traditions, villagers are engaged with religious communities or brotherhoods, also called neo-tarikats, which have raised their level of conscious involvement in Islam. These groups are engaged in a deprivatization of Islam, the result of the rise of public Islam, that is, politically motivated Islamist movements that counter elite Kemalism, the ideological movement that legitimizes the nation of Turkey and its republic, founded in 1923.

As well as describing religious life in villages and transnational connections to Germany, I discuss villagers' decisions to migrate. Many of the young people I knew in the early phases of my fieldwork in 2000–2001, later decided to move and settle in Manisa or Izmir. By considering their lives in these new places, I show that they understand the stakes of involvement with secularism, the deprivatization of Islam, and Islamist movements, in a way unusual for their relatives in the villages. Because Islam was never made private in the rural world, through state-mandated secularization policies, and therefore has not undergone a deprivatization process, villagers who migrate experience a different social geography of piety. When they move, they often make choices about whether to take on a public Islamist stance or a secularist one in which Islam becomes a personal and private practice. Thus, the movement from village to city often involves existential questions confronting the nature of secularity and Islam. This causes those who make this move to make choices about their own worldview.

By demonstrating the social geography of piety, this book challenges the rural-urban distinction in categorizing religious practice and critiques the easy dismissal of rural Muslims by urban Islamists, secularists, and scholars who overlook how Sunni Islam is experienced by people living in different areas of the country. As Asef Bayat suggests,[14] there is something urban about Islamist movements, but I would add that there is something rural about them as well. Olivier Roy, Dale Eickelman, and James Piscatori all argue that people become involved in purifying movements after they migrate because migration has created a sense of cultural alienation, which purified religion addresses.[15] Here, I describe how rural people are involved in purifying movements in their home regions, whether they migrate or not. I am not arguing against Roy, Eickelman, and Piscatori's important insights into global Islamic movements, but pointing out that villages are not isolated from Islamic cultural transformations.

The distance which Islamists often emphasize between their purified practices and those in villages demonstrates their efforts to create a layer of social distinction between rural and urban piety. This distinction draws upon temporal associations between cities and villages, in that villages are widely dismissed as "backward," living in a different era, whereas cities are modern, engaged with the present and shaping the future. This distinction resembles the one made between Islamists and Kemalists (often confusingly referred to as secularists). Muslims involved in purified Islamic movements and politicized Islamists align themselves against Kemalists in a counterhegemonic political movement in cities. But Kemalists often charge that Muslims, regardless of their ideological stripes, are backward and are working to drag Turkey out of modernity and into the dark ages. Islamists, then, to gain greater prestige, work to strip any association with rural Islam. They work to match the westernizing, secularizing, and modernizing claims of Kemalists with purified Islam, demonstrating its engagement with modernity, religious freedom, and human rights. These categories of time and cultural progress are ideological weapons in a political battle for state power and economic domination.

It is important to make a distinction between this battleground and the meaning of rural spirituality. In a kin-based rural community, with a collective sense of the past, Islam, as we find in Reinhold Loeffler's work on an Iranian village,[16] and in Magnus Marsden's on a town in Pakistan,[17] is a living and evolving body of practice. I am primarily interested in learning to interpret the traces of history in the patterns of everyday life. In this regard, this book adds a historical dimension to studies of rural Islam to show that rural people are engaged with social change, the state, and political configurations of power. I have been especially influenced by Erik Mueggler's work on a village in China,[18] and

by Margaret Paxson's on a village in Russia.[19] Both have expanded my understanding of rural experiences of social change caused by state policies. Turkey,
like Russia and China, experienced major cultural revolutions during the twentieth century. While all three countries enforced policies of rapid economic
change, modernization, and secularization, Turkey did not eliminate religion.
Instead, early policies of the Republic attempted to contain and control Islam
and thereby create a private space of individual belief and practice.

While the Turkish state implemented policies of radical secularization,
modernization, and westernization in the early twentieth century, after the
1980 coup, religion became a useful source in new policies for reformulating
an ethnic and sectarian national identity, that of being a Sunni Turk. These
later state policies, therefore, invested in the wealth of cultural memory to create a sense of national unity. Not surprisingly, religion has played an important role in China and Russia in re-creating a sense of national identity based
in cultural memory. Thereby, after secularization or policies of state atheism
were adjusted, religion was reappropriated for cultural and moral ends.[20] In
Turkey, the state deprivatization of Islam in the 1980s facilitated the establishment or the reemergence of numerous Islamically oriented foundations
and associations, creating a gray zone in laicism. Though these groups were
registered legally, they were not under the control of the Diyanet. Villagers
have not yet caught up with the fact that groups, which were once illegal, have
entered into the gray zone of legality in the post-1980-coup era. It is for this
reason that many are uncertain about them.[21] Villagers react to these groups,
the state, and their own local cultural practices as they reflect on their spiritual
lives. Their involvement with Sunni Islam is not, therefore, a private and personal matter or even a matter of tradition, but it is inflected with local and national history, political ideologies, camps of power and control, and domains
of influence, some local, others national, and many global.

THE RURAL YUNTDAĞ

Lifting a branch wedged into the wire gate, I pushed it open and stumbled onto
the path leading to Ayşe *nene*'s (grandmother's) house. Walking past the stone
fireplace where we fried dough as a good deed (*hayır*) for the week of her husband's mourning ten years ago, and stepping onto the spot where her son had cut
the throat of the sheep she sacrificed for Kurban Bayramı, the Sacrifice holiday,
that year, I continued to the staircase leading to her tiny house, a single room

with a small anteroom. The doves in the fig tree cooed, in the distance a donkey brayed, a cow lowed in reply, somewhere a cat screeched, and a van zipped around the bend in the curve of the road from the neighboring village of Yeniyurt. Ezan, the call to prayer, started with an unpleasant electronic noise, as the broadcast system from the central mosque in Manisa made its connection. The professional tones of "Allahu Akbar" began as I stuck my head into the low doorway, slipping off my sandals. When I called out, "Hello," Ayşe replied from inside her house. My bare feet pressed the cool stone floor, past her spinning wheel. The neat balls of finely spun yarn showed the fruits of her recent labors. With a hand on the carved wooden door painted green, I entered the room.

She was sitting cross-legged on layers of floor cushions and blankets by the windowsill, her prayer beads beside her, listening to religious hymns on the radio. Ayşe nene greeted me and said we would have tea, but first she needed to pray. I sat on one of the low cushions, adjusting my şalvar, and pulled out my notebooks to reflect on the conversations I had had that day as she got up to perform the *aptes*, or ritual wash before prayer. Water trickled from the spigot into the low stone platform in the anteroom. Ayşe nene returned, her headscarf flipped up, showing wet skin. Running a towel around her neck, she dried herself and retied her cotton scarf. Praying in the room where I sat, her whispered prayers and creaking joints were punctuated by the loud ticking of the clock hung on a nail from one of the beams forming the ceiling of the room.

Afterward, Ayşe made tea and we talked about heaven and hell, the need for prayer, and the impossibility of knowing one's fate. She reflected on her son, the former director of the carpet-weaving cooperative, who had died five years earlier from cancer. "Why," she asked, "did she continue, elderly and tired, making do each day, when he had been young and vibrant?" For the elderly, reflections on life often lead to discussions about the need to perform duties, questions of one's fate, and the incomprehensible mystery of life itself. She had performed the pilgrimage to Mecca decades earlier with her husband, their trip funded by their son's success. Reflecting on her life, she suddenly announced that she would "burn in hell," because she could read neither the old nor new alphabets. Startled, I made some noises of assurance, which she waved away. She felt that the radically secular state policies of her childhood, under the İnönü regime (1938–50), had damned her.

Sitting with Ayşe nene, I thought, not only about the everyday importance of piety and practice, but about the stakes involved, and about her family and the range of experiences she and all the people discussed in this book have as

Sunni Muslims. Though her children and grandchildren shared her thoughts on fate, they looked to their futures differently, seeking spiritual legitimacy in diverse ways. The neoliberal context of the post-1980 military coup d'état and the development of public forms of Islam had changed the playing field. One son argued that state control of religion was essential to prevent terrorists from organizing in divergent and secretive groups. In a similar vein, a granddaughter showed me the stamp the Diyanet put on all its Qur'ans, so that one would know, she said, that it is "real." A grandson was studying at an Imam Hatip school in Manisa, a public school combining a secular curriculum with Qur'anic study. There was hope he might become an imam.

Yet, support of the state version of Islam and laicism is not the only path they followed. One of Ayşe nene's granddaughters and I attended a festival outside the village of Recepli, to venerate a holy man, a newly minted saint, Muhammed Zühdü,[22] who, she said, had turned into a bird each day to fly to Mecca for the morning prayer and returned afterward to his village. She described how Muhammed Zühdü communicated with people from his grave, one of the reasons why people visited his tomb each year to participate in a communal prayer service with a feast for the community. The Diyanet administers neither the tomb nor the mosque; the organization is registered as an association, and is thereby a civic organization with a spiritual bent. But for villagers in the region, it is a holy site that allows them to express fellowship and practice venerating a local and very new Sunni saint. Two years earlier, with one of Ayşe's daughters, a woman in her sixties, I attended a women's celebration for the holy man associated with the neighboring village's mountaintop. We enjoyed the Mevlut, a prayer service commemorating the Prophet's birth, under the shade of a massive oak tree. The women read sonorously in Ottoman from texts they had preserved from their ancestors, and we gathered a bagful of sweets from the event to share with people in Kayalarca. This event also had no ties to state Islam. In fact, women are often involved in practices that are dismissed as heterodox by those who follow official Islam and as heretical by those involved in objectifying Islamist movements and brotherhoods. But they are meaningful spiritually and locally, invoking cultural memory and religious doctrine in texts.

In addition to involvement with culturally Islamic practice, legally tolerated religious brotherhoods also played a role in Ayşe's family. A grandson had married a quiet woman who had studied the Qur'an and basic principles of Islamic ritual and morality for a year with the Süleymancı community at a boarding school in a provincial town near Manisa. They had celebrated the engagement and wedding rituals with sermons delivered by a female *hoca* (meaning a teacher or preacher). Both the boarding school and the work of the female preacher fall outside the state definition of Islamic authority and knowledge. The grandson made it clear that he thought of music and dance as sinful, and thus he expressed an opinion common among Islamists, who believe these experiences diminish self-control and therefore lead to sin. In contrast to this view, there are those who dabble in a form of secularism that places worship in the private sphere and allows youth a margin of freedom from the rigors of devout practice. Though still too young to know for sure what path she would take, this man's sister wanted me to photograph her in her secular high school uniform in coquettish poses. In the distance, a man observing the event mirthfully called out, "Are those pictures for your boyfriend!?" In the process of making representations of herself in a secular high school uniform, worn in a government school in the city, her head uncovered, and physically demonstrating a flirtatious attitude, she resembled a number of other village girls. As many elderly people critically noted, all these girls who achieved a high school education married outside the village and assumed a secular lifestyle. Education, then, is an important focus of this book because it inculcates a secular or Islamist worldview.

This brief look at a few members of Ayşe's family demonstrates the diversity in approaches to religious authority and dimensions of spiritual transformation, including reverence for the Ottoman past, evident in rural Turkey today. While some support laicism, others sustain Islamic traditions from the past. Some prefer the cleansed and objectified practices from religious communities, while others seek a secular world, in which Islamic practice is a private, individual affair, separated from the more public aspects of life. People combine approaches and experiment, depending on their spiritual needs and stages in their lives. They are not expressing narrowly defined ideological positions, as one might conclude is the case among people in Turkey because of the prevailing discourse of bifurcated identities, secular and Islamic, about which one can be lectured in towns and cities in the most casual of settings.

How did I find myself in the Yuntdağ region, a mountainous area north of Manisa, conducting ethnographic fieldwork? As a doctoral student, I had studied the DOBAG (Doğal Boya Araştırma ve Geliştirme Projesi, or the Natural Dye Research and Development) project. Harald Böhmer and Josephine Powell, two expatriates living in Istanbul, who founded the project during the 1980s, introduced me to Kayalarca village. As I wrote on the cooperative and the transformations in rural life relating to it, however, I repeatedly was distracted by Islamic practice, which I had experienced in the village from 1998 to 2001. Before entering the fray of the job market, I was able to make return visits in 2002, 2003, and 2004. Upon finding a job at Buffalo State College in 2007, I began studying Islamic practice during the summer of 2008, and, with support from my institution and some grants, I extended this research from July to December 2009. I returned in 2010 for a month. My inquiries into Islam were informed by my interests in cultural transformation, memory, and systems of social categorization. I did not inquire into theological debates or particular doctrines, but considered the role of Turkish laicism in relation to rural spiritual practices and the possibility that both local memory and political transformation had informed the manner in which rural people create a pious space separate from secular worldviews and Islamist ones associated with urban life. While, during my early research, I found the villagers to be slightly uninterested in discussing the cooperative—especially because they were flooded with researchers, journalists, documentary filmmakers, and tourists—they were very interested in discussing Islam. In fieldwork, I settled on a system of writing quick notes while discussing topics with people. I found people to dislike tape recorders, and for this reason my material is not in the form of transcribed conversation. I regret this because many villagers have a charmingly direct and emotive style of speech, which I am unable to fully capture. To collect information in interviews, I typically use two notebooks. One contains the questions and topics I am exploring at a particular time and the second is used for writing individual responses. I keep both open on my lap as I sit with someone in conversation, usually on the floor. My notes are written in a chaotic mixture of Turkish and English. On rare occasions, I was able to write long descriptions of events in English as they transpired. I spent each evening writing up the day's conversations, interviews, and experiences. In the morning I reviewed these and considered whom I would visit next. As I researched, I selected a topic and explored it by visiting as many people as possible until the answers I got led me to a new question. This means I asked many people the same questions, and because news of my topics of interest spread quickly, villagers often knew what I was interested in before I arrived at their houses. I generalize in the text by often describing individuals as "villagers," because responses coalesced in agreement among a large number of people. Being in a village meant I could easily visit people without making appointments. Women, the main focus of my interest, were often at home and willing to converse with me while they were doing housework or weaving. I also interviewed men, especially those who had studied with the Süleymancıs, at government Imam Hatip high schools, or had become imams. I visited them in their houses, accompanied by their wives, in mosques, or by daring to visit the coffeehouses, the domain of men. They were remarkably tolerant of my efforts to talk to them. During 2009, I worked in sets of three weeks in the villages and then returned to Istanbul to consider what I had learned and to explore these same practices in Istanbul or other cities, such as Konya, before returning to the villages for another stint of three weeks. I also regularly visited a particular town in the Balikesir region, which I call Tepeli, where a village woman had married, thereby meeting new people to talk to, and I often visited Manisa, where many villagers had migrated. I followed the research where it took me, as far as Bamberg, Germany, where I spent two weeks on separate visits in 2009 and 2010. I have changed village place names and those of informants.

COMPETING CLAIMS TO RELIGIOUS AUTHORITY

In making decisions about what kind of life to have, villagers in western Turkey explore the remembered and forgotten, state-based and transnational, and gendered sources of Islamic authority. The region where these villages are located, the Yuntdağ, north of Manisa and south of Bergama, is known among carpet dealers and textile experts for a women's carpet-weaving cooperative based in Kayalarca village. Locally, the area is regarded as a bastion of formerly nomadic, Yörük people, who maintain a residual nomadic economy, making cheese, herding on a small scale, and visiting the city of Manisa to shop in the big markets and gather goods for marriage. The Yuntdağ, in other words, is not regarded internationally or locally as a hotbed of Islamic activism.

From the perspective of Manisa, the mixtures of spiritual practices rooted in cultural, state, and new Islamic movements are unremarkable. Indeed, people in Manisa engage in similar practices—one of the reasons why so many villagers comfortably migrate to the city and commute between the two. Yet, rural places provide a different perspective on engagements with the meaning and purpose of the state's secularization program through the production of laicism. By considering villager perspectives of this process, I shift the focus of the many debates and discussions about secularism and Islam in urban Turkey to rural communities, which have their own histories and legacies of spiritual practice. Communities are not composed of people who choose piety on an individual basis, but of collectives, connected to each other, across multiple generations, with a particular local rendition of the past, which relates to how Islam is understood and practiced. Members of these communities address and debate the meaning, goals, and purposes of laicism, the statist goal of producing a secular society, as well as newer alternatives, such as an Islamist future, in which Islam is wrested from state control, and alternative communities, brotherhoods can practice openly. They also consider cultural Islamic rituals and whether they should continue these.

All the people I met in the region identified themselves as Sunni Muslims. Americans find it surprising, when I discuss my research, that no villagers professed atheism or openly disagreed with their fellow villagers about the nature of God's interest in their lives. Though I describe many debates and discussions in this book, none involved people who refused to identify as Muslims or who would rather have joined a different religious tradition. Rather, the most significant disagreement was about who was the better, more devout, more knowledgeable Sunni Muslim. Turkish people often ask me about the ethnic and sectarian makeup of the villages. Though all the villagers I studied present themselves as Sunni Muslim Turks, there is evidence of greater mixture, of Kurds, Alevi, Yörüks, and Greeks who lived in the region in the past. These are details which often are unmentioned because people identify as Turks.

In both villages, Yeniyurt and Kayalarca, exploration of forms of Sunni Islam gives rise to debates on state authority, spiritual efficacy, the nature of orthodoxy, and the role of culture and memory. Through an examination of these diverse legitimations to practice, I argue that women and men are involved in distinctly different forms of Islam because the Diyanet mediates their orientation toward the state and its interest and ability in providing spiritual resources for them. State productions of orthodoxy are gendered and skewed toward men's needs. Men find the mosque and thereby the state's official Islam a home for their practice; but women, who avoid the mosque, locate spirituality in places and times outside the mosque—the Ottoman past in Yeniyurt or neo-Islamist future in Kayalarca—and thereby outside the state control of Islam.

The social geography and coherency of rural communities creates a different field of vision for the future, past, and present. The ideological machine of progressive modernity, discussed in the next chapter, implemented through state policies, weighs less heavily on rural people. In part this is due to the late arrival of public education in the region, the villagers' ability to live without full engagement with wage labor and the monetized economy, and the ideological construction of rural spaces as premodern. The state project of modernization, secularization, and westernization was implicit ideologically and explicit geographically as urban in design.[23] While cities were made according to plan, villages were mostly ignored because state officials—secularist elites—imagined modernity as an urban project. Geographically, then, villages are constructed to be and actually are a bit distant from centers of power and authority.

Being a villager has become an existential question, rather than a fact of existence. Leaving is a choice, but staying is as well. Those on the fence debate the benefits of living in rural areas where spaces are encoded as "domestic" and shared among villagers who are "the same" (i.e., homogeneous, that is, Sunni Turks, not Alevi or Kurdish). Rural spaces are more relaxed because villagers assume everyone is engaged in the same pious and moral project. This assumption has distinct benefits for women, who can walk from village to village, visit freely, and move about without needing to fully cover (i.e., wear a manto). They always, however, wear headscarves. In addition, many men and women note that in the cities, relationships are negotiated through money, whereas in the rural regions it is possible to live without full-time employment. Though socioeconomic differences exist in rural areas, villagers promote ideals of social egalitarianism. They expect fellow villagers to have the same material resources and opportunities, though this is not in fact the case. High ideals of social egalitarianism contrast with their experiences of city life and city people, whether secularist or Islamist, as devoted to self-promotion through an engagement with fashionable commodities and professions.

Though some argue that rural life has distinct benefits, others point to drawbacks. Young parents argue that Manisa, the nearest city, has jobs for men, markets, schools, and health care resources. These are reasons for leaving. By making migration a choice not only of where to live but who to be, villagers face existential questions about themselves, their identities and their futures, as well as about the lenses through which they choose to view and interpret the past. Rather than coherent and isolated socially and geographically, villages are more fluid, ideologically constructed spaces. They are also, however, imagined by many villagers and urban people to be insulated, morally, socially, and geographically. Thus, rural life is not always regarded positively.

KAYALARCA-YENIYURT DIALECTIC

Yeniyurt and Kayalarca villages, a mere kilometer apart, differ significantly in forms of Islamic practice. The difference relates to how each village locates spiritual legitimacy and authority temporally. Over Yeniyurt looms Kaplandağı, a mountaintop where a holy man from the Ottoman era once lived. Not to be outdone, Kayalarca village's crown of rock cliffs is also associated with a holy man, one who has largely been forgotten. That villagers in Yeniyurt would continue to remember their holy man while those in Kayalarca would have forgotten theirs is no accident. The villagers in Yeniyurt deliberately sustain old and traditional practices, taking pride in their active memories. Kayalarca villagers scorn this attitude, saying it is backward-minded. In Kayalarca, people work to erase the past and forget cultural traditions.

The two villages represent two paths to modernization and secularization available to Sunni villages and peoples within the ethno-national narrative of the Turkish state. One path, Yeniyurt's, includes a sustained cultural connection to the Ottoman Empire, Islamic devotion, and disciplined study, features which translate well to achievement in secular education and the professions, including that of being an imam. The other path, Kayalarca's, focuses on innovation—in both the economic and spiritual spheres. The female villagers have allowed neo-tarikats, especially the Süleymancı community, to influence their spiritual activities, and women have been instrumental in economic development and the commercialization of a heritage product, carpets, for the international market in a cooperative. Men in Kayalarca, like those in Yeniyurt, abide by the state's construction of Islam as located in the mosque, but few of them at the time of this study, in comparison to village men in Yeniyurt, have achieved success in the professions, such as imam.

Yeniyurt is the larger of the two villages, with a population of about five hundred. Kayalarca's population is in decline, as more families migrate to Manisa, but there are still about three hundred people in the village. The people of Yeniyurt recall where they had once lived on two different *yayla*s (pastures) during the Ottoman Empire. That is, the village is composed of two migrating groups, probably clans or descent groups of different Yörük and Türkmen tribes, which merged together and moved further upslope. The name of the village underscores its newness because *yeni* means new. Some claim that Greeks once inhabited their village. Looking at the surface effects of the village, there are no material indications that Greek Christians lived in Yeniyurt. The old houses are similar to those in Kayalarca, simple stone constructions with flat earthen roofs or newly tiled ones, which resemble solidified tents in their interior use of space. Though precise evidence of former Greek occupation is hard to come by, one supporting indication is the remarkable grapes cultivated in tiny vineyards by both villages. An older man from Kayalarca claimed that

Greeks had once made wine from the grapes they now use to make *pekmez*, grape molasses. The historical records, written in Ottoman and located in Ankara, have been out of my reach,[24] but it would not be surprising if the Ottoman government had encouraged or required nomads to occupy a permanent place, as the imperial government settled migrating groups and moved them to control taxation and conscription.[25]

The villagers from Yeniyurt refer to themselves as "Yörük." As Halil Inalcık writes, the term *yörük* has a complex origin. ". . . 'Yürük' was originally an administrative word commonly used for nomads of various origins who arrived in Ottoman controlled lands during the 14th and 15th centuries and who over time had appropriated this name for themselves."[26] The term does not indicate a coherent ethnic, linguistic, or religious group, but a subsistence strategy, nomadic pastoralism. The term is often confused with an ethnic one, as Kasaba argues,[27] and in some ways, the villagers interpret it as such because those in Kayalarca deny being Yörük, saying, rather, that they are "Turks"—an expression of patriotic allegiance to the state.

In Yeniyurt, memories connecting people to the past are active. For example, material culture demonstrates a sustained link in the form of small shepherds' bags called *torba* and flat weaves, overwarp reverse tapestry, *cicim*s, referred to as *kilim*s throughout the villages. While a few elderly women in Yeniyurt make kilims for the cooperative, it is notable that none in Kayalarca do; instead they make carpets. Due to the technical differences between cicims and carpets, the former involve the reproduction of traditional designs while the latter provide a freer surface for the innovation of patterns—and also their simplification. Though cooperative dealers regard both carpets and kilims as cultural heritage, the structure of kilims transmits cultural memory through the exact reproduction of designs, whereas carpets do not. Thus, in the material culture, the weavers in Yeniyurt actively pass on the skills needed to create torba and kilims. Those in Kayalarca have ceased to make these designs and produce carpets on order by dealers, experimenting more freely with design. Comparing the cultural value of these two kinds of textiles, furthermore, shows how deep the different orientations to the past are in the villages. Yeniyurt weavers value the traditional kilim patterns and pass them down to the next generation relatively intact, whereas because the production of traditional material culture is not valued in Kayalarca in the same way, the skills to create kilims have not been passed down. Instead weavers pursue innovation, especially pleasing to customers, such as the addition of small pictures like cats or looms in carpet patterns.

In terms of Islam, villagers in Yeniyurt are oriented toward tradition. This tradition is grounded in relationship with state configurations of Sunni Islam, both from the Ottoman and republican governments and from cultural memory. These villagers proudly recount miraculous tales about the founder of their Ottoman-era *medrese*, or Islamic school (these were all closed in 1925), preserve and read Ottoman texts, recall the legacy of preachers who settled in their village from the Black Sea region. They also tell stories of a saintly figure, a hermit who was told by God in his dreams to travel from Central Anatolia to their mountaintop. These memories and practices, which would be regarded as heterodox by purifying Islamist movements, do not diminish their respect for the state construction of Sunni Islam through government administrations, the office of the caliphate during the Ottoman era, and the republican Diyanet. Their interest in official Islam is also evident in the "countless" imams and religious teachers who have come out of the village.

In addition to Yeniyurt's rich sense of its own history, women are involved in rituals that draw on Ottoman texts, the veneration of local saintly figures, and in the men's and women's practice of Sakal-ı Şerif. Women and men in Yeniyurt, in other words, maintain "cultural traditions" associated with Islam. Their interest in recalling and sustaining memory of the distant past is unusual in view of their neighbors and co-nationalists, many of whom have worked to eliminate the past in a state project to westernize, modernize, and secularize government, law, and society, starting in the early twentieth century, or to purify Islam in Islamist movements. However, a new view of the Ottoman past is sweeping the country among the devout, referred to as Neo-Ottomanism.[28] This imaginative rendition of the Ottoman past locates an era before secularization as a historically legitimizing foundation to new political and public forms of Islam. This new trend makes Yeniyurt's particular regard for the Ottoman past very current, though their neighbors in Kayalarca believe it to be evidence of their backward viewpoint.

The people in Kayalarca see themselves as looking to the future. Though the carpet-weaving cooperative commodifies a heritage product, clearly a link to a nomadic past, the villagers emphasize that it is a commercial not a cultural undertaking. Harald Böhmer, a German chemist, founded the cooperative. He became interested in plant dyes used in older Anatolian textiles. By testing fibers from these textiles, he was able to identify the plants used to make them and create easy-to-use recipes for the dyes. He and his wife traveled to villages in Anatolia, where they taught villagers to dye their wool using plants. He hoped that new weavings using these plant-dyed fibers would help villagers earn money. Seeing that weavers needed more assistance in selling their products, he established the DOBAG project in Ayvacık, a market town near the western Aegean coast. Later, he and Josephine Powell, an American photographer, amateur ethnographer, and textile collector, founded the Yuntdağ cooperative in the early 1980s, as a women's cooperative, the oldest one in the country.

The cooperative benefited from a neoliberal softening of the state-run economy after 1980. The government supported industries, which brought in foreign currency, and for this reason the cooperatives were only allowed to sell their textiles abroad. Through work in the cooperative and also because a road was built around the same time connecting them to Manisa, villagers improved their material conditions. But as I learned in a survey of households in 2004, families do not earn their main source of income from weaving. Families who have administrative roles in the cooperative or are dyers, however, have earned significant amounts. Though not earning the most money, weavers often note that weaving is a better way to earn money than the alternative: field labor.

Kayalarca villagers have worked hard to improve their living conditions as they earned money. As Harald Böhmer often noted, one of the first improvements villagers made was to replace their flat earthen roofs with pitched tiled ones. Trousseaux, once composed of handwoven textiles and meager household goods, were now filled with pots, pans, furniture, bedding, and masses of decorative goods, far outstripping in quantity what their parents or grandparents ever enjoyed. By 2005, the village created a water system through collective labor, linking households to pipes that brought water. When I first began my fieldwork in 1998, villagers seemed to never eat chicken or have sweets. Now, the addition of a chicken from time to time and enjoying ice cream is routine. Meat (beef and lamb) is still only eaten for special occasions and during the month of Kurban. By 2009, women had begun to abandon making their own bread; instead they purchase white bread from the market, bread once despised and derided as unhealthy, unwholesome, and a symbol of womanly laziness. Now, having white bread instead of sour dough is "normal," and women no longer talk about the moral "impossibility" of relying on market bread for this dietary staple. Villagers have also purchased washing machines, televisions, cell phones, and satellite dishes. As media was privatized in the 1990s and consumers throughout the country enjoyed these new sources of information and entertainment, villagers were not left behind. Now villagers enjoy watching dozens of television channels, including Kanal 7 and Samanyolu, two

Islamically oriented networks, the latter owned by the Gülen movement. By 2009, many households had begun to buy computers and get Internet connections. These resources are enjoyed by the children, primarily, who surf the Web, join Facebook, consume pop culture, and post photos of themselves, their relatives, and the village online, tagging each other, like other children and teenagers around the world. I should point out that villagers in Yeniyurt also have begun to enjoy the same material comforts as those in Kayalarca. In addition to all the labors that villagers engage in to earn money, field labor, cultivating grapes and olives, selling milk from sheep and cows, and working in cheese workshops, they have exported their children as imams, religion teachers, and members of other professions, such as police.

As such, village life has undergone radical transformations since the 1980s. In Kayalarca, these transformations are, in part, due to the efforts in establishing and running the cooperative but also interest in other forms of entrepreneurship. The biggest effect of the enterprise has been the change in how Kayalarca villagers view themselves. Looking at the amounts weavers earned shows that they could not sustain a household single-handedly through women's labor—weavers earn little—but villagers, through the daily rational engagement in quantifying and connecting their work with the benefits they receive in monetary terms, transformed their self-perception. As I discuss elsewhere,[29] weavers who once viewed themselves as lucky peasants who had found a way to sell carpets now view themselves as underpaid employees who do not receive the same benefits as men performing comparable labor in factories in the city. In contrast, Yeniyurt villagers sustained a cultural link to a rich past of Islamic scholarship, a path they continue to follow when they seek a better life for themselves and their children.

The fact that the villagers in Kayalarca allowed foreigners to transform the local economy demonstrates their relaxed and open attitude toward influences coming from the outside. In Yeniyurt, villagers point out that they do not need foreigners to succeed, and for this reason their village feels more closed to outsiders.

Also, unlike their neighbors in Yeniyurt, Kayalarca villagers do not link themselves to the material culture of the nomadic past. Though the homes of the elderly are furnished with handwoven goods, just as those in Yeniyurt, villagers in Kayalarca react strongly to the notion that these are markers of "tradition," calling this tendency *müzelik*. Müzelik, as the term is used by villagers, refers to the objectification and fetishization of material goods as cultural and historical markers of identity, which have been uprooted from their former context and placed in museums. Unfortunately, by running a carpet-weaving cooperative that draws on the notion of tradition and heritage, the question of cultural authenticity constantly brings up the issue of the past, its meaning and implementation, because dealers and carpet tourists remind villagers of this, expecting an authentically "traditional" village experience.[30] Villagers in Kayalarca find this embarrassing because it demonstrates a connection to the past, something they are eager to let be forgotten. They would prefer to be seen as savvy businesspeople. In addition to ignoring the material cultural connections to a nomadic past, the villagers in Kayalarca also have no memory of one. This may be due to being one of the oldest villages in the Yuntdağ, according to some amateur Ottoman historians, high school history teachers in Manisa who said they had read the archives before they were transferred to Ankara.

Recall that, in Yeniyurt, villagers openly described their roots as Yörük. I asked many in Kayalarca in the early stages of fieldwork in 2000 whether they were Yörük, and many claimed that the Yörük are somewhere else. Others considered the possibility that they may have been Yörük in the past, but now were Turks. The suggestion of difference, of being Yörük, troubled their sense of loyalty to the nation. All agreed that the question of Yörük identity was hidden in the deep recesses of the past and not worth dredging up. But the notion of a nomadic identity was strategically employed when rug tourists and dealers came to the village. This underscores that Kayalarca villagers refer to a nomadic past when they know that nomadism heightens the romance of woven carpets for customers; they are savvy businesspeople. The fact that they sustained the cooperative despite the problem it raises vis-à-vis heritage, identity, and the past, shows their interest in innovating and doing well financially.

The same disregard for cultural heritage and eagerness to cast off memory and replace it with new practices relates to how the female villagers in Kayalarca treat Islam. They want to cleanse Islamic rituals of cultural practices that appear backward and underclass from the stance of the modernizing, secularizing state, and sinful from the standpoint of modernist Islamist movements. Though the orientation to the past is fraught with anxiety, the future is less so. The villagers in Kayalarca allow innovation in Islamic practice, such as women visiting graves during Arife Günü, the last day of the holy month of Ramazan, and allowing Islamic associations or tarikats to enter the village for special occasions, engagement and marriage parties.[31] Children are also sent to Süleymancı Qur'an schools. In contrast, Yeniyurt is utterly closed to the influence of these

groups and Yeniyurt villagers disapprove of the innovations that Kayalarca
women engage in. They do not send their children to Qur'an schools run by
tarikats but to state-run Imam Hatip schools.

Despite these differences, the two villages share a Sunni identity, patriotic *in common*
dedication to the nation-state, and an uncritical merging of Turkish ethno-
national and Sunni Islamic identities, as is common throughout the country
among Sunni Muslims who were taught in school according to the Turkish-
Islamic Synthesis. They consume similar forms of media, which are the product
of the privatization of the media, which resulted in a proliferation of independent broadcast channels beginning in the 1990s. Their villages are also similar
in physical layout, house construction, and a lack of reference to republican nationalism. Neither, for instance, has a "square" with an Atatürk statue, though
there is one at the two elementary schools.

Like most people who are very close culturally and geographically and who
compete for resources, including spiritual authority and legitimacy, the villagers in Kayalarca and Yeniyurt fight over land, vineyards, and pastures, as well
as doctrine, cultural memory, and worldview. Both villages have many who
migrated to Manisa and both have kin who migrated abroad, some as workers,
in the case of villagers from Kayalarca, or as imams, as is the case with villagers
from Yeniyurt. Looking at the lives of villagers in these two dialectically opposed but intertwined villages, neighbors, enemies, relatives, and in some cases
friends, reveals the broader complications for locating sources of religious authority and legitimacy for Sunni Turks through ideas of the past.

An examination of two small communities will lead us to consider the political history of Turkey in the twentieth century. This is a story of how ideologies of modernity, secularity, and westernization were used by the state to create
a certain kind of person, one expected to emerge as a result of state policies.
Instead, different kinds of people emerged in the decades of struggle, coups,
new ideologies, and globalized media. Today, some work to revitalize Islamic
practice in public urban spaces, some sustain cultural traditions of spirituality
in rural and urban places, and others seek a life that separates worship from
public life. That is, the reality is of plurality, even if the ideology is of singularity.

There are many books on Islamic movements and ethnographic case studies of Muslims in Turkey. Cihan Tuğal,[32] Yael Navaro-Yashin,[33] Jenny White,[34]
and Nilüfer Göle,[35] all focus on Islamist movements and developments in
Istanbul; Esra Özyürek on secular Kemalists.[36] I learned a great deal from reading these studies, but also frequently have reflected on the fact that there is

more to the story of Turkey's unfinished and much-contested modernization, secularization, and westernization program happening beyond the geographic center of the former empire, as Michael Meeker also argues.[37] It is not merely the dearth of books on rural and provincial Anatolia, and indeed the other big cities, but the Istanbul-centric assumption—usually unacknowledged and untested—that the city is the relevant location of all study. In fact, Istanbul may be an exception, though the saying goes, "Istanbul demek, Türkiye demek [Istanbul means Turkey]." That is, the city is a remarkable and special place. Its unique position in the nation needs deeper interrogation. Here I respond simply by asking: what about other places?

1 SECULAR TIME
AND THE INDIVIDUAL

THE REPUBLIC

An overview of the history of the Republic during the twentieth century high-lights the relationship between the state and Sunni Islam. Through an examination of this relationship, I will show how Sunni Islam was contained and controlled by the state in what is referred to as laicism (government control of religion). As I trace three of the most important moments in this history, the Atatürk revolution, the 1950 election, and the post-1980 coup, I discuss how unstable and intertwined with political ideologies this relationship between the nature and meaning of secularity and Sunni Islam has been. By considering this history, I can then compare it to how villagers understand time, the nation, and Islam.

The first era under consideration is the transition between the Ottoman Empire and the Turkish Republic. The Ottoman Empire fought on the side of Germany during World War I. After its defeat, its vast territories were occupied by victorious European powers, the Allies, many of whom had an interest in the religious minorities, especially in Christians, who had an emergent sense of national identity as Greek, Georgian, and Armenian. The War of Independence, led by Mustafa Kemal (who later took the last name Atatürk), was fought against this occupation by Europeans. There was widespread dread over the anticipated dismemberment of the remaining Anatolian heart of the former Empire.[1] The ensuing triumph of the national army was remarkable, considering their state of exhaustion following decades of war and epidemics.

Many Turks, like the villagers, consider this victory a miracle. They refer to the fallen as martyrs, *şehitler*. As is evident in descriptions of journeys that villagers make to Çanakkale, where Mustafa Kemal was a general in the battle at Gallipoli against the Allies in World War I, this location is treated as a place of pilgrimage. For instance, when asking a woman to list the important tombs one can visit in Turkey, she mentioned the cemeteries at Çanakkale alongside the Mevlana's tomb in Konya. To further justify the sacred nature of the site, another woman explained to me that they do not visit the cemeteries of *gavurs* (infidels), only those of Turks. This battle, then, is understood as one between Muslim Turks and Western Christians.

Many other Muslim citizens also conceptualize this late Ottoman era in religious terms, as I realized while visiting a packed temporary museum in a tent by the New Mosque in Istanbul in 2012. People crowding over glass cases treated the artifacts of the battle excavated in Çanakkale as religious relics, viewing fragments of uniform, shoes, weaponry, and soldiers' personal effects with hushed reverence. Interestingly, by treating this battle and its relics as sacred, they legitimize Atatürk's leadership as an Ottoman military leader. This imbues his later leadership in the War of Independence with spiritual import, as if the nation were predestined. They thereby create a foundation of continuity between the sacred nature of the Ottoman and republican states and legitimize Atatürk's role as a *gazi*, a holy warrior, who was victorious against infidels. Thus, pious people understand the state from its inception, as founded by a gazi (as the Empire was as well), in sacralizing terms. This is regardless of the fact that the Republic was founded as a secular state, one which was based on laws constructed by people (imported from the Swiss legal code), not God.[2] This means that for some there is either a refusal to recognize the full import of secularization, which includes the privatization of religion,[3] or that this never happened and instead of experiencing a rupture with the Republic, they choose to see continuity with the Ottoman past.

The Republic was founded in 1923 and Mustafa Kemal became its prime minister. He commanded immense power and was able to introduce a series of secularizing, modernizing, and westernizing programs, aimed to utterly transform society or actually re-create it, since the remnants of the former Ottoman life were in disarray. In addition to these reforms changing law, language, the way people dressed, and education, the people of Anatolia were managed through a population exchange with Greece; millions of ethnic Turks who had been living in Greece migrated to Turkey, and concomitantly millions of Ottoman Greeks migrated from Anatolia. Meanwhile, Ottoman Muslims migrated

from the Balkan territories. The government settled many in villages in western
Anatolia, where they continue to retain a sense of their former Balkan identities. Many millions emigrated—Armenians, Jews, and Georgians—as it became
clear that the population would be reconstructed by the state as being composed of ethnically homogenous Turks. People would either have to conform
to this idea, concealing their former identities, or leave. Thus, the composition
of the population changed substantially from being, in contemporary language,
multiethnic and multisectarian, to being composed primarily of Turkish Sunni
Muslims, many of whom were immigrants.

unified

Substantial numbers of Alevis and Kurds, indigenous to Anatolia, remained. The Alevis are a Shi'i-related Islamic group that venerates Ali and that
does not use mosques for worship, fast, or pray five times a day. They include
music and dance in their key ritual of the Cem, and they do not seclude women
or forbid drinking alcohol. Kurds are ethnically different from Turks, being
Indo-European. They are Muslim, either Alevi or Sunni, but have been systematically discriminated against as ethnically and linguistically different.[4]

Through the founding ethno-national idea, that of being a Turk, this era
ushered in a vigorous sense of national identity, creating the foundation of a
new world, and fighting off divisive forces from within and without. The indivisibility of the state and the homogenous nature of its people are core concepts
in Turkish nationalism. Groups which threaten the indivisibility of the state,
such as religious and ethnic others, are regarded as threatening to national
unity. Since the 1990s, this era has been reexamined, reinterpreted, and reprocessed by scholars and through books on minorities; in Kurdish, Sephardic,
and other folk music; in films and television shows exploring the Ottoman Empire; and in museum exhibits. A new understanding of the Ottoman Empire
and a notion of a reconstituted multiethnic society are being actualized, but it
has been long and hard in coming.

For our purposes, of special interest is the caliphate, once the worldwide
seat of Islamic authority. Atatürk disbanded this office in 1924 and the Diyanet
was established, taking over some of this previous office's roles. But because
religious schools, communities, and shariat courts, which controlled domestic issues of marriage, divorce, and inheritance, were also disbanded, the role
of the Diyanet was significantly modified from that of the previous Ottoman
administration. Islamic practice, without courts or communities, and allowing only state-controlled training, was truncated and contained by the secular
government. The aim was to restructure what it meant to be Muslim, making

why?

religion an individual private practice but one regulated by the state. Thus, a Muslim was meant to become an individual believer who practiced under the leadership of state officials who were bound by civil law. This was a radical departure from the worldview of the Empire, in which the individual Muslim was bound by laws from God interpreted and administered by Islamic legal scholars, the *ulema*, whose power was legitimized by their spiritual knowledge.

In the Republic, the authority to rule was secularized and the spiritual tasks of the Diyanet functioned within the secular framework of state control. Sunni Islam was thereby managed by a government office. State employees hired to lead prayer, imams, would not have the power to make legal decisions, to legally marry people, or to determine issues regarding inheritance, for instance. This institutional framework for Turkish Sunni Islam, one which produces secular law in secular time, and which encompasses what predates the state, Islam itself, is called laicism, drawing upon but not reproducing the French model. As Elizabeth Hurd argues, "Laicism insists upon a singular and universal set of relations between sacred and profane dimensions of existence that holds regardless of cultural or historical circumstances. This is achieved in part through exclusionary practices that represent Islam as antimodern, irrational, and tyrannical."[5]

Confusingly, laicism is often translated as "secularism," without qualification. In fact, Turkey's legacy of state control of Sunni Islam is different from the American form of secularism, in which the government theoretically cannot establish religion, as outlined in the First Amendment, and from French laicism, in which the government claims to protect citizens from the intrusion of religion in public life in order to protect the unity of the nation.[6] In Turkey, the government protects itself from the intrusion of Islam in its institutions, by containing and pacifying religion within one of its ministries. In so doing, the government shields itself from unruly Muslims and attempts to pacify them by making illegal forms of Islam which exist outside state controls. Thus, in Turkey, the secular state creates Sunni orthodoxy and puts a stamp of legality on it. As Jeremy Walton demonstrates, the contradictory and uneasy relationship the secular state has to the production of religious orthodoxy is not only a contradiction but a source of dispute and debate among Muslims.[7] These debates are a subject of this book.

As Esra Özyürek argues, political debates about the meaning and purpose of a Kemalist worldview and an Islamic one are mediated through the deployment of historical eras: Ottoman, republican, Neo-Ottoman, and their conceptual foundations: Islamic, secular rationalist, and spiritual.[8] Cultural memory, therefore, is a battleground in which political positions about the meaning of the past are used in the present and projected into an uncertain future.

If Sunni Muslims have trouble swallowing the total control of Islam by the state, what do non-Sunni Muslims and non-Muslims do? In Turkey, non-Sunni Muslims are by and large the Alevi, a Shiʻi-related, Anatolian-specific community, often dismissed by Sunni Muslims as not "really" Muslims at all. Others, minority religious communities, Jews and Christians, have a tenuous position within the state system and for this reason they are reluctant to draw too much attention to themselves.[9]

In short, the laicist state creates an official Sunni orthodoxy by funding and running mosques, disseminating sermons, and training imams. These institutional controls make Islam "into a religion,"[10] marginalizing and privatizing it, codifying and controlling it. Because Sunni Islam is made by the state, it follows that Islam is de facto secularized—contained within state institutions. Through the institutionalization of religious practice, the orthodox subject is created through the discipline of the body (prayer and other actions), putting that body into a temporal and spatial frame where Mecca is the center but where the Turkish state has a shadowy presence. The Diyanet extends its jurisdiction over the meaning, role, and purpose of Turkish Sunni Islam by working among Turkish immigrants abroad. The Diyanet İşleri Türk Islam Birliği (DITIB; the Türkisch-Islamische Union der Anstalt für Religion e.V., or the Turkish Islamic Union for the Institution of Religion), for instance, in Germany, is a branch of the Turkish Presidency of Religious Affairs, which appoints imams from Turkey to work in mosques for four years serving Turkish migrant communities. In this way, being a Sunni Muslim is an expression of a national identity, connected to expressions of citizenship and related to the negotiation of immigrant identities abroad.

Villagers in the Yuntdağ, argue that the Diyanet is the descendant of the Ottoman office of the caliphate, thereby suggesting a connection between the republican control of Sunni Islam and the Ottoman one. Rather than seeing the laicist containment of Islam within a secular state, many praise Atatürk for replicating Ottoman structures in the Republic. They consider the authoritarian control of religion important to the maintenance of order. In a contradictory fashion, though villagers see continuity between the Ottoman administrative structures of Sunni Islam and republican ones, they are critically wary of the early republican reforms, which included disbanding the caliphate, changing the script from Arabic to Latin, transforming the calendar, replacing Ottoman and Islamic legal codes with ones imported from Europe, revolutionizing headgear for men, discouraging the wearing of headscarves for women, putting the call to prayer in Turkish (during the early decades), forbidding the teaching of the Qur'an to children during the difficult early years of the Republic, eliminating unofficial imams, closing saints' tombs and brotherhoods, eliminating Islamic schools (medrese), and replacing these with secular education and so on.[11]

They note backpedaling on some policies before the first democratic election in 1950, twelve years after Atatürk's death, including the reopening of saints' tombs, the introduction of religion classes in public schools, training for imams, the return to the call to prayer in Arabic, and support for making the pilgrimage. Villagers' assessment of this early history is contradictory, based as it is on a primary understanding of continuity rather than disjuncture between the two governments. Many are quick to assert the legitimacy of the state, but also make critical note of past actions, which controlled the role of Islam in daily life. On the other hand, though villagers critique some early reforms, they praise Atatürk for controlling unruly Islam. That is, Islam, from their view, should be purified by state control but not to the extent that Islam itself is changed. This means that there is an essence of Islam, orthodoxy, which many expect the state should protect, such as certifying that Qur'ans are "real" via a Diyanet stamp in each book. They therefore do not always interpret laicism as the state production of orthodoxy, as Walton argued, but as the governmental protection of orthodoxy.

The fact that it is illegal to criticize Atatürk makes it difficult for people to say that Atatürk's secularizing policies were detrimental to Islam itself. Instead, many look to İnönü, Atatürk's successor, as the one who caused problems. Atatürk died in 1938. The law protecting speech about Atatürk was passed in 1951, after the 1950 first multiparty election, a time when Atatürk's legacy was being reevaluated, especially in the provinces.[12] Rather than open a space for discussion and reflection, the state nervously closed the lid on this discourse. Villagers demonstrate their fear of voicing illegal or "wrong" (yanlış) opinions. Many of the contradictory statements people make about their view of secularizing reforms and the role of the state in controlling Sunni Islam come from a fear that they will be interpreted as having said something against the state or against Atatürk's legacy.

Why was Sunni Islam regarded as such a threat that it needed to be controlled by a state institution? Islam in the Empire, in both its official capacity within the institutions and in its decentralized, mystical form among brotherhoods (tarikats), had posed a threat in the newly laicized, nation-state of the Republic. In the Ottoman era, Islamic brotherhoods and other Islamic orders were not only powerful, but they had important roles in provincial cities and

towns less tied to the imperial center, Istanbul. They decentralized religious authority. Furthermore, brotherhoods were involved in revolts and uprisings before and after the establishment of the Republic, creating alternative networks
of political power.[13] The main fear was of alternative political organizations,
which would undermine the state, as well as pluralistic sources of religious authority which would decentralize Islam.

Though Atatürk successfully changed social, governmental, legal, and linguistic life in the Anatolian remnant of the former Empire, the political power of
Muslim leaders and Islamic brotherhoods never completely vanished. Most went
underground.[14] Despite the closure of all religious orders, tarikats, new groups,
the exact definition of which is now contested, variously called tarikats (brotherhoods) or neo-tarikats, Islamically oriented civil-society associations (dernek),
or Islamic communities (cemaat), developed within the Republic, often building on former Ottoman communities. Some, like the Nurcus, reformulated
themselves within the context of the Republic, where the state project of modernity with its emphasis on positivistic science, rationality, and progressive
modernity inspired them to argue that Islam was a source of modern science.
An offshoot of the Nurcus, the Gülen movement, led by Fethullah Gülen, who
is in semi-exile in the United States, is a global religious community that uses
schools, dormitories, media outlets, and businesses as platforms for the dissemi-
nation of its ideological interpretation of Turkish Sunni Islam. Others, like the
Süleymancı community, emerged during the early years of the Republic in reaction to secularization policies. The Süleymancı community is important in the
villages I study, more so than Gülen, although Gülen is admired by rural people
for his message of global humanitarian brotherhood and many watch his television channel called Samanyolu (the Milky Way). Overall, Gülen's movement has
less influence in rural regions because this movement cultivates wealthy, urban
Muslims, and creates a powerful upper middle class of Islamists in urban areas.
The Süleymancıs, in contrast, reach out to rural and poor Muslims.

Turkey emerged from many decades of difficulty after the establishment
of the Republic. There was an urgent need to build infrastructure, to create a
sense of common identity in a region fraught with traumatic memories of the
recent past, of war, depopulation, and repopulation. During Atatürk's lifetime,
the Cumhuriyet Halk Partisi (CHP; Republican People's Party) ruled without significant opposition, due to Atatürk's charismatic legacy. After Atatürk's
death in 1938, his successor, Inönü, opened the opportunity for Turkey to seize
upon a real multiparty democracy. Inönü's generous allowance of political

multiplicity caused the CHP to lose the 1950 election. Many of the supporters of the Demokrat Partisi (DP; Democratic Party), the party which won, were provincial and rural Muslim voters. The result of this election showed that provincial and rural Anatolians did not strongly support Kemalist policies which suppressed Islam.[15] In particular, rural and provincial Anatolians did not support secularism, specifically a form of secularism that is against religion and attempts to privatize it through government mandate. It is not that voters were unpatriotic: they wanted both Islam and a strong nation, similar to what they experienced during the Ottoman era. With the change in government in 1950, radical secularization policies were relaxed. Infrastructural changes, like roads, drew villagers closer to cities, prompting mass rural-urban migration.

This is one of the most significant stories of the Republic in the twentieth century: mass migration, which completely transformed the urban centers and emptied out villages, especially those with little viable economic life. With mass migration came economic and political change, and the development of a cultural ethos called *arabesk*. Though often used to exclusively refer to a musical style, arabesk culture expresses cultural loss and social alienation resulting from rapid economic change, mass rural-urban migration, and a perceived collapse or confusion in morals.[16] Arabesk made its mark in mass media expressions, in music and cinema. It is disliked by secularists for being degenerate and by Islamists for blaming God for one's bad fate.[17] Though arabesk cultural expressions seem old-fashioned and quaint in the big cities of Turkey now, village youth continue to be inspired by this era, the music, movie stars, their style and sorrowful expressions of cultural loss, hopeless love, sin, and moral confusion. For instance, young villagers post songs by Orhan Gencebay like his great hit, "Batsın bu Dünya" (Let This World End), from YouTube and use photographs of these musicians and movie stars to identify themselves on Facebook. It would seem through their continued engagement with arabesk cultural forms that they feel that the (imagined) piety, rigorous discipline, and comforting references to rural life are crumbling into a state of moral chaos and cultural loss. A primary focus of this emotional ethos is unattainable, hopeless love.

THE VILLAGE

The early republican reforms were meant to transform Ottoman state and society into something, which looked like and eventually would become a westernized, modern, secular society. That is, visible demonstrations of modernity have been key to how people perceive social progress. Through the introduction of westernizing values, traditional society was expected to become a modern progressive society, which looked western. Implicitly, this new society would be constructed on notions of social evolutionary progress leading to the development of "civilization." This new world was imagined as urban, with modern forms of transportation, factories, electricity, communication technologies, wide boulevards, rows of official buildings housing new government institutions, public parks, statues depicting great leaders, and museums, where the former world would be housed in display cases, safely divorced from former contexts.[18]

Though reverence for the state and the nation was privatized and personalized by secular Kemalists,[19] many citizens never fully accepted this vision of a progressive secular modernity and were marginalized economically, socially, and politically. In fact, the geographic edges of the big cities, including the illegal settlements or *gecekondu*s, provincial towns, and villages, became the margins of progressive urban modernity and those living in them regarded as behind the times, trapped by tradition or backward (*geri kafalı*). Urban settlers like villagers saw themselves, in contrast, as experiencing a world in which people loved and looked out for each other, fulfilled meaningful social roles defined by gender and age, and practiced Islam. For this reason, arabesk expressions are so poignant for villagers, because they point to a lost world in which Islam created social meaning.

Kadioğlu points out an interesting paradox: "While originally, the Kemalist project was based on a split between the modern and traditional cultures, its very success diminished the physical distance between these two cultures. As a result of massive international migration, big metropoles became the very location where the modern and traditional cultures found themselves in a position to coexist."[20]

A piece of evidence for the degree of anxiety that this mixture causes is the common complaint in Istanbul, as voiced to me by an enraged cabdriver gesturing toward pedestrians jumping into the fray of traffic trying to cross the busy street, clearly rural in their dress, "they have made Istanbul into a village!" "They" being migrants, primarily, or anyone deemed "other" Islamists, poor people, and so on. It seemed especially telling that the cabdriver, a frequent motif in arabesk film as an intermediary to the rural world, identified himself with the elite Istanbul natives. Villagers would see this scene very differently: poor people, down on their luck and exhausted, struggling to cross a street where people encased in expensive vehicles heartlessly prevent them from crossing. That is, the city has become a world peopled by gavurs.

If cities are expected to be "modern" though they are filled with people who do not look modern, what is the village? "The village" is a screen upon which imaginative metaphors of national belonging and identity, as well as revulsion and disgust, coalesce. In the national imaginary, the village is a morally and socially pristine location of true ethno-national identity,[21] a backward hell of ignorance and dirt, a place filled with superstition, a nostalgically and sadly remembered homeland lost to the bulldozers of modernity, and a place of real piety and true faith. These contradictions are fodder for countless films and television programs about villagers migrating to cities, where they lose their innocence to loose women, conniving conmen, and cold relatives. Rurality, in other words, remains a politically charged category of being, one understood to be at odds with urbanity, due to differences in "culture" and "civilization" on the one hand and morality and sociality on the other.

Villages are actual places, of course, not merely imaginary motifs for constructing stereotypes or the material for movies and heartrending arabesk songs, blank screens onto which nationalists can project racist and culturalist ideologies, or a curse used in anger to disparage folk one does not like, such as the "the uncivilized." Villages are the smallest social units recognized by the state; they are run by an elected headman (*muhtar*) and overseen by a council of elders or managers. Though both men and women vote, men run villages. Villages manage on few resources and often draw upon collective labor to achieve projects, called *imece*, such as the construction of water systems. They are cohesive social units, both actually and ideologically, in which members are devoted to the collective welfare of the whole. While some villagers complain about the suffocating social atmosphere in which everyone knows everyone else's business, many villagers praise how rural life allows one to be disengaged from the monetized economy. These are places where people feel a sense of collective solidarity, are somewhat removed from the pressures of employment and money, but are also neglected by the state in the lack of basic services, such as schools, water and sewage systems, and health care. For some these characteristics translate into a life free from the constraints of money, and for others they translate into too much distance from the excitement and sustenance of the city.

At the inception of the Republic, the population was predominantly rural. Beginning in the mid-twentieth century, the distribution and concentration of the population changed dramatically—as it also grew exponentially.

Transforming the orientation of the nation, millions migrated to cities seeking economic opportunity and the benefits of the state, and millions emigrated as workers especially to Germany in the *Gastarbeiter* (guest worker) labor program. After this program ended in 1973, many of these workers were able to bring their family members to settle more or less permanently in western Europe. In the dense networks of kinship and friendship across these different geographic domains, rural identities and outlook were stretched into urban and international contexts.[22]   *Taifeh*

Villagers are ideological markers of the family of the nation. They are a racialized ideological motif of an ethno-national project. Before the establishment of the Republic, rural Anatolians were idealized as the source of the nation-state's ethnic identity. Ziya Gökalp, an early-twentieth-century Turkish sociologist influenced by Durkheim, advocated for a pan-Turkic nationalism, which would be grounded in the people of Anatolia, linguistically, socially, culturally, and racially and would include people of all the Turkic nations: Azerbaijan, Uzbekistan, Tajikistan, Kazakhstan, and Kyrgyzstan.[23]

Intellectuals in a movement known as the "Blueists" (Maviciler), beginning in the 1930s and influential until the 1960s, distanced themselves from Gökalp-inspired theories of a primordial Turkish race and instead located an authentic Anatolian rural culture in villager life. "Starting from the 1950s the Alevi-Turcoman village for paradoxical reasons came to be seen as an ideal if politically portentous topic of humanist folklore: its supposed syncretism in integrating the ancient religions of the land with Islam made it a survival of the ancients in flesh and blood, just as its isolation in the mountains, inflicted by centuries of persecution, made it supposedly impervious to modernity."[24] Among nationalists, fascists, and even secularists, somewhat paradoxically, rural Anatolians are imagined to be the pure origin of ethno-national identity, that of being a Turk, apparently unsullied through association with the decadent Ottoman past.

In the Ottoman era, the term "Türk" was used disparagingly to refer to "Turcoman nomads or the ignorant and uneducated Turkish-speaking peasants in Anatolia."[25] I encounter these theories of race and culture when talking to people in Anatolian towns, cities, and villages, that Turkish is the origin of all languages (and by extension all people), a debunked theory of the early Republic, the Güneş (sun) language thesis,[26] and/or that Turkish villagers (especially the Yörük) are the true Turks of the race. It is surprising that these openly racist ideas and debunked theories continue to thrive. In terms of villagers being the true "Turks" whether they are Yörük or Turkmen is very slippery since these are quasi-ethnic designations often describing a former nomadic way of life.

While in their "pure" form, villagers were regarded as the genetic core of the nation, this did not mean they were considered ready to take part in the new nation as citizens. Accordingly, a number of state projects in the early twentieth century attempted to engineer villages and villagers, to transform their sense of self—their minds and their bodies. These projects included the People's Hearths (Halk Ocakları), established before the Republic in 1912; People's Houses (Halk Evleri) established in the 1930s, replacing the Hearths; and the Village Institutes (Köy Institütleri), established from 1937 to 1950, which educated rural children. The houses and hearths taught modern, more efficient agricultural practices, established cooperatives, and created small rural-based industries. The Village Institutes were run by Kemalist secularists—leftist reformers who educated villagers in special boarding schools located in towns. Newly educated young people were expected to become teachers in villages, not to migrate to cities, where they might utilize their new educational skills in other professions. A number of intellectuals—authors and artists—emerged from this movement. It was the leftist character of the institutes, as well as the expectation that educated villagers were still villagers in some essential sense, and therefore should not seek a life in the cities, which led to villagers' suspicion of the project.[27] After involvement in these projects, villages were meant to continue, cleansed of superstition and ignorance, improved through economic development and infrastructure, and marked by the imprint of a secularist, westernized political regime.

These programs which attempted to modernize villages were closed when the DP took over in 1950. Kemalist secularist social engineering projects were accused of socialist tendencies and the Village Institutes were closed. The leaders of the program were put on trial.[28] A number of the leftist intellectuals who had supported the spread of Kemalist principles were embittered by their experiences, only to worsen when, in the 1960 military coup, 147 of them were forced out of the universities.[29] Thus, the national orientation toward villages, villagers, and rural life changed a number of times. First, the early Republic implemented state-led modernization, westernization, and secularization policies to change how rural people saw themselves, behaved, and oriented themselves. Second, programs led by leftist nationalist intellectuals attempted to educate villagers and thereby develop rural areas. And third, villages were cut off from these developmental programs, while cities developed. The result of this was mass migration. In each case, villagers were an object of social engineering, and their civilizational status was assessed in terms of cultural and racial authenticity.

Villagers have not, of course, merely been the subject of reforms, they have also been leaders in reshaping contemporary society, especially with the deprivatization of Islam following the 1980 coup. Religious leaders and followers, many of whom came from rural areas, helped create new Islamist movements with political, educational, business-centered, and spiritual goals. Mass media have greatly enhanced the role of public Islam in building networks and communities. Notions of secularity changed with these developments, expanding to include a sense of individual freedom of public religious expression. Many secular, urban, young people raised in the atmosphere of stifling Kemalist ideology, seeking new freedoms and forms of expression, look to Islam, especially Sufi groups, with curiosity not fear. And through this new sense of openness and curiosity, rural pious life is rehabilitated as interesting and meaningful, an alternative to both Kemalism and urban Islamisms.

In considering the political and historical ideas about rural life in Anatolia, alluding to the lively rural world itself from which urban and immigrant populations come, it is important to note that ties between rural and urban are deep and complexly intertwined through kinship, economic exchange, and forms of dependency. These bonds keep lively the relationships between villagers, townspeople, and city folk. In other words, moving away from the ideological categories "rural" and "urban" and looking at actual people—their families, friendships, histories, and experiences—one finds many connections, confounding easy generalizations.

Rural life is outwardly defiant of an urban secular worldview, yet villagers are drawn to cities. The urban world represents the pleasures of consumption, the promises of education, the liberating possibilities of alternative lifestyles—not wearing head coverings, drinking alcohol, and making trips to the beach. But the urban world is also populated by prestigious demonstrations of orthodoxy in massive new mosques, women's Islamist fashions, big new dormitories for all stripes of Islamist students, and prosperous Islamic businessmen creating invigorated local economies. In other words, the urban world, from a rural perspective, offers the opportunities to be either publicly secular or publicly Islamist. These characterizations of the two sides of urban life describe Manisa, the closest city to the rural Yuntdağ.

In contrast, "the village" is a bounded social space. People who have been separated from it, whether temporarily or permanently, know they have to re-conform to its mores upon reentry. There are no lifestyle options. The village is a devout space. Young women who wear tight clothing and go with heads uncovered while outside the village put on şalvar (baggy pants) and a headscarf when they return. Annoyed elderly people note that clothing can so easily be donned and then discarded. Once, chatting with some women in the village about my choice to wear şalvar, I said with impertinence, "It's just clothing; I can take them off." An older woman shot back, "Why don't they change your inside?" For those who leave more permanently, the actual and symbolic border of the village becomes a point of no return. Though they may long for the comforts of their village, fresh air, and view of the mountaintops, they know "being a villager" is no longer an option. A woman remarked on her decision to leave the village upon marriage, saying, "I couldn't do it, be a village woman." Another who married a man in a town said, "I knew I didn't want to be a village woman. I wanted a different life." The village becomes a place they re-create in Facebook postings and visits for holidays. In this way, place is associated with a specific way of life, which is imagined as unchangeable. Social geographies are existential. People feel they need to make a permanent decision about whether or not to be a villager.

In part, the belief in the immutability of rural spaces is a demonstration of the acceptance of the state's ideological construction of the nation as urban. While some feel they cannot be villagers, others who choose to remain feel marginalized from the nation. The choice to be a villager removes them from many of the benefits of urban life: jobs, health care, and education. But some praise the option to live in relative comfort without pressures in the fresh air.

MILITARY COUPS AND THE POST-1980-MILITARY-COUP ERA

The insecurity of political life in the cities has stemmed in part from conflicts over the role and purpose of public and political Islam. From 1950 to the present, public and political expressions of Islamic authority have been thrashed out in the dialectic of coups d'état, events which ended parties and forced the reframing of Islamist political messages within the context of military control. Coups in 1960, 1970, and 1980 were instigated to restore Kemalist secularity and social order, as parties on the right, nationalist, and conservative political parties clashed with leftist socialist and communist parties. The military stepped into the political arena and changed the scene, instigating coups, disbanding parties, and forcing parties to reframe their platforms. The history of coups demonstrates unresolved contradictions in the role that Islam should have in public life and how secularism should be framed and implemented. As parties closed and opened, and programs were reformed, ideas about Islam and secularism, state power, and legitimacy were reshaped. But the left was crushed and has yet to be reinvigorated.

After decades of political struggle between Kemalists, leftists, fascists, and emerging Islamists, the political scene settled down somewhat after the 1980 military coup. Instrumental to the transition was the opening of the economy under Özal, who was elected in 1983. The 1980s brought a structural reorganization of cultural ideologies, political parties, and the economy. As Richard Tapper explains, "A tacit admission of the failure of the ideology and forms of Kemalist republicanism led to a reassessment of its elements and a perception of the need for reinforcing an unchanging national culture and eliminating foreign influences."[30] The general sense that Kemalism had failed was reinforced by the Turkish-Islamic Synthesis, the product of a rightist think tank called the Intellectuals' Hearth (Aydınlar Ocağı). Sam Kaplan describes the work of this organization: "To them, only a synthesis of Islam and Turkish nationalism— what they branded the Turkish-Islamic Synthesis—could bring about political stability and national unity."[31] They believed that there was an implicit contradiction between secularizing, westernizing policies, ethno-national identity, and a tabooed past Ottoman Islamic society, which needed to be addressed. A new social-engineering program would create a revitalized Islam combined with national identity, and this would fill the psychic gap in the Turkish national social order, which had been fragmented during the chaos and violence of the previous decades. The Intellectuals' Hearth "based its Turkish-Islamic Synthesis on the pillars of family, the mosque, and the military, three pillars that were to produce a disciplined and unified society."[32] Thus, Sunni Islam was deprivatized and merged with the nation. This new approach to structuring a national identity and creating a national ethos was in direct contrast to earlier movements like the Village Institutes, which had believed in liberal education rather than Islam as a means toward creating a new society.[33] In the turn to the right in the 1980s, the state relaxed controls over Sunni Islam and tied state structures to Islamic leaders, creating a space for Muslim cultural expression.[34] This change opened a public space for Islamic piety as being a national expression of citizenship and a political power as well. As Ümit Çizre describes, "The military welcomed and supported the new Turkish-Islamic synthesis because it believed that this ideology strengthened national unity and social solidarity, eased the dislocations caused by the full liberalization of Turkish capitalism, and defused potential opposition by the left."[35] Yavuz argues that after the 1980 coup, in order to solve the problem of state legitimacy, "state officials did not hesitate to adapt the model of the umma in their articulation of state ideology."[36]

Religion was thereby re-visioned as modern, rational, and a national expression, not a source of tradition, superstition, or irrationalism, at odds with scientific empiricism. A component of this synthesis was the revival of the former Sunni Islamic sense of global unity that had been lost after Atatürk disbanded the caliphate in 1924. "According to the Hearth, rapid Westernization in Turkey was a mistake, which led to the alienation of the Turkish people from themselves."[37] The neoliberal restructuring of Islam was intended to resuture the rifts created by the imposition of a westernized secularist worldview. The Turkish-Islamic Synthesis was implemented in public school curricula, creating a new version of Turkish nationalism that conflicted with Kemalist, positivistic-secular, western-leaning, modernizing reforms. In schoolbooks, the two contradictory philosophies are awkwardly combined, including the claim that Islam is the only rational religion. Furthermore, just as a homogenized Turkish ethnicity has become the foundational racial identity of citizens, Sunni Islam is taught in the public schools, not as one "religion" among many, but as the only true form of religion.[38] From a multi-ethnic, multi-sectarian Empire, the nation is now homogenized in terms of ethnicity but also in terms of religious identity. By definition antiliberal, this version of Islamic-Turkish national identity is now widespread. There are significant questions raised, therefore, about the legitimacy of those who are not Sunni Turks. Though subtleties and complexities of ethnicity, if not religion, exist in the rural Yuntdağ, most people label others as gavurs (i.e., infidels) or terrorists (i.e., Kurds).

As a result of state attempts to transform society, Muslim identities since the early Republic have been in a state of radical flux, from maligned and decadent Ottoman social remnants attacked for being backward and premodern to an acceptable foundation for a sectarian, nationalist, modern identity. State control of Islam was not new, but this era introduced a significant difference: public Islam. The relaxation of state control after the 1980 coup facilitated the rise of Islamist parties (Adalet ve Kalkınma Partisi, AKP, or Justice and Development Party; Refah Party; Fazilet Party; Saadet Party), Islamist movements, and the development of Islamic communities (cemaat) and brotherhoods (tarikat) under the legal cover of associations (dernek) and foundations (vakıf). Thus, the role of Sunni Islam in Turkey today refers not merely to a flourishing of private and personalized faith and spirituality, but to particular religious communities, parties, and organizations that gained political power under the watchful gaze of the military.

A Muslim urban middle class now exists and holds political power, as well as significant business interests. The AKP won the seats of prime minister, which Tayyip Erdoğan holds, and mayor in major cities and neighborhoods in 2004, 2007, and 2011. In 2007, AKP won control of Parliament. The acronym AK is clever. *Ak* is an old Turkic word for white. AK symbolically appropriates the whiteness of the "white Turks." White Turks are meant to be modern and urban, in contrast to other Turks, meaning the rural ones, who are regarded as backward. Using "whiteness" to describe elite urban identities gestures toward American-style racism.[39] In this way rural people are racialized. AKP's icon is a light bulb, illustrating enlightenment through modern technology. The incandescent light bulb could be interpreted as referencing the Nurcus, a Sufi group. *Nur* means light and radiance, with spiritual overtones. Because the Nurcus believe science and technology are not incompatible with Islam,[40] the light bulb illuminates through science, thereby enclosing an Islamic reference to enlightenment in a product of modern science. The light bulb used by the AKP also plays upon Kemalist formulations of "enlightenment" as secular, coming out of the western philosophical tradition of empiricism's triumph over religion.[41] The light bulb prosaically gestures to the symbolic discourse of other Islamic groups that employ light as a symbol of spiritual knowledge. The Süleymancı, as Yükleyen explains, believe that God manifests in light. "God has transmitted His divine light (nur) to the Prophet Muhammad, who is the source of all divine light on earth."[42] The Alevi employ fire. *Alev*, meaning tongues of fire, has spiritual overtones of wisdom achieved through Ali's passion, his martyrdom. Later in the book, I discuss miraculous candles and the significance of handheld lamps in the villagers' spiritual hagiographies. AKP thereby draws upon a range of cultural and spiritual referents to light: intellectual and spiritual enlightenment.

AKP continues to wield remarkable power even as it takes a "post-Islamic" form. As Asef Bayat argues, "post-Islamism represents an endeavor to fuse religiosity and rights, faith and freedom, Islam and liberty. It wants to turn the underlying principles of Islamism on their heads by emphasizing rights instead of duties, plurality in place of a singular authoritative voice, historicity rather than fixed scripture, and the future instead of the past."[43] In 2008, for example, the AKP attempted to expand the ideal of Turkish ethno-nationalism to include Alevis and Kurds and to respond to "human rights" issues via EU initiatives. But not all pious Muslims yearning for a moral society understand the post-Islamic turn or support unraveling the Turkish-Islamic Synthesis. Many villagers with whom I discussed these transformations during the heat of the *Mavi Marmara* affair,[44] were aghast that a party of Muslims would reach out to Alevis and Kurds. They concluded that the AKP is an "ordinary" political party, which works to promote its self-interest—the consolidation of power—and not a party devoted to the foundation of an Islamic society. As the AKP distances itself from its former Islamist message, it loses support among patriotic, pious citizens while it gains support among secularists.

Despite the AKP's frequent reframing of its message, it is important to recognize that the AKP's moral Islamic economic framework for transforming society is built upon a legacy of earlier political transformations, an amalgam forged in the dialectic of political parties and the military coups and legal actions, such as the "soft coup" of 1997 in which the Refah Party was dismantled. Clearly, political voices, allegiances, and approaches to transforming society changed over the decades as radical secularization policies of the early Republic softened and were modified to include a moral social foundation in a newly deprivatized but also newly politicized Sunni Islam.

2   ISLAMIC TIME
    AND THE VILLAGE

Constructions of time influence and shape understandings of the self and, as Carol Greenhouse argues, agency, our ability to act.[1] These notions of time create the context of meaning within which individual lives and collective experiences of a group—in this case, village communities—are experienced. As I discussed in the last chapter, secular time is constructed through the republican project to modernize, secularize, and westernize Turkish society. State reforms of the early twentieth century, as Hakan Yavuz argues, severed links to the past, creating a state of amnesia, and establishing a secular religion, Kemalism, which was meant to take the place of Sunni Islam. "The Republican state was an 'educating' and 'civilizing' state with the goal of getting people to 'forget' their history and shared language of politics."[2] That is, secularism as made through state reforms created a new cosmological system of belief and practice. While secular time is made through the state, a parallel understanding of time is built through what I call Islamic time, as framed through God's construction of eternity with a beginning and an end, and through the life course of individual lives, falling within God's cosmology. This linear understanding of spiritual time is parallel to secular time and popular acceptance of progressive modernity as a foundational idea for structuring one's life. The state construction of secular, linear time parallels Islamic time, in form if not substance, in that both have imaginary end points. Islamic time on earth ceases with the end of days, Kıyamet Günü, the Judgment Day. The telos of progressive secular time is an apex of modernity, when one can declare that modernity has been achieved.

Both the imaginary end point of modernity and Kıyamet Günü are times when the self is realized and actualized as either modern, westernized, and secular, or in the case of the devout Muslim, judged to an eternal fate in heaven or hell. The self-realization as modern and/or Islamic is the outcome of intense personal struggle and discipline. The trouble is that, unlike Kıyamet Günü in which one knows earthly time has ended and one is about to achieve a resolution to one's fate, the end point of modernity is constantly shifting, reconfigured, reimagined, and pushed through involvement with international codes and standards, such as those the European Union requires for Turkey's application for membership in the union.

Being modern, then, is enigmatically impossible; one is strapped to an engine designed to frustrate, because there is no point when one has definitively achieved the end. Though the modern state's progressive rendering of secular time implies a forward movement into a future and thereby suggests the possibility of radical change, in practice it achieves the opposite. The struggle to prove that Turkey has achieved a modern status puts people on a wheel of pain as they reflect on and compare their lives to an imaginary, idealized West, as Zeynep Gürsel's brilliant documentary *Coffee Futures* (2009) implies.[3] The achievement of a modern self and modern state might better be read in coffee grounds than in objectifying measurements set out by the European Union. As Pamuk suggests through his writings, the desired end point of modernized westernized Turkey is a paradox. If, as those who torture themselves with comparisons assume, the west is the location where modernity happened, what occurs in places where there is a longing for being modern and western is merely a semblance, a shadow facade masking a deeper authenticity—the maligned and detested eastern self. The result is widespread frustration with the republican project of secular time, and its insistence that modernity is western, a nostalgic longing among some Kemalists to re-apprehend the idealized modern future, which they never experienced,[4] and among Islamists and many frustrated secularists, a disgusted refusal to continue the race, which is rigged because the end point is always changing. This explains the recent turn to the Ottoman Empire as a legitimizing foundation for an Islamist future, called Neo-Ottomanism, a temporalized response to western modernity. It also explains the heightened nationalist defensive response to westernization, that Turkey does not need the west and cannot be compared to it because the nation, understood through a blood-based ethnicity, is exceptional.

I turn to the cosmological construction of Islamic time in village life as it relates to the life course of the individual, as punctuated by rituals and the work of daily prayer, fasting, and worship. I am not implying that Islamic time of village life is timeless or more authentic or traditional but that village life includes a temporal conceptualization of the individual within the framework of Islamic cosmology. The linearity of Islamic time places each individual Muslim on the same path as every other Muslim. The ultimate goal is for every Muslim to achieve a record of good deeds and correct practice so that on Judgment Day, one can go to heaven after an examination period, amounting to an application—as one woman put it, "like the university exam"—for the next world. I am not arguing that Islamic time as experienced and ritualized in the village is an authentic social time, whereas state time of secularism is not; but rather, that people manage both systems and have parallel understandings of time, often linked through their experience of a sacralized state.

I will discuss the everyday experiences of Islamic time through prayer and major life-course events: naming babies, initiating boys and girls, sending young men to military service, and burying the dead. These events connect villagers to a cosmological experience of Islam. They concretize what is otherwise abstract. Instead of dwelling on the abstract cosmology of Islamic time, people embody and practice it in ritual.

TIME AND MEASUREMENTS

I was struck in the early stages of my research by the number of calendars in homes. I often found myself in a sparse room, sitting on a cushion on the floor, faced with six or so calendars on the whitewashed walls. My informant would sit with me, often sharing tea, and I would be momentarily distracted by the proliferation of calendars. Later I realized that calendars, as in the United States, are given out by businesses at the beginning of the year. They both mark time and become decorations. Instead of the calendars from banks and hardware stores, which my mother and grandmother had on their walls, villagers had calendars from cheese workshops and feed stores, illustrated with cows and sheep. Other calendars were from religious dormitories for children in Manisa, and those printed by the Diyanet. The later calendars have big pads of paper attached to them. Much like a farmers' almanac, each sheet gives helpful tips on baby names, recipes, historical facts peculiar to that day, and the times of prayer for cities in the region. Religious holidays, the dates of which change each year because the Islamic calendar is lunar, are listed alongside national holidays. These calendars, the numbers of them lining walls and the variety from many years, caught my attention because they mark time, as regulated and linear, measured according to the Gregorian calendar, otherwise at odds with the Islamic system. The calendars are secular artifacts. They place the Islamic calendar within the framework of the Gregorian one, adopted by the Republic. These tools for measuring time repeatedly remind one of scales of measurement, discordantly displayed and utilized. They represent a link between the state and the cosmos, the individual included in the practice of marking time by ripping off pages, consulting curious facts from national history, looking for advice on practicing prayer or for a recipe for dinner.

The Gregorian calendar was adopted during the state-led reforms in 1926. As Özyürek describes, her elderly informants living in Istanbul used two calendars, the Islamic and Gregorian, for recounting their lives.[5] Many told the date for personal and intimate events by the Islamic calendar but told events in national history, such as witnessing Atatürk, according to the western calendar. In my experience, it was infrequent that a villager would describe a date from the previous system, but it did happen. As an ever-present artifact of state reforms, Diyanet calendars mark the manner in which state secular time and Islamic time are united in people's lives and experiences. One sees the date on the calendar as marked in secular terms for months and years, and the parallel indicator of the Islamic month and year on the same sheet. Rather than contradicting each other, this parallel representation shows how Turkish society combines them. The banality of each sheet on the calendar—torn off by a child or woman keeping track of the number of days until her husband returns from a job, for instance—underscores how ordinary it is for people to fuse both systems.

The proliferation of calendars, even those that fuse two systems, does not mean that Islamic systems for marking time are irrelevant. To the contrary, daily life in rural places is measured in relation to the call to prayer, not by the clock. The middle-aged and elderly rise with the first ezan (call to prayer), called güneş (sunlight), and pray. Some return to bed, but many begin their day's work. Women make tea, take the cow to the pasture, feed the sheep, sweep the house, prepare bread dough, and so on. The children go to school. Some of the men leave with the minibus for their jobs in Manisa. Others, if it is summer, have returned from pasture with their herds and are ready to sleep after working all night. In the winter, they go out with their sheep to tend them in the lush pastures on the mountains. Women begin to prepare lunch an hour before the second call to prayer, oğle; lunch is eaten after this call to prayer. The afternoon is a time when more work can be accomplished—weaving, doing laundry, building a fire for baking the bread, sorting beans for dinner, winding yarn in balls, spinning wool, working in the garden, and so on. The male dyers for the cooperative return to their jobs, other men sit in their houses relaxing and drinking tea, smoking and watching television before heading to a coffeehouse to chat with their male friends. In the late afternoon, a couple of hours before the third call to prayer, *ikindi*, people relax and drink tea. The children come home from school and play. Some eat a small meal with tea, bread, and cheese, with their mother and her female visitors. The elderly men make their slow journey to the mosque courtyard, leaning on their canes. Then women begin to prepare the evening meal in preparation for when the men will return home after the fourth call to prayer, *akşam* (evening). Many pray and then eat. They have an hour or less, depending on the season before the fifth call to prayer, *yatsı*, and thereafter many go to bed after watching a few hours of television at home or in a coffeehouse.

Not only is the day experienced in relation to the calls to prayer, but these move every day in relation to the position of the sun. By this standard, the exact time, as measured by the clock, for some events (getting up, cooking, eating, working, etc.) changes every day, but events relating to the state, media, or the formal economy (going to school, watching television, or going to work) do not. This creates parallel systems for measuring and acting in the world. The only television programs that run in relation to Islamic time are those held during the month of Ramazan on the two mainstream Islamically oriented television stations most watched in the village, Kanal 7 and Samanyolu.[6] Villagers manage these two systems of time seamlessly. Each day of the winter shortens the time between calls to prayer and the amount of work, which can be accomplished between them, until the encroachment of spring lengthens periods between prayers. This daily rhythm of prayer happens without anyone consulting the calendar or clock. The waning or waxing sunlight is the indicator of when the next call to prayer will happen, and without anyone needing to think about the progression of the hands on the clock, people and animals move seamlessly with the passage of daylight. I mention animals because once I was stranded in Manisa after a trip from Istanbul, not realizing that the minibus driver and all his passengers did not recognize the change from daylight saving time. Having missed the bus, I asked around as to why the time for the minibus's departure would suddenly change. I was told that the time had not changed at all, because the people I spoke to were not measuring time in relation to the clock. Thinking from their perspective, I realized my question was absurd—time does not change but our measurement of it does. After I made the problem clear—that the rest of the country had changed its clocks— someone pointed out that the minibus went back to the villages "early" because the cows come home with the call to prayer for milking: "they do not have watches!" I later heard a young woman point out how the animals in the villages, roosters and donkeys, give the call to prayer. She was making the argument that Islam is thoroughly engrained in the natural world and thereby true and correct. The popular perception is that time as it is measured through the passage of the sun around the earth is unified with spiritual practice, one which is so evident and obviously correct that even the animals perceive it.

NAMAZ

The call to prayer prompts prayer itself, the *namaz*. One day in Yeniyurt, I observed Şehriye nene performing the namaz. She gave me a plateful of figs from her tree and remarked that she would say her prayers. Outside her door on the open platform in front of her house, she sat on a low wooden stool in the open performing the ritual washing. Her scarf was bunched up on her head as she washed her face, arms, feet, behind her ears, and spat out water from her mouth, snorting it from her nose. Picking up the blue plastic pitcher, she entered her house, taking a hand towel from a nail on the wall to wipe her face. Finishing, she hung the towel back up. As she prepared herself, she breathed heavily, saying, "Allah'ım çok şükür" (Praise be to God), a common refrain spoken in a whisper. She performed the namaz in the next room, breathing her prayers, her joints creaking with each prostration. I sat writing these observations, noting the sound of the wind blowing through the tree branches outside. Her break for prayer is peacefully meditative and solitary but directed at the collective act practiced worldwide.

Children learn to perform the aptes (ritual washing) and namaz at a young age. As one woman pointed out, girls start at seven and boys at twelve. I asked why. She answered, "Ne bilim ben [How should I know]?" Her granddaughter, who was sitting with us and who had more formal training in Islamic knowledge, said, "Künahlar ortuyormuş [To cover their, implying girls' sins]," and her grandmother agreed.[7] This brief conversation revealed two important points about the degree of religious knowledge and training across the generations and the expectation of male and female duties. In terms of the first question, the elderly tend to have less training in Islamic learning and practice for political reasons relating to the regime under which they were born and lived as children. I will discuss how different political leaders enforced or relaxed secularist policies and how these filtered into rural regions later. For now it is useful to recognize that the young have a more standardized Islamic training than their grandparents. Therefore, in an inversion of typical structures of authority, they have greater confidence in providing explanations for religious practices than do their elders. Second, this conversation revealed how girls and women are expected to carry a heavier burden of devotional practice than boys and men. Females are regarded as having more sin by nature. Therefore, they need to be more devout and careful than males. For children, this means the namaz is learned and practiced at different ages. As well, girls are recognized as being more mature at a younger age and therefore more responsible and able to perform the namaz. Girlhood carries greater maturity and sin. Both features of femaleness are addressed by the earlier age at which girls learn the namaz.

The intensity of religious practice is experienced in relation to one's life course. Though children learn the namaz, they rarely pray. As children grow, they enter a new stage, that of being youth (*gençler*). Youth refers to individuals who are unmarried teenagers and young adults in their early twenties, an age that is regarded as problematic by the middle-aged and elderly. Youths are imagined to be carefree, adventurous, eager to find enjoyment, not especially responsible, and not fully conscious of the implications and import of their actions. Middle-aged and elderly people ruminate on the things they did in their youth and the consequences thereof. They regret their carefree ways, even their former tendency to laugh and smile. While conducting research during Ramazan, I noted the numbers of extra namaz beyond the daily five and additional sets of prostrations many of the elderly and middle-aged performed. While sitting with a middle-aged woman, Fatma, I asked her about this. She said, "Because in our youth we didn't do it. We enjoyed ourselves, laughed, and didn't perform the namaz; we now need to make up for that." At a later date she expounded on this point, saying that she had enjoyed herself and laughed in her youth and thereby had accumulated many sins, which needed to be eliminated. Though she had enjoyed herself in her youth, she added that in middle age she no longer had any desire for these forms of enjoyment. Given the sobriety of the older generations and their increase in numbers of namaz, I asked her why older people intensify their religious practice, and she responded that it is because they have become fearful of their fate in the next world: "They worry about whether they will burn in hell or go to heaven." She said that they fast and pray more: "We ask that God will forgive us."

While many older people remarked on their frivolous youth, passed in laughter, fun, and indiscriminate pleasures, I wondered about the perception of joyful pleasure in everyday life. Another middle-aged woman, Çevriye, went much farther in her analysis of the dangers of fun, claiming, "Muslims are not supposed to laugh out loud or cry in excess." I was surprised about her remarks on laughter, though I had noted that people constrain their sorrow at funerals. She said that she had never mentioned laughing before to me, as had no one else in over ten years of research. She seemed to think that no one had wanted to reveal this to me because I had laughed on occasion. She remarked that it is acceptable to smile with a closed mouth but not to laugh—and demonstrated the difference as she told me this. A soft chuckle was acceptable in her demonstration, but loud guffaws and knee slapping were not.

Middle-aged and elderly villagers' preoccupation with sin as expressed through seemingly innocent practices like smiling or laughing calls to mind Asef Bayat's "Islamism and the Politics of Fun,"[8] which, focusing on Iran, asks why everyday pleasures such as listening to music, dance, fashion, mingling innocently with the opposite sex, and watching films, flying kites, and so on would be threatening to the political power of regimes. "The fact is that fun, whether foreign or commoditized or indigenous and innocent, can be subversive. And the threat is not simply a perception but a reality. Fun disturbs exclusivist doctrinal authority because, a source of instantaneous fulfillment, it represents a powerful rival archetype, one that stands against discipline, rigid structures, single discourse, and monopoly of truth. . . . Fun builds on joy of immediate and instant pleasures rather than on those distant and abstract referents such as the hereafter, the sacrosanct, and the untouchable—the very referents on which the authority of the doctrinal movements and regimes rests."[9]

The villagers in the Yuntdağ live in a nation-state, where people are not averse to fun. Provincial cities, even ones known for their conservatism such as Konya, are filled with families strolling around in the evening, visiting parks to drink tea, eating ice cream, and engaging in innocent forms of fun. Bigger cities have additional forms of fun, where Muslims from oppressive regimes, such as Iran and Saudi Arabia, are often spotted enjoying the fun of shopping, going to the beach, visiting nightclubs, and flirting. It is not the villagers' perception that the world beyond their carefully tended moral space is subversive to their sense of propriety, but a reality. The regime they live within is suspicious of innocent practices such as laughter and smiling. These are scrutinized, as are elopement, premarital sex, and the pleasures of consumption. Young people enjoy themselves, but they expect they will become more sober and pious as they age. Thus, the category of youth is one in which fun is possible, yet as people age, they enter into the weighty responsibilities of life and in the process they conform to regimes of aged authority, in which they lose their taste for youthful pleasures.

Though one might expect that the world beyond the village is filled with morally subversive activities, these excesses (drinking, dancing, casual sex, and excessive consumption) do not seem to warrant comparison with laughter and smiling. Yet, the middle-aged and elderly painfully dwell on innocent pleasures, such as the many times they laughed in their youth. Bayat argues that fun is often conflated with youth culture, despite the fact that everyday pleasurable activities are enjoyed by people of all age groups and by different classes.[10] The villagers enjoy, as do Muslims around the world, what are regarded as heterodox forms of Islamic folk ritual, such as performing Mevluts, attending festivals for saints, performing rain prayers, and so on.[11] They suffer because these activities are categorized as being lower class and heterodox, but they do not specifically define them as sinful, though there is contentious discussion on the merits and efficacy of these activities. Rather, youthful enjoyment is reflected upon regretfully as transgressive of Islamic behavior.

Youth are, as Bayat argues, feared as subversive to regimes. While young women are under constant surveillance by their parents, neighbors, and relatives, young men are not. Young men, *delikanlı*, literally meaning the "wild-blooded," effectively defy patriarchal authority and for this reason, parents justify the control of daughters—to protect them. Older people attempt to control the young by sending them to Qur'an schools; policing the use of technology, such as cell phones; and critiquing popular television shows, such as *Aşk-ı memnu* (Forbidden Love). They are able to gain a foothold over young people's activities to some extent, but youth find a way around these measures when they want. Young men and women are able to navigate modern pleasures, such as texting, chatting on the Internet, talking on telephones, and channel surfing with more fluency than the middle-aged and elderly. Because parents and grandparents cannot access the technological pleasures that youth enjoy, which bring them closer to interacting with the opposite sex, they express anxiety about the fate of the young. I should add that media, television, radio, and the Internet are not simplistically demonized as sinful. In fact, these media are

Neda

often praised by the middle-aged and elderly for their educational value, but the activities of youth, especially those that are concealed (such as texting) or hard to access (such as secretive phone calls), are looked on with suspicion because they imply illicit sexual activity. The era of youth, before marriage, therefore is considered dangerous, and older people reflect upon their own youth, as they witness the activities of the young around them, as harmful to their "applications" to heaven.

Contradictorily, older people often regret the fact that they did not have a chance to enjoy themselves while young. While talking to an elderly woman about the dangers of transgression and fun, I asked her, if she could live again, in what era would she prefer, the one she grew up in or another. I was surprised when she said, "Now"—adding, "Now there is everything!" In comparing the pain of poverty and struggle in her youth to the pleasures the young now enjoy, she would choose the dangerous pleasures of today. Similarly, a middle-aged woman who worried that her son and his fiancée would "blacken her face" by having sex, complained that she was married off at sixteen. She was not arguing that she should have had subversive fun of premarital sex, but that the burdens of adulthood and motherhood came on her too soon. Though in retrospect many older people would have preferred to experience their youth in the present, they are fearful that their children and grandchildren will lose control in innocent fun and digress into sin, ruining their lives. As one mother, after we had had a discussion about the need to control girls, and after an elopement in the village, which proved her point, remarked: "You see, it is their lives." Older people's feelings about their own lives and their concerns about their children and grandchildren are complexly intertwined with memories of suffering in the past, the pleasures of the present, and the fear of the future.

Considering the full import of these anxieties, the namaz provides relief. People believe they can accumulate acts of namaz to offset the numbers of sins they have committed. Though in the case of significant sin (such as adultery, *zina*) or numbers of sins, "extra" namaz cannot fully wipe the slate clean, but the rigor and quantity of acts of namaz can offset the weight of sin. I mention weight because sin is conceptualized as being weighed on scales by the angels of heaven against the weight of good deeds, on the Judgment Day. The namaz thereby has a utilitarian effect upon the case to enter heaven. Given the cleansing effects of the namaz, many young people expect that they can employ it later in life to offset their youthful indiscretions. For example, a woman in her thirties who moved to Izmir after marrying (for the second time; the first was by elopement) acknowledged that she owes many debts to God because she does not perform the namaz and because of her past. She said she knows that she should do it, but she feels she is still young (and therefore inclined toward enjoyment), and can do it when she gets older. It should not be surprising that some disagree with this utilitarian approach to the namaz, arguing that it cannot be applied post hoc to youthful bad behavior.

Until I began to ask people what they felt when they performed the namaz, I was not fully aware of how the namaz could address actions from the past. I received a number of different answers to this question: "How do you feel when you perform the namaz?" A few people were puzzled. One woman said, "Whatever comes to mind." She then added, "What would I feel?" It seems she did not understand that I was asking about sensations and feelings. An older man replied, "Müsliman öğle dir [Muslims are like that]." He took it as self-evident that Muslims perform the namaz and any sensations beyond the obvious did not seem worthy of comment. Another woman was openly confused by the question, and searching for an answer said, "Eve bereket gelir [It brings prosperity to the house]." Her response put aside the individualistic interiority of the question and emphasized practical utility—prosperity to her family. For some, then, the question did not make sense or at least not in the manner I had intended. There was no need to interrogate the interior and personal experience of the namaz; it is merely something one does. But these responses were in the minority.

Most replied that performing the namaz gave them sensations of *huzur* (quietness or peace), *rahatlık* (comfort), and *ferahlık* (relief). I could have let these answers suffice, but I probed further and asked why they felt these sensations. One older man explained that he felt a sense of relief and calm when he performed the namaz because it was as if "he had paid a debt." And a middle-aged woman said that she feels comfort when she prays because she has paid a debt. I asked where this debt comes from, and she replied that Muslims have to pray five times a day and when they do not, they generate a debt. "These unpaid debts pile up and then God will not accept them." I began checking these answers with other people and found that most people believed that performing the namaz pays a debt to God. One woman explained she had heard this from the *hoca*s (learned men) but she also thought that the Qur'an said this.

As part of this research, I visited a mosque in Bamberg, Germany, where the imam, from Yeniyurt, is appointed by the foreign branch of the Diyanet, the DITIB. While I was talking to his wife, she remarked, "We are slaves to God," explaining that our purpose is to worship God and then to have God collect our records for the "real" life, which begins after this one. I asked if she thought, as I had learned from people in the villages, that when they (meaning Muslims generally) perform the namaz, they feel they have paid a debt to God. She said yes, and enthusiastically described how we have to worship to accumulate good deeds in order to pay our debts and create a record of good deeds, which will be weighed against our sins in the next world. She used the term Hesap Günü (the day of accounts) in referring to the Judgment Day, also called Kıyamet Günü.

The villagers commented on the conditions under which missed prayers can be made up. They believe that missed prayers from their youth can be made up in later life. The local imam said that people accumulate debts from God beginning at age of twelve. He explained, "Nevertheless, youth do not pray regularly; so the debts from youth are high." Older villagers struggle to keep up with the demand of these prayers, including the debt from youth, remarking that they are çok görevli (very charged with duty). Prayers mark each day's passage and accumulate in a personal account of one's duties and debts. These accounts matter because they are used to assess one's entry to heaven. A man in his thirties pointed out that after death, the first question a person is asked by angels is "whether or not we performed the namaz." An elderly woman expressed, as do many villagers, uncertainty and fear about whether she had accumulated enough acts of prayer in her lifetime. She said, "We hope that God will accept them. We need to pay our debts."

Villagers' discussions of their fear that they have sinned interestingly relate to Saba Mahmood's examination of the role of fear in cultivating a pious self who is ever aware of the relationship between one's actions and God's intentions. "Repeated invocations of fear, and practices that evoke and express that fear, train one to live piously (act as a spur to virtuous action) and are also a permanent condition of the pious self (al-nafs al-muttaqi)."[12] Like the women involved in the purifying mosque movement in urban Cairo described by Mahmood, the villagers constantly reflect on their actions and assess these, perform prayers and fasts to address and attempt to counterbalance the effects of sin in their program to enter the next world.

Despite the overwhelming consensus in the villages (and beyond) that keeping account of one's actions cultivates a pious self, the further assumption among many villagers is that keeping track of the number of times one prays is foundational to being a Muslim and is an essential set of data used to support one's case for entry into heaven. This materialist view of the role of prayer is contested. A woman and her husband who had migrated from Kayalarca to

Manisa in the 1990s argued that "all this running after the namaz does not mean anything to God, but what does, is to give a fly a drop of water from one's fingernail." That is, they argued that showing kindness to a living creature is more important than running after the accounts with God in a selfish manner. Both were involved with alternative religious communities (in a relaxed fashion), neo-tarikats, and perhaps from conversations with people from these groups they had picked up these ideas, which stress one's commitment to creating a just world based on human compassion rather than a selfish accumulation of points for entry into heaven. Another woman in the village also implied that there is another way to think about the accumulation of namaz. She said that though she felt peace when she performed the namaz, and that she knew that this was a way to pay her debts, she revealed that she did not pray consistently. She said, "I can't tell a lie. God knows how often I pray. I did it during Ramazan but now I stopped." "But I'll start again," she added. "For sure, I feel less guilty when I pray." Somewhat like the couple in Manisa who looked askance at the materialist conceptualization of the namaz as an individuated payment of accounts, she said that she does not like "those people who make a big show of their piety by announcing that they are going to go pray!" She said, "One prays for God, not to make this show for others." Thus, the materialist accumulation of acts of piety is not always regarded as a sign of true piety. In a provincial town I visited an elderly woman and her daughter. When I asked the elderly woman how she feels when she performs the namaz she said, "Comfortable." I was comparing what I had learned about practices in the villages to practices in towns and cities, and explained to her that the villagers (whom she did not know) feel they have paid a debt to God with each namaz. Her daughter was in the room at that time and she said, "Yes, we feel like that, but these are spiritual debts." The daughter steered me away from interpreting what her mother was saying as literal. Nevertheless, the mother said, "We are çok görevli [charged with duty]."

It would be an easy conclusion that villagers' views of namaz differ from people who have a more sophisticated and worldly experience of Islam. But the diversity of views from people who are from villages or cities, in Turkey and Europe, prevent this simplistic interpretation of rural Islamic practice. Yükleyen, for instance, describes how a Turkish Nakşibendi preacher visiting Boston from Germany described the namaz as a payment for a debt to God. "Ritual obligations are like debt, he explained."[13] All these reflections on debts and the duties of prayer underscore a dimension of work Muslims perform for God. This work may take the form as Mahmood describes, of a conscious cultivation of perpetual awareness, or as the villagers and the imam from Germany argued, of a more materialist numerically based accounting of numbers of acts. Clearly there is a degree of difference in how one assesses these acts, but whether they are understood as the cultivation of an advanced state of spiritual awareness or a more mundane form of spiritual accounting, the act is the same: prayer. And one can easily see how keeping track of prayers can lead one to develop this more sophisticated understanding of a state of perpetual pious awareness.

Nevertheless, there are divergent views about the legitimacy of practice, in this case based on counting numbers of prayer versus showing compassion for people and animals in this world and cultivating piety. The disagreement is about what God is especially concerned with. Ideally, one would pray regularly and perform good deeds, which help people and animals, and spread good will generally. Nevertheless, the point of disagreement is important to recognize. The divergence of views does not merely demonstrate that there is a diversity of opinions, but that within the so-called Islamic world, there are disagreements about how people practice and whether faith and practice are correct or not. When distinctions are made between correct and incorrect practices, the charge is not merely that some people have misinterpreted practice, but that they are wrong and therefore heretical. These heresies are regarded as direct paths to hell.

LIFE COURSE RITUALS

Prayer is a constant in villagers' daily lives, and certain rituals mark their life course. The first ritual that brings a person into the community is birth, but birth itself is not marked other than by the prayers people offer to help protect the mother and baby through the arduous process. The naming of the baby, however, is an important occasion, the first moment when the baby is brought into the social world by means of Islam. In 2010, a young woman had recently given birth, and for a week afterward there was discussion about when the name would be given. I asked the baby's great-grandmother how this would happen and she said the baby's father's father would speak ezan into the baby's ear three times and then say its name. I asked what would happen if the baby did not have a paternal grandfather or for some reason he was unable to give the name. She replied casually, "They'd get a grandfather [*dede*]" (dede literally means grandfather but also can be used to refer to any older man). She emphasized, "Women cannot give the name." A mother does not have the authority or power to give names; not only is she not a member of the child's lineage, but one who joined her husband's lineage as an outsider, a wife, she has less spiritual power as a woman. Clearly, women's biological capacity to produce human beings is tempered by their spiritual incapacity to name them. This does not mean that motherhood is denigrated—to the contrary. Rather, men have a role in creating the social and Muslim person through their ability to name.

THE SIXTH-MONTH HENNA

Women celebrate the lives of girl babies after they have passed their sixth month. The ritual of *altı aylık kınası* or the sixth-month henna celebration, genders girls by spreading henna on their hands and feet, the same treatment given to brides on their Henna Night (Kına Gecesi) and to female corpses before burial. In each of these moments, babyhood, bridehood, and burial, older women or one's peers perform the rite. In 2009, I had the chance to participate in a sixth-month henna event in Kayalarca. Many pointed out that this event was a recent addition to village life (as far as my informants know, applying henna to brides and female corpses is not new). While I was sitting with Ayşe nene on the morning of the event, she said that she was going to go collect firewood and wouldn't be going to the celebration. She said she never went to these events because "in the past they didn't do this. Now, they gather together and do these things." Clearly, she did not think this newly introduced practice was legitimate. Her remarks somewhat deflated the importance of the event, but many women attended, including relatives from nearby towns and villages.

As with most village events, the exact time when something will happen (as measured by the clock) is never specified and there is some confusion about when the event will begin. For this reason, I arrived early and sat in a room waiting with other women who had also come early. Slowly, women began to gather and crowd into the room, each carrying a small present wrapped in newspaper, which they tucked by their side when they found a place to sit on either the crowded floor of the room or the divans lining the walls. As the crowd gathered, women began to debate what they should do to mark the occasion. Because the ritual is a fairly recent addition to village life, the exact parameters are uncertain.

In the small living room, twenty women and two children sit on three sofas and on the floor. They begin by greeting those who came from a neighboring village, whom they had not greeted for the last holiday, talking amongst themselves about their workloads, the pistachios which mysteriously did not form in their shells, their children and grandchildren who are going to school, those who married and returned for the holiday with their children, their cows, and so on. Some have brought Qur'ans covered in colorful protective papers, an embroidered or a plastic bag. The women who can't read in Arabic, the elderly, did not bring prayer beads. A few complain, "We thought this would be a henna event. We didn't know we'd need prayer beads!" That is, they were considering this event to be a cultural ritual not one which was Islamic. Çevriye, a middle-aged woman, widely recognized for her leadership, though often critiqued for being overbearing, takes charge of the discussion and commands, "We will do what we do for our Friday gatherings [Cuma Toplantısı]. We will read the Yasin forty-one times!" She, in other words, creates the religious parameters of the event. They begin with a prayer. A young woman schooled by the Süleymancı community in reciting the Qur'an begins with a long recitation in a nasal tone. Everyone listens. In the next room, we hear the sounds of the children and younger women and girls. Their occasional cries and shouts reach the middle-aged and elderly women sitting quietly, listening to the recitations. Their infectious chaos underscores the fact that religious events are expected to be somber and quiet. After the young woman finishes reciting, a middle-aged woman begins reading the Yasin, one of the chapters of the Qur'an.[14] As she reads, the elderly and middle-aged who cannot read in Arabic, listen. As one recites, the ones who can read in Arabic turn their pages in synch. As the reading progresses, the sound of ezan rings from the loudspeaker outside the mosque. It is the midday call to prayer. They do not pause in reading the Yasin for the call to prayer, as they normally stop and listen to ezan. This is unusual. I am struck by how the woman's voice passes through the sound of a man's voice reciting the ezan. At that instant, a woman claims spiritual authority on a par with a man. I reflect on the fact that these women's gatherings are giving women greater religious authority.

There are nine women sitting on the sofas who can read the Qur'an in Arabic. I note that they are all young, in their thirties or forties. There is only one older woman sitting on the sofa, from Yeniyurt, where the culture of religious training enabled people to learn to read the sacred book, though the state imposed a ban against teaching it in the 1930s. The elderly from Kayalarca, who say that it was forbidden in their youth to study the Qur'an, sit listening. They never had the chance to learn it.

Younger women are outside with the children, who are playing, running, and shouting. Outdoors, where big cauldrons of food are simmering on fires, a

few older women watch the pots. Because fall is approaching, everyone is wearing layers of clothing. Their loose şalvar in multicolored patterns is made of cotton, rayon, or thick cotton flannel. I notice how the elderly wear bright and fresh
flannel şalvar. This is because the cloth was given to them at the end of Ramazan
as a good deed. Most wear long underwear with their socks tucked into the cotton jersey pants peaking out around their ankles. Though the latest fashion in
shirts is horizontal stripes, only the middle-aged wear these; the older women
wear fashions of the past few years, flowered shirts, closed with button plackets
in muddy colors. Many have the odd safety pin pragmatically attached for some
future emergency. They wear long vests of knit polyester yarn, mostly machine-
made; only a few have the more expensive and thicker hand-knit vests. The vest
keeps one's back warm against the constant wind in the mountains.

Despite the crowded atmosphere in the room, an elderly woman closes the
window tight against drafts, and all the women keep their vests on, as they
squeeze their limbs and sit with their feet and knees tightly packed, folded and
squished together. It is impossible to stretch one's legs or stand. Their heads are
covered, some in multicolored polyester edged with fanciful *oya* (decorative
crochet edging), others in white cotton scarves. The elderly women wear the
old-fashioned *alın bez*, a black headscarf with striking beaded oya wrapped
around their foreheads. The visitors from Yeniyurt have sprigs of basil tucked
into the black alın bez. Flies wander around, touching down on noses or foreheads. They are brushed off or ignored as the reading continues.

One woman stumbles on the Arabic. The women learn to read the alphabet in
order to speak the words, but they have not progressed to studying their meaning. This does not reduce the words' power or importance; the words are God's,
and human speech brings them to life. Most wear rings of tin or brass, incised or
plain, in layers on their fingers. These *hacı yüzüğü* (pilgrim rings) are gifts from
those who made the journey to Mecca and demonstrate a network of relatives
and friends all now carrying the title hacı. Some also wear a gold wedding band.
A few hands have traces of henna on their nails, from the holiday or from the
last wedding. Thus, examining women's clothing and jewelry demonstrates many
links to Islamic practice, beyond that of the typically noted headscarf.

As the readings continue, we listen, and many sigh. The women pray after
each reader finishes a round of the Yasin. Someone asks during the short interval if the soup has been stirred well. The reading begins again. The plan is
to have five women take turns reading the Yasin out loud, while eight others
follow along, totaling forty turns, which, along with the first recitation, makes

forty-one. After reading the Yasin, they continue with another section of the Qur'an. From the outside room, a woman with a shovel spewing incense smoke approaches. The room is filled with the heavy scent. After the readings are finished, Çevriye pulls out one of her well-worn books in Ottoman Turkish, the Mevlut. She and a woman from Yeniyurt will read it together. There are no other women in the room who can read in Ottoman. The poem is widely available in modern Turkish, but the women continue to use the Ottoman text printed on cheap newsprint during the late Empire. Using the text in the old script gives it greater spiritual legitimacy, since it is connected to the holy Arabic alphabet. The two voices form a chant with small cadences and ornamentations. One takes a higher tone, the second forming a low minor tone in a dirge. The women put their hands on the book, sharing it. The women put their hands on their hearts when the name of Muhammed is sung. Çevriye decides that the sound of two voices is discordant so, taking charge, she says they should sing separately. The other woman follows along, moving her mouth to the words without raising her voice. In bits and pieces, the meaning of the Ottoman poem filters to us. The poem is about Muhammed's birth—he is a human being but also the Prophet.

Everyone struggles in the packed room to disentangle limbs and stand together at a high point in the ritual. They face Mecca, with their hands crossed low over their chests. The women all recite in unison, "Allahu Akbar," and the lines of the poem. They end with a brief prayer, wiping their faces and sighing.

The women sit again. Girls bring rose water. They squirt it out of plastic bottles and we wipe it over our faces. Then they Turkish delight (*lokum*) and paper napkins. The women take the big blocks of sweet dusted in powdered sugar, wrap it in a napkin, and secrete it in their pockets or bags. The flies buzz around. The woman from the neighboring village takes the book, but the other wants to add her voice to the recitation with the line, "Merhaba." With this word of greeting to the newborn babe, the women all turn to each other in the room, extending their hands, they clasp their neighbors' hands in greeting, wipe their faces, and turning to another neighbor, repeat the greeting.

Two women, the mother and her *yenge* (the mother's husband's sister), enter the room with the child. The baby girl is dressed as a *küçük gelin* (little bride), in red with a red headscarf and flowing red chiffon scarf topping off her headdress. A few helpers bring a sheet and a bowl of henna, some rags, and paper napkins. When the child is brought into the room, the women who had been sitting outside with the children squeeze in. The poem continues but with the new arrivals, everyone turns to the next task, which is to put henna on the hands and feet of the child. The mother and her sister-in-law begin spreading henna on the child, who looks at them in surprise. They cover the wet henna paste with rags, covering them with cotton headscarves, then they begin work on her feet. The child who recovers from her surprise, begins to cry. The women in the room look on in half sympathy, half amusement. Someone pops a pacifier in the baby's mouth to calm her. Another says, "She's turned into a regular baby now," whereas a moment earlier they had praised her intelligence, meaning her self-contained demeanor. They finish applying the henna and take her out of the room.

The Mevlut poem is left unfinished. Çevriye complains, listing the many occasions when they began to read the Mevlut but broke off before finishing it. She said this was "*olmaz*" (impossible), implying it is wrong, and that, "in the future they should finish the poem before turning to the next task." Few pay attention though she has made a stab at being the spiritual leader of the group. In the meantime, the sister-in-law brings in prepared packets of henna. Everyone takes one. They will apply henna to their hands at night before going to bed. Girls with tablecloths enter the room, spreading two on the floor. Many women have left the packed room to find a place to eat—the bedroom, kitchen, entry room, or the porch outside. Girls bring two large metal trays filled with metal bowls of food: flat green beans, potato and chicken stew, soup, and a dessert made from *kadayıf* (batter cooked in long threads resembling shredded wheat), soaked in sugar syrup. Another brings in large chunks of bread. Everyone sits around a tray, takes a spoon and a chunk of bread. From the next room we hear a prayer being recited loudly over the food. Everyone joins in the prayer, quietly reciting the words, then wiping their faces before beginning to eat. We eat politely, taking a spoonful of food from the bowl on the edge nearest to us, being careful not to cross or collide our spoons over the tray. Once done eating, everyone gets up to leave, saying to the hostess, "Allah razı olsun": May God approve.

I return to the house with Çevriye, where she describes the event to her husband complaining that the Mevlut poem was not finished. I say, in defense of the group, that they had read so many things that it had become too much. The husband asks what was read and we list them off. He is surprised, remarking, "If you try to read so much people will start to hate it." He adds, "Men would never stand for so much reading." Mühettin, Çevriye's husband, highlights a clear difference between men's and women's pious practices. Men attend the mosque and listen to sermons delivered by the imam or conveyed through the loudspeaker system from Manisa. Therefore, they do not make choices about what they will

read but listen passively to what is addressed to them. Men have nothing to prove about the legitimacy of their practice since it takes place in the mosque. The women, however, gather on their own in a house. For this reason, they create their own program of worship and determine who will lead the event. Because their practice takes place outside the mosque, the space of religious le-
women:
gitimacy, they need to prove that they are correctly Islamic by showing their enthusiasm and efforts at covering a lot of material. Çevriye is eager and excited to participate in these events because she is regarded as a leader in the village and because she wants to increase the rigor of women's pious practices, but as her husband warns her, she should not force her fellow worshipers into doing too much. As he argues, this sours their experience of worship.

That night Çevriye and I apply the henna to our left hands. The next day, the village is filled with women with red-stained left hands. I meet up with women on the village paths and we compare how well the henna stained a bright circle in the middle of our palms and our fingertips. The signs of the henna celebration color our hands for weeks and remind us of the collective ritual of fellowship and celebration for the baby girl.

The sixth-month henna celebration is a recent import to village life. Like many recent additions, such as rituals proceeding marriage, the engagement and promise (*söz kesmek*) ceremonies, the sixth-month henna is expensive. The baby's family invested in food, including store-purchased sweets and henna. The ritual underscores the celebration of the birth of a girl, which, I hope the reader realizes, is rarely publicized in literature on childbirth in the so-called Islamic world. Contrary to the many bleak descriptions about the value of girl children and the reported despair many women feel when they discover they have "only" produced a daughter, women in the Yuntdağ are pleased by the birth of a girl. They emphasize that their ideal family consists of one girl and one boy. Many attempt further births when they have two boys or two girls. Mothers point out that their daughters are "friends" with whom they share their daily lives, the household chores, and the experiences of being a woman, including getting married and giving birth. Sons are valued and loved, but daughters are as well, and the sixth-month henna celebration expresses the joy they feel for their daughters.

Considering more closely the meaning of the henna celebration, one has to point to other occasions when henna is used: the circumcision celebration (*sünnet*), the Henna Night (Kına Gecesi) of the wedding, the celebration of a son returning from military service, women's burials, and personal and individual occasions when women want to decorate their hands with henna. It is widely believed that using henna is a good deed and that henna appears in the Qur'an and was used by the Prophet. Staining one's hands with henna therefore brings one's body closer to Muhammed's. This is similar to men growing beards, which they shape in a characteristically rounded manner, in reference to Muhammed's. Using henna, then, is an embodied form of worship. This ritual for baby girls has many intervals during which a collective fellowship among women is enacted: sitting together, sharing books, participating in the ritual movements, listening, gesturing, greeting, sharing food, always a component of the generation of fellowship, and the collective process of staining hands at night and comparing them the next day. And this event is particularly touching in that it welcomes a new girl into the community.

BOYS TO MEN:
CIRCUMCISION AND MILITARY SERVICE

While girls' lives are celebrated with the sixth-month henna, boys are made into men through circumcision (sünnet) and military service. Girls are made into women only through marriage. For men, both sünnet and departing for military service have rituals attached to them, which are Islamic in character. Boys' circumcision is celebrated any time in their lives before their eleventh birthday. The sünnet is almost as eventful and expensive as the village wedding ritual (düğün) and not surprisingly, the sünnet also is referred to as a "düğün." Like a wedding düğün, the sünnet requires that the son's mother spend years creating decorative handiwork in headscarves and embroideries, which are used to decorate the sünnet bed, where the boy will be circumcised and rest afterward for several days. An expensive costume, usually a white satin soldier's suit with matching feathered cape and baton, all liberally decorated with sequins and embroidery, is a notable purchase. Unlike in the cities, though, village boys do not parade around for many days in advance of their sünnet wearing this costume, but only wear it during the event, which usually lasts two or three days.

The düğün requires slaughtering an animal, a sheep or calf, so that keşkek (discussed below), also served at weddings, can be prepared. Slaughter involves a prayer recited over the animal before cutting its throat and collecting the blood in a pan or hole in the ground. Slaughtering an animal is a sacrifice because it is expensive and spiritually arduous. Women do not participate in or witness the animal's death, though I noted elderly women witnessed the death of an animal, which they sponsored for sacrifice for Kurban Bayramı (the Sacrifice holiday). Keşkek is a dish made from pounded wheat berries (to remove the husk), boiled with meat and bones, a mixture which is then beaten with long paddles until it forms a mush resembling oatmeal. It is one of the only foods requiring male assistance. Men stir the big pots with paddles and an elderly man, the keşkekçi, supervises.

I was a guest at a sünnet in 1998, during two weeks of preliminary fieldwork. This circumcision feast was for two sons from a household, which had members who had migrated to Manisa and France. The relatives from both Manisa and France came for the occasion. The main festivity began on a Saturday. After eating in the late afternoon, the young unmarried women excitedly dressed for the dance, which was to be held in a former coffeehouse. I was with Hatice, a young woman with whom I formed a close friendship. She loaned me a pair of heavy velvet şalvar, which all the young women would be wearing. In my notes, I described that I wore blue velvet şalvar, a black linen shirt, and a red headscarf. The red headscarf was an unfortunate choice because brides, or young women who pointedly demonstrate a desire to become a bride, wear red. I did not know that then. Embarrassingly, my headscarf was remarked upon. After we dressed, Hatice in her sparkling red şalvar and decorated headscarf, we went to the coffeehouse where women were waiting outside and a group of young men had assembled by the steps where they could look at the women as they entered the building. The place filled up and became hot quickly. All the women and girls were there, as were the sünnet boys, some of their friends, and the younger male children (themselves uncircumcised). The sünnet boys were dressed in their ivory costumes with feathered capes and special hats. Arabic dance music played loudly on a cassette recorder. The young men were gathered outside the building in front of an open window.

At first, the girls were very shy about dancing. The adolescent girls started and then the older girls joined them. The older girls would only dance in a corner of the room, directly opposite the window, with a line of girls standing between them and the window. I noted how they emphasized their shyness and reluctance, but then strategically danced directly across from the men who were gathered outside by the open window. We could see the many glowing red tips of cigarettes in the darkness outside the open window and occasionally the shining eyes of the young men. I joined the older girls. Finally, as the dancing progressed, the young women began to relax and dance more openly. It seemed that their initial shyness was real and a necessary prelude to their more expressive dance later. It became clear that it would have appeared shameless to boldly dance in front of the open window, where all the young men had gathered; they needed the line of young girls shielding them from the window.

I noticed on this first occasion when I danced in the village that the married women did not dance, but sat in chairs or squatted on the floor with their children as they examined the younger girls dancing. I learned that girlhood is a period of time when one can dance and have fun, but that this period of lighthearted celebration ends after marriage. Married women only dance for specific reasons and in a constrained and formal manner. Dancing for this generation is a pointed illustration of their joy for some specific reason, such as their sons being circumcised or married. There are few occasions when unmarried young men and women dance together, though I witnessed some striking exceptions, which I will discuss later in the book. The sünnet boys danced with the young women for a brief amount of time, then with their mothers and the mother's female relatives. After this dance there was a break during which female relatives of the sünnet boys pinned money and small gold coins on the boys' costumes. As at all such events, the gold and money helps the family offset the costs of the event and anything remaining is given as a gift to those who are being honored, in this case, the boys.

As the party began to disperse, Hatice urged me to accompany her outside to catch a glimpse of the young man she was in love with. As we were standing on the balcony, the party suddenly ended and all the women decided to leave. We followed them, but in order to get away from the coffeehouse we needed to pass through a crowd of young men who were lined up on either side of the path. I bit my lip and passed through, never looking up to see who was staring at us. Probably, I would have seen the important exchange of glances among the young women and men, which constitutes many relationships before they are formalized through the procedures of engagement and marriage, lasting many years. The next day the woman I was staying with, Arife, said that she had been afraid for me, saying, "The village was filled with men. I was alone and anything could have happened!" This sense of fear of disorder contributes to the tension at celebratory events, which include music and dance. People are afraid that fun loosens social control and leads to sin, and it is the case that many young people elope after exchanging meaningful glances at weddings.

The next day was filled with visits to houses, tours around the village, lots of tea drinking, lunch at the sünnet house, and sitting and waiting in the late afternoon for the circumciser. After the circumciser arrived, the boys were paraded

around the village on the back of a decorated horse. Their young friends, uncircumcised boys, created obstacles by running and shouting and trying to prevent
the horse from going forward. By the time the horse, led by the boy's father,
reached their house, a mob of children rushed and screamed around them.
From the balcony, the boy's mother and relatives threw sweets into the crowd
and trays of fried dough (çörek) were brought out to distract the children. Abandoning the ritual protection of their friends, the boys dashed to grab the candy
and snatched the fried dough from the big trays. The parade of the boys on
the horse and the obstacles the boys' friends create are similar to the strategic
barriers put in the path of a groom's family taking the bride by the bride's male
relatives and her fellow male villagers (ones who might have been her spouse).
Both ritualized obstructions demonstrate the love and loyalty of one's peers and
relatives and a sense of protection they symbolically express. The parallels between the two rituals, sünnet and weddings, are further stretched by the experience, shared by both brides and circumcised boys, of bleeding from the genitals.
Both, as a result of this blood and pain, are transformed into adults.[15] The structure of the ritual, in other words, conforms to the rites of passage described
by Arnold Van Gennep.[16] The düğün is a liminal period of disorder, fear, and
danger, enacted through the chaos of music and dance, the parade on a horse
(or car), ritual barriers, payments to appease the resisters, and the final stage of
pain and blood, which changes the social status of brides and boys. The boys
were taken to the gate of their house, but they ritually refused to dismount from
the horse. To coax them, the father promised them bicycles and watches. Suf-
ficiently appeased, the boys agreed to descend and were taken inside, where the
circumciser was waiting. The adult men stood outside and said a prayer as the
boys entered the house. This moment of prayer as the liminal actors cross the
threshold exactly parallels the men praying as the bride exits her natal home and
gets into a car, which takes her to her marital home and the prayer men say as
the bride crosses the threshold to her new marital home. A few hours after the
operation, everyone in the village visited the sünnet house, which was now somber and quiet. Each visitor brought a small gift, some money, an embroidered
headscarf, or a small gold coin. They visited the bed where the boys were resting,
their legs open, showing their bloodied underpants.

Circumcision makes boys into men, regardless of their age, as measured by
the calendar. The ritual creates the physical adult male body, though most boys
still have a lot to live through before they are grown men. While circumcision
makes little boys into men, military service makes unmarried male villagers

into male citizens—men who belong to the nation. In Turkey, all men are conscripted. Men can postpone and shorten the eighteen months of service by paying a substantial sum. According to a recent bill passed in 2011, men over the age of thirty and who have worked or studied abroad are able to pay 30,000 TL (about $16,800) to the government to avoid service.[17] Avoiding service is beside the point for village men, who look to become soldiers with dreaded excitement and a sense of patriotic duty. They accept it but are often afraid of where they will be posted, given the ongoing civil war in the southeast. Mothers sob for months before sons leave. They fear that their son may become one of the martyrs, announced each night on television, young men killed in ambush in the mountains in the southeast by members of the PKK (Kurdistan Workers' Party).[18] The soldier is therefore not understood in secular terms merely: he is a potential martyr.

In the villages there is a subdued ritual marking the young soldier's departure. The village men meet at the mosque for the morning namaz. Afterward, they say a prayer outside, and the young man greets the older men with respect according to age, by in turn kissing their hands and raising them to his forehead. He then embraces peers, says goodbye to his mother, and boards the minibus for the journey to his training site.

The practice of sending soldiers to military service in the Yuntdağ is interesting when contrasted with an account of these events in a town in Thrace, in the far western European portion of Turkey, near the border with Greece. There, townspeople refer to the weeks before the young man's departure as a soldier's wedding, and the event is capped with a celebration held at night with drum and "clarion" players.[19] Young men and women dance, sometimes together, openly demonstrating their relationships in public, often for the first time. The practice ends with a prayer on the morning when the soldier leaves, much like in the Yuntdağ. Unlike the Yuntdağ, the townspeople in this Thracian region describe that they "marry" their young men to the state, his departure for military service paralleling that of a bride leaving her natal home, but like in the Yuntdağ, the soldier is a potential martyr.[20] The evening event, like marriage, is celebrated with music and dance, and young couples are given space to explore their relationships in the open, due to the heightened sense of danger surrounding the soldier's departure. In the Yuntdağ, many young people get engaged just before the young men leave for the military. This creates a link between girls' path to womanhood through marriage, and men's path to manhood through the military service.

The subdued village rituals in the Yuntdağ are notably unlike those in towns and cities, where the soldier's farewell is celebrated with *davul* (bass drum) and *zurna* (double-reed wind instrument) music and dance. As Yael Navaro-Yashin argues, "these boisterous events are a ritual for the state."[21] As I discuss later, davul and zurna are regarded as sinful in the village. For this reason, they are replaced with a sober prayer. In the villages, many families also sponsor Mevluts for their son's departure and his return. These Mevluts, unlike the Mevlut for the sixth-month henna celebration, are held in the mosque because they are performed by men. That these rituals mark military service underscores the fact that villagers experience the state as sacred. As Robert Bellah famously argued for the United States, and Talip Kucukcan for Turkey, civil religion sacralizes the state.[22] As discussed in the previous chapter, through the Turkish-Islamic Synthesis, Sunni Islam has become connected to national ethnic identity. The prayers and Mevluts for soldiers at departure are demonstrations of how rural people venerate the state, sacralize their son's service, and mark entry and exit from the village establishing its sacred borders.

SENDING THE DEAD TO THE NEXT WORLD

The end of adulthood is death, marked by mourning rituals that socialize the corpse and incorporate the dead into village society. By socializing the corpse, I mean that villagers assess the person's life, examine the body, prepare it for burial, and mourn the deceased person, thereby transforming the social identity of the dead individual. Mourning combines economic practices and Islamic rituals, which help villagers express their ideal of an Islamic society based on compassion. The socialization of the corpse reveals how religious meaning is created through physical acts and how grief is structured, shared, and consumed. Importantly, death marks the end of the living person's work for God. The deceased can no longer expiate his or her sins by performing good deeds or performing the namaz; instead, burial begins a period of assessment when the deceased faces his or her actions in this world, waiting to travel to the next. Often, for this reason, villagers say that someone has migrated (*göç etti*) when they died.

The social rite of passage of death begins with the acknowledgment by the mosque, communicated through the *sala*, the prayer for the dead. At the first plaintive notes sung by the imam over the mosque loudspeaker, everyone stops and listens. The imam announces the deceased person's name, his or her social relationship to others, and the spiritual status, if the person had performed the pilgrimage to Mecca and therefore had earned the title hacı (pilgrim).

After the imam's announcement, villagers gather at the deceased person's house. Elderly women prepare women's corpses and elderly men prepare men's. The body is washed and wrapped in a shroud. Men take it to the graveyard's gates where they put the wrapped body on a stone platform, designed for this purpose. There they pray over the body until the grave is dug. Then they bury it. In the meantime, women have been watching the activity at the graveyard from inside their homes. Women never accompany the body or enter the graveyard for funerals. These initial steps take place within a few hours of the announcement of the death. During this time, the village is filled with tension and anxiety. People feel an overwhelming sadness when they lose a person they have known their entire lives and who played a vital role in the community. Living as we do now, moving frequently, settling in towns or cities because of work rather than because we were born there, it is difficult to imagine what it is to live with a group of people all of whom knew you from your birth and, for people younger than oneself, whom you knew from their births. In the world I inhabit, very few people have known me from my birth and most of these have died. In the village, I began to gain some understanding of the meaning of such a community, in which everyone knows their place in a long narrative of births and deaths, and in which they share every event of each individual's life collectively. Though I had never experienced this powerful sense of collectivity in my own life, I especially began to understand it when someone died because suddenly a piece of the whole story was missing. After the burial, women and men gather at the deceased person's house and begin mourning. In the evenings, they gather in the house to read the Qur'an. These rites continue for many days, depending on the circumstances. The elderly, whose death was anticipated or at least was not a surprise, are mourned but not with the same intensity as younger people whose death was sudden. Young people, especially those who die in tragic accidents, whose deaths were the result of suicide, or who suffered prolonged illnesses, are mourned intensely, sometimes for up to a month.

ELVEDA'S UNEXPECTED END

On the morning of March 21, 2000, the elderly Fatma nene noticed that no smoke came from the chimney next door. After knocking, she found Elveda ebe, her sister-in-law, lying peacefully dead, wrapped in her quilt, on her meager pallet. She had died in her sleep, alone, in her small, one-room house. Even though she had been the oldest person in the village, over ninety years, she had shown no signs of sickness or any sign of impending death. Fatma nene found Elveda on the first morning of my fieldwork in 2000. On this early morning, Fatma nene informed some neighbors, and as word spread, the imam was told. He gave the prayer for the dead from the mosque. Immediately, the elderly women gathered in Elveda's house to prepare her body. I did not witness the preparations— indeed on my first morning of fieldwork, I was unaware of them. Later, people described how they prepared the body. The women washed her and wrapped her in a white shroud. Her face was covered, except her eyes. Her hands were covered in henna and wrapped in cloth. The bodies of women are prepared for burial as they are prepared for marriage, with hennaed hands and feet. The fourteen-year-old daughter of the family I lived with, Zübeyde, remarked to her mother, Çevriye, while we discussed death, "Don't they go beautifully, Mommy?" The application of henna and the connection between death and marriage may seem surprising given American and more broadly western notions of marriage as a happy occasion, but death as sad. Michael Herzfeld argues that villagers in Crete make an analogous relationship between marriage and death in both funeral and wedding rituals. "Death may be represented as a marriage with the earth."[23] I understood, based on what people had said, that death is the end of one life and the beginning of another, held under the ground, waiting, often while being interrogated by angels, until the Judgment Day. In this new state, the bonds of marriage are dissolved. For the villagers, both marriage and death for women and death for men are sad events (marriage for men is not sad). Both marriage and death are rites of passage, which are regarded as de facto difficult and emotionally painful. Marriage for a woman is painful because she has to symbolically and actually separate from her kin. It is not geographic distance but separation from the woman's natal lineage that marks the ritual with mourning. Marriage for the bride, then, is a social death followed by rebirth as another person. Death also separates one from kin and, more intensely, isolates the person from networks of assistance, though as I discuss later, relatives are attentive to the needs and feelings of their dead relatives in their graves.

After her death, Elveda, a widow and mother of nine children who had left dozens of descendants in the village, was washed, prayed over, and buried. After breakfast on the day of her burial, I went with Hatice, one of Elveda's many granddaughters, to her grandmother's tiny house in the narrow, cluttered older section of the village, built around rocky paths. We entered the one-room stone house, with its flat earthen roof, characteristic of her neighbor's houses, the homes of elderly grandmothers and grandfathers. When we entered the doorway, I made out women in the dim interior light, sitting on the floor before the open hearth. I remembered to say, "Başınız sağ olsun [Health to your head]," offered to people who have lost someone. The women made space for us by the fire. They were cooking çörek, a typical food made as a good deed. Later we ate some of these with white cheese and tea, and the women prepared them throughout the day for distribution to all the houses.

The women talked about Elveda, while one of her daughters, Sultan, sat beside the fireplace cooking, lamenting, "Anneciğim, anneciğim [My dear mother, my dear mother]," wiping tears from her cheeks and stirring the hot oil. Although we might imagine that Elveda's death was the best one can hope for— she was over ninety years old, had not been ill or suffered, had not died in a hospital but peacefully in her sleep at home—the women gathered by her fireplace felt otherwise. They stressed that she had been alone despite the fact that eight of her nine children were living near her. Villagers never want to be alone and elderly widows often sleep beside one of their granddaughters who each night make the trek to their grandmothers' modest homes to sleep on the floor with them. These discussions about the details of Elveda's death passed in waves among the women as they struggled to accept her absence. They sobbed quietly, letting tears roll down their faces, wiping their cheeks with the corners of their scarves, softly moaning over the certainty of death and the suddenness of Elveda's. Sultan cried out, pausing in her work over the pot of oil, "Anneciğim!"

After they grieved for a period, they stopped crying and conversation went on to happier subjects. The day passed, and at the evening call to prayer, everyone rose to go home. The village recognized Elveda's death as they sat down to eat dinner with the çörek. This was the beginning of the process of mourning. On the second day, the women mourners prepared et aşı, a meat dish. This particular form of et aşı was keşkek, described above, a special food made for wedding and circumcision celebrations. The food was served to the men at the mosque for the midday prayer and to the women who came to Elveda's home for the second day of mourning. Dishes were also distributed throughout the village, and that night we had a small dish of et aşı with our dinner. On the third day, Elveda's death was again recognized through the cooking, distributing, and eating of foods. Women prepared pide, which they call bide. Unlike the urban variety of pide, which resembles pizza, in the villages, this is a flat bread cooked over a fire, stuffed with onions, greens, and sheep cheese, cooked on a metal dome supported by a three-pronged metal stand. On the last day, a sweet, *saraş*, was made from wheat.

Although the circumstances surrounding every death are unique, the rituals of mourning follow a predictable path. The days after death are marked by intense activity. Though the mourning family has to contribute the majority of the foods, especially meat, women bring a contribution on the days when meat is not cooked: a bowl of olive oil, flour, or some greens. In addition to bringing people together, cooking, eating, and distributing foods, these activities are rituals of spiritual fellowship uniting men and women, young and old, in sharing their grief and memories of the deceased. Through the collective act of eating foods cooked in memory of an individual, mourning is an intimately embodied experience.

In the villages, death is ever present, often discussed and reflected upon, visible in the landscape, in the division and ownership of land, as a motivation for performing good deeds and in having children. I noted how villagers cared for the graves of the deceased by visiting, weeding, and watering them. It was also significant that many who could read Ottoman were able to decipher the words on old graves, thus resolving a long-standing barrier people in secular Turkey experience: due to the change in language, they cannot read the gravestones made during the Ottoman era and therefore they have no knowledge of where their ancestors are buried.

Both due to the long wait in one's grave and the difficulty of dying, villagers state that it is necessary to have children. They expect their children to care for them in their old age and to be with them when they die. They also expect their descendants to pray at their graves, to comfort them while they wait for the Judgment Day. An elderly woman in Yeniyurt remarked that they perform good deeds, such as the collective production of wrapped grape leaves and their distribution throughout the village in spring (called *dede sarması*), so that "the dead know we have not forgotten them." She implied that acts in this world reverberate back in time, as people perform the same rituals as in the past, maintaining cultural memory. These actions engage with the imagined continued existence of those people, now dead, as they wait in their graves, so that by performing cultural rituals, the maintenance of a temporal continuity to the past is sustained.

Employing modern technology, many elderly people asked me to take their pictures so that their children and spouses would have something to look at and cry over after they died. Most houses have one or two photographs on their walls, portraits of deceased parents or spouses. Some of these were enlarged identification photographs; others I recognized as photos I had taken over the past decade. The presentation of the self is concretized in photography, in the practice of making a portrait of oneself as a future memorial portrait. Death thereby permeates everyday life.

Islamic time supersedes the time of the state. By reflecting on death, villagers remind themselves of their life project for gaining entry into heaven after the Judgment Day, that is, that eternity is the framework for their lives. In contrast, the secular state sees itself as the harbinger of temporal meaning. Kezer describes, for instance, how the dead were concealed in Ankara's landscape when cemetery lands were appropriated to build the ministries for the new republic. Though these cemeteries were owned and administered by religious foundations (vakıf), they were treated as if they were empty. "Minister of the Interior Şükrü Kaya stated, 'In the past, for some reason, respect for the dead was shown at the expense of the well-being of the living. The most beautiful portions of urban real estate were . . . use[d] as cemeteries'. . . . More than lending a strong support to modern urbanism, his words reveal a profound shift in the view of life, death, and spirituality."[24]

In the republican era, Islam was wiped off the landscape in an effort to secularize society and create a new temporal framework in which the living would dominate the dead. State administrators' cold words about the practice of maintaining cemeteries and caring for the dead parallel testimony in Winnifred Fallers Sullivan's book *The Impossibility of Religious Freedom*, in which popular and multisectarian expressions of piety and grief were deemed individualistic and idiosyncratic, not formally religious by the judge in Boca Raton.[25] In the Turkish case, religion is made invisible but in the American case, religion is allowed, as long as it conforms to what religion is expected to be, which in practice means it is also not allowed. In both cases, cultural rituals of caring for the dead challenge state authority by pointing to the fact that people live outside and beyond the state.[26] Because death is perennial and maintaining care for the places where the dead are buried involves imagining a time before and after the state, death attacks the legitimacy and sovereignty of state time. It is for this reason, that cemeteries for people whose lives were lived outside the framework of a particular state are often destroyed or, as is also the case in secular Turkey, made illegible.

3 GOOD DEEDS AND
   THE MORAL ECONOMY

INTRODUCTION

Charitable practices are an intrinsic component of Islam. They relate to the individual quest for salvation at the end of time because people offset their sins with good deeds. Here, I consider how good deeds function in relation to events in this world: state policies of economic development as experienced on a local level in a carpet-weaving cooperative. In Kayalarca, villagers implement good deeds (*hayır*) to respond to the social effects of economic change, as well as to address their personal quests for salvation. In the post-1980-coup era, Prime Minister Özal implemented policies that opened the national economy.[1] These included laws regarding cooperatives, enabling small enterprises, such as the cooperative in Kayalarca, to earn foreign currency, more stable than the Turkish lira. Part of the logic behind these policies regarding cooperatives was the expectation that rural and provincial people would improve their lives in villages and towns, and not migrate to cities.

Özal's policies created a second wave of major social transformation in the Turkish state—the first being the Atatürk secularization policies. Like the first wave of government policies, this second wave addressed a question of time within the state. On the one hand, villagers emphasize the primary importance of personal salvation, undergirded by the knowledge and practice of Islam. On the other hand, the time of the state demonstrates that economic progress and accompanying social change is important. Notions of progress and civilization, as configured by the state, are experienced and expressed through a transformation in individual bodies and attitudes toward modernity. Gaining personal wealth, for instance, is interpreted as a demonstration of success. From a rural Islamic standpoint this same success shows how one has acted selfishly, because unless one chose not to share one's surpluses, one could not have accumulated that wealth. For this reason, wealthy people are regarded with suspicion.

Though policies that opened the national economy were designed to develop the country, this second wave was implemented around the same time that the Turkish-Islamic Synthesis was formulated. Connecting economic development, the opening of the national economy, and a reinvigorated conceptualization of ethno-nationalism with state support of Sunni Islam enabled the rise of prosperous Muslim businessmen. Turkey now has a powerful Muslim middle class and a society transformed through consumerism and consumption.

Villagers who have not become members of the Muslim middle class continue to be marginalized geographically. But more importantly, many villagers try to maintain a social distinction between urban people (whether secular or Islamic) and themselves on moral grounds. Villagers frequently express the idea that urban people are selfishly opportunistic and value their own socioeconomic opportunities over the welfare of others. For this reason, many villagers argue that rural life is better and more moral because it is not defined by the need to make money and the pursuit of status through wealth.

Taking the moral high ground has not been so easy in Kayalarca village, where, since the late 1980s, the commercialization of weaving has improved the financial circumstances of a handful of families. Overall, the cooperative improved the perceived value of women's labor, as it also raised the usefulness of a residual nomadic economy based on sheep herding. But everyone has not benefited equally. Though Kayalarca is the home of the cooperative, it has members from six villages in the region, including a few in Yeniyurt. Among these villages, the greatest financial gains have been experienced in Kayalarca because the head of the enterprise, dyers, managers, and the president all live there. These individuals are paid more than weavers and spinners, who are paid by the knot in finished carpets or by the kilogram in spun wool. The male head of the cooperative and male dyers have been paid a salary including benefits, called *sigorta*, a bundled retirement and health insurance package. Not surprisingly, other villagers, men and women, have viewed the inequitable distribution of wealth and benefits with envy and anger. Nevertheless, the cooperative is a source of pride.

While the cooperative has made life comfortable, villagers worry that this has led to greed and social isolation from humanity. By addressing these concerns with hayır, they perform piety and express love for the community while also celebrating their newfound prosperity. The practice of good deeds or informal alms critiques the monetization of the local economy, the emergence of socioeconomic difference, and modernity as an economic and social system predicated on individual success, the accumulation of property, and a savvy engagement with commodities. Hayır calls attention to the need to maintain a pious community. These practices create a pious modernity or, as Cihan Tuğal categorizes it, "moral capitalism."[2] As other scholars argue, Islamic modernity is not antimodern—that is, a reversion to an Islamic golden age—or against social change and economic development,[3] but against heartless disregard, selfish accumulations of property, and exploitation. The villagers refer to this modern world of empty western modernity as *gavuristan*—the land of the infidels. By locating this selfish form of economic success elsewhere and identifying it as specifically related to infidels, they differentiate their practices from those of gavurs. However, their reactions to economic development and the creation of a consumerist economy lead one to wonder if they are not afraid that the effects of gavuristan have seeped into village life.

Sunni belief and practice in this setting includes the traditional creation and maintenance of community through rituals and networks of sharing, as Reinhold Loeffler also shows in an Iranian village.[4] This rural form of pious collectivity is different from the urban-based Islamist mobilization movements. Sunni Muslims as mobilized in Islamist movements, in the form of a national political movement, nongovernmental organizations (NGOs), and civil society organizations are forums of spiritual, economic, and political expression, in which practitioners demonstrate their expectations about pious modernity and political change. In villages and, one can certainly argue, in all Muslim communities, pious modernity requires a consideration of how God has helped people achieve a new level of material comfort, but in this rural context, the formation of pious modernity is not connected to a formal political party. By utilizing traditional practices of hayır and responding to trends at the national level, villagers create networks of charitable activity, distributing goods, many of which are symbolic of modernity. Through pious expressions of sharing, the villagers position and imagine themselves as part of a global community of Muslims and a national and transnational community of Turks, but they are not involved in these practices in order to further the goals of a political party or Islamist community. Rather, they are interested in a more diffuse, less ideological notion of global humanity and the specific and very particular survival of people they know.

ZEKAT AND HAYIR

I will distinguish between what the villagers refer to as hayır, good deeds in Turkish, *sadaka* in Arabic and *zekat* or *zakat*, the annual tithe.[5] Sadaka is voluntary, but zekat, one of the five pillars of Islam, is mandatory for those who qualify. Zekat is a tithe of 2.5 percent of individual annual income and assets, once one has fulfilled one's basic requirements. It is understood as an act of reciprocation. It "is owed by those who have received their wealth as a trust from God's bounty, to the poor."[6] In this sense, devout Muslims are "earning" because God is willing to give. Ownership of earnings is contingent upon recognizing God's capacity to make income possible. One is only required to give zekat after earning above what is needed to maintain oneself. Without reciprocation both to God and community, one cannot "freely" own that extra amount. Zekat "purifies that portion which remains, and also oneself, through a restraint on one's greed and imperviousness to others' sufferings. The recipient, likewise, is purified from jealousy and hatred of the well-off."[7] Not giving zekat means withholding the "forbidden *riba* or tainted income."[8] Islamic scholars of banking argue that zekat cannot be charity because the amount is determined by income. Rather than charity, it is a tax. Furthermore, zekat resembles other protective measures, which secure good fortune and wealth, such as amulets against the evil eye, *nazar boncuğu*. In this sense, zekat seems to justify economic inequalities. The rich contribute to the community, but their contribution is a fraction of their income. Thus, zekat is a symbolic gesture, which expresses interest and concern but does not dismantle the social structures that have enabled an accumulation of surplus.[9] As a mandatory tax and not a voluntary charitable act, it has a moral rather than revolutionary effect on the community. In Kayalarca, most do not pay zekat because, as villagers point out, few have gained that amount of wealth. For this reason, good deeds rather than zekat are the primary form of economic redistribution.

I hasten to add that good deeds, like zekat, do not transform the social structures from which inequalities emerge. Good deeds make a gesture toward acknowledging inequalities and making amends. Hayır is voluntary, and for this reason resembles charity, rather than a tax.[10] Although sadekat and zekat are distinct practices, in "the key verse of the Qur'an (9.60) . . . the word sadaqa is actually used in the text but it is generally interpreted as referring to zakat."[11] Although the two terms are used interchangeably, there is no question that zekat is a mandatory tax, while sadaka is a voluntary act. As Maurer says, "It is not required of the believers, but recommended."[12] Unlike zekat, good deeds are not focused on material wealth exclusively. Hayır can be expressed by offers of assistance and expressions of care. It is not charity only, but a practice and a duty, which maintains community. "'If you straighten out some trouble between two individuals, that is an alms. If you help a man with his beast, mounting him thereon or hoisting up onto it his luggage, that is an alms. A good work is an alms. In every step you take in walking to prayer there is an alms. Whenever you remove something harmful from the path, that is an alms.'"[13]

As Amy Singer points out, "'Sadaqa' comes from a root which means 'to be sincere' and charity is a reflection of the sincerity of the donor's belief."[14] Alms in this sense are a demonstration of the consideration for others, which can be performed through small deeds. These gestures infuse everyday life with meritorious actions, linking individuals to community and God. Since hayır includes gestures of concern and offerings of assistance, as well as material distributions, the overall effect is broader than zekat. Hayır does not separate rich from poor, dividing donors from recipients. Assuaging envy and anger are not motivations for the gesture. Since the poor can make gestural contributions, hayır is spread across small acts, the accumulation of which show attention to all needs, not only material inequities. Marcel Mauss points out that "the Arab sadaka originally meant exclusively justice, as did the Hebrew zedaqa."[15] Embedded in the practice of giving is the desire to create social justice by leveling difference. As Tuğal argues, "All Islamists see justice not only as a good solution to the extreme inequalities created by the system, but also as the foundation stone of Islam."[16] In the village, hayır is both a traditional religious practice, which creates community, linking the secular economy to a spiritual one, and a critique and response to economic development and modernity.

ECONOMIC DEVELOPMENT AND COMMUNITY

The intensity with which the villagers practice hayır can be explained by their experiences in the cooperative. In ethnographic literature on cottage industries, it is common to discover that the commercialization of traditional, heritage products, such as textiles, leads to social discord.[17] Some villagers prosper, while others languish. Social and economic differences develop in communities which value egalitarianism and as a result, well-intentioned development projects can have unexpected effects. In my discussions with the villagers about the cooperative, they showed that it was not merely economic development they wanted, but a socially conscious and just economy.

The business is a source of anxiety because it has raised the standards of living, creating differences between households and individuals. The conundrum, which the villagers attempt to manage, is that two programs of social change work side by side. One, the cooperative, was established on western notions of economic development. The other, Islamic morality, attempts through spiritual practice to create communal solidarity and a concern for the welfare of the group, which includes redistributing surpluses. While Islam does not categorically forbid surpluses or wealth, the villagers have cultural expectations about social egalitarianism, which they believe are Islamic. Capitalist accumulation, such as that which has resulted from working in the cooperative, upsets this culturally defined balance. They see this as spiritually, socially, and economically unsettling—sentiments that are not unique to the village. As Tuğal writes, "In Turkey, the influence of world capitalism and the modernization projects of the local elites have created institutions and relations (the real) that radically differ from the moral order envisioned by Islam (the imaginary): they have introduced objectifying relations (those of class) among religious populations, which contradicts what is expected from human bonds within a religious framework."[18]

Like many in Turkey, the villagers are ambivalent about capitalism and the new wage economy. They comment on the fact that they have to work within the capitalist system, showing that they are observant and reflective about economic development. For instance, they often say, "Parasız bir hayat yok [There is no life without money]," and, "Para yok, ekmek yok [No money, no bread]." I was struck by the number of times I heard people of all ages, when describing how the village had changed over the decades say: "İnsanlık yok [There is no humanity]," "Ben seni tanımıyorum, sen beni tanımıyorsun [I don't know you, you don't know me]," and, "İnsanoğlu ölmüş [Humanity is dead]." These expressions showed that villagers thought the community was fragmenting. Many claimed that neighbors and relatives no longer helped one another, by sharing work, food, and money. As one elderly woman remarked, "Gençler hepsi bok! [The youth are all shit!]." When I asked why, she said, "They don't help their parents." She was referring to the expectation that children should assist their parents after having been raised by them. These remarks critique the monetized economy and its effect on individuals, who seemingly no longer honor parents, strive for social egalitarianism, or communal solidarity.

From an ideal standpoint, members of households are not expected to act autonomously or independently, but are bound to networks of family, kin, neighbors, and others. Jenny White identifies how establishing unpayable debts among members of households and communities binds people to each other. These debts are framed in such a way as to avoid the implication that one created the debt in order to profit at another's expense.[19] In the village, it now appears that when children, for example, do not honor their parents and seek to pay the unpayable debt owed them for producing and raising them, children attempt to get off free.[20] To the villagers, then, not recognizing these debts and acting freely means acting without regard for others, being selfish, individualistic, and egocentric. This behavior is often glossed as being like that of a gavur, an infidel.

These critiques of economic development rest on a rosy construction of human generosity in the past. I wondered if it was true that before Kayalarca began to develop there was less socioeconomic difference. In response to this question, the villagers argued that there were fewer economic differences in the past because everyone was poor. That was not what I learned, however, through a survey of trousseaux from the 1940s to the early twenty-first century. While generally all villagers were poorer in the past than in 2004 (when I conducted the survey), this did not mean that there were no economic differences. Wealthy families, of which there were two, drove camels and as one elderly man exclaimed, "We were the truck drivers!" They had more wealth than other villagers, owned expensive animals, and were traders.[21] Considering economic differences in the past, it is hard to know whether people were more generous and caring. Faced with a nostalgic construction of the past or a reflective and insightful commentary on how things have changed, I noted that many remarked as did one man, "People are different and it is money that has changed everyone." These expressions demonstrate the importance of the concrete and material bases of an Islamic society, as well as the ideals of community and communalism, which include distributing wealth.[22] It seemed that the cooperative had created discord, even though I had expected that as a collective development project it would have brought the villagers together. The paths to economic development, which would seem progressive, had enabled some to become successful entrepreneurs, but the majority to be low-paid laborers who were managed and directed by their fellow villagers.

Relationships within households have also been affected. The cooperative has infused village households with capitalist relations of wage labor. As a cottage industry, the home is a workplace, open to the market influence of production and consumption. This means that people who manage wage labor in the household (mothers and fathers) and those who perform it (mothers and daughters) relate to each other vis-à-vis cultural notions of gender and social roles, but also as workers and managers. Villagers are conscious that daughters are important contributors to the household wage pool and have little recourse in protecting themselves from the potentially exploitative interest their parents have in sustaining their earnings by lengthening the time before marriage. Considering the possibility for exploitation in this situation, as researchers on workshop labor and kinship have done,[23] village women comment on whether parents exploit daughters' labor.[24]

As the result of economic needs and interests, the communal space of the village, in which egalitarian ideals are regarded as social goals, has become a place where individuals have divided interests and compete against each other. The middle-aged are seeking to gain wealth, amass property, educate and marry off their children at higher levels than they experienced. The elderly ponder their retirement without a social welfare safety net—a retirement that ideally would include making the pilgrimage to Mecca and securing care from their adult children. Young people play the marriage market: daughters strategize how to marry someone they love while marrying into property, and sons work to locate a girl who will comply with their desires, possibly causing her to act against her parents' wishes and elope, forcing her to relinquish her trousseau.[25] Considering the pressing need and escalating uses of money and goods, neighbors, friends, and enemies spend time considering who is making more and how they managed to do it. They measure the kinds and amounts of gifts given at ritual exchanges, how willingly individuals give labor, and the intensity with which they work at festivities to gauge greed and selfishness. They examine the bride's trousseau at her wedding, calculate its value, and consider whether her parents were generous or stingy. These calculations, observations, and gossip about what happens inside a given household, and the common knowledge about how much each family makes through weaving and other labor, create the collective impression of how exploitative, selfish, and greedy individuals are. It is in part through these social observations and commentary that the moral community is established.

PIETY AND PROSPERITY

In this climate of ambivalence toward the effects of economic development and social change, I began to notice good deeds, hayır. One day, Cennet nene, Çevriye's elderly mother, put three biscuits on the windowsill as she got up to leave, in a gesture so modest and unassuming it almost escaped my attention. After she left, I asked Çevriye about this small act. She said, matter-of-factly, "She wanted to give you some hayır." Her act intrigued me because of its economic and spiritual meaning; it seemed a gift, which carried consequences beyond our personal interaction. Intrigued, I watched Cennet nene more closely and realized she performed a lot of good deeds, as well as extra fasts and many rounds of long prayers before the month of Ramazan. I learned how this elderly woman's pious behavior was connected to her past. When I asked her about her marriage, during a time when I was interviewing all the married women in the village about this, she blushed and shrank in shame. The circumstances were typical of women of her generation.[26] Her father had wanted her to marry someone whom she did not love. In an act of panicked desperation, Cennet nene had approached an itinerant trader who walked from village to village. It is true that he was strikingly handsome, as he retained his looks into his elder years, but above all she was trying to escape her father and an undesirable marriage. She approached the trader, offered herself in marriage, and left that day with nothing from her childhood home. Together, they walked to his village in the mountains. Describing the journey, she seemed to relive her elopement. She looked down at her şalvar and nervously picked at the cloth, as if trying to hide the pain of retelling the experience, in what seemed to be a confession. I understood that her strenuous piety was a way to make amends for her youthful act of disobedience fifty years ago. Though her father was long dead, she could address her emotion to God through performing pious acts. This simple offering—dry biscuits, clearly a small sacrifice—was one of many that she gave to various people, which together constituted a rigorous program of good deeds and performances of namaz, the sum total of which were weighed against her elopement. As she was preparing for the other world, by managing her accounts with God, her acts of charity were directed with conscious intensity, pointing to their greater significance in a spiritual economy of actions and amendments.

Understanding how Cennet nene's piety and personal history were linked revealed the deeper meaning and purpose of others' actions. The fresh-cut oranges Arife offered me with the comment, "Let me give you some hayır," had new significance. Before leaving in 2001, Fatma nene pointed out the debts I owed for the hayır given in each glass of tea I had drunk in the village. I shrank at the load of my burden. Through seemingly minor, but by no means casual acts of sharing and in more formal rituals, I began to see how hayır infuses life with spiritual significance. It enables individuals to express attention simultaneously to God, to one's future in the next world, and to the material condition of one's neighbors. Hayır is a bridge, in this way, linking the seemingly secular concerns of economy and fortune to a spiritual economy. Without acknowledgment, the villagers argue through demonstrative acts that both sacred and secular networks may fail.

OLIVE OIL

Local sayings involving olive oil are part of expressions used to describe greediness. Villagers critically remark, with a gesture of squeezing and licking, "When so-and-so squeezes her fist, olive oil runs down her arm and she licks it up again." Olive oil is an important source of wealth, but it can cause contentious relations. Keeping it to oneself is regarded as greedy, sinful, and shameful. Despite the fact that the villagers live in the Aegean region, known for olive cultivation, olives have only recently become an important component of their diet and economy. About thirty years ago a government-development project encouraged the cultivation of olive and pistachio trees. Both foodstuffs are symbolic of modernity, because they were introduced by the government and can be sold. Before olive oil, the villagers made oil from the fruit of the *çitlembik* (nettleberry) tree, which is indigenous and grows wild. Although these seeds are useful and tasty, they have no market value. Olive trees are planted in low-lying areas but pistachios are grafted onto the çitlembik tree. While çitlembik is now a product of the poor, olives are new, modern, and expensive. For these reasons, olives inspire ambivalence. The villagers are acutely aware of how many olives each family gathers at the biannual harvest, and family members often bicker about who owns the trees, how much labor was contributed to the watering and cultivation of the olives, and how much each adult child expects as a share after the harvest.

In response to these conflicts surrounding this product of modernity, luxurious consumption, and potential wealth, the villagers perform hayır by donating olive oil to the mosque. The imam gives some to a local Qur'an school and distributes the rest to the needy. Women gather and make çörek, which they distribute to the houses in the village. I saw a similar practice in Manisa. Men from a local mosque gathered to cook çörek on the street and distribute it to passers-by. Making and distributing food, especially foods that utilize costly ingredients like olive oil, is a concrete demonstration of a willingness to incur costs and to share. It is important to see the significance of these seemingly ordinary acts, like distributing oil or fried dough. Gains inspire ambivalence. Being happy about success without distributing some portion of the gain by giving to others is shameful. Even though olives play an ambivalent social role, villagers rejoice over abundant olive harvests. This is because economic success is considered a sign of God's blessings. The problem is not success, but the refusal to recognize that God is behind that success. There is also the need to make a return to God, by giving to others, in order to acknowledge God's blessings and to ensure a continuation of them into the future.

These expressions of care and concern for individuals, and by extension for the community, whether expressed economically or through pragmatic social intervention, are not open or free. They are strategic tools for social control and are political because they are intended to change individual behavior and action through moral pressure. The application of moral force is not limited to Kayalarca. Scott describes how villagers gave zekat as a reward for those whose reputations as good workers were sound.[27] Benthall also attests, in the decisions about how zekat be distributed, that "the consensus seems to be that Islam calls on all people to work and the characters and reputations of poor people may be taken into account in deciding whether or not they deserve help."[28] The tithe is not an open-ended gift to those in need, but a means to control labor and enforce social conformity.[29] The selectivity of the tithe makes it political, by rewarding or punishing. In Kayalarca, the selectivity in providing assistance includes social action as well. The villagers consider the morality of the person, who might be in need of assistance. They did not, for instance, actively mourn the death of a baby who had been conceived out of wedlock. They were not punishing the baby, who was "innocent" since she "did not witness the sin" which resulted in her conception, as one woman remarked, but they were punishing the parents. They did not intervene when a young woman isolated herself by eloping and later was tormented by her mother-in-law. They did not assist poor families when the husbands had been difficult and resentful of the cooperative in the past. They actively avoided individuals with whom they quarreled, even on holidays, when people are expected to exchange greetings. These social sanctions are expressions of disapproval and they are meant to check the behavior of others. I did not find more violent threats, as did Stirling in his research on a village in Central Anatolia during the 1950s.[30] There were no cases of honor killing, nor did men physically fight. Yet, in a community which is small and relatively removed from larger towns and cities, and where people frequently comment on the need to be with others, social isolation and the refusal to assist by contributing labor, compassion, or other assistance is a stinging punishment.

It is important to recognize that through both the practice of good deeds and the selective withholding of social support, community is not vaguely situated in a loosely defined public space but is grounded in households, which are linked together by ties of kinship, neighborhood, and friendship. Individuals and families are connected through exchanges of labor, assistance, moral and emotional support, and through redistributions of wealth, such as olive oil, milk, and cheese. These dense networks show that the villagers do not regard a private space of the household as separate from a public space of the community. Islamic morality in the village is based on how community levels a distinction between public and private. This formulation contradicts Göle's argument that "the culture of Islam . . . is established not only on the invisibility of the *mahrem* (literally, 'forbidden' but also meaning private or domestic) sphere and that of women but also on the 'secrecy' and 'nonverbalization' of the affairs taking place in the *mahrem* realm; it is a society of silence, thus, it is antiliberal in its very organization."[31] Göle is describing elite Islamists, who are attempting to revitalize Islamic practice in Istanbul, and therefore individuals who are self-conscious of the need to reinvent traditions, including dress, spheres of activity, and moral action. In my understanding of the construction of a rural Islamic society, the public is not separate from the private in the same manner. The elision of public and private is not unique to rural Turkey. White describes how Islamic charity workers in Istanbul visit families in their homes to learn their intimate economic situations.[32] Few who have been integrated into these networks of support are hidden from view. Contrary to Göle's claims about the role of Islam in isolating women, in the village and as White also shows in poor neighborhoods in Istanbul, Muslim women are not living in seclusion. In village homes there are no separate spaces within the house for men—the *selamlık*, or the *harem* for women. Women move outside the home and are influential leaders in the cooperative and village. This is not to say that there is not an understanding of "home" or domestic space or of gendered distinctions of place and behavior. Rather, the village and the entire space of the Yuntdağ are conceptualized as "home," in which there are no strangers.[33] Women freely visit each other's homes, facilitated by the fact that husbands are rarely in them. Rural spaces create different forms of gendered piety. Thus, in the domestic social space of the village and the Yuntdağ, a sense of trust is generated through concrete exchanges, redistributions, acts of caring, and consideration—practices that are knitted together with discussion about other people's behavior.

One might argue that the politics of economic redistribution in village life are cultural, distinct from religious practice, but this implies that for a practice to be correctly religious it must be drawn from texts, not from social practices. And this, in turn, is the crux of the problem I have been examining: the definition of what is regarded as religious. A narrow, doctrinally based definition sweeps away most of the material discussed in this book. Clearly, while not drawing a border around religion per se, I am including culturally religious practices, thereby challenging a narrow definition of religion.

White shows how the collective well-being of the group can be used by a community to create solidarity and networks of mutual economic and political support which are interpreted as being a moral foundation of society grounded in religion.[34] In the household and community, individuals are expected to subvert their individual desires for the welfare of the group.[35] Loyalty to the group secures assistance and support among its members. The community protects and controls (and prevents), as well as assists the individual in achieving goals, which are seemingly individualistic but can be collective investments, such as obtaining an education or getting married. The return on a collective investment for individual well-being requires that the individual be socialized in a system of mutual indebted assistance,[36] or in some way be required to make a return to others within the group. These burdens of expected return are created through moral socialization taking place within an Islamic context. Individuals, who are socialized in the need to reciprocate, express their gratitude for help and assistance from others via the cultural rendition of religion as they understand it. For instance, children are expected to assist their elderly parents not only because they raised them, but because this a spiritual duty.

The structures of Islamic behavior create a moral framework within which individuals reciprocate. A couple that enjoys a bountiful yield contributes a part of their olive oil for redistribution to the poor in the village. This informal contribution is distinguished from giving their children, who assisted in maintaining the trees and harvesting the olives, a part of the crop which was due them. This is understood as a payment in kind. In other words, villagers recognize collectivity, the bonds of duty, in spiritual terms and distinguish these from payments for debts for labor. Thus, villagers expect a return for labor equaling the work performed, but a generalized moral support for the community, especially the poor, in economic terms. In this way, villagers cultivate a perpetual attention to piety through practices of good deeds. As Loeffler also describes with regard to a village in Iran, villagers respond to virtually every occurrence in everyday life with "innumerable offerings, sacrifices, dedications, contributions, alms, vows, *sufrahs* (meal offered for a religious purpose), invitations, and gifts made to obtain favors, ensure well-being, secure protection, avert evil, help the dead, give thanks, or simply show compassion."[37]

Islamic practice, as it is popularly understood, encompasses these many small acts, which punctuate everyday life and infuse ordinary acts, like sharing a bowl of fruit, donating a bucket of milk, saying a brief prayer when passing the graveyard, pinning an amulet, making tea for visitors, throwing out vegetable scraps on the road for cows, as spiritual gestures of compassion and care. Villagers draw upon these expressions of care to distinguish "real Muslims" from infidels. Thus, the test of being a good Muslim is connected to these cultural acts, not only ones codified in texts. Loeffler's discussion of village life in Iran seems less troubled by the purifying movements of Islamism than the period I discuss. "Being a true Muslim does not come from saying the prayers but from having compassion: to give to the poor is better than to make the pilgrimage to Mecca. Thus, while the religion's normative structure as well as the thrust of the clergy's presentations projects [*sic*] the strict observance of prayers and fasting as criteria for a good Muslim, in the peasants' view a good Muslim is one who does good to others."[38] Though villagers in the Yuntdağ are concerned with standards of orthodoxy as measured by the ability to read the Qur'an in Arabic, performing at least five prayers per day, and fasting, the culturally and spiritually defined attentiveness to others is also fundamental to Islam, as in the villagers in Loeffler's case. Reciprocation is supposed to assist in the making of community through mutual indebtedness,[39] as well as securing one's position in the next world—"to give to people to please God and so obtain favors many times greater in value than what was given away."[40] Individuals, inspired by a sense of collective good, create a political constituency of Muslims who act to mobilize communities in politically, spiritually, and culturally moralistic ways.[41] These social networks and bonds of dutiful reciprocation make Islam a tool for political mobilization, which generates a framework for establishing political and moral agendas for social change in communities both large and small. People expect that God notices these activities, demands that returns be made and surpluses shared, and also records these deeds through angels who populate the unseen world around us. Ultimately, the record-keeping activities of angels are used to assess one's deeds on earth when one attempts to make a case for entry into heaven after the Judgment Day.

In the cooperative, the villagers have worked to develop the village and region to make it prosperous. Through their work with western expatriates in the foundation of the cooperative in the 1980s, they expanded their view of the world by meeting foreigners, traveling to other countries, and success-fully running businesses. In so doing, they have experienced improvements in their material lives, as well as the revitalization of carpet weaving. While economic development has enabled some to enjoy a more comfortable life, it has intensified discord, ambivalence, and envy. Economic difference, which stems from success, is not easily concealed. It is clear that some have gained wealth: satellite dishes sprout in gardens, washing machines relieve women from drudgery, olive oil is always available, and some families afford the occa-sional chicken in their diet. Meanwhile, others languish eating sunflower seed oil and pulling their children out of school to weave. Piles of çitlembik drying in the sun in front of the houses of the poor, which resonate with the sound of the beater on the warp as daughters dutifully weave carpets, mark them as poor. They know that even after marriage, when many enjoy the fruits of their parents' generosity, they will be carrying water from old wells and scrubbing their laundry by hand.

An intensified turn to the Islamic practice of good deeds helps assuage the inequities that villagers see displayed before them. In intimate interactions and exchanges, hayır addresses concerns about the loss of humanity. However, it does not transform the social structures, upon which inequities rest, or return village life to a nostalgically imagined egalitarian past.

Nevertheless, the particular concern with olive oil shows that hayır is not only a traditional practice, but a critique of a new economy. In the villagers' efforts, they show an interest in formulating a pious and sustainable capitalist economy, which is not predicated on the separation of individuals from the group or the selfish accumulation of wealth. As Tuğal points out, the proponents of moral capitalism are not effective in reconciling their desire for economic development on the one hand and an Islamic and just society on the other.[42] Caught between these two tendencies, they are ambivalent about the effects of capitalism—the tendency within it for individuals to act based on self-interest and as a result, for community to fall apart under the pressures of envy and greed.

The consequences of this contradiction are played out in everyday life. In 2004, a few weavers were traveling to towns to work in factories. By abandoning weaving, they were seeking factory wage labor that would free them from the social and moral pressures that working at home with their mothers, mothers-in-law, neighbors, and friends put them under. Given these few who were breaking away from the old system in favor of the more intensely capitalistic structure of factory work, the division between those who desire a return to an imaginary socially egalitarian and just rural society, and those who wish for greater wealth and individual freedom cannot be reconciled easily. A consideration of these struggles shows that through practices that appear to be traditional people work to construct a pious modernity.

4 CONSTRUCTING ISLAM
Mosques, Men, and the State

The history of mosque construction in Yeniyurt and Kayalarca villages demonstrates how, over the course of the late nineteenth and twentieth centuries, villagers have become more involved in urban-based, state-directed Sunni Islam. Villagers support the Diyanet and its activities, including mosque construction, in part because they see it as an extension of the Ottoman office of the caliphate and therefore a link to the Ottoman past and contemporary state. In contrast, among non-Sunni Muslims, especially the Alevi, the Diyanet attempts to redefine non-Sunni practice and build mosques to regularize and assimilate non-Sunnis into a state-defined form of religious practice. Unlike Sunni villagers, the Alevi feel threatened by state assimilation policies.[1] Villagers in the Yuntdağ support the construction of local mosques—usually undertaken through local initiative.

The expression of state orthodoxy includes the shape and style of mosque architecture. In western Europe and the United States, the construction of new mosques and Islamic cultural centers is often blocked due to Islamophobia. In western Europe the proliferation of new mosques implies to some that the landscape is being conquered by a minority, immigrant population, radicalized and unable to assimilate. In 2009, in Switzerland, a referendum against the construction of minarets was passed.[2] In Cologne, Germany, there is controversy over the construction of a new Turkish mosque, sponsored by the DITIB.[3] And in the neighborhood of Kreuzberg, Berlin, there have been controversies and misunderstandings from both Europeans and Turks over the size, shape, and form of mosques.[4] In the United States, the controversy over the construction of a Muslim community center in Manhattan, which would also house a mosque, enraged people who thought of Islam as a religion of terrorists and the land around the former Trade Center sacralized by the martyrdom of the victims of the 9/11 attacks.[5]

In Turkey, a majority Muslim country, one might expect that the construction of mosques would be uncontroversial. But there too, the construction of mosques is interpreted as a political tool wielded by Islamists who plan to geographically dominate the city. To people beleaguered by a growing population of devout Muslims from the lower middle classes, often with roots in rural and provincial Turkey, many fear that the urban landscape is being used to express the growing power and influence of devout Muslims who are politically mobilized and organized. Mosque construction is regarded as a symptom of the re-Islamicization of public life, a movement from secularity to Islamism. High-profile mosque construction projects, such as one proposed for Taksim Square—the historic European center of the city, dominated by a theater, a Greek Orthodox church, a luxury hotel, and an Atatürk statue—underscores the polarization of the debate between secularists, who want to symbolically uphold the principles of the Republic, and Islamists, who want to counter these with the symbolic presence and visibility of mosques.[6] Additionally, the huge numbers of Neo-Ottoman-style cement-form buildings in lower-class neighborhoods in Turkish cities and provincial towns are pointed to as a sign of increased public religiosity. In short, the building of mosques—in Europe, the United States, and Turkey—inflames debate about who should visually dominate the landscape, and whether Muslims should be visible and audible. These debates point to the more general observation that the use of space is an expression of power. The construction of mosques in Turkey, in both the republican and the Ottoman eras, Islamicizes public space,[7] while the demolition of these sacred spaces for republican structures secularizes them.[8]

MOSQUE COMPLEXES, KÜLLIYE, AND ISLAMIC SOCIAL SERVICES

Due to the secularist policies of the Turkish Republic, the socially meaningful, politically powerful, and symbolically productive *külliye*, or mosque complex, has been pared down to a mosque. Mosques contain worship, but the range of buildings in the Ottoman külliye included services to communities, founded on principles of pious collectivity. The paring down of külliye to mosques thereby underscores the meaning of Islam within the context of the Turkish secular state. That is, Islam becomes a private practice controlled, contained, constructed, and funded by the state, a matter of individual prayer, rather than social services supported by vakıfs, private pious endowments. These endowments created services for communities—thereby establishing the social and geographic foundations of collectivity with buildings to house them: soup kitchens, orphanages, schools, libraries, mosques, baths, hospitals, cemeteries, tombs, and shops. The vakıf ensured that these social services would extend the viability of the institutions into the future, insulating them from political control. As Amy Singer describes, vakıfs were legal contracts made by an individual or a group of individuals to fund a "valid pious purpose, which could be the support of Muslim ritual, social and cultural institutions (their buildings, staffs, and activities), public works, poor and needy persons, or even family members. Once constituted, an endowment was irrevocable and unalterable, except according to conditions laid down in the original deed or otherwise approved by a judge."[9] Singer notes that attempts to reform the system began in the eighteenth century, but the most decisive step in reform came in the nineteenth century. "The destruction of the Janissary Corps in 1826 made possible the incorporation of all Janissary *waqf* holdings under the ministry, as well as the further expansion of the ministry's authority over imperial waqfs to include those under the control of the chief eunuch, the grand vizier, the shaykh al-Islam, and the Istanbul *qadis*."[10]

The Bektaşi order, closely associated with the Janissary Corps, was abolished and all their property appropriated in 1840.[11] In other words, attempts at appropriating vakıf property, including that held by tarikats, had begun long before the Republic was established. At the time the Republic was founded, the new government, which needed funds, took over vakıfs. Singer points out that the Vakıflar Bankası (Vakif Bank) was founded in 1954 using capital from the former vakıfs. As part of their service, the bank provides funds to support monuments, students, and dormitories, which previously were founded by vakıfs.[12] There is some attempt, then, to recognize the vakıf contracts.

Though many of the services have ceased, the former buildings of Ottoman külliye in contemporary urban Turkey are often standing. Though many spaces are being renovated, they are not used to house the same institutions they once did. In many instances, in any case, this is impossible. Medreses (Islamic schools) were disbanded, for example. The socially meaningful Islamic communities of the past are thereby safely reprocessed as a lost history of Muslim communities, not a living Islamic present.[13]

The Süleymaniye in Istanbul, built in 1550–57 by Mimar Sinan, is one of the few complete külliye remaining. There is, in addition to the mosque, a cemetery, widely visited for its important tombs, including that of Sultan Süleyman Kanuni or Süleyman the Magnificent. I noticed while visiting the tombs in 2009 that a number of ordinary-looking graves were being visited enthusiastically. I saw that these were Özal's mother's grave and beside it that of her sheik, as people visiting the tomb explained to me. The physical association of the neoliberal leader's mother's grave, and that of her Nakşibendi sheik, with Sultan Süleyman Kanuni (the lawgiver) (r. 1520–66), should not escape our attention. The close proximity of the graves aligns republican Sufi influence with the greatest Ottoman sultan. As one man pointed out to me, "Though they would like to say these groups are finished (meaning the Nakşibendi), they exist and are important."

On one remote corner of a wall of the huge complex far from the cemetery is Mimar Sinan's (1490–1578) grave, the famous Ottoman architect, who built this külliye as well as many other significant structures, tombs, and mosques in the Empire. Now the tomb is closed and one can easily miss the structure in the maze of shops on the edge of the complex. Buildings that have been repurposed include a former hospital, guesthouse, caravansary, several schools (medrese), soup kitchen, shops, and bathhouse (*hamam*).[14] As of 2010, while massive renovations of Ottoman structures were being carried out in celebration of Istanbul's European cultural-capital status, many of the buildings, such as the guesthouse, were unused and locked shut. Others, such as the former hospital, now a café, cater to tourists and local visitors. The medrese can be rented for big events, such as weddings. The hamam remains in use but now men and women wash together there. Traditionally, hamams have separate male and female areas or are open to different sexes on different days; the exception to this rule means that tourists prefer this one. Interestingly, the many small restaurants outside the wall of the mosque and cemetery region, housed in a former medrese, serve beans and rice, a dish similar to those served to the poor in soup kitchens. Mosque complexes, as well as smaller local mosques, also had fountains (*çeşme*) and sometimes a *sebil*, a booth where fruit juice and water were distributed as a pious deed.[15] Fountains were often built as memorials after someone's death or endowed by a wealthy person to serve a neighborhood. Much wealthier people, such as the sultan and his wives or mothers, endowed soup kitchens, as Singer's interesting book on an Ottoman soup kitchen in Jerusalem endowed by Süleyman's wife Hurrem Sultan testifies.[16] Considering the variety of services mosque complexes offered, it is no wonder that they were active centers of public life.

There was even commerce in small shops. Founded as pious deeds by wealthy individuals who privately endowed buildings and services through vakıf, the külliye served the public. The current structures of the külliye demonstrate that their former purposes have been undermined. No longer are the poor fed, boys schooled in the Qur'an, the sick cared for, or travelers hosted. Even the fountains do not work. The library, however, continues to function and has about seventy thousand Ottoman manuscripts as well as thousands of printed books.[17]

With the founding of the Republic, the külliye and all the services associated with it were truncated in the push to secularize society. The mosque became the only standing building representing Islam, a bastion of male activity. As Kezer describes the effect of the erasure of Islamic life from the spaces of cities, "It was as though a layer was forcefully being peeled off of the landscape. As a result, what had once been busy street corners or tucked away congregational spaces, shrines, and other sacred sites—were sealed away from the patterns of everyday use."[18] There are some exceptions: a few soup kitchens survive, such as the one at the great mosque and tomb complex in Eyüp in Istanbul and the one described by Singer in Jerusalem. The imperial mosque complexes, which lasted hundreds of years,[19] were taken over by the new republican regime and in the process, the social world of Islam, visible in public spaces and forming the foundation of community spaces and services, were "peeled" off. They were replaced with republican institutions, public schools, hospitals, and so on. In this way the "welfare societies" of the Ottoman era were incorporated in the welfare state of the Republic.[20] Mosques came under the jurisdiction of the Diyanet, founded in 1924.

In rural Turkey, where these grand complexes never existed, state reforms affecting foundations and endowments did not disturb the annual cycle of charitable activities. Obviously, the scale of social service was smaller but the rural areas were less affected by secularist policies that aimed to confine faith in a mosque, because orthodox practice and Muslim social services were less dependent on the imperial order of the state and less tied to their endowments. Furthermore, the Islamic concept of the welfare society, as Singer argues, was not secularized by the state in rural places where Islam was never privatized.

FROM OTTOMAN TO NEO-OTTOMAN MOSQUES

The classic Ottoman mosque structure both contains and constrains Islam literally, but it broadcasts an implicit symbolic message visually, through the style of architecture, design, and decoration, as Gülru Necipoğlu-Kafadar argues in her examination of the political message of the Süleymaniye complex.[21] The political message of the mosque building is carried into the present in the design of new mosques. Considering the typical form of most newly constructed Turkish mosques, one cannot fail to notice their allusion to Ottoman architectural styles.[22] The exuberance of these structures expresses a sense that Islamic legitimacy, not only of a spiritual private variety but of a public one, is derived from reference to Ottoman structures, and by extension to the Empire. However, these buildings are not historical replicas. These new mosques construct Islam, deliberately and literally, as a combination of Turkish modernity and a glorious empire. The singularity of the form is not accidental. Turkish mosques in Anatolia rarely evoke an Arab past, nor do they propose something new. Rather, they reproduce in cement the classic domes, the multiple minarets, and the arcade-like terrace of columns. They rarely attempt an interior courtyard, an important feature of Ottoman mosques, which created an intimate space for fountains, a respite from the bustle of the city where men could rest on shaded platforms and pray outside while protected from weather. Instead in Neo-Ottoman-style mosques, space for protected but external prayer is pushed outside. The door to the interior is exposed; on Fridays, the exterior overflows with praying men spilling into the streets and sidewalks outside the mosque. Men performing the namaz in public spaces is a pointed act of rebellion against secularist power, as the masses of men around Yeni Camii ("new mosque"—which does have a courtyard) in Istanbul for the Friday sermon attest.

Keeping in mind that mosques via their architectural form broadcast political messages, I will consider the particulars of mosque construction, deconstruction, and reconstruction in the rural region of the Yuntdağ. Villagers began to construct village mosques in the late nineteenth and early twentieth centuries. One might wonder why villages did not have their own mosques, given the prevalence of mosques throughout Turkey. Until recently, Islamic practice did not require a building to contain and control it, and activities now regarded as heterodox were common, such as prayers to holy men on mountaintops (*dede duası*) and rain prayers (*yağmur duası*). However, as state authority and power represented through Sunni Islam gained greater influence, even in relatively remote rural regions, people began to build mosques. The mosque itself demonstrates the official construction of Sunni Islam. As Necipoğlu-Kafadar argues, the Süleymaniye was constructed to politically legitimize state power and Sunni authority over heterodox Anatolian political movements.[23] Similarly, the village mosque demonstrates a tie to legitimizing state orthodoxy.

In addition to being an expression of local acceptance of state authority, mosques are spaces of male domination. When I asked women why they did not go to the mosque, they were quick to point out that they pray in mosques during the month of Ramazan and for Mevluts. However, women in the Yuntdağ treat the mosque, including its courtyard, as a male domain. In Kayalarca, women take the long way round the mosque, when they could take a shortcut across the courtyard, in order not to tread on male space. In 2005, some men in Kayalarca built a stone-paved path, which parallels the mosque staircase so that "women and animals," as one put it, would not have to cross the mosque courtyard. One reason why women do not enter the mosque is because they menstruate. A menstruating woman pollutes the mosque. I had trouble convincing village women in Yeniyurt that I should be given permission to enter their mosque in order to photograph it. They reluctantly allowed me to ask the imam, a young man from Urfa. Because he is a student, he respected my status as a professor and invited me into the mosque. He was eager to learn about my research and discuss his job as imam in the village, far from home. I was heartened by his open welcome and understood that village women police the mosque to ensure the purity of the mosque. This rural attitude toward mosques as being male space is different from urban mosques, where there are women's sections with separate doors. These are usually in the back of the mosque or in a small room (without a view of the main mosque), in itself a marker of women's lesser status and men's reluctant accommodation to women's piety. Yet, despite the side entrance, women have a way to attend the mosque in cities if they want. In villages, this is quite different; women feel they should pray at home, and they avoid making demands on men to allow women entrance to the mosque.

While women visit the mosque during the month of Ramazan, Mevluts and Kandils,[24] men often pray in the mosque, especially for the Friday sermon and for the last namaz of the day. Elderly men spend their final decades sitting in the mosque courtyard waiting for the call to prayer and performing the namaz several times a day. Women remarked to me that they "wished" women also could go to the mosque because this would make it easier to pray. Maintaining a private practice at home requires discipline, and many felt that prayer would be easier if shared with others and performed in a public space. Women also praised the mosque for having miraculous powers. As one young woman remarked, "In the mosque, one's bodily aches and pains do not hurt." She explained, "Kuş gibi olup camiye giden insanlara [A person feels like she has turned into a bird when she goes to the mosque]." Developing her remarks, the same young woman mentioned how during Ramazan, when one fasts during the day but eats at sunset, one's stomach swells. She said she often didn't want to go to the mosque then because she felt physically uncomfortable, but once inside the building, she did not feel discomfort and was able to perform the namaz easily. She attributed the disappearance of physical discomfort to being inside the building. In other words, she imagined the building had powers.

For years I had difficulty reconciling women's lack of concern that they were shut out from the mosque, as I saw it, with their piety. It seemed to me, especially given the movement of many Muslim women to gain access to mosques, such as that described by Mahmood,[25] that the women in the Yuntdağ were being prevented from practice inside the mosque. I thought this because I wrongly equated the mosque with a church, and I expected that religious practice needed a building and a clergy. But as I studied women's piety more systematically, I began to consider an alternative perspective, to which I have already alluded: women's piety is less contained by mosques and therefore less codified and contained by state constructions of orthodoxy. For this reason, women maintain connections to the past through heterodox activities and cultural Islamic traditions. Being outside the mosque and apart from state control, they have the freedom to create their own expressive and innovative practices. The state is less concerned with women's piety and its association with or against the state.

The history of mosques in the region demonstrates that men's spirituality was not always contained by a building, and by state renditions of correct practice, as it is now. In the gendered construction of Sunni Islam, which relates to the encroachment of state power, men's piety is contained by state institutions and the mosque, while women can choose whether they want to engage with official renditions of Sunni Islam. Men experience the disciplining rigors of state constructions of Sunni practice, while women, practicing at the margins of this power, dabble, innovate, and maintain links to the past. This means that men's practice is regarded as an official representation of state orthodoxy.

FROM PRAYER HOUSE TO MOSQUE

Before there were village mosques, men gathered in a simple *ibadethane* (prayer house) on Fridays on a plain a kilometer or so north of Kayalarca village. The region called Maşatla is dominated by an ancient oak tree, which is always mentioned in descriptions of the place;[26] for instance, a young man from Kayalarca posted a photograph of the tree on Facebook, in his collection of important features of the landscape around his village. There are two small cemeteries where people from a number of villages are buried. A few have continued the practice with recent graves. The flat space near the tree was once used as a threshing ground, but villagers no longer thresh their wheat; instead they take it to a mill. The area is still frequented, however. The shepherds use it to water their sheep in stone bowls which they use to hold water they draw from wells close by. One woman noted the diligence of their ancestors who carved the bowls out of rocks. The plain is dotted with the remains of small fires for making tea, also the work of shepherds who spend the nights grazing their animals during the summer and during the day in winter. Before the tree was struck by lightning about five years ago, one of its large branches was used to support a rope swing, a game for children during holidays, weddings, and other ritual occasions, and for rug tourists visiting in groups organized by the villagers.

Several men described the prayer house as resembling a stone and earthen house. This would have been a one-room building with thick stone walls and a flat earthen roof. There are no visible traces remaining. Villagers described how men from a number of villages in the region prayed there on Fridays. The dates when the prayer house was used are not clear, but it would seem to predate the village mosques and possibly the settlement of some of the villages, such as Yeniyurt. According to some amateur Ottoman historians I met in Manisa, whose day jobs include working as high school history teachers and managing charitable endowments, Kayalarca is one of the oldest settled villages in the Yuntdağ. These men said they had read the Ottoman notebooks on the region, before they were transferred to Ankara, to the main state archive. Though Kayalarca was a settled village early, it seems it did not have a mosque until later. Yeniyurt's mosque was built in 1319, according to the Islamic calendar, 1901 by the Gregorian conversion. This means the prayer house was used during the nineteenth century, before the foundation of the Republic. As I described earlier, the villagers from Yeniyurt recall that they settled in their present location when two migrating groups, who inhabited different yaylas (summer pastures) joined together. They built a village mosque during the reign of Abdulhamid II (1876–1909), an era of significant social and religious institutional reform.

Maşatla's association with a now-vanished prayer house does not fully account for its spiritual status. The oak in the plain, always mentioned in descriptions of the area, is significant. Though it may seem a stretch, trees were revered in central Asia and in Anatolia in pre-Islamic shamanistic practice, often assimilated into Islam. Though the prayer house is gone and no one reveres the tree, Maşatla is still used as a gathering place for rain prayers, yağmur duası. Rain prayers are conducted in the spring or during a time of drought. There are two forms: those instigated by women, usually in spring, and those led by men, usually in times of drought. Women's rain prayers involve gathering to cook bide, as they do at funerals. Women pause in their cooking, say a prayer, and then eat together, distributing the rest of the food to households. In times of drought, men take over the rain prayer. They invite an imam to deliver a sermon in the mosque, sacrifice an animal, and make keşkek. They also perform a Mevlut in the mosque. The entire village gathers to feast at Maşatla. Both men's and women's styles of rain prayer in the Yuntdağ differ from descriptions given by Ilhan Başgöz, demonstrating that the ritual in this region has been cleansed of cultural practice and Islamicized.[27] In addition to rain prayers, many elderly men visit the graves on Arife Günü, at Maşatla at the end of Ramazan. The space retains, therefore, spiritual significance in the local landscape.

YENIYURT'S MOSQUE AND MEDRESE

Villagers in Yeniyurt are proud of their mosque, for its solid stone construction, beautiful decoration, and old style. In 2010, while visiting Orhan, who works as an imam in Bamberg, Germany, I shared photographs from Yeniyurt's mosque interior. The interior of Yeniyurt's mosque has striking calligraphic paintings in the shape of boats on the walls. These seem quite old and newer whitewash has been carefully applied around them. Orhan experienced a wave of nostalgia looking at the photographs. He read the calligraphy to his wife and me. I had not realized that the words, intertwined and flowing to form a picture of a water vessel, could be read. His love for the interior of his childhood mosque was evident. In addition to these striking old decorations, there is a wooden *minber*, or pulpit. Above the curtained doorway is a container holding the Sakal-ı Şerif, a hair of the Prophet. A wooden balcony at the rear of the interior is the women's section. Wooden lattice screens shield men's and women's gazes from each other in the women's section. These also obscure women's view of what men are doing downstairs, though they can peek through the diamond-shaped holes.

As well as a mosque in Yeniyurt, there was also a medrese. There is some confusion in people's stories about which building was constructed first. In any case, Ali Hacı, the former imam in Kayalarca who is native to Yeniyurt, told a story about how the medrese was founded. In the Ottoman era, there was an orphaned boy in Yeniyurt living with his grandfather, who had a herd of goats. The grandfather wanted his grandson to look after the goats but the boy wanted to study. "To study" *okumak*, as I previously discussed, means in village parlance to study the Qur'an and other religiously oriented books, and to pray. Therefore when Ali Hacı told the story, he merely said that the boy wanted to study (*okumak istedi*) and I understood this to mean that he wanted to study the Qur'an, not a secular subject. In order to study and also avoid caring for the goats, the boy ran off to a town near Şakran, on the Aegean Sea, called Çandarlı, where there was a medrese. Because this was before electricity, the room in which he lived, as Ali Hacı pointed out, had no light. Naturally, he might have had an oil lamp, but for some reason, there was none. He used the light coming from a hole in the wall to read the Qur'an. This hole opened to the neighboring room where a Jew lived. According to Ali Hacı, the Jew, realizing that the boy was using the light coming from the hole in his wall to study the Qur'an, stopped it up. The boy, unable to read the Qur'an in the dark, asked God to provide him with light (*nur*), upon which God lit the boy's little finger like a candle. In exchange for this miracle, the boy promised that he would return to his native village and establish a medrese once he became an imam.

The miraculous tale of the boy with the lit finger sacralizes the establishment of the medrese and establishes a lineage of scholarship in the village. It also alludes to an era when provincial Ottoman society had a mixed population. Though people lived side by side, clearly there were hostile feelings. The villagers in Yeniyurt are proud of the many imams who have come from their village. As one man said, when I asked how many imams have come from Yeniyurt, "sayılmaz [countless]!" The medrese created a "culture of learning" in the village, as one imam put it, a culture that accounts for the many imams, *vaiz* (a religious leader higher than imam) and public school religion teachers who came from the village. It also is used to account for the success of those who have pursued a secular education to become lawyers, police, teachers, and doctors. The medrese was closed along with all others in the new Republic in 1924, but the building was not razed. As many recalled, the building was allowed to slowly disintegrate, until it fell in the 1970s. The slowly disintegrating building evokes ambivalence toward the state reforms. While villagers did not resist the state's power by keeping the medrese open, they also did not enthusiastically raze the building. Instead, the memory of a miracle story, the culture of Islamic learning, and the state's power to control this was symbolically represented through the slowly disintegrating structure. After the building collapsed, a lodging house for the imam was built in its place.

THE MEN FROM OF

One evening in 2000, while eating dinner with the couple I lived with in Kayalarca, Çevriye and Mühettin remarked in our conversation that they were Laz. I laughed, thinking I had misheard or they were pulling my leg. The Laz are the brunt of jokes in Turkey, similar to Polish immigrants in "Polack" jokes in the United States. Where Laz are located and who they are is confusing and sometimes comically mysterious. While traveling along the Black Sea coast in the 1980s with a Turkish friend, we would ask if the people we met were Laz. Invariably, the answer was "no," but we would be told that over the next mountain or around the next bend, the people "over there" were Laz. This answer was so common, that we would ask out of a sense of fun rather than a real interest in locating these elusive peoples. As Michael Meeker writes, "Any mention of the Laz should be understood with respect to the situation of the speaker using the term. Although all peoples of the province were considered Laz in Istanbul, the peoples of the further eastern sectors, Rize, Of, and Surmene, were considered Laz in Trabzon. The Lazi-speakers of the coastal region inhabited the valleys still further east of Rize."[28] As Meeker reveals in this quote, the Laz have their own language. The peoples from the Black Sea region also have a reputation, which they live up to, for industriousness and a willingness to migrate long distances for work. As I found in the Black Sea region while visiting a remote and beautiful yayla in the lush mountains, accessible only by foot, there were a number of men who worked half the year in Istanbul. I was not expecting to meet people who worked in Taksim while in such a remote place. These men pointed out that their region was famous for pudding makers, and that pudding shops such as the famous Sütiş chain in Istanbul were manned by them.

Though the Laz are a distinct ethnic and linguistic group, they are reluctant to be contained and labeled as such,[29] which accounts for why everyone I met in the region was reluctant to assert a Laz identity. Rather, as is the central argument of Meeker's book, the multiethnic peoples of the Black Sea region (though they would not have thought of themselves in these terms at the time) adopted an imperial identity, eliminating ethnic difference in deference to a state identity. Denying difference assisted their entry into the local imperial elite. Similarly, to claim a distinct ethnicity in the republican era would be disadvantageous, since to identify oneself as a Turk is an empowering marker. The denial of difference for the Laz is similar to the denial of a Yörük identity in the Yuntdağ, and is related to a homogenizing influence of state-constructed Turkish ethno-nationalism. The capacity to integrate different regions and multiple peoples enhanced the statist orientation, as Turkey made the transition from empire to republic.[30]

For these reasons, I was bewildered that villagers in Kayalarca were calling themselves Laz. Recall that they deny referring to themselves as Yörük, a more obvious identity marker. Exploring the question further, over time I uncovered a curious story. In the late nineteenth century, there was a pious and learned man, called Hacı Ahmet, who was married to a woman in the province of Of, on the Black Sea. They had a fight and separated, but apparently did not divorce. Hacı Ahmet traveled from the Black Sea region and settled in the village of Yeniyurt. It is worth pointing out that he was already a pilgrim, a man with sufficient resources to make the pilgrimage to Mecca, before he settled in Yeniyurt. His two grown sons, Hasan and Mehmet, arrived later and also settled in Yeniyurt. All three men married locally, including Hacı Ahmet, who abandoned his previous wife. Many in Yeniyurt are descended from the unions of these men and women from Yeniyurt. Because Kayalarca often took brides from Yeniyurt, one of the daughters of one of the men from Of, Havva, was taken as a bride in Kayalarca. While talking to Havva's daughter, Kiymet, now an elderly woman, I estimated that the date of Havva's father's birth was about 1885. Havva was the mother of a number of then-elderly people in Kayalarca. Havva's great-granddaughter (descended through her mother and father's side because her parents are first cousins) is named after her, thereby carrying on the name of this single Laz descended bride into Kayalarca village.

By talking to people from Yeniyurt about descendants from these men in their village, I learned that the men from Of settled in regions where Islamic knowledge was regarded as weak. They were missionaries, of a sort, who spread Sunni Islamic study and understanding. Ali Hacı explained that the men from Of settled in Yeniyurt, rather than Kayalarca, because there was a medrese, which facilitated their work. Meeker's book helps explain why men from this region would have been trained as religious leaders and why they would have left the Black Sea area for a relatively remote village near the Aegean. "During the later Ottoman Empire, the largest numbers of professors, academies, and students were to be found in the upper western valley-system, which had later become the district of Çaykara. This part of the old district of Of had not been settled until the sixteenth century, at which time it became a place of refuge for Pontic Greek-speaking Orthodox Christians who subsequently converted to Islam."[31]

It would seem that people of the region of Of had been devout Christians, with many priests who converted to Islam while retaining a high degree of religiosity. Conversion was most likely, as Meeker argues, a way to integrate into the power structures of the Empire. After describing the poverty of the region, he says, "under such circumstances, its villagers had been pressed to use whatever skills they had to make up for the lack of material resources. These skills appear to have included reading and writing and, quite possibly, even before conversion, religious teaching and learning."[32] Meeker's description of the poverty of the region combined with a high degree of religious learning describes Yeniyurt today. Assuming that the imams from Of helped intensify a culture of Islamic learning in a village which had a medrese, it would not be surprising if the villagers who descended from them would have learned that Islamic training opens many doors within the state system. This explains the tendency of men from Yeniyurt to study to become imams and to seek rank within the republican system. However, Meeker also sheds some light on the range of practitioners who came out of the Of system.

> The religious academies . . . exported large numbers of graduates, both Oflus and non-Oflus,[33] in the manner of any contemporary university system. A few would continue their studies in the more prestigious religious academies in the major cities. A few would become religious officials in the middle to upper ranks of the imperial religious establishment. But most would seek appointments as prayer-leaders and sermon-givers in the towns and villages of Anatolia. It was the latter, the very large majority, who had come to be known as "hodjas from Of" famous and infamous throughout Asia Minor during the Empire and then again during the Republic.[34]

Meeker describes how many of the students from the region became low-level unofficial imams who would do a little spiritual service for a small fee and cobble that work with others to get by. He adds,

> By my own experiences during the 1960s, some of them would have been relatively thoughtful and educated. Others would have been "şeriatçı," subscrib-

ing to an interpretation of the sacred law of Islam so literal as to bar any kind of music or dancing, not to mention the use of alcohol and tobacco. And still others would have been "cinci," engaging in shady practices such as casting spells for the lovelorn (*büyüme*), performing cures (*okuma*) for the possessed, and selling charms (*nuska*) to fend off the evil eye.[35]

Meeker's description of the range of Islamic practitioners coming from the region of Of describes the imams, official and unofficial, and hocas who work in the Yuntdağ today. Some are intelligent young men who become imams and vaiz, gaining posts and even working abroad within the Diyanet's system of national and international appointments. Others become imams in village mosques, while some manage to gain a more prestigious post in a town or small city. Then there are those who never achieve an official post, but practice unofficially and illegally. And there are a few (though not in Kayalarca or Yeniyurt) who are regarded as "powerful" though unofficial and illegal, who make *muskas*,[36] diagnose illnesses, cure with holy water and other methods, and cast spells. Still others become imams through neo-tarikats, such as the Süleymancı. In short, during the Ottoman era as now, rural regions have been filled with a variety of religious experts and professionals, religious communities, and brotherhoods: individuals known for spiritual power and efficacy, many professing a connection to legacies of learning and importance from the past.

As I have described, Yeniyurt village with its medrese was the center of Islamic training in the region, attracting learned men from the region of Of and creating a powerful culture of Islamic training. The village continues to be an important center of Islamic learning and practice. The mosque with its Ottoman calligraphic adornments contains the Sakal-ı Şerif, venerated by villagers throughout the region. Yeniyurt's remarkable heritage of Islamic learning includes the story of a holy man who lived on its mountaintop. This man is reported to have carried a lantern to the mosque each day to perform the namaz, and was told by God in a dream to migrate across Anatolia to live in that place. The important themes and tropes of dreams and a light illuminating the wisdom and spiritual power of a holy figure play a significant role in creating a spiritual aura around the mountaintop, just as the miracle of the boy's lit finger legitimates the medrese. In addition, many women and men are able to read religious texts in Ottoman and the Qur'an in Arabic. These features of the village, as well as the numbers of imams and vaiz that this culture of learning has produced, made the village a venerable institution of Islamic learning and knowledge in both the Ottoman and republican eras. Understanding the competitive atmosphere between the two villages, let us turn to Kayalarca to see how its villagers respond to Yeniyurt's impressive legacy.

A NEW MOSQUE IN KAYALARCA

While walking from Yeniyurt one day in 2009, I was struck by Kayalarca's mosque, which loomed above me as I entered the village. The location of the mosque, at the entrance of the village, makes a clear statement about the villagers' interest in presenting themselves as prosperous and devout. The statement of the building seems to address Yeniyurt, with its old mosque, tucked within the sprawling village. This aggressively competitive stance was not always how villagers in these two places approached each other through their mosque buildings. From an ideological perspective, the villagers in Kayalarca have taken on an aggressively modernist position with regard to the meaning and purpose of the past in their daily lives. While villagers in Yeniyurt remember, recount, and ritually practice features of their past culture of Islamic learning, villagers in Kayalarca are quick to disparage not only their neighbors for this "backward" (*geri kafalı*) attitude but anyone who would be foolish enough to wallow in the murky realm of the pre-republican past. These different stances toward the past and the construction of modernity are echoed in their mosques.

The villagers in Kayalarca demolished their old mosque and constructed a new one in the mid-1980s. I first heard the history from Josephine Powell and Harald Böhmer, who had founded the cooperative in Kayalarca. Both were a bit bewildered that the villagers would have invested time and energy in demolishing an old, quaint mosque to replace it with this bigger edifice. They described with nostalgic regret the loss of the building, including its painted, wooden interior, and the courtyard filled with big oak trees, which shaded benches where elderly men sat waiting for the call to prayer. They also noted the fact that the old mosque had been filled with carpets of local design donated to the building by weavers. They contrasted the unnecessary expense of the new building with more pressing issues which could have been addressed, such as constructing a water system.

Having heard this story, I tried to understand it from the villagers' perspectives. After interviewing a number of people, I understood that once the village had begun to make money in the cooperative, they wanted to perform a good deed that would express their thankfulness to God for their newfound prosperity. The villagers gathered money from donations within the village, from other villages, from businessmen in Manisa, and from male attendees of mosques in Manisa. As one man described, it is typical that after the Friday noon prayer, men are asked to open their wallets and make a donation to help a village build a new mosque. Ahmet, the former cooperative director, according to his eldest son (this conversation took place after Ahmet's death), was one of the principal donors. Clearly, as soon as they could afford to do so, the villagers made a clear statement about the strength of their belief and its orientation toward state-defined, urban-oriented Islam. In contrast, the old mosque represented a rural legacy of practice. Villagers of different ages and genders explained that the former mosque was "old" and "narrow" and needed to be replaced with something better and newer.   *why?*

As I have learned over the years, villagers in Kayalarca consider old things useless and new things important and desirable.[37] Interestingly, the handmade textiles in trousseaux were not especially valued as cultural artifacts, examples of local nomadic heritage, or the artistic works of one's mother. They were "old" and, as such, expendable in exchange for mass-produced carpets and kilims, woven fiberglass sacks and plastic bags when traders came by the village. Traders passed on their loot to carpet dealers who sold them to collectors, foreigners, and city people. While one might be shocked by the theft of cultural heritage, one has to recognize that villagers did not want it. Similarly, villagers traded their old tinned heavy and handmade copper kettles, trays, and pots for cheaply made mass-produced aluminum pans. Earthenware cooking pots, now fetishized in the cities for their culinary authenticity were smashed in garbage heaps. The old mosque fell into a similar category in the minds of those in Kayalarca: it was wooden and hand-painted, narrow and crowded, and so had to go.

Building a new mosque not only gained Kayalarca villagers a sense of their modern Islamic identity but also earned merits from God. From this perspective, the new mosque was an expression of thanks to God for newfound prosperity, a result of the commodification of weaving heritage in the cooperative. As such, they regarded it as a necessary return for their material success. Though they stress the good deed in building the mosque, this may seem confusing in light of the good deeds I discussed earlier, which focused on redistributions of a surplus or profit to the community to assuage anxiety about the emergence of socioeconomic difference. Does the new mosque perform the same kind of function? Does it assist the poor or redistribute wealth? It would seem, on the face of it, that the new mosque does not directly help the poor. The new mosque does not even serve the female members of the community, though all are proud of the building and would never mention—as I do—that it does not serve them. Building the new mosque does not redistribute wealth; rather, it concentrates it in a new, ambitious building. However, if we reconceptualize the meaning of assistance to that which is not direct and material but ideological, used to create a community, with a particular vision of itself, we can see that the new mosque directs this message to God and neighbors. The mosque was meant to demonstrate thanks to God and create an assurance from God for sustained future prosperity by giving to God a new mosque rather than using that money for personal gain. The villagers, then, conceptualized their success in the economy via a reciprocal relationship to God. The new mosque unified and clarified the spiritual expression of the community—as pious, modern, prestigious, and aligned with statist constructions of Sunni Islam.

Most village mosques have a pitched roof and are small, square, one-story, stone buildings with wooden, painted interiors. Kayalarca's new mosque, in contrast, is a massive, two-story building crafted from stone, shaped by hand by local stonemasons. It has a large, metal-plated dome, which shines brightly and, as the villagers point out, can even be seen from airplanes as they pass overhead between Istanbul and Izmir. The strength and authority of rural Islam thereby is visible to urban air travelers zooming overhead. Villagers proudly note that their new mosque was the first in the region to have a metal-clad dome. Now many villages are replacing their old mosques for ones with metal-clad domes. Commentators in Kayalarca consider themselves the leaders of this new shape of rural and prestigious Islamic architectural expression.

The mosque in Kayalarca is an expression of a particular Islamic identity, an urban-leaning, state-constructed Sunni Islam. In contrast, the mosque in Yeniyurt draws on a culture of religious learning by maintaining Ottoman calligraphic decorations, which can be untangled and read. In Kayalarca, the design and decoration of the building, with serigraphed tiles and a crystal chandelier conveys a political message about the role of economic development, a product of the carpet-weaving cooperative. While their neighbors excel in higher Islamic education, Kayalarca has focused its resources on the carpet-weaving cooperative, opening the village to foreigners, tourists, researchers, journalists, and carpet dealers. An effect of this economic-development project is that Kayalarca is oriented toward Islamist modernism—with references to the Ottoman Islamic past but firmly located in the present.

Though Kayalarca's mosque clearly projects a collective sense of the community as modern and urban, the fact of the building also demonstrates a worry about the spiritual effects of new wealth. The building thereby embodies a contradiction: Islamic modernity can be the product of economic development even as it can assuage selfish materialism. The new mosque also demonstrates the efficacy of charitable contributions from a Manisa-based Islamic community. The villagers in Yeniyurt have chosen not to follow the same path. When I asked villagers in Yeniyurt if they have thought about tearing down their old mosque and replacing it with something bigger, one woman remarked pragmatically that the village is "shrinking," so why the need for a new mosque? While villagers in Yeniyurt enter the world outside the village, they do so as religious professionals. They open up their village to others when they visit for Sakal-ı Şerif, for instance—but they do not make themselves indiscriminately available to outsiders, foreigners, and infidels. This is another way of describing what from the Kayalarca perspective is a closed attitude toward humanity more generally—a point often used in Kayalarca to argue that the villagers in Yeniyurt are not really the good Muslims they claim to be. The fact that the villagers in Yeniyurt choose to retain their old mosque only confirms to those in Kayalarca that their neighbors are hopelessly backward, closed, and old-fashioned, while Kayalarca's mosque convinces villagers in Yeniyurt that those in Kayalarca are blinded by wealth and modernist prestige.

Kayalarca's mosque is part of a history of Islam in the region, an articulation of newfound prosperity and a modern outlook, as well as a demonstration of the pious economic expression of good deeds. While Yeniyurt's mosque is from the Ottoman era, Kayalarca's makes reference to Neo-Ottomanism, a movement that draws nostalgic reference to the Ottoman-era to project the style, power, and piety of that era onto an Islamist rendition of contemporary republican Turkey. These Neo-Ottoman expressions demonstrate an Islamist legitimization of the Ottoman Empire, as a new source for a national past, a direct attack on Kemalist amnesia.[38] Kayalarca's mosque, because it draws upon this political imaginary of the Ottoman Empire, is a place designed for the projection of fantasy. The dome in particular makes reference to Ottoman grandeur, though the building lacks minarets. The fund for building the mosque was not large enough to cover the construction of a minaret.

The political import of the building became clear to me in 2001 when I visited the elementary school and reproduced an experiment I had conducted among second- and third-generation Turkish schoolchildren in Mannheim,

Germany, in 1996. In Germany, I asked children to draw pictures of their lives in Germany one week, and of their lives in Turkey the next. I interviewed each child about what they had depicted in their drawings. All the children had visited Turkey during the summer months. The children's images of Turkey were filled with nationalist iconography—pictures with flags and portraits of Atatürk. One boy solved the problem by filling the whole page with red, creating the crescent moon and star of the flag by dotting white paint directly from the paint tube, eliminating any reference to people or geography—his depiction was pure nationalism. Pictures of Germany had more prosaic references to childhood, such as ice-cream cones, swing sets, and football games, but hovering over these scenes were flags, German and Turkish, referencing a world where people are perpetually conscious of their national origin even when swinging on a swing set or kicking a soccer ball. I was not expecting any nationalist revelations when I repeated my experiment in the village. In Kayalarca, I asked the children to draw pictures of their lives in the village. Like the drawings of life in Turkey, as illustrated by the immigrant schoolchildren in Germany, the Kayalarca children's drawings of their village were filled with political symbols. Though I provided no direction or suggestions, the majority of the children drew large and impressive mosques and pictures of their school but tended to skip over what I thought were the main characteristics of village life: people, houses, and animals.

Confused, I showed the drawings to a group of the children's mothers. The mothers seemed unsurprised by their children's artistic representations. They pointed out that the children chose to draw the most important buildings: the mosque and school. It is notable that no children drew pictures of their homes or families. Their drawings were representative of how they wanted me to see their village. Because the children chose to draw state institutions, the mosque and school being the only two in the village, and thereby the public face, rather than the intimate world of village families, they demonstrated the state's important role in village self-perception and identity projection—which includes the official construction of Islam represented in the mosque. Because the school building is on the outskirts of the village, surrounded by a wall and festooned with national imagery, with an Atatürk bust and a national saying on the side of the building, it is unlike any other building in the village. In this way, the children expressed the self-evident purpose of public education: to create secular citizens.[39] But they also showed the other pole of state power: the construction of Sunni Islam in the mosque.

The children's renditions of the mosque were striking because they drew on imaginative renditions of Ottoman urban mosques, not accurate depictions of Kayalarca's particular mosque. This disjuncture gestures toward the ideological role of the mosque in the children's minds. The children's drawings were of buildings resembling Ottoman imperial mosques. Whereas Kayalarca's mosque has no minaret, the ones in the drawings had multiple minarets, such as the Süleymaniye in Istanbul. Kayalarca's mosque has an impressive dome but the children's had huge central domes with the cascading multiple supporting domes of an iconic Mimar Sinan masterpiece. Not surprisingly, the school-children know implicitly that the ideal mosque should be Sinan's. Thus, in their less sophisticated and unscholarly minds, they already know that this architect is deployed as a symbol of Ottoman masterworks.[40] But this is not to say that the children have not seen impressive Ottoman mosques. A smaller version of Istanbul's grand Mimar Sinan mosque complex, the Muradiye, is in Manisa. Because the city was once the training ground of the future Ottoman sultans, it has a number of impressive Ottoman mosque complexes. A notable complex, especially for the children, is the Sultan Mosque, built in the sixteenth century in honor of Süleyman's mother.[41] Every year, a spiced candy paste, *mesir marcunu*, according to legend a medicine devised for Süleyman's mother, now revamped as "Turkish Viagra," though the children are unaware of the sordid association, is tossed from the minarets during a spring festival. Many village children who have attended the festival recounted their excitement at candy being thrown into the air from the minarets into the courtyard of the mosque and the mass scramble to grab the colorfully wrapped paste. For the children, then, their association of classical Ottoman mosques is mixed up with the famous and impressive imperial buildings in Manisa, their experiences at the Sultan Mosque, and the proliferation of Mimar Sinan–style buildings in Istanbul used on television to promote a particular view of Turkey's Ottoman heritage.

In the children's imagination, their village mosque is as prestigious and important as one of Mimar Sinan's masterpieces. The children merely reflect what their elders feel. The mosque responds to attitudes about rurality and social status generally and religious efficacy in rural spaces particularly. Kayalarca villagers are acutely aware of how geographic categories are signs of class, religious, ethnic, and social identities, and how they are used as a shorthand to categorize people who live in rural places as being traditional and thereby unsophisticated, uneducated, and backward. Places and buildings, as well as practices and beliefs, are connected to ideas of time and progress. The villagers in Kayalarca react against the paternalistic interest, concern, and involvement of city people, who imagine them as belonging to a "traditional" world marked by geographic and chronological barriers. But the past, as it is employed in this politics of identity, is not fixed in content or meaning. Neo-Ottomanism references the past by bringing some of the luster of the Empire into the present. That other past, though, the one of the actual ancestors of the villagers, roaming nomads who had no impressive buildings and poor villagers who had modest prayer houses, is erased from the landscape. In this elective configuration of history, villagers reject the nationalist intellectual construction of Anatolia and Anatolians as a primordial expression of ethnic authenticity, that of being "pure" Turks, and instead embrace the Islamist use of the Ottoman past to render their landscape as historically meaningful, spiritually efficacious, and politically legitimate.

THE "MERKEZ" AND FEATURES OF STATE CONTROL

In my discussion of the spread of mosque buildings in the Yuntdağ, replacing simple prayer houses and the gradual collapse of the medrese in Yeniyurt, the role of the state as an outside actor influencing village life was evident. My rendering of the state appears as an un-deconstructed entity, which directs actions, influences through policy, and controls practice. This disembodied state is an ethnographic description of the villagers' perception via their discussions of how the state works. It is not my theoretical intention to imbrue the state with a disembodied, essentialized power. From villagers' discussions of the state, it would seem a superhuman force behind imperfect real-world entities, politicians and institutions, often expected to be corrupt and with little interest in rural areas. The state requires obedience; villagers rarely make prolonged critiques. In their reluctance to elaborate, they express that the state can only withstand a limited degree of critique and resistance. Villagers' rendition of state power is similar to how they describe God's power. Like God, this superhuman entity directs lives and can call one to account for actions, delivering punishments and consequences, prison or hell. Unlike God, the state has many representatives who are all too human and therefore unlikely to inspire full trust. Villagers who have little pull or influence in the world beyond their region tend to put their faith in God and the ultimate judgment of the next world, rather than in the imperfect and partial humans who embody the state.

Implicit in my discussion of mosques has been the Diyanet's power. The Diyanet trains imams in Imam Hatip schools and employs them in mosques in Turkey and abroad. The mosque is a state institution. The local imam is referred to as a *memur*, a civil servant. A further example of the Diyanet's overarching power in mosques is the recent domination of aural space around them in rural regions. In 2008, the village mosque was hooked up to a broadcast system from the Hatuniye Mosque in Manisa, which broadcasts ezan, the call to prayer, and sermons. As a result of this centralized system, the village imam would no longer perform the call to prayer, deliver sermons, or perform Qur'an readings.[42] He would merely lead the prayer.

I wondered about this obvious demonstration of state involvement in the aural space of the village and the imam's authority and began asking people about it. Ali, an imam native to Kayalarca appointed in a town close to Manisa, explained that his mosque was also connected to the center in Manisa and that all mosques in the Manisa region, but not those inside Manisa, are connected to it. When I asked why, he explained that when each imam reads ezan, they start at different times, resulting in cacophony. Though this is certainly the case in cities where many mosques exist, in villages there is typically one mosque. He added that in addition to the problem of timing the ezan, there is the fact that some people do not read it well. He said that this makes some uncomfortable, and that to eliminate this problem the Diyanet decided to connect all the villages and regions to one center. In fact, the Diyanet instituted singing classes for urban imams, so that they would deliver the ezan more melodiously.[43] It would seem that providing these lessons to rural imams was beyond the financial capacities of the Diyanet or their interests, so instead the Diyanet decided to replace the local reading of ezan with a centralized system. Ali added that sermons and Qur'an readings could also be broadcast, thereby educating the public about religion. During the month of Ramazan, a time of intensified piety and religiosity, the centralized system broadcast long sermons and Qur'an readings every day. Villagers, when the weather and the sound system permitted, could listen to these broadcasts.

Perhaps, feeling nostalgic, I missed the simple villager renditions of ezan, when not only the imam but many men sang the call to prayer, and even small boys whose clear and unornamented performances seemed to me pleasing and inspiring. This democratic rendition of the call to prayer, one in which village women and men paused and appreciated the skill of one of their own, seemed a different expression in comparison to the state's official version projected from

Manisa, performed by an unfamiliar man into the aural space of the village. On the occasions when the system was broken, I was glad we did not have to listen to the electronic screech of the system starting and stopping or the heavily arabesque ornamentations of the urban imam, who, delivering the call from an urban center, did not know us, the village mosque, or any of the people living in the village. To me, this was yet another demonstration of the intrusiveness of the state, but I never encountered a villager who critiqued the call, the readings, or sermons, even when they echoed incomprehensibly off the mountainsides, or were distorted by electronic noises. To the villagers, the state's obvious concern about the accuracy and predictability of Islamic practice, even in the call to prayer, but especially in the delivery of sermons, was a welcome sign of their greater urban connections.

During the month of Ramazan in 2009, I realized that the aural space of the village was becoming a mosque itself. The Diyanet's domination of this space turned the mosque inside out. While the building would seem a demonstration of an interest in state orthodoxy, as I argued in the construction of these spaces, the state's power in projecting its teachings aurally extends beyond the building, thereby reaching people, such as women, who do not typically enter the mosque or listen to sermons from official sources. Women mentioned that they were glad that they were able to listen to the daily sermons during Ramazan because they felt they were included in the official expressions of orthodoxy coming from the central mosque. Men noted this as well. As one said, "Now everyone can be educated in Islam."

5 WOMEN'S TRADITIONS AND INNOVATIONS

In rural Turkey, the mosque is a male domain, as well as one controlled by the state. Women do not challenge men's authority in the mosque, as congregants or professionals. Though women enter the mosque for particular occasions, during the month of Ramazan, for Kandil, and for Mevluts, they do so with the attitude that they do not belong there. They climb the rickety metal staircase affixed to the outside of the building after the men are inside. Once inside, they quietly gather and never look over the railing draped with cloths, which conceals the upper balcony where they pray. Women leave if they cough because any audible sound of a woman is expected to distract men from their prayers. This all means that women's Islamic expressions in daily prayer, ritual, and good deeds, as well as the embodied habitus of piety expressed through dress, behavior, and speech, happen outside the mosque and therefore outside of the domain of state control.

I do not mean to imply that men are uninvolved with cultural Islamic traditions, which happen outside the mosque. On the contrary, men perform a benedictory role at many rituals, including naming babies, marriage, burials, circumcisions, and rain prayers. For instance, men's rain prayers are held when there is a drought but women's rain prayers are held annually regardless of the weather. Women attend rituals, which men lead, but adult men rarely appear at women's rituals. Thus, in terms of cultural Islamic rituals, those led by men are considered more important and efficacious. From both the perspective of state orthodoxy, as expressed through the Diyanet, and from that of uncodified cultural traditions, men have greater authority and spiritual power.

Women work to create a community of practitioners, whereas men have ready-made structures and institutions that accommodate and valorize their spirituality. In reference to the daily discipline required to perform the namaz, one middle-aged woman said, "If only women also had to go to the mosque to perform the namaz, as men are expected to do on Fridays. . . . It is difficult," she said, "to do it alone." Not only do men benefit from the mosque building, but, as she pointed out, "it is *daha sevap* [a greater good deed] to perform the namaz in the mosque." Rural women's understanding of the greater efficacy of male practice is shaped by their expectation that gendered activities are physically separate and differently valorized. Unlike many Muslim women who participate in mosque movements in the Middle East, western Europe, and North America, such as groups described by Saba Mahmood,[1] and by Laura Deeb,[2] rural women in the Yuntdağ and in western Turkey generally do not challenge male authority. They work to create their own spaces of female practice, similar to the women in Tone Bringa's work on a Bosnian village.[3]

Women's constraint in challenging male space and authority does not mean that women's activities are politically innocuous. For instance, in women's sixth-month henna celebration and collective rituals of good deeds, these celebratory, charitable, and distributive practices underscore women's concern for the construction of community and care for the less fortunate. These expressions of concern are the foundation of a moral Islamic community. From the perspective of political economy, women's efforts to invigorate empathy for the unfortunate are political in that they instruct people in the community through model behavior to pay attention to excess, surplus, and greed. But however political these activities may be, they are regarded as cultural practices that are not revolutionary, contentious, or orthodox.

In this chapter, I consider debates about female practice in Kayalarca and Yeniyurt, and in reference to differing formulations of Islamic legitimacy, located temporally, in the Ottoman era or an Islamist future. In Yeniyurt, women engage both in cultural traditions and in state-constructed orthodoxy by sending their children to Imam Hatip schools. Yeniyurt women's concern for keeping tradition alive is political as well as spiritual; as one elderly woman argued, "We do this so that the dead know we have not forgotten them." In a national culture of amnesia,[4] and a regional culture of Islamic innovation, Yeniyurt women's dogged efforts to perform cultural traditions, which point to deep ties

to the Ottoman era, has a political effect. Through these practices women rein-
terpret the national narrative of republican laicism and the Ottoman past. But
these activities are implicitly not explicitly political, easily dismissed by villagers in Kayalarca as curious holdouts of tradition and/or old-fashioned rituals,
however pleasing they are to attend. By contrast, in Kayalarca women keep a
few cultural practices alive, such as rain prayers, but for the most part they have
turned their backs on traditions and allowed them to be forgotten because they
suspect that such practices from the past will mark them as culturally backward. Instead, they have introduced new practices that they learned from female relatives who live in Manisa and from female hocas from the Süleymancı
neo-tarikats. Both innovations in practice and activities with tarikats are highly
contentious and debated and discussed in both villages—and in Turkey generally, as well as among Turkish immigrants in western Europe,[5] because the existence of these groups suggests that there are multiple forms of Islam, and that
the Turkish state's control of Sunni Islam may be unnecessary, if not illegitimate.

THE KAYALARCA YENIYURT DIALECTIC AGAIN

My comparison between Yeniyurt and Kayalarca is for analytical purposes, to
explore differing notions of time in constructions of Sunni Islam, but it also
is meant to convey the thoroughly engrained local discourse of difference,
attitude, and orientation. Though this chapter is about differences between
women's practices in the two villages, it is necessary to explain that, seen from
the outside, Islamic practices among women in these places do not appear different. All women fast during the month of Ramazan, perform the namaz, make
the sacrifice for Kurban if they are able, participate in ritual occasions, and
comport themselves in conservatively Islamic ways. If they have financial resources, elderly women, often with their husbands, go on pilgrimage to Mecca.
More recently, several are making the umre, a trip to Mecca, because this is less
expensive, though also less efficacious. In 2010, I was impressed to learn that
two elderly widows made the umre together. Both are quite poor, living in very
meager houses, just single rooms attached to their married sons' homes. Somehow, they gathered enough resources to have this adventure together. While
elderly women are active and engaged in Islamic practice, the young are as well.
Young girls study the Qur'an with the imam during the summer months. A few
have begun Imam Hatip school and several have studied with the Süleymancıs.
Girls increase the intensity of practice as they age and approach marriage. All

women take care not to be seen wandering around aimlessly, and cover themselves, leaving only their faces, hands, and feet exposed. All women cultivate states of perpetual attention to piety and talk about God, the next world, their fear of sin and potential damnation, and the need to care for others daily.

One practice unique to women in both villages—not practiced by men—is healing. I was reminded of how certain elderly women develop a reputation for healing powers in 2010 while visiting the elderly Makbule ebe (*ebe*, meaning midwife, is used to describe a great-grandmother, older than a nene). Makbule ebe and I were sitting in her tiny one-room stone house on her threadbare kilims. She was lecturing me on Islam, using one of her big Ottoman books to illustrate. She had rested the worn book on a cushion so she could read it comfortably and show me the illustrations. Beside her was a pile of tattered paperback Ottoman texts, blackened by age and by the smoke of decades of fires on her open hearth. I had been introduced to her while visiting Yeniyurt. People regarded her as a local scholar of Islam and also of the village's history, who could talk until most were dizzy in this normally reticent village. While we sat together, a middle-aged woman entered the room requesting some healing prayers. She sat on the floor, with her back to Makbule ebe. Makbule began to pray and, to keep track of the number of repetitions, she ticked them off on her fingers. Once done, she blew the efficacious healing power of her breath on the woman's back, around her neck, and head. The woman being healed sighed often, deeply, releasing the tension caused by her ill health. Though in the process of being healed, the woman turned to me in curiosity to ask me questions, such as whether I had come to Turkey by airplane. After the prayers were finished, both sighed and wiped their faces. Comforted, the woman left.

YENIYURT'S PRAYER TO SÜLEYMAN HOCA

In the summer of 2009, I learned that the women in Yeniyurt were going to have a prayer service on the top of the mountain, Kaplandağı, which overlooks their village, followed by a meal. This was to be a dede duası, or a mountaintop prayer for the grandfather. The middle-aged couple I live with described the dede duası as an old practice, one neither had witnessed. The husband, Mühettin, remarked that it is a "tradition that they are doing to pass down to the younger generation." After attending the event, I learned from Mühettin's father that in the past in Kayalarca they used to have a prayer on their mountaintop for a grandfather, called the *oncak dedesi*.[6] Like the Yeniyurt prayer, I learned that women would make sarma (rolled grape leaves), bide (a stuffed flatbread), *börek* (layers of flat pastry fried in oil), and other foods that they would bring to the mountaintop, where they would have a Mevlut and read prayers. He said they used to have it in May or June but they had not done it for the past two years. Unlike Kayalarca, then, where this summery rite among women to celebrate the life of a holy man associated with a mountaintop has died out, in Yeniyurt the practice continues.

On the day, Çevriye, Saadet, and I walked the kilometer to Yeniyurt in the burning heat and then to the top of the mountain. It was a difficult climb for us. I managed to fall once after stepping on a loose rock. Falling backward on some more rocks, I landed on top of a thorny bush. The thorns pieced my şalvar, and after picking myself up and recovering from my humiliation, I more gingerly tested rocks before setting my foot on them as we ascended, picking bits and pieces of thorns out of my pants along the way. We were overheated and worn out by the time we reached the top. When we got there, we saw that there were some women sitting and milling about with children on a plateau shaded by a large oak tree.

Asking later in Yeniyurt about the mountain and its associated holy man, I learned two stories about the hill. The first is of a shepherd boy who was given a piece of bread by his mother in a time of extreme poverty and hunger. He didn't want to eat it and threw it away. Instantly, he was turned into a rock. Supposedly, there is a rock on the mountaintop that looks exactly like this young boy. The story is a morality tale told to children to terrify them into not wasting food. Furthermore, throwing bread on the ground is a sin. Throughout Turkey one sees little piles of bread along walls on the side of sidewalks in the cities and towns. These, though hardly palatable for a person but acceptable for a rat, prevent the bread from touching the ground. As Çevriye once admonished me, because I shake out the tablecloth over the ground, angels land on every bread crumb on the ground to protect it. If one were to walk on that crumb, the wings of these tiny angels would be broken. This is another reason for not allowing bread, even crumbs, to land on the ground. The folk belief that bread is sacred is memorialized in the *çoban taşı* (shepherd rock) on the mountain above Yeniyurt.

The second story is of an old grandfather, a dede, Süleyman Hoca, who reportedly "knew a lot" (*pek biliyordu*), meaning he knew the Qur'an and about Islam generally. Kayalarca's former imam, Ali Hacı, a native of Yeniyurt, described the story. This man came from Kırşehir, a city in Central Anatolia. It was not clear why he left Kırşehir or when this happened. In Ali Hacı's rendition, it seemed to have been a very long time ago. Süleyman Hoca, Ali Hacı described, as we sat together in his spacious enclosed porch drinking tea and looking out over the mountains in the distance, had a series of dreams in which he was told to travel. Spurred by this dream, he began walking. Each night, after walking all day, he asked God before going to sleep if this was the right place to stop, but each night he was told in his dream to continue walking. So he did. He continued walking until one day he reached Kaplandağı, the mountain above Yeniyurt. By this time, he must have walked for many weeks. Before he went to sleep that night he again asked God if this was the place to stop. In his dream, he was told to stay. So he did. He began living on the mountaintop. He lived there above the village away from everyone as a hermit. But each night he descended from the mountain to go to the village mosque, carrying a lantern to light his way down the rocky path. He lived there until he died. He was buried on one of the lower slopes of the mountain, where his tomb still stands, apart from the village cemetery.

This story was repeated to me many times by people in Yeniyurt. When I talked about it to people in Kayalarca I heard a different story. Somewhat critically, a man in Kayalarca claimed that the holy man had been a *yabancı*, a foreigner—a Christian, maybe a Greek. He thereby insinuated that the man is not a legitimate saint because he was not a Muslim.[7] Given the competitive tension between the villages, it is not surprising that a man from Kayalarca would want to downplay the Yeniyurt holy man's status. It goes without saying that no one in Yeniyurt mentioned this. A similar attack about the Islamic character of the village came from an elderly woman, originally from Kayalarca, who now lives in Manisa. When I met her in the village while she was visiting her adult daughter, she said that in "old times" one of the names given to Yeniyurt was Kızılbaş. That is, she was claiming that the villagers in Yeniyurt were not Sunni but Alevi, an Anatolian, mystical and Shi'i-related form of Islam. She implied that the form of Islam practiced in Yeniyurt is heterodox. This was a serious attack considering Yeniyurt's reputation for being the center of Sunni Islamic learning and authority in the region.

While not agreeing with these attacks and rumors, the terminology used to describe saints as dedes suggests that the villagers in the region, not only those in Yeniyurt, may have been influenced by Sunni orders, such as the Bektaşi, who are closely associated with the Alevi.[8] As David Shankland describes for Alevi villages in Central Anatolia, the Alevi have dedes, who are elder men who have spiritual authority in the community and also who intervene in disputes.[9]

Various Sufi orders, such as the Mevlevi, use the term *dede* to describe a particular rank among the members. It is possible that villagers were influenced by a Sufi order or by Alevi practices when they chose the term dede to describe their saints. In either case, it is significant that all the dedes in the region are deceased and are venerated at their tombs rather than being living individuals who guide villagers in Islamic knowledge and practice.

The story about the Yeniyurt dede descending from his mountaintop with a lantern to perform the namaz in the mosque addresses an ambiguity about local identity. Alevi do not perform the namaz or have mosques; therefore the holy man's dogged use of the mosque asserts, somewhat heavy-handedly, a Sunni identity. In Sunni Islam there is no need to perform the namaz in a mosque, and it is unclear why of all the namaz one might perform, the mystic hermit would choose the evening namaz. Though men use the mosque, and attending mosque for the midday Friday sermon and accompanying namaz is regarded as the most efficacious, they can perform the namaz in any place. Perhaps a more insightful reading of the story is allegorical. The holy man (with some ambiguity surrounding his identity) holds a lamp, thereby illuminating his path, both actual and spiritual, as he makes a daily pilgrimage to the site of orthodoxy and state power, the mosque. In this way, the story describes a holy man who asserts both a Sunni and state-centric legitimacy to his practice, while also living as a mystic hermit on the mountaintop, thereby incorporating popular and potentially heterodox Islam. Furthermore, because he is revered after death as a dede and therefore a saint, this story underscores all reverence of him as legitimately Sunni, cleansed of association with a Sufi order or the Alevi. Finally, one can read the story as an allegory about the kind of Islam developed and practiced in the village of Yeniyurt itself because state practice, Ottoman and republican, is valorized even while popular beliefs and rituals continue.

A few points in this story resemble narrative devices in other Islamic hagiographies. First and foremost is the role of the mountain. Irene Melikoff, scholar of Sufism (Islamic mysticism) and the Alevi writes: "We know it was a custom of the ancient Turks and Mongols to pray on mountain tops [*sic*] where they felt nearer to Gök Tenri, the God of Heaven."[10] As I learned, it was not only in Yeniyurt and Kayalarca, but in many villages of the region, that villagers associated mountaintops with holy men. For example, Muhammed Zühdü has been established on a mountaintop near the village of Recepli. The Web site for the association promoting him includes several other local saintly figures whose tombs are on mountaintops.[11] The tombs located on mountaintops, associated with particular holy men, are visited for special occasions, especially in the spring, when visitors also have rain prayers.

A second hagiographic element is Süleyman Hoca's dream. As Mittermaier argues, the dream-vision is a liminal space within which Muslims engage the imagination to interpret the future. Furthermore, the dream is a device through which God speaks to men and women and directs actions in this world, rather than exclusively delivering rules governing correct behavior leading to salvation in the next.[12] While dreams in Islam are legitimate mediating mental devices for God's transmissions, they also lead us to pre-Islamic practice. Ilhan Başgöz argues that the dream motif in Turkish folklore explains the initiation of a shaman, a pre-Islamic holy person who could travel to the spirit world in his or her dreams. "A youth is called to be a shaman by the souls of dead shamans or by spirits. The youth goes through a psychological crisis, becomes absent minded, seeks solitude, sings in his sleep, and easily loses consciousness. His soul is carried away from his body during sleep to meet celestial spirits, demigods, or gods. . . . He learns shamanistic treatment, technique and the culture of his new future life."[13] The initiate then drinks a cup of wine, which gives him a vision.[14] The Yeniyurt story only uses the dream in the mystically driven journey to the saint's final destination, the mountaintop of Kaplandağı. The fact that this dream-vision is recounted today sacralizes the mountaintop and connects the villagers' perceptions of the depth of their Islamic heritage to the Ottoman past, a past that resonates with a worldview different from rational modernity. And women's rituals in reverence of the saint, reveal practices at odds with state-certified activities allowed by the government at tombs.

The third element is the lantern. Similar to the story about the founder of the medrese in Yeniyurt whose little finger ignited to assist him in reading the Qur'an, the holy man's lamp that lit the way to the village mosque is significant. The lamp enabled him to literally and figuratively follow the correct path of Islam, down the mountain to the mosque. Light symbolically refers to cultural and spiritual enlightenment. Sunni and Alevi used to burn candles at the tombs of saints, but this practice has been forbidden by the state.[15] Fire and light, then, are not insignificant but symbolic referents to spiritual wisdom and clarity from a Sunni perspective, and to passion and mystical love for God from an Alevi standpoint.

A final point needs to be made about the sacralization of the nation and the use of mountaintops in expressions of reverence for the army and Atatürk. Above many provincial cities and towns, nationalist slogans are spelled out in white rocks along the sides of mountains by the military, claiming the space as a tablet for nationalist expression, reminding the population that would read these slogans every time they look at the landscape, that the nation, backed up by the army, is ever present. As Esra Özyürek discusses,[16] and as does Yael Navaro-Yashin,[17] mountaintops are among the places where Atatürk is venerated. Both authors argue that the appearance of an Atatürk silhouette on a mountaintop "naturalizes" his political power in the landscape. The naturalization of Atatürk's image certainly unifies him with the country itself, but there is another way to view this apparition. These silhouettes associate Atatürk with saints, who are associated with mountaintops. His spiritual status as a *gazi*, a warrior for Islam, is further legitimized, underlining the sacred nature of the nation.[18] In this way, a figure who stands for the nation above all others can be interpreted by religious nationalists as connected to Sufi and Alevi mysticism.[19]

Another example of how Atatürk is associated with mountains is a famous photograph showing him when he was a leader of the nationalist forces in the War of Independence. The photograph depicts Atatürk in deep contemplation, alone, smoking a pipe, struggling to climb a rocky mountain slope. Originally, the photograph showed Atatürk walking on level ground bent in contemplation, a few soldiers in the background. As Walter Denny describes, the image was transformed when the soldiers were removed and the flat plain was tilted to make it seem that Atatürk was climbing.[20] Atatürk's struggle to create the nation is obviously highlighted by his efforts in climbing the (fictitious) mountain. Nationalist slogans and the association of Atatürk with mountains and slopes sacralize him. The mountaintop has a pre-Islamic spiritual significance, which is carried into Islam and state ideology, creating an icon in the civil religion. In the Yuntdağ, where state imagery has yet to intrude on the mountains, their peaks are the location for the saints' tombs but not nationalist slogans.

I return to the story about my trip to the mountaintop with Çevriye and Saadet. As we reached the flat area under the expansive oak tree, a few elderly women were sitting on some rocks, which formed a small desklike structure. They had brought their books with them and had begun to read and recite. The crumbling papers of these old Ottoman texts showed that they were repaired many times, covered in cloth, with homemade bindings, and almost black from wear and use in smoke-filled one-room houses for over a hundred years. They included the *Muhammediye*, texts of the *Mevlut* and *ilahi*, hymns to Muhammed. The Muhammediye describes Muhammed's life, with illustrations of Muhammed's personal possessions, the gates of heaven, scales used by the angels at the gates of heaven to weigh one's sins and good deeds, and the Ka'bah in Mecca.

Talking to tradesmen of religious books set up outside the famous Ottoman tombs in Eyüp in Istanbul, I learned that there are many such texts written about Muhammed's life. I was hoping to purchase a modern Turkish rendition of one of these books or one reprinted in Ottoman as a gift but the bookseller dismissed the books that village women read in Ottoman as "unimportant." He was comparing this text to the main sources of Islamic knowledge, the Qur'an and Hadith.

Though easily dismissed as unimportant, I thought the Muhammediye the women read in Yeniyurt significant for a number of reasons. Turkey underwent a language reform beginning in 1928, which involved changing not only the Arabic script to Latin, but purging the language of Arabic and Persian grammatical structures and vocabulary. One can easily detect a person with an Islamist bent when they pepper their speech with Arabic and Persian words. Villagers often use older words, such as *yavuz*, meaning good; *talib*, meaning student; and so forth. Though they use old words, villagers do not use these words as a demonstration of their allegiance with the deprivatization of religion, as is often the case in the cities, where the politics of Islam and secularism are more intense. As a living tradition, rather than a political statement, I found the use of these words even more interesting because they are evidence of sustained cultural memory. Using Ottoman connects the women in Yeniyurt to the Empire, to the pre-republican past. This is a profound commentary on the republican language reforms which cleansed the language and secularized it. As is widely known, Qur'anic texts, whether written in an artistic and learned calligraphic script or with a ballpoint pen, are regarded as having curative and protective power. Preserving the old books keeps alive the Arabic script linking Ottoman to the holy Qur'an.

As we sat and recovered from climbing the mountain, we watched as women and children arrived from Yeniyurt. The Yeniyurt women's comportment was striking. Many had big torba or shepherd's bags slung across their backs, filled with food they had prepared for the meal, which would follow the prayers. Coming from Kayalarca, seeing these bags in use was striking because these old-style bags are no longer woven in Kayalarca; everyone devotes the looms to cooperative weavings and regards handmade woven bags as old-fashioned and easily replaceable with plastic bags. The women in Yeniyurt, in contrast, continue to make and use torba. From a material cultural perspective, their continued use of handwoven goods connects them to past practices. Also, we were impressed by their fitness, since we had arrived exhausted and sweaty after hiking up the mountain. The women in Kayalarca tend to spend most of their time working at their looms trying to make money, a lifestyle that has a detrimental effect on their physical fitness.

After arriving, the women gathered under the oak tree to recite the Muhammediye, hymns, and for a brief interval the Qur'an. Çevriye participated in the recitations, and though she was proud of having taught herself Ottoman using her grandmother's books, she was not as skilled as the women from Yeniyurt. Her grandmother (her father's mother) was Havva, the direct descendant of one of the men from the region of Of. Çevriye's self-directed labor to learn to read Ottoman directly connected her to the legacy of Islamic learning imported to the region by the imams from Of, of which she was proud. The women from Yeniyurt could easily read the verses and chant them in unison. I overheard one woman telling Çevriye that there are Ottoman courses each week in Manisa, which are taught as a good deed. No one remarked that this was strange. Clearly, the interest in Ottoman is alive in the city as well as in the countryside. The fact that villagers do not see a division between their practices and those in Manisa is important in light of my discussion about how they easily migrate to Manisa and how the relationship Manisa has to the villages is quite different from the ideological role that villages play in Islamist and nationalist ideology. For villagers in this region, it is self-evident that people in Manisa can relate to their interests in Islamic scholarship and study of Ottoman. For people in Manisa, it is clear that they share a similar Islamic, national, and cultural worldview, as men cooking and distributing çörek on a street in Manisa explained to me. These shared attitudes are quite different from the sense of a cultural gap as expressed by people in Istanbul between themselves and "uncivilized" villagers.

The women began to read a Mevlut. The chronology of Mevluts I have discussed needs to be explicated because it relates to an argument I am making about the construction of practices as male-oriented and orthodox versus female-oriented extra-statist, as they have developed over the period of my research in the region from 1998 to 2010. This book presents female-led and male-led Mevluts out of the chronological order in which I observed them. Chapter 2 presented the first female-led Mevlut I witnessed in Kayalarca, at the sixth-month henna celebration. Female-led Mevluts are very recent in Kayalarca—the one described in Chapter 2 is one of the first, according to a woman in the village. This chapter presents the first female-led Mevlut I witnessed in the Yuntdağ, predating, in other words, the one in Chapter 2. After attending the Mevlut in Yeniyurt, I asked women in Kayalarca about why they did not have Mevluts. One woman remarked that it was because the women in Yeniyurt "know more." Thus, the Mevlut in Chapter 2 represents an effort by women in Kayalarca to learn more about Islam, and it is not insignificant that a woman from Yeniyurt helped lead the prayer service. In Yeniyurt, female-led Mevluts have a longer history because the poem is in Ottoman, which many women can read. The next chapter discusses Mevluts as I observed them from 1998 to 2008. All of these were male-led rituals held in the mosque. Considering, then, that the first female-led Mevlut I attended was in 2008 on the mountaintop in Yeniyurt, the event was especially remarkable, because it was performed to venerate a local saint.

As the readings went on, we became tired and the children restless. I began to wonder about lunch, since it was well past one-thirty (according to the clock, which only I was eyeing). I went with Saadet to survey the scenery from the top of the mountain, and I took a panoramic set of photographs to represent the landscape. We could see the Aegean Sea to the east, a lake formed from a dam, a modern wind farm, and a number of other villages in the distance. Saadet pointed out the different villages she knew, many of which I had visited over the years. She gazed down on Yeniyurt, her mother's natal village, for a long time, remarking on how close it was to Kayalarca, though the two places are very different. When we got back to the oak tree and the group sitting in the shade, lunch had materialized from all the bags brought up the mountain. We ate together, sitting at common tablecloths spread on the ground under the shade of the tree. The lunch consisted of green salad, macaroni, beans, a dish of fried eggplant, potatoes, peppers and tomatoes, yogurt, honey, bread, *ayran* (a dish made in the oven—not the yogurt drink—made of cornmeal, greens, onions, and *kaymak*, or clotted cream), and more sweets. I list all the items here because they indicate the labor, care, and expense of the meal. The meal was shared together as a good deed. Like all village ritual events, a shared feast is an important feature in how community is established. After lunch, the readings continued, but the children ritualistically interrupted them with collective chants demanding sweets. The women responded to the chants by stopping the prayers and distributing candy and biscuits to everyone. We ate some and gathered big piles of candy and biscuits into plastic bags to share later with people back in the village. The children's ritual interruptions showed that the event was meant to include them and a sense of fun, as well as sober prayers.

In the late afternoon, after the burning sun of midday had cooled, we descended the mountain. Çevriye and Saadet caught a ride with a truck on the way back but I elected to walk. When I arrived at the house, Çevriye was strug-gling to cool off. She had made tea, which we shared, and we lounged about resting and discussing our day in Yeniyurt.

Yeniyurt women's prayer for the grandfather is a rite in which women en-gage, but men also know the story of Süleyman Hoca, and respect women's concern for and acknowledgment of the saint. But men do not participate in venerating the saint, except as children. Whether the saints are old or not, as in the case of Muhammed Zühdü, women in villages, towns, and cities are enthusiastic participants in celebrating and visiting them. One might argue that this is because the veneration of saints is often an event involving feasts and visits, giving women a chance to put aside their domestic chores, as Mary Hegland argues is the case among female participants in Muharram rituals in Pakistan.[21] But why wouldn't men also venerate this local saint? Men visit other tombs, Muhammed Zühdü's, the Mevlana's in Konya, and many significant sites in Istanbul, but they avoid the local saints' tombs in their own villages.

My view is that visiting major saints, such as the Mevlana in Konya, is not merely a visit to a holy man, but a way to venerate figures which are politically charged and associated with national, state-oriented versions of Sunni Islam and the nation itself. The Mevlana was an important figure in the Empire, and though the Republic closed his tomb and *Mevlevihane* in Konya,[22] it was later reopened as a museum. The Mevlana has recently been included in a pantheon of nationalist symbols. In recent years, the green dome of his tomb, or the image of him sitting cross-legged wearing a turban, is often paired with an Atatürk portrait. The inclusion of images of the Mevlana shows the deprivatization of re-ligion in the national imaginary. In contrast, the shrine in Konya does not fully incorporate popular Muslim interest in the saint as an Islamic figure. Rather, the place uncomfortably attempts to reconcile the two groups who visit: pilgrims and tourists (many of whom are foreigners). Guards try to enforce use of the space as a museum, not a shrine, a place to look but not to pray. The tombs are fenced off, preventing pilgrims from touching or circumambulating them. All visitors wear plastic covers over their shoes, as if the place were a shrine, but not a mosque, where one removes one's shoes. Tourists mill about looking at the displays while pilgrims treat these as housing for relics, not museum exhibits. The tension in these contradictions, between these two groups and the guards' efforts to regulate their behavior, increases the political value of this pilgrimage.

The state "museumification" (drawing upon the term *müzelik*) of the tomb in Konya is notable when contrasted with the shrine at Eyüp, also a government-controlled mosque and complex of tombs. There, pilgrims' enthusiasm is only slightly reined in with signs posted by the Diyanet, setting rules for correct behavior. At Eyüp, it is possible to make a sacrifice—not at the actual shrine and tombs, but in a separate area. Nevertheless, quite a few sheep are slaughtered and the meat donated to the poor. At Eyüp, the candles were cleaned up some decades ago, but people circumambulate the tomb, touching the metal gates, praying at the tomb, distributing candies as a good deed, and so forth. A notable use of the tomb is as a place where sons about to be circumcised are paraded in their fine costumes in the days leading to the actual event. Given the activities of men and women at these tombs, it is striking that local village events venerating saints are the domain of women.

Çevriye, who later accompanied me to the festival for the newly minted Recepli saint in May 2010, used the ritual in Yeniyurt as a counterpoint in critiquing Recepli's. One point of her critique was that the event in Yeniyurt was better because it was shared among women. The event in Recepli, in contrast, was problematic she said, because men led it, thereby marginalizing women. In particular, the shrine complex is designed to accommodate men, and women's spaces are an afterthought. Women, thus, are either prevented from exiting or entering the mosque when throngs of men block the way when they spread their prayer rugs around the entry to the mosque. Women cannot easily collect a share of the feast distributed. The men's side is paved and spacious, but the women's side is a rocky, muddy slope, crowded with families who set out small picnic areas, some even sleeping in tents. Because women were not spatially accommodated, village women regarded the event in Yeniyurt as "nicer" because it was for women, led by women, without any men in attendance. There was no problem in where to pray, sit, or eat. Thus, in the configuration of gendered efficacies, women prefer to attend local saints' tombs, where they can worship without being restrained and constrained by men. Men stay away from women's events, perhaps in deference, or because their attendance requires them to take over the place and proceedings, and thereby completely transform the nature of the ritual.

YENIYURT'S SAKAL-I ŞERIF

Yeniyurt, as I have described, represents a local heritage of Islamic training and practice. Further supporting this heritage, Yeniyurt is one of the few villages in the region where there is a Sakal-ı Şerif, or a ritual in which a hair from the Prophet's beard is venerated. This practice is contested by orthodoxizing movements, which see the veneration of the Prophet's body as dangerous to the purification of Islam. Venerations of the Prophet dangerously toy with the deification of Muhammed, challenging God's singularity. Like other forms of veneration of Muhammed, such as the worship of his footprint or cloak,[23] the Sakal-ı Şerif demonstrates popular attachment to the Prophet's body in the present.

There were a few stories about the origin of the hair in Yeniyurt. The story with the closest link to a living person came from Makbule ebe, who said that her father purchased it in Mecca when he made the pilgrimage. Makbule's father was a descendant of one of the imams from Of, which she noted in telling the story because it gave weight to the significance of his pilgrimage and the decision to bring back a relic from Mecca. Ali Hacı, also a descendant of one of the imams from Of, said the hair was brought to the village in 1953. If Makbule's story, supported by Ali Hacı's dating, is correct, the pilgrimage was taken after the Democratic Party won the first multiparty election. This would correspond with the softening attitude toward radical secularization policies after many decades of struggle following the War of Independence, state reform, and a period of extreme poverty in the 1930s. It is surprising, though, that a group of village men coming out of this era would have had the means to make the pilgrimage. Nevertheless, as Makbule described, her father brought back the Sakal-ı Şerif after making the pilgrimage by steamboat.

The veneration of the hair is an addition to village spiritual life, post-Republic. It takes place on special occasions during the year, Kadir Gecesi, the Night of Power (or Night of Destiny) being the most important.[24] Kadir Gecesi, the Night of Power, the twenty-fourth night of the month of Ramazan (the month of fasting) is when Muslims believe the first chapters of the Qur'an were revealed to Muhammed. In the villages, women and men gather at the mosque to celebrate a Mevlut in the evening after breaking the daylong fast. After the Mevlut, villagers from the region make the trek to Yeniyurt.

On Kadir Gecesi in 2009, I was sitting in the house after Çevriye and her husband had left to go to the mosque to perform the namaz, before the Mevlut.[25] Hatice arrived to take me to the Mevlut. Following her, I climbed the rusting metal staircase attached to the exterior of the mosque to the women's section upstairs. Though a chilly night, the mosque was warm from all the people crowded together, the men downstairs and the middle-aged and elderly women upstairs. Young women and masses of children were outside, sitting on benches in the courtyard. Because they cannot have the children running around the mosque, their mothers have to stay outside looking after them. As the women got up to perform the namaz, I scooted to the rear of the gathering. Midway through, the candies and cakes were readied for the crowd. Children and young girls distributed them. The last section of the Mevlut followed, but the distribution of candy and cakes had made the children restless and it was hard to concentrate because they were now inside the mosque, running from place to place. Young girls of a slightly older age than the noisy children stood beside their mothers dutifully and quietly performing the namaz. I left the mosque as everyone exited.

I went to the house with a big crowd of women, all of whom would go to Yeniyurt for the Sakal-ı Şerif. Later, I learned that not everyone from Kayalarca went to this event because through their involvement with the Süleymancıs they learned to critique it as heterodox. Some performed the aptes (ritual wash) again before we left. A group climbed into Mühettin's car and drove off. I waited with Çevriye and Arife and a few others for Mühettin to return and give us a ride, but I actually wanted to walk. I got up and said I would walk, and Arife said, "Tamam, haydi! [All right then, let's go!]." I caught up with Hatice's mother, who was walking with another woman in the dark, and then passed her to walk with Fatma, Hatice's sister, a middle-aged woman. As we walked together, she remarked that it was nicer to walk instead of go in a car and I agreed. I knew she would say this because she walked all over the mountains carrying firewood and collecting wild plants. She had a small flashlight, which gave off a blue glow. The stars were out.

From the middle point of the road, halfway to Yeniyurt, I looked back to see Kayalarca, a brilliant cluster of cool fluorescent streetlights. Villagers remark, especially when the wind knocks out the electricity, on how beautiful the bright streetlights are. I was reminded of the many conversations I have had with the elderly who complained about how they once lit their homes with oil lamps, which gave off a dirty, dim glow. Electricity and the paved road came late to the region, in the 1980s. The kilometer of road seemed to get longer in the darkness.

We arrived at the edge of Yeniyurt, passing the sağlık hoca, the local health clinic, and the first few houses. Then we turned into the village, careful not to stumble in the dark on the unpaved rocky path, and came to the mosque, where we could hear the men chanting inside. A crowd of women and girls gathered at a wall that circles behind the mosque. Many looked over the wall to watch what was happening inside. But as I joined them in peeking over the wall, I saw a group of five or six women who were standing beside the mosque with their backs turned to it, so they would not be able to see what the men were doing. Seeing the line of women with their backs like this surprised me because it showed how decisively they respected the spiritual authority of the men who were viewing the hair of the Prophet in its glass vial, uncovered. On the other hand, the wall seemed to imply that it would be fine, since there was an external constraint, to look over it at this scene. Though the mosque was some distance from us, I watched the men marching in a circle in it, chanting Allahu Akbar.

In the darkness, the women waited until it seemed the men were done. Then they began to approach the building from all directions. From our position behind the mosque along the road, we were able to climb through a small set of steps set into a hole in the wall. Many women did this, but it was very crowded and I decided to circle the building and enter at the front gate. There, a mass of women began pushing through the gate. In the meantime, the men were trying to squeeze out. The jam at the main gate explained why there was a "back door" to the courtyard of the mosque, so that it would be possible for men and women to enter and exit without running into each other. I bumped into Çevriye just as she was loudly remarking how women from "our village were mixing with the men as they exited." Clearly, she thought the women from Kayalarca were less skilled and educated in correct, gendered comportment than those from other villages. I looked around, as I tried to push my way in the gate with everyone else. The mosque and its courtyard were packed with women who had come from villages throughout the region. They wore clothing distinctive of their villages. Women from the northern part of the region were wearing their long black cloaks on their heads with skinny symbolic sleeves flying behind them like long ears (they do not put their arms through the sleeves). Others were in fancy, beaded, heavy black-cotton headscarves, and some were dressed in an Islamist fashion in polyester headscarves and overcoats. This was one of the only times I was in a group of women from all over the region who were mixing together indiscriminately. On occasions when women from different villages arrive for an event, such as weddings, they cluster together according to their kin, lineage, or village groups in strategic political blocks representing either the bride or the groom's side. At weddings, one does not mix with the opposing party. This event had dissolved those corporate bonds, and all the women were gathered together in an atmosphere of single-sex fellowship.

After getting through the carved wooden doors decorated with crescent and star designs painted green, I entered the mosque through its front door, slipping off my shoes in the entrance hall. The women filled the mosque. Since the men had left, there was no need to stay in the women's section. To view the event, I stood on one of the platforms at the back. The women formed a long line, circling the interior. They approached Elif Hacı, Ali Hacı's wife. She held the Sakal-ı Şerif, covered in a cotton headscarf over a high table. There was a pile of colorful cloths under the object on the table, which were ready to wrap the object. A woman would approach the table and Elif would present the wrapped object to her. She then kissed it, touching it with both cheeks, as if in greeting. Another woman to Elif's side would wipe the cloth with another cloth and the next woman in line would approach. The one who had just greeted the object went to the back of the mosque or upstairs to perform the namaz. I watched this for a long time, trying not to get in the way of those who wanted to mount the platform, perform the namaz, and leave. I was noticed and those from Kayalarca, in their cheerful joking way, greeted me. Deciding to go upstairs to the women's section to observe without distracting anyone, I discovered that there were many girls upstairs who were looking down through the wooden lattice screen to see what was happening.

A young girl sat beside me and began to ask me questions. She said she was from Yeniyurt and asked if I had kissed the object. I said no. She made the assumption that I had not kissed the glass vial holding the hair of the Prophet because I had not performed the aptes.

I replied, "I am not a Muslim and so I would not do this."

She and another girl who joined in the discussion urged me to become a Muslim. The girl said, "Our religion is so wonderful, you should become a Muslim."

She spoke so fluently that I asked her if she went to Qur'an courses. She said that she studied on her own, at times with her older brother but mainly alone at home. As we began a discussion, I realized that there were few people from Kayalarca downstairs. Just then a few girls appeared, one of whom said that Çevriye was looking for me. I went with them, thanking them, and said, "I wouldn't have known how to find her in this crowd." Çevriye was anxious about where I had gone. I found, as I often did, that my role as a researcher had to be put aside to not cause anxiety for the people I lived with in the village. We piled into the car and drove back to the village.

Once back, I realized that there was more planned for Kadir Gecesi. Çevriye and I went to Arife's, her sister-in-law's house. The plan was to stay up all night, reciting the Yasin seven hundred times and make rounds on prayer beads. Unlike Yeniyurt's somber and contained ritual, the women in Kayalarca introduced this practice from the city but they had not planned it well. They began by complaining that among the women who can read the Qur'an, few had come, thereby creating a heavy burden for those who could read in Arabic, to finish the many hundreds of rounds. It became clear that many people were exhausted, after having fasted all day, attended a Mevlut and then the Sakal-ı Şerif in Yeniyurt. They wanted to sleep. It was decided that the women who had gathered would make rounds on prayer beads rather than attempt to read the Yasin. Arife did not have date stones, which are used to keep track of the number of rounds said on the beads. These date stones are from fruits imported from Saudi Arabia and are consumed to break the fast during Ramazan. They therefore are associated with the holy city and the arduous work for God during the month of Ramazan. The women looked on in shock when Arife brought out a bag of beans instead. I was given the task of making tea, because I would neither be making rounds on prayer beads nor reading the Yasin. Sabiha, a young, recently married woman trained at a Süleymancı Qur'an school, began to read the Yasin to begin the prayers. Then the women, many of whom were elderly, began to make rounds on their prayer beads, intending to make seven hundred total. When I distributed tea, I started on my right, with Arife. I didn't realize my error until she said, "Why would you start with me, the owner of the house, and not the guests?" Realizing my mistake, I apologized and gave everyone tea. Then I sat as they talked, chatted, and made rounds on their prayer beads. I was cross-eyed with exhaustion.

Havva nene, Arife's mother, said I should help out by making rounds on the *tespih*.

I said weakly, "You say, 'Bismillahirrahmanirrahim [In the name of God, the most beneficent and most merciful]' for each bead."

Someone exclaimed, "She knows!"

Çevriye said, "Of course she knows, Kimberly is working to become a Muslim!"

I said as I lay on the floor, "I'm working on writing a book, not on becoming a Muslim." I had said this many times to her because I did not want her to be confused about the fact that I was doing research to write a book, and not to disappoint her because she did not succeed in convincing me to convert.

Fahriye said, "It is so easy, all you need to do is say the *shadaha* ['La ilaha illa Allah wa-Muhammad rasul Allah (There is no God but God and Muhammed is his messenger)'] . . . and then you can go to heaven."

I responded, "I think there is a lot more to it than that."

As I got up to refill the tea glasses, Arife playfully slapped me on the butt for my insolence. While I was in the kitchen, I could overhear a scattered discussion about religious difference, which they were working out. They established that there were different religions and different practices. But faced with the epistemological conflicts these differences would pose to the single statement of faith they had encouraged me to recite, their discussion tapered off in confusion. Returning with the teapot, I lay down on the floor again. Finally, not being able to stay awake any longer, I left to go to sleep.

I asked Çevriye when she got up the next day what they did after I left. She said they made seven hundred rounds on the prayer beads, read from the Qur'an, said prayers, ate, then left. She came home, made tea and food, got Mühettin up, ate with him, said the namaz, and went to bed. She got up after only three hours of sleep because the carpet tourists from Norway were arriving in the village. I persuaded her to go back to bed for at least another hour and told her I would help with the massive cooking project we faced, making lunch for the thirty visitors.

In the days after Kadir Gecesi, I asked men and women in Kayalarca about whether they had gone to Yeniyurt for the Sakal-ı Şerif. In my visit with a young man who had studied with the Süleymancıs, and his wife, Elif, who did not study with this group and is less aware of the debates about heterodoxies, we discussed the event. The young husband, after Elif had described how she enjoyed the evening, remarked, almost sneering at her, "But do you believe this is really the hair of the Prophet's beard?" She answered in the affirmative, clearly unaware that there was a debate about whether the hair was the Prophet's or not. Her husband said he did not believe it and thought it wrong. Elif was flummoxed by his disapproval, and bashfully repeated that she thought the ritual was beautiful. He asserted that he would never participate in the ritual. Though many men and women enjoy the Sakal-ı Şerif and believe that the glass vial, concealed by layers of cloth, is the hair of the Prophet, others, especially men in Kayalarca and those who have studied with the Süleymancıs, critique the occasion and discount its importance. Other men made jokes about how the men from Yeniyurt were cheated in their purchase by a merchant in Mecca and were fooled for believing that the hair was from the Prophet.

In disenchanted secular Turkey, I have seen many tiny glass vials containing the hair of the Prophet in former medreses and mosques, now converted into museums. Examining one at a museumified tomb in Konya, I wondered what my village informants would say about the display of the hair, for all to see, itself contained in a glass case, stripped of its context and sacred atmosphere. Would they support the desacralization of a heterodox practice? Would they feel shocked at how relics become museum pieces, revealing how it is not only the heterodox aspect of the relic but the sacred character of Islamic belief itself which is deconstructed? Though some with training from neo-tarikats critique the practice, the tie to the past via a relic brought from Mecca by a descendant of the hocas from Of is regarded as authentic and sacred by many in the region. The ritual captures the sense of awe all devout Muslims experience on the Night of Power. Our brief pilgrimage to the neighboring village helped us make a connection to that distant past, the sacred event of Muhammed's prophecy.

KAYALARCA WOMEN'S FRIDAY GATHERINGS, CUMA TOPLANTISI

Women's Friday gatherings, which resemble the one I described in the last section for Kadir Gecesi, are new practices in Kayalarca. The gatherings were introduced by Sultan nene, a woman who had migrated to Manisa from Kayalarca about fifty years earlier. Because about thirty years ago her husband arranged for her daughter to marry her first cousin back in the village, Sultan frequently visits her daughter, granddaughters, and great-grandchildren in the village. Due to these close ties, Sultan, who had been influenced by women's gatherings in the city, introduced the idea to women in the village.

In 2008, I began to attend the Friday gatherings. On one occasion, I wrote about it in my notebook:

> When I arrived, about five older women were sitting on the floor in a room in Esma's house praying with their tespih (prayer beads). Thirteen more slowly arrived. The middle-aged and younger women carried Qur'ans or paperback books of the Yasin. The elderly women, however, brought only prayer beads. All the women with books could read Arabic, but as I asked them later, they do not know the meaning of the words. Fatma, with whom I walked to Yeniyurt for the Sakal-ı Şerif, was the only one with a Qur'an that had a Turkish parallel text in the margins. I asked her if she read this and she said, "Sometimes." After beginning with a single oral recitation of the text, the ones who could do so began to read the Yasin to themselves. They used date stones to keep track of the total number of times they read the prayers and verses, taking about forty minutes to complete them. All this was conducted in silence. The elderly women fin-

ished much sooner than those reading the verses from the Qur'an; restless, they waited for the others to finish. Then everyone prayed, read the same verses from the Yasin out loud, and finished, after which they allowed two little girls who had been running and yelling outside to enter the room. The girls passed around little dishes filled with sugar or salt. We dipped our fingers in each bowl to taste a bit of each. Then the host set out the trays of food and we ate.

I asked Fatma if she understood the verses and she said no, but that it was a major meritorious act to read them. I asked if they read other verses on different weeks, and Fatma told me that they always read and did the same things. Later I talked to a man who studied to become an imam but who never gained a position. He asked me if I had liked the Qur'an reading and I said yes, but that I wanted to know what the Yasin is and why that is the only chapter the women read each week. He said that the Yasin is a complete shortened version of the Qur'an and that when one needs to read the Qur'an during a short period of time, this is the part to choose. I asked if the women understand and he said, very confidently and patronizingly, "Very little." I asked if he thought reading these verses without any understanding was useful and he said yes. "To read the Qur'an is to know it," he remarked. We breezed past the contradiction in his belittling attitude toward the women, whom he had quickly affirmed as having had done something significant. He emphasized the main practices: the five daily prayers and fasting, rather than particular beliefs that one professes to know or have faith in. His emphasis was on the discipline and performance of practice rather than on textual interpretation and scholarly study, or individualized faith, though his condescending attitude toward the women's intonation of the verses did imply that there is more to knowing the Qur'an than reciting it.

After having attended many of these Friday events, I began to realize that women are moved by the sound of the words. The event is serene and quiet, unlike most village occasions. The ritual represents a disciplined collective practice, enjoyed by women among themselves, and thereby establishes a community of women who are striving to improve their recitation skills and connection to doctrine. It thereby is markedly different from the cultural rituals, such as good deeds and rain prayers, in which texts play little part. The Friday gatherings provide women with an opportunity to express a collective concern for purified, doctrinal Islam, inspired by urban practices. They also create a platform for young women who have been trained in recitation to display their skills. These demonstrations inspire other mothers to send their children to Qur'an schools, whether run by the government or not. Finally, the fact of the performance encourages many to make the next step in learning more about the meaning of the text.

ARIFE GÜNÜ IN KAYALARCA AND OTHER PLACES

In making a distinction between Yeniyurt and Kayalarca, I am not only explaining differences between two villages but am making a commentary about paths to Islamic modernity. Women in Yeniyurt have a striking attachment to the past, to holy men and miracle tales, rituals to venerate the Prophet, and a remarkable degree of scholarship, which keeps Ottoman texts about Muhammed alive. The women in Kayalarca, in contrast, choose to abandon saintly figures associated with the land and seasonal rites, such as sarma dede (making stuffed grape leaves for the "dede"). They continue rain prayers and good deeds, as do villagers in Yeniyurt, and believe in the healing capacity of certain elderly women. Women in Kayalarca are eager to introduce new rituals, such as the Friday gathering, the sixth-month henna celebration, and, as I discuss in this section, visiting graves on Arife Günü, the last day of Ramazan.

On the last day of the month of Ramadan, Arife Günü, men visit the graves of their deceased relatives to read the Yasin or say a prayer. A young imam from Kayalarca, who works in a mosque near Manisa, explained that going to the cemetery on Arife Günü is an opportunity to ask forgiveness to one's relatives. He explained that when the person was alive one might, for example, not have visited during holidays and just called on the telephone. This visit provides a chance to express regret for these occasions. Men clear the grave of shrubs and weeds, water it, and place myrtle on the grave or insert it into the earth by the headstone. I asked many why they put myrtle on the graves. Several men explained that myrtle smells good, and this is why they leave it at the graves. According to some sources, myrtle represents immortality, and sprigs of myrtle were often buried with the dead to aid the soul in its journey.[26]

Women's visits are a new practice, and very striking because most village women are reluctant to go near graveyards. In cities, women often attend funerals, though even secular women often stand away from men and some cover their heads. Women also visit graves in cities such as in Istanbul. Rambling among the thousands of graves on the hillside at Eyüp, stopping to visit those of fallen gazis or one's own relatives, is a popular weekend activity. Village women, however, describe graveyards as filled with the spirits of the people buried in them. Many women shudder in horror and fear at the thought of entering a graveyard.

The mixed feelings that villagers express about graveyards, visiting graves, and venerating saints at their tombs relates to theological debates in Islam about the visits, the dangers of men and women mingling in these spaces, and engaging in heretical traditions, such as candle lighting. On the one hand, "based on the sayings transmitted from the Prophet which encourage the visitation of tombs, and notwithstanding the fact that there were reports to the contrary, this practice was in general seen as permitted by later Sunnite scholars, with some of them even promoting it."[27] But on the other hand, "after the time when the practice of visiting tombs in Islam had given rise to different usages which could be easily marked as abominable 'innovations' (viz. the lighting of candles, touching or kissing the tomb, circumambulating the shrine, etc.), later scholars and preachers found still more reasons than the early authorities why the visitation of tombs should be severely condemned."[28] Though men permitted and, some scholars argue, encouraged or even required tomb visitation, women visiting graves were scrutinized. The Prophet had not condemned Ayşe for visiting her brother's tomb, a historical precedent that is used as evidence that women should be allowed to visit graves. Yet, "a negative dictum reported from the Prophet and referred to by Ibn Hagar says that he cursed the female visitors of tombs."[29] This curse, however, is often interpreted as referring to women who visit graveyards excessively to lament. Lamentations, as well as other funereal practices of the pre-Islamic era, are forbidden, including sacrificing animals at the grave, ripping one's hair, sobbing excessively, scratching one's face, or playing music. Due to the rich discussions and debates among theologians on correct practices at graves and the ever-present Shi'i variations on lamentations and mourning which are forbidden in Sunni Islam, villagers are understandably concerned about the orthopraxy of women taking up this activity.

Until 2009, women never entered graveyards, for funerals or any reason, and so it was a surprise to see them discuss and debate among themselves about whether or not they would go on Arife Günü. Women began going because, as Zübeyde, Çevriye's daughter, said, she had wanted to visit her grandfather's grave. He had died in 2008. Because she did not want to go alone, her mother agreed to go with her. Çevriye has been a leader among women, elected as cooperative president every other year for over twenty years. She has also been an influential leader in women's efforts to improve their knowledge of Islam. Her daughter has also set a benchmark for girls, being the first girl in the village to graduate from high school. It is not surprising that they would have made this bold step together, expanding women's spiritual activities.

In 2009, during the month of Ramazan, as we approached Arife Günü, I visited Elif, the recently married young woman whose husband studied at a Süleymancı Qur'an school. She is a devout believer and talks in a touchingly innocent manner about spirits, angels, God, and cultural Islamic practices without fearing that these are unorthodox or embarrassingly rural. When I asked her whether she would be going to the cemetery on Arife Günü, she said, "Kıyamet olacak ya biz dua onlara [The Judgment Day will happen, we will say prayers for them (the dead)]." A few days later I returned to her house and we talked about her visit to the cemetery. She described how she went to say a prayer and to read the Yasin. She did this because, as she said, "özledim [I was sorry]." Much like the young imam who explained that one visits graves on Arife Günü to ask forgiveness for times when one failed to visit or call a now-deceased relative, she felt she needed to tell her deceased uncle and grandfather that she was sorry if she had failed them in life. Although she had made the visit, she added that she had only gone inside because she saw me there. (I was there taking advantage of cemeteries being open to women on Arife Günü, so I could photograph some of the old tombstones.) She said that her mother and grandmother were both afraid to go inside but that she was not afraid at all: "What can the dead do to us?" Then she added, "They aren't there anyway. They are with God. Only their bodies are there."

The next day I asked a middle-aged woman, Saadet, if she had gone to the cemetery for Arife Günü, and she answered no, adding, somewhat in explanation, that women don't go much—"though they could," she said. She thereby indicated that she had absorbed the transition in attitude in the village regarding women visiting graves. Instead, she said, she read the Yasin at home for her late father and other dead relatives. She remarked, "When we read for the dead, the deceased feels relief from the pains of entombment for forty days each time the Yasin is read for them. For this reason, many read the Yasin a number of times on behalf of a dead person." She said that when one prays for others, one is doing it correctly. "One should not," she said, "pray for one's own self-interest." Saadet's interpretation of what happens in the grave was different from Elif's, who said that the dead are not really there, only their bodies. Saadet described how the dead feel physical pain in their graves, whereas Elif believed that dead bodies are insensate. This difference in how the two women imagine existence in the grave may help explain their interest in visiting the graveyard. Elif did not seem troubled by the fact that dead bodies, which do not feel, were buried around her when she visited the graves of her relatives, and yet she seemed to think she could communicate her prayers to them even if their spirits are with God. In contrast, Saadet expected that the dead are present and feel in the grave. Their spirits are active in that space. Saadet's position on the state of the dead being tormented in the grave is a more common viewpoint in the village.

Many discuss the physical pain a recently buried corpse feels on the fortieth day when it is believed their bones separate. It is a common practice to say a special prayer on the fortieth day to ease the disintegration of the body. Others remarked on how certain people had spread rumors in the village in their lives and how they would have "hard work" to do in the grave, answering for their sins. They implied that one is tortured physically for each sin in the time one spends buried underground before the Judgment Day. Others seemed to think that spirits are active after death and travel beyond graves. For this reason, women say a prayer and hurry past graveyards.

The attitude toward women visiting graves was very different in Yeniyurt. Elif Hacı said, very forcefully, that women "never" go to the graveyard because they are more sinful. She emphasized that they can pray from outside the grave-yard. Surprised that women in Kayalarca prayed inside the graveyard—she had not heard about it until I asked her what women in Yeniyurt did—she remarked on the peculiar innovations allowed in Kayalarca. I also spoke to some other women in Yeniyurt about the new practice. An older woman suggested that there was no reason why older women could not go, but she thought it inap-propriate for younger ones to do so. Someone in the group mentioned the issue of menstruation as a reason why women should not go, which was obviously implied in the distinction being made between older and younger women. The imam from Kayalarca, however, approved of the practice. To summarize his very long answer to my question about whether it was regarded as correct for women to go to the cemetery, he said that in the past, during the time of the Prophet, women were told not to go to the cemetery because they have soft hearts. "Later, we began to consider this an old idea and that women should go." In short, in Kayalarca, innovations in practice are under debate and people make a distinc-tion between past practices during the golden era of Islam and the present. Be-cause practices can be updated, women have been able to push the boundaries of acceptable behavior, making demands to be allowed to care for their dead relatives on a par with men. Women in Yeniyurt, however, unamenable to mod-ernizing practice, maintain the old distinction. Entering the cemetery, like en-tering the mosque, sacred sites maintained by men, pushes the boundaries of female behavior in a manner that women in Yeniyurt are reluctant to imagine.

Viewed from afar, these debates about whether women should be able to enter a graveyard may not seem very important or interesting. After all, women in cities go to cemeteries regularly. But however innocuous and politically insubstantial women's practices may seem, cumulatively they have political effects, in that they loosen old practices, suggest innovations, and provide an imaginative space within which people begin to consider variations in practice and worldview. In Yeniyurt, the tendency is to guard against any change that could topple the structure of rural life and the social roles it contains. In Kayalarca, the attitude is quite different. New practices—from women visiting graveyards to foreigners buying carpets—are interesting and potentially good or at least worth a try. As they say, "Haydi bakalım! [Alright, let's see!]." In terms of women's Islamic practices, any effort to improve and intensify practice, to expand on knowledge and skill, is viewed positively.

Without a secure and intense context of Islamic scholarship, as women enjoy in Yeniyurt, those in Kayalarca are naturally directed toward innovation and alternatives because they cannot engage with state-controlled, mosque-based Sunni Islam. As their interest in intensifying practice and scholarship increases, they need to find ways to accommodate this. Rather than seeing themselves as rebellious, as Asef Bayat argues, they engage in "nonmovements." These nonmovements change social practices by accumulating many seemingly mundane and ordinary acts, motivated by practical needs and desires. The overall effect is political because they cause social transformation.[30] Furthermore, women in Kayalarca do not want to associate themselves with cultural traditions and the past, as women in Yeniyurt do. They consider these practices backward and outmoded, counterproductive to the creation of an Islamic modernity, which is progressive and therefore engaged with a very different notion of time. Finding no space in official orthodoxy, and eschewing the cultural traditions of the murky past, they create a middle way, where they dabble in innovations.

Though women's spiritual practices in both Yeniyurt and Kayalarca are contested and debated among women and lead to striking social change, because spiritual expression is gendered and hierarchically ordered, men pay little attention. Women's practices play in the background of male mosque-centered duties. While women gather for prayer services or the veneration of local saints, men's activities are unaffected. They visit the mosque to perform the namaz or do it at home, the only potential interruption being whether or not their wives will cook lunch that day.

Boys riding a ceremonial horse for the celebration preceding their circumcision. Their male relatives and all the men and boys in the village surround them. Kayalarca, 1998. (All photos by the author.)

Mosque with a striking metal-covered dome. Kayalarca, 2008.

A woman greets her elder by raising her hand to her forehead after kissing it on Şeker Bayramı, the holiday following the month of Ramazan. Kayalarca, 2009.

A grave of one of the imams from the Black Sea region of Of, stuffed with myrtle during the month of Ramazan. Yeniyurt, 2009.

A lone oak tree on the plain of Maşatla, where a simple prayer house was once located before mosques were constructed in villages. 2010.

Women surround a baby as they put henna on her palms and feet. Kayalarca, 2009.

Women gather on the mountaintop to read from the religious texts they have preserved from their ancestors. Yeniyurt, 2008.

Women gather on Friday for a prayer meeting in the house of an elderly woman.
Kayalarca, 2009.

A young woman prays at the grave of a relative on Arife Günü during the month of Ramazan. Kaplandağı, the mountain above Yeniyurt village, is visible in the distance. Kayalarca, 2009.

A boy delivers rings of fried dough from his mother. This is an expression of a good deed. Kayalarca, 2010.

Islamism - Is not traditional Islam. It is very modern. Intirely new

— How is this an example of moving away from traditional past

6 RITUAL PURIFICATION AND THE PERNICIOUS DANGER OF CULTURE

hetropraxy - having 2 different types of schools

— Womens religios practicing
Non-state religious interpretations and traditions
— Ottoman practice
— Visiting graveyards
— celebrating saints
— deciding what is pure & what isn't

In Yeniyurt and Kayalarca villages there is a debate about correct religious practice. As we have seen, villagers draw from a variety of sources and time frames to shape contemporary practice. In so doing, they demonstrate how past practices are either sustained or forgotten, how innovations are explored or deplored, and how men and women relate to Sunni Islam in profoundly different ways. Villagers therefore engage with debates about practice in a manner similar to purifying Islamist movements in cities, in that they assess the validity of their activities and worry about the veracity of the paths they take to the next world. There is not, then, a radical difference between rural and urban Muslims, as both are engaged in questions about orthodoxy and orthopraxy. *→ State, to have the power over religion as well*

To consider the intellectual connections among urban and rural Muslims is to challenge the scholarly interpretation of the rural-urban distinction in assessing Islamic practice and the meaning of a global Islam. As I show, Muslims who live in rural places and are native Muslims, not converts; who live in closely knit communities, not ones in which families have contracted to isolated nuclear households; and whose social world is informed by patterns of Islamic worship and charitable practice, as opposed to fragmented migrant and immigrant groups, are also thinking about and reforming Islamic practices. While scholars of globalizing Islam have looked to migrant and immigrant communities in cities and the urban context more generally to explain the attractiveness of Islamist movements, this chapter describes one rural community's decisions to purify ritual from culture. It explores the perceived dangers of enjoyment and fun in wedding rituals.

In Kayalarca village, transformations in the purification of wedding rituals took place in two stages. This is partially due to the fact that weddings have two distinct and separate but parallel celebrations—that of the groom's family and that of the bride's family. In the first set of transformations, relating to the groom's wedding, villagers were not directly influenced by an Islamist group. As far as I could determine, they made decisions on their own, though probably influenced through association with the imams from Of and the legacy of Islamic training they established. But in the second set of changes, relating to the bride's wedding, which happened fifty years later, they were influenced by the Süleymancıs. This group did not set out to transform them, as Kristen Ghodsee describes is the case in a Bulgarian city of non-Turkish Muslims, whose form of Sunni Islam was changed by Wahabi missionary groups.[1] Rather, villagers were influenced by the example of purified rituals the Süleymancı presented. Though the changes in men's and women's rituals cannot be attributed to the missionary zeal of Islamists, both were clearly affected by national and global developments in self-conscious reflection on and pointed criticism of culture as an untamed category that diverts from true Islam. The effects of a global movement to purify Sunni Islam is a recurrent theme in recent ethnographic works on Islam, as Ghodsee's work in Bulgaria;[2] Cihan Tuğal's work in Turkey,[3] as well as Brian Silverstein's work there;[4] and Amira Mittlermaier's in Egypt all attest.[5]

The national ethos of self-transformation, in which cultural traditions of the past become threatening to projects of progressive secular modernity and an Islamist future, has made Islam into an object of modernization. That is, both global Islamist movements and state secularizing, westernizing, and modernizing policies intensify the ideological stance that rural Muslims take toward themselves, leading to their critical and anxious assessment of the efficacy of Sunni practice, and of their own past and its value in sustaining an Islamic society. Villagers thereby begin to think, as do many scholars and Islamists, that rural Islam is different: popular, traditional, or folk, unconscious of modernizing and globalizing influences. For this reason, villagers in Kayalarca replaced cultural rituals involving dancing and music with emotionally constrained Mevluts and *sohbets* (literally meaning a conversation but referring to sermons in this context). But there were other things that happened as well, of local importance—a fight at a wedding and resulting bitter feelings between Kayalarca and Yeniyurt villages.

Looking at when, why, and how the villagers in Kayalarca decided to replace men's performances of davul (bass drum) and zurna (double-reed wind instrument) music and folk dancing with Mevluts, and to replace women's dances with sohbets, is instructive of the agency of local communities to engage in religious change. Replacing music and dance with sober Mevluts is not unknown in the scholarship on Turkey and other parts of the world,[6] because the fear of fun, as Bayat puts it, is related to global Islamicizing movements. Cihan Tuğal,[7] for instance, describes how, in a neighborhood in Istanbul, people feel pressured to have Islamic weddings, eliminating music and dance. The decision to transform ritual practice in the case I observed relates to villagers' concern with cultural traditions that mark them as rural people, with their engagement in Islamic movements at both national and global levels, and with individual fates in the next world. They express worry about damnation, explicitly and directly, and are concerned with national ideologies of cultural progress and development, modernity, and class position. I argue that these concerns are linked.

As the Kayalarca villagers work to transform cultural practices that appear backward from the perspective of state-based ideologies of cultural progress, and heretical or incorrect from the perspective of Islamists,[8] villagers show that they accept that the past should be separated from the present. In Kayalarca village, unlike Yeniyurt, there is a rupture rather than a continuity in how the past and future are imagined to be related to each other. Villagers' quests for sacred and secular salvation are connected to an understanding of progress as an apex in a temporal order. Thus, they support the state's construction of modernity leading to an apex of westernized, secularist modernity, and Islam's construction of sacred individual progress as leading to one's fate in the next world.

In these dual and parallel configurations of time and legitimacy, the state is included in how individual fates in the next world are achieved because the government controls and creates Sunni orthodoxy. Thus, the time of the state includes state-approved Sunni practice narrated through history rather than experienced through cultural memory or tradition.[9] As the vague past of cultural memory is replaced with codified, linear, historical narratives, cultural rituals need to be replaced with practices that are certified by some authority, giving them a coherent and "official" character. By following the implicit logic of social change that comes from some authority, villagers have learned to be suspicious of their own cultural memories and traditions. They rank the implicitly old traditional practices of their collective past against new practices and evaluate these according to their understanding of the legality of Islamic practice vis-à-vis the state.[10]

A suspicion of the cultural past leads to an open attitude toward religious change, framed as a purifying movement. It is not, in other words, that Islam changes but that it is cleansed of practices which prevented correct belief and practice. Being able to purify Islam requires legitimacy, that is, the changes undertaken need to be certified and accepted as real, in the same way that Qur'ans stamped by the Diyanet are accepted as "real." But if the Diyanet's legitimacy is challenged, or if its legitimacy seems ambiguous in any way, then some other authority may be able to gain acceptance. Currently, villagers in Kayalarca are undecided about who should have the authority to claim what is orthodox, and because they are undecided, they have an open attitude toward alternatives. For this reason, villagers in Kayalarca have been welcoming to Islamists: practitioners from the Gülen movement, the Süleymancı community, and others who legitimize their version of Islam through the interpretation and use of texts.[11]

The purification of Islamic practice to ensure its spiritual efficacy and political legitimacy is well known in literature on the Islamic world. Lara Deeb calls this, in the Shi'i context of Lebanon, the pursuit of "authenticated Islam."[12] Following Talal Asad, I call it orthodoxization, though orthopraxization would be more accurate, because these changes relate to purified Sunni practice.[13] As Mandana Limbert points out, as pious practice is controlled and contained in rural Oman, "paradoxically, perhaps, as more people claim 'religion' is a way of life, fewer things qualify as properly 'religious.'"[14] Thus, many activities that were once regarded as legitimately religious, such as burning candles at tombs or making offerings to saints, are now heterodox. The work of codifying and purifying religion can be seen as a secularist movement because it allows for human intervention into the definition of what is regarded as religious.

I was inspired to study Kayalarca village because it is the base of a women's carpet-weaving cooperative, founded by Harald Böhmer and Josephine Powell, expatriate scholars in Istanbul who had an interest in revitalizing plant dyes and women's artistic textile heritage. The project implicitly engages in notions of economic development and the revival of tradition, the paradoxical aim of which is cultural progress (i.e., women's emancipation), as June Anderson describes in her early book on the projects.[15] The villagers are economically embedded in discourses of progress, and one aspect of my research has been to study how they react to these ideologies. At times they are ambivalent and therefore make accommodations. In the process of studying the cooperative, I traveled to other villages in the region where cooperative members or relatives and friends of Kayalarca weavers lived. As a result, I was often invited to spiritual events, Mevluts, celebrations of return visits from pilgrims, and other ritual events such as engagements, weddings, funerals, and circumcision parties. From 1998, I witnessed the concerns the villagers have about the role of music and dance in wedding feasts, listened to their debates about what should and should not happen at happy ritual occasions, and considered their attempts to contain and control youthful exuberance through sober Mevluts and sohbets. I collected stories about past wedding rituals from the elderly and middle-aged, some of whom were critical of changes and some of whom insisted on their importance. And I heard discussions among young people about personal salvation, the "costs" of enjoyment, and, on the flip side, the importance of enjoying one's youth. These discussions constitute a debate about how, when, and why ritual occasions should be celebrated and the relationship between these celebrations and local notions of modernity and class prestige, as well as their weight and significance among the angels of heaven, who observe and record all of one's actions in a book that is used to assess one's fate after death.

Although achieving a perfected Islam is probably not cosmically possible, the villagers begin with the problem of tradition. As a young imam from a neighboring village argued, the villagers in the region are only now becoming schooled in real Islamic practice, as they put aside cultural traditions that they once imagined were Islamic (such as using henna), but that were, in fact, based on superstitions and incorrect understandings of Islam. Significantly, the newer practices that villagers in Kayalarca prefer are legitimized by texts (the Qur'an, the Mevlut poem, and texts about Muhammed's life written in Ottoman). The Mevlut is not at all new, as it is based on a poem written in the fifteenth century, but the villagers' replacement of men's music-and-dance celebrations with Mevluts is a response to debates on practice. Islamists would consider the Mevlut ritual a poor attempt at purifying Islam because the Mevlut is not based on the Qur'an and is in the vernacular. It also leads to the veneration of the Prophet. Texts require study, which many villagers acknowledge takes too much time and effort, especially when in a foreign language. This may account for their use of texts in modern and Ottoman Turkish. Yet, as Tuğal points out, "The need to learn the meaning of the Qur'an rather than only reading and memorizing its Arabic original, is one of the most pronounced principles of Islamism in Turkey."[16]

Although they would like to become Islamists in this sense, able to read the Qur'an in Arabic fluently, many villagers feel they cannot take the time for this study. Instead, they worry about what they can change: immoral acts, cultural rituals, and incorrect forms of prayer, all of which stem from a lack of schooling, ignorance, and a lax attitude toward the cultural past. There are consequences for not doing so; as one woman said, "We don't know what will happen in the next world." Villagers fear damnation. Because cultural traditions are so dangerous, infected with uncertainty and contaminated by fun, villagers grapple with what might be correct: practices codified by texts, approved by the state, enhanced by global debates among Islamists, and purified from questionable traditions.

BY DRUM OR BY PRAYER?

The significance of davul and zurna music and dance in villagers' lives, and their decision to eliminate these celebratory performances and replace them with Mevluts, illustrate a change to sober and contained ritual. The villagers' perception of correct practices and their concern with maintaining and transforming these practices show how ideas about spiritual practice are manifestations of agency, as deliberate containment and control and individual subjugation to God's will. To echo Talal Asad, orthodoxy and orthopraxy are not a fixed compendium of doctrines and rituals, although these terms imply the contrary, but they exist in a state of flux in relation to social and political debates. They are marked by historical contingencies.[17] Thus, the effort to be orthodox paradoxically involves change.

In 1998, as I prepared to visit Kayalarca for preliminary fieldwork, I heard from Harald Böhmer and Josephine Powell that the villagers had banned all music in a radical endeavor to transform Islamic practice. A few days later, I was genuinely surprised when Ahmet, the director of the carpet-weaving cooperative, inserted an audiotape of Turkish folk music into the truck's cassette player as we drove to the Yuntdağ. Ahmet switched off the music as we entered the village. I thought I had cracked the code: music is acceptable outside the village but not inside it. But, as I visited looms in homes where women wove for the cooperative, I met many who passed the time listening to cassette tapes. I quickly learned that young daughters listened to heartrending arabesk, and middle-aged mothers and elderly women listened to folk music or religious hymns on the radio. Yet as Martin Stokes argues, "Music as a whole falls into the juridical category of *mubah*—neither specifically approved nor forbidden but merely tolerated in Islam."[18] For this reason, I would not have been surprised to find that the villagers were ambivalent about music, but my observations did not, at least initially, demonstrate this to be so.

Two years later, in 2000, the rumors circulating among expats in Istanbul about the villagers' apparent fundamentalism had not ceased. Although, at first, I discounted these discussions and pointed out that the villagers often listened to music, I decided to investigate more closely. Back in the village, after talking to people about music, I realized that there was something of a ban in place. Although music, in itself, was regarded as unproblematic, music played by davul (bass drum) and zurna (double-reed wind instrument) was seen as cause for concern. I heard many conflicting opinions about the merit and role of this music. During 2000, the most common response to my question about why davul and zurna music was not heard in the village was that the players charged too much. Others said playing davul and zurna was sinful. Although in the past davul and zurna players were hired for the Kına Gecesi (Henna Night) at wedding rituals and circumcision parties, they had been banned from these occasions several decades ago. Surprisingly, this ban did not ease villagers' minds about the problem of music and dance. Families having one of these events would debate among themselves about whether they would permit the women to dance, whether there would be live or taped music, where the event would be held, and when it would occur. Young women getting engaged or married usually had no idea what form their ritual celebration would take until just beforehand.

In the earlier form of wedding rituals, davul and zurna players performed from three days to a week for the groom's side, and all the men from the groom's side danced while women watched from the earthen rooftops of the houses. Meanwhile, the women of the bride's side danced together, playing an upturned washbasin and singing folk songs. In its contemporary form, the bride's friends and female relatives on the groom's side attend the bride's kına gecesi to dance to taped or live music while men watch from the periphery. The men on the groom's side dance to taped music on the evening before taking the bride to her new home, while the groom is given a shave by one of his friends. This is an occasion, the *damat traşı* (groom's shave), for the women to watch the men dance. However, male folk dances, folk music, and folk plays, once the core entertainment of wedding rituals, have been eliminated.

Underscoring the tremendous diversity in rural life as villagers engage in a lively debate about ritual practice and spiritual legitimacy, the tension and anxiety in Kayalarca about celebratory feasts is not replicated in neighboring villages, many of which continue to employ davul and zurna (often clarinet) players and allow male dancing, although women are not permitted to watch. For example, in Pınarköy village to the north, I was only able to videotape five minutes of men's folk dance around a fire during one wedding, after repeatedly requesting the father of the family I lived with to accompany me. I had been with women of the bride's side, who were dancing to cassette music in another part of the village. Though a researcher, as a relatively young unmarried woman I had to conform to many restrictions, and this meant I could not wander around and videotape at will in areas where there were no women.

But other more liberal events also occur. At a wedding I attended in another village in the region, for a young man from Kayalarca who married a woman from this other village, unmarried men and women at times danced in separate halves of a field, but simultaneously to music by a harmonium and a davul player; and at other times, married men and women danced together as couples, waltzing to taped arabesk music. Many villagers from Kayalarca praised this event afterward, saying it was fun. The groom's mother from Kayalarca, however, was disturbed that the bride's family had hired a davul player without telling her.

These variations show the state of flux relating to local debates about practice. And in terms of the details of this particular transformation, whereas the wedding ritual once centered on the groom's side dancing to folk music, it now centered on the bride's dancing to live or taped music. I pondered these differences and asked in Kayalarca about Pınarköy, where villagers employed davul and zurna players and permitted male folk dancing. One response was that people in that village have "hidden gold" that they use to pay for davul and zurna. I was not convinced by this explanation, although I heard it many times, because families in the village in question sell pekmez (grape molasses), which is neither highly profitable nor more prestigious than weaving. Both weaving and pekmez are traditional products and thereby tainted in the configuration of time and value. The villagers in this nearby but parallel universe dress conservatively and wear polyester clothing from their trousseaux, rather than purchasing new clothes, as do villagers in Kayalarca. They also have fewer expensive appliances, such as televisions, washing machines, and satellite dishes. For these reasons, I was unsatisfied with the explanation that the other villagers are rich, and that instead of buying the typical creature comforts, they spend their money on davul and zurna players. Finally, while attending a wedding there, I learned another piece of the puzzle. When men dance to davul and zurna, they drink alcohol. The musicians arrive on Friday and stay until Sunday. The drinking, therefore, lasts several days. Banning the musicians in Kayalarca, thus, also eliminated alcohol consumption at weddings. Consuming alcohol is regarded as a major sin because it causes one to lose self-control.

The common practice of drinking alcohol while the davul and zurna played and men danced explained why the villagers in Kayalarca were reluctant to allow this practice in their village, but I continued to ask about celebratory music and dance. A year or so later, during a period when I was interviewing the elderly about their wedding celebrations and trousseaux, I asked a couple, Hatice and Hasan, about davul and zurna. Hatice, who was in her sixties, had come from Yeniyurt to marry Hasan. In their elder years, they were notably close; I often saw them in the fields together or working in the house, and on this day they were shucking a big mound of pistachios they had harvested. They described how they had married in 1962 in a double wedding. The plan was for Hatice to be married into Kayalarca at the same time that another woman from Kayalarca was to be married into Yeniyurt. Hatice and Hasan described how, at the big wedding, there were davul and zurna players, drinking, and a knife fight. Their memory of the event was vivid. At the wedding, the youth from Yeniyurt opened fire with guns to celebrate. Hasan exclaimed that in Kayalarca someone yelled, "Why are you opening fire inside the village?!" Then a knife fight ensued between some young men. Hatice added, "Someone was stabbed, but not killed." In anger, the Kayalarca family took their daughter back from her new marital family in Yeniyurt, which started a bitter feud. Villagers in Yeniyurt also remember the event vividly, but they blame young men from Kayalarca. Since Hatice and Hasan's wedding, there has been only one wedding between the two villages, which once freely exchanged brides. This event is cited by villagers in Kayalarca and Yeniyurt as the moment when they became enemies.

Learning that davul and zurna had been eliminated as a result of this event dated it. I returned to elderly villagers who had married before and after the elimination of the music and asked them how they had celebrated their weddings. Interestingly, elderly women distinguished the style of their marriages by coining two verbs: *davullandık* (my nonliteral translation: we were married by drum) and *duallandık* (we were married by prayer). I learned that, in 1963, after Hatice and Hasan's wedding, there had been one more marriage in Kayalarca celebrated by davul and zurna. Thereafter, the imam forbade this music and accompanying celebrations, saying "it was a sin." I spoke to the Deveci, the son

drinking led to a fight @ a double marriage between 2 villages. No more drinking ordinm @ weddings & villages are enemies of this imam, who at ninety-six is the eldest man in the village. He explained his father's authority in making the ban. The imam had made the pilgrimage to Mecca, was well respected, and apparently had his theological roots in the imams from Of, with whom he would have studied in Yeniyurt, who condemned music for its "association with drink, dance, and sexual impropriety."[19] Whereas some villagers now question whether davul, in particular, or all music is sinful, members of the elderly and middle-aged generations consider only davul to be sinful. A few elderly women said this was not true at all; as one said, "It's just music." In 2008, the Deveci breathlessly confirmed to me that davul in particular is a *günah* (sin). Though the elderly may disagree on this point, their children, the middle-aged parents of those marrying now, do not. They consider davul and zurna to be sinful, without exception. Davul and zurna music was replaced with Mevluts to celebrate the groom's wedding feast. However, the bride's düğün was still celebrated with dance and music.

THE PRACTICE OF THE MEVLUT

The Mevlut is a deeply aesthetic and moving ritual that centers on the performance of a poem, sung in the vernacular, commemorating Muhammed's birth. According to Nancy Tapper and Richard Tapper,[20] around the year 1400 Süleyman Çelebi wrote what is the best-known Mevlut poem in Turkey. As I became accustomed to village life in 2000–2001, I realized that most important ritual occasions were met with Mevluts: marriage, death anniversaries, circumcisions, leaving for military service, returning from military service, and rain prayers. These were utterly unlike the Mevluts I experienced in Yeniyurt on the mountaintop. The seeming universality of Mevluts in providing a public ritual response to special occasions is well substantiated in ethnographic literature on Turkey,[21] as well as on the Balkans,[22] but the use of Mevluts for all ritual occasions in the Yuntdağ seems a recent development.

Mevluts play an interesting role in ethnographic literature. Tapper and Tapper, Tone Bringa, and Julie Marcus describe Mevluts as women-centered, emotionally moving, and often held in private homes, followed by meals shared among women.[23] These Mevluts resemble the one I attended for the holy man associated with Yeniyurt's mountaintop, though it was outside and was a component of a full day of prayer, including Qur'anic recitation. Recall that I also described an unfinished Mevlut held in Kayalarca, one of the first of its kind, during the sixth-month henna celebration. In the literature, women-led

Mevluts are used as examples of heterodox practice and therefore regarded by the people living in those communities as less important and powerful than orthodox practices led by men. The Tappers, Bringa, and Marcus, departing from their informants' opinion of the heterodox nature of the practice, use the Mevlut to demonstrate the vibrancy of women's Islamic practice. In contrast, most Mevluts in Kayalarca (prior to 2008) are held in the mosque, led by men, and are emotionally contained.

At the first Mevluts I attended, I remained outside the mosque with "daughters" (i.e., women of my status) and young married women (of my actual age). I learned that, from their perspective, the Mevlut is not an interesting experience. It was impossible to hear the beautiful recitation, and we were with the children, who were running and screaming through the mosque courtyard. Part of the rite includes drinking a glass of şerbet (a sweetened red drink), being given rosewater, and having incense smoke wafted over one's body. Outside the mosque, we were included in these sensual experiences, but it was not possible to understand what was happening inside the mosque. Because piety increases with age, older women become more active in Mevluts and enter the mosque. However, their involvement only extends to listening silently inside the women's section. They never look at the men in the main part of the mosque below their balcony, for fear that they will distract them. The gendered and structured forms of these Mevluts are surprising, given that the Tappers, Marcus, and Bringa describe the Mevlut as a specifically and powerfully female, though heterodox, ritual. Unlike the cases described by these scholars, in Kayalarca the Mevluts held in the mosque are dominated by men and regarded as an important ritual. Interestingly, given that the women in Kayalarca have recently (ca. 2010) begun to conduct their own Mevluts in houses, they have appropriated what otherwise is a male ritual practice. Though boldly claiming rituals of their own, they are not so brazen as to consider conducting these in the mosque, which continues to be a space for male piety.

BY SERMON OR BY MUSIC

Although I returned to Kayalarca for visits in 2002, 2003, and 2004, I had not gathered any material that suggested that women had begun to consider their cultural practices with the same critical eye that men had several decades before. But by 2008, women had become more concerned with their fates in the next world, the correctness of their religious practice, and their class-based position in the national imaginary. In part, I connect these changes to the decline of the carpet-weaving cooperative's power in employing women and keeping families in the village. The village's somewhat closed perspective, as I understood the place in 2000–2001, was due to cooperative director Ahmet's efforts to prevent women from gaining employment outside the village. In 2003, however, Ahmet died. I returned to mourn his death on the fortieth day after his burial, in October 2003, and again in January 2004 to survey household economic strategies. At this point, the villagers had only begun to process Ahmet's death and its implications for the future of the cooperative. But by 2008, dramatic changes were in place.

Kayalarca is a small village; in 2000–2001, there were only eighty-seven households, and by 2008 twenty-five families had migrated. Once-occupied and thriving houses stood empty. All of the families that had left were young, either newly established or with children reaching the age of middle and high school, when families face an educational crisis. There are no high schools in the region. Sending a child to a high school in Manisa is therefore complicated and expensive. Parents need to have relatives in the city who are willing to take in their child, an apartment of their own, and a parent able to live in the city part-time—or enough money to board their child in a dormitory. The last option is a common solution, but parents then worry about their children wandering the city unsupervised. Moving the whole family to the city is, then, a reasonable solution to all these problems. In addition to established households that migrated, young women who remained in the village described how they would prefer to marry a man in a city so they could time their marriage with migration. This would help them avoid the labors of rural life, including weaving. Thus many young people sought to abandon the drudgeries, inconveniences, and the lack of state services that characterize rural life. Meanwhile, those who remained in the villages had become more involved in urban life. The connections and exchanges between city and village were denser than in the recent past. The minibuses, for example, had previously made a single round-trip per day, but by 2008 they were making three round-trips per day. Improved transportation led to livelier exchanges with former villagers in the city, and with urban friends met through former villagers, relatives, and co-workers. Increased networks led to invitations to ritual celebrations, including women's gatherings, Mevluts, and sohbets, in the city. And through this process, women began to import urban-style Islamic rituals to the village.

Although the first wave of religious purification focused on men's activities, in 2008 women had begun to transform their spiritual practices to become more educated in Islam, conforming to the construction of the doctrinally astute modern Sunni Muslim, who eliminates suspect cultural events. One woman explained why they had instituted the Friday gatherings in their homes: "Of course, women are more educated." This woman relied on the Islamist position that the study of religious texts is a demonstration of increased piety. Another said these new practices came from the city: "We saw them there and decided to do them ourselves." Just as middle-aged and elderly women met to read the Qur'an and pray on Fridays, young women planned to have *sohbetli* (with-a-sermon) engagements and wedding rituals. As I had once asked elderly women whether they had married davullandı (by drum) or duallandı (by prayer), I now began asking young women if they had chose a *sohbetli nişan* (engagement with sermon) or a *çalgılı nişan* (engagement with music and dance).

In July 2008, I learned that a twenty-three-year-old woman was going to celebrate her engagement with a sermon rather than music. This would be the third such engagement in the history of the village. Upon arriving at her house, I broached the subject of the nature of the party with her father, a shepherd with whom I had had many conversations about global humanitarian unity, realizing belatedly that he was referring to the Turkish Sunni leader Fethullah Gülen and not to liberal multiculturalism. The family, clearly, was engaged in global Islamist movements. The father said, "You need to ask Elif. It was her decision." Elif said that she had decided to have an engagement with a sermon because she was "planning for the next side," that is, the next world.

Typically, engagement parties consist of a feast, followed by the women gathering in the teahouse, with the groom attending. The bride and groom wear gold rings, tied together with a red ribbon that a relative from the groom's side cuts. The bride's future mother-in-law gives the bride gold coins, earrings, and, possibly, bracelets and a watch. The bride's female relatives pin gold coins and bills to her dress. Previously, they sang folk songs and played an upturned washbasin as a drum, but more recently the women used taped music.[24] In the events I witnessed, the bride, mother-in-law, sisters-in-law, and sometimes the groom danced in a circle. After this ritual dance, the young women in the village dance in celebration. They then have a ritualized trousseau event, at which the mother-in-law presents the bride with each item she is contributing to her trousseau by placing it on the bride's head, as if to remind her of the many good deeds she is performing on the bride's behalf.[25] All the guests toss their gifts (they are always cloth) to the center of the packed room, and the mother-in-law places each item on the bride's head, announcing the giver. This gift-giving practice ritualizes the transfer in personal textile property (i.e., cloth and clothing) to the new bride. The event ends with more dancing. Elif's engagement did not follow this pattern. There was a feast in the late afternoon at which gold was given. Very late, around ten o'clock in the evening, two female hocas who belong to the Süleymancı community, arrived from Manisa. They had been invited to a previous engagement in the village, which is how Elif knew them. On the one hand, the appearance of women from a Sufi order seems extraordinary, especially considering that such groups are technically illegal, although tolerated. On the other hand, there are no female imams, and though there are female vaiz trained by the state, they have yet to visit the rural regions. This means that as women become more concerned about religious practice, they involve themselves in religious communities outside the Diyanet's control.

The women's and men's ability to combine multiple practices and ideologies is surprising. Mixing them means disregarding the state's control of Islamic practice and not paying much attention to intellectual and ideological differences. As Ali Hacı in Yeniyurt remarked, "There are differences between tarikats, but all Muslims are brothers." This statement summarizes an attitude of tolerance toward differences between and among different Sunni authorities, including state-based orthodoxy.

At Elif's engagement party, many of the women and children in the village assembled in the teahouse. The female hocas began by chanting a greeting and then a prayer. They then sang ilahi (songs venerating Muhammed's life) and greeted us. They addressed us saying that we were gathered together with our husbands' permission to learn a few important words from the Qur'an. One of the women recited passages from the Qur'an in Arabic, in a stylized nasal tone. This was the only textual recitation at the event. The woman then began to preach in Turkish. One detail in the long sermon struck me, given my interest in davul and zurna. The hoca said that we might enjoy dancing and enjoying ourselves at a wedding, but imagine how many sins we accumulate. She said that all our sins are weighed against all the good things we do and that both are taken into account when we try to enter heaven. She described the angels at the gates of heaven, who hold scales loaded on the one side with our sins and on the other with our good deeds, and described how we needed to balance the scales in favor of the good things. "Even though we may enjoy dancing and music, we have to take account of the next world, tomorrow, not yesterday, which is over." She also argued that davul and dancing might be enjoyable, but they are costly, "and is it worth paying the price for sin?" She asked,

"How can we explain why we paid so much money to dance when it weighed against us, on the side of our sins?"

The women sat silently, listening, at times quieting their children. They finished with a prayer and passed around rosewater and candies before leaving. The village women pinned money and gold on the bride, and, with less ceremony than at previous engagements, they tossed their contributions of cloth into a big sheet in the middle of the room, without the bride's mother-in-law putting them on the bride's head or announcing the giver. They treated these older practices as unseemly. When I asked about it, a woman said, "This is how we do it now."

The next day, I went to Elif's house to find out what she and her family thought about the event. Elif and her mother were overwhelmed with dirty dishes, but both paused to say that they thought the sermon "was very beautiful." By chance, I was included in the ritual of taking trays loaded with baklava and gifts to the mother-in-law's house, which reciprocate for trays the mother-in-law sent to the bride on the day of the engagement. This was fortuitous because I went with a group of young women, all of whom were married. None of them had had sohbetli engagements or weddings, and yet they felt the need to praise the previous night's event, so markedly sober and emotionally contained, and to justify their decision not to have had such an event at their own engagements and weddings. At the mother-in-law's house, while having tea, the groom asked how the sohbet was.

The youngest woman, Elif's sister-in-law, said, "It was very nice." She said wistfully that she wished that she had had an engagement and wedding with sermons instead of with music because "having music was so chaotic. This was much nicer. Everyone sat quietly and listened, then they got up to give the gold and leave."

The groom replied, "Yes, we often like to have music and dance, but these things are for this world. We need to think about the next world."

Later the middle-aged couple I live with, Çevriye and Mühettin, echoed this conversation. The wife praised the sermon and felt the need to explain why her daughter had chosen to have a wedding with music. She said that she had talked to her daughter about having a sermon at her engagement and wedding, but "she didn't listen." On a separate occasion, her daughter explained her decision herself, exclaiming in annoyance, "Oh, Mommy, forget about these hocas! I am young and want to have fun and dance!" It came out at that moment that her father had been a davul player in his youth. Bolstered by his daughter's opinion, he added, "No one wants to go to a wedding if there is no music and dance. It isn't fun." The debate echoes Asef Bayat's discussion of the politics of fun, in which he argues that the censure of enjoyment is not merely a fear of the chaotic joys of youth culture, but that fun is subversive to fundamentalists' maintenance of power. "The adversaries' fear of fun revolves ultimately around the fear of exit from the paradigm that frames their mastery; it is about anxiety over loss of their 'paradigm power.'"[26] Considering that the household is also a domain of control and power, the mother sought to enforce an antifun politics of control over her daughter and husband, and for this reason tried to convince her that she should have an Islamist wedding ritual. The daughter, refusing her mother's attempt at control and asserting her independence by marrying a boy from the town of Tepeli, outside the village and region, responded by choosing to celebrate her wedding with music and dance.

At the daughter's new home, we watched hours of video footage from her engagement and wedding parties. As we watched the different rituals of marriage in this other place, her mother asked me rhetorically what I thought about them: "Wasn't it bad that they had a davul and that men danced?" Later that week, a neighbor was having a circumcision feast in the unpaved street outside the newly constructed apartment buildings on the edge of town. The mother shouted in horror when the *mehter* band (an Ottoman-style marching band) played the davul and zurna: "When the davul is beaten the devil appears!"[27] Because her daughter no longer lived in the village regime of control but in a town where davul and zurna were played, she felt she had cast her daughter into a foreign territory where strange and spiritually dangerous ritual activities occurred. The complex dynamics of this mother-daughter relationship, struggles over authority and power regarding who chooses correct practices and whether one can be devout but also enjoy one's life, are echoes of the struggles about the meaning and purpose of religion and debates about orthodoxy itself.

These occasions and the discourses surrounding them underscore a series of anxieties about spiritual practices and the implications of music and dance for people's fates in the next world. The villagers in Kayalarca chose to eliminate ritual expressions of fun and to replace them with the Mevlut to sober up wedding celebrations. This substitution demonstrates that a repositioning of practiced identities and reformulations of ritual have taken place. Considering the Mevlut gives clues as to how and why these political reinterpretations have occurred and what they mean in terms of how the villagers wish to imagine and practice cultural traditions and Islam. Replacing men's folkloric expressions of dance with a Mevlut shows the villagers' engagement with discourses and practices of modernity, in which fun cultural practices seem lower-class, heretical, and backward. The Neo-Ottoman mehter band, replete with men in Ottoman-style costume who perform amid huge banners and tents, should not be treated in the same category as village davul and zurna players, whose style of music, costume, and dance make no reference to court practice of the former Empire. Yet even this upscale Neo-Ottoman version of davul and zurna horrified the village mother. She assured me that the family holding the circumcision would be having a Mevlut as well. She did not actually know that family or what they were planning to do, but she wanted to convince me that they would cleanse the dangerous davul music with a Mevlut, which she regards as being an orthodox practice. In the village, the Mevlut is a public forum for the performance of a modern, rural sensibility. In the early years of my research, I saw how women attended and enjoyed Mevluts held in the mosque. These were unlike Marcus's, Tapper and Tapper's, and Bringa's depictions of Mevluts because they were not for women and were not regarded as heterodox. For this reason, the village mother assumed that a Mevlut would cleanse the troubling effects of davul and zurna playing, even when these came from the upscale Ottoman-style band. This modern, rural sensibility shows a reformation of local Islamic practices to make them correct, a concern with emotional sobriety and decorum, which the villagers view as part of being enlightened, modern people.[28]

The early transformation in the groom's village wedding rituals reinforced the notion that women are associated with folkloric practices because the bride's ritual was not examined with the same critical eye. Though urban women were the objects of Kemalist progress, rural women were not. Now, women everywhere are symbols of an Islamist future. For this reason and for spiritual ones as well, women have found they need to change their ritual practices, to make them pious, contained, and sober. In the process, women have defied the stereotype that their practices are more closely linked to the past, tradition, and folklore, as they have also begun to seek purified rituals based in textual "authenticated" legitimacy, as Deeb argues for Shi'i women in Lebanon.[29] They thereby dabble in the symbolic role of women as Islamist markers of moral and spiritual progress. In Turkey, pious women feel marginalized by the state control over the domain of the mosque, and like the middle-class Muslim women Mahmood describes in the mosque movement in Cairo, they want to gain textual knowledge of Islam that underpins their legitimacy as Muslims.[30] Though Islamist movements exist in rural spaces (such as the

Süleymancı community), the politics of difference and discord as experienced in urban space is less intense because there are no secular people who live openly in the villages (except for state officials, of course). Within this pious space, unencumbered by secular worldviews, women are free to work on their practice and knowledge through intensive study, collective ritual practice, and individualized piety. In so doing, rural women might look outside the official and constrained institution of the mosque to find religious authorities to guide them. Their heightened interest in an authentic, purified practice leads them to alternative religious communities such as Sufi brotherhoods, or away from them, to the enjoyment of music and dance.

The most striking aspect of villagers' struggle to locate alternative practices is their tendency to act like the *bricoleur* who mixes discordant activities without regard for their epistemological contradictions. For instance, though the young couple had a sermon at the engagement party, they decided to have music and dance at their wedding. When I asked the wife about this decision, she said her husband wanted to have fun at their wedding. Because marriage involves many ritual stages, it is possible to have one's cake and eat it too by combining an Islamist engagement with a fun bride's wedding and a somber groom's Mevlut held in the mosque.

◇

In considering the construction of the rural subject as a modern Muslim in Kayalarca, villagers have reformed rituals, stripping them of cultural traditions. I have demonstrated how these changes link them to Islamist modernities, which seek sacred progress, and to state ideologies of modernity, which seek secular progress. These forms of progressive constructions of time, piety, legitimacy, and modernity are not limited to Turkey or to the (unbounded) Islamic world, but relate to the construction of "alternative modernities,"[31] parallel to, reflective of, and often formed in relation to western secular modernity. In this case, an Islamist alternative modernity constructs legitimacy in texts, state institutions, and religious communities but not by sustaining cultural traditions. The villagers in Kayalarca seem enmeshed in local dramas, but the institutional structures of the state, which include Sunni Islam, play a role in how they live. The villagers have intentionally and willingly embraced state structures, identities, and opportunities. Rather than being a traditional, rural peasantry, remote from the politics of urban life, as many Kemalists and Islamists would assume, they are agents of spiritual as well as economic and infrastructural transformation. Sunni orthodoxy and an attention to correct practice, in their view, are part of this modernity. I would argue, however, that their understandings of Islam and configurations of correct practice are in a state of flux; they borrow from state-approved Sunni Islam and the teachings of various religious communities, and they maintain some traditional practices.

The villagers' interest in a revamped spiritual practice relates to a self-reflexive application of ideas of status. For instance, Nilüfer Göle describes Islamists' project of "introduc[ing] the 'real Islam' to social groups with lower levels of education and culture who otherwise experience 'folk Islam.'"[32] And as Cihan Tuğal argues, "Radicals attack popular rituals, labeling them 'traditional religion,' which they claim they will replace with 'real Islam.'"[33] For the villagers, who are not under direct attack by secularists or Islamists, introducing a purified Islam in local practice entails a reflexive critique of rural Islam and an assessment of how these practices measure up from the viewpoint of Islamist others, such as those described by Göle.[34] Although there is considerable debate and flexibility among religious scholars in Turkey and in other parts of the Islamic world about what should be retained and what transformed, powerful prejudices in Turkish society are at work to marginalize rural people, devout practitioners of all varieties of Islam. In Kayalarca, villagers feel that everything they do is labeled as marginal with respect to the nationalist project of modernity. In discussing the villagers' understanding of an Islamist modernity, I have described how they imagine orthodox practice as distinct from local, folkloric or traditional, alternative ritual celebratory, or spiritual expressions. Whether a product of the Diyanet or religious communities, the villagers rank such practice higher and see it as more real, authentic, and orthodox than their cultural traditions, which refer to an indeterminate past. It is not the state that they resist but cultural heritage, which places them in a low position in secular progressive modernity. They thus work to eliminate or forget traditions, which are socially contaminating and spiritually damning.

From an analytical perspective, it is important to avoid essentializing practices as either official or folk, orthodox or heterodox. These are distinctions that anthropologists rightly critique. Social theorists critique the process of categorization as distorting because it solidifies what otherwise is fluid. Categories of culture,[35] the state,[36] class,[37] gender,[38] and so on, when bounded, subsume the fluidity of social arenas of power and its contestation through individual and collective agency. Categorization and reification destroy holism and the acceptance of ethnographic fluidity and ambiguity. The processes of categorization are political, as they create domains of occident and orient, as James Carrier,[39] as well as Edward Said,[40] have taught us. Geographic constructions of civilization and development are pitted against and mirror each other. As they are deployed, these categories create a sense of nostalgia for what imperialism, colonialism, and capitalism have destroyed.[41] In the distinction between official and folk Islams, villagers as well as scholars, state officials, middle-class urban dwellers, and the elite categorize practices in relation to dichotomies of urban–rural, male–female, Kemalist–Islamist, and traditional–modern. Whereas ethnographers and theorists can afford to deconstruct these classifications, the villagers in Kayalarca are invested in these notions of worth. They attempt to gain power over categories and in the process of categorization and instead of resisting, they select those practices that gain them the most prestige, in this world and the next.

The villagers situate themselves in the historical framework of the Republic, which was constructed on the notion that positivistic scientific rationalism could transform a broken, backward, and eastern society into one that looked western, progressive, secular, and rational. The Atatürk revolution put the necessity of rupture into the imaginary space of the nation.[42] This is enacted in the performance of fragmentation, the self-conscious worries of class and status, the troubled and alienating sense of not being quite modern enough and of needing to catch up.[43] Orhan Pamuk poignantly evokes the feeling of melancholy of the people of Istanbul, who, in striving to attain a (self-constructed and imposed) modern, secularized, and westernized level of civilization, desire the darkness of night, which cloaks the ruins of the Ottoman Empire dispersed throughout the city.[44] While he describes their shame at not having attained western modernity, they wish they could cast off these ruins but they also want to protect them. The process is reflexive: "Whenever I sense the absence of western eyes, I become my own westerner."[45] Many urban Turkish people who visit Kayalarca often are caught between these conflicting desires. On the one hand, they wanted to be sure that I understood that they were modern, urban people, not what they assumed the villagers to be—traditional—and they wanted to protect the villagers from me, assuming I would exploit their innocence and expose that untainted authenticity to the crude western gaze, to the academic audience that would not be able to understand, with the same degree of intimate concern they felt for traditional village life. This position echoes Michael Herzfeld's formulation of "cultural intimacy" as shared sets of beliefs people apply to themselves to explain stereotypes of national character, thereby defensively creating a feeling of commonality.[46] The villagers apply this reflexive process to defensively claim a space for themselves. They know that the politics of identity and culture are interlaced with geographic stereotypes, that is, that devout Muslims are seen as poor, rural people, who have infiltrated the cities or who remain mired and isolated in their provincial locales. These geographic and class prejudices are reproduced in state ideologies of progress. Hakan Yavuz asserts, "Kemalism based its raison d'être on the perception of its Islamic 'other' as backward and conflict-ridden."[47] And Richard Pfaff argues, "Kemalism is essentially an urban ideology, and, while the peasant could participate in the Turkish transformation proposed by Kemalism, the object of that transformation was to create a Turkey within which the peasant would be disengaged."[48] Conforming to the state construction of correct Sunni Islam forces rural people to assess themselves and view their cultural practices critically. Yet it also empowers them, allowing a degree of resistance to Kemalist secularity while making a claim to the state and an Islamist future because they can engage with state power via the Diyanet. In addition to its implications for the politics of modernity in this world, Islamic practice has meaning and power in the next world. Theorists have to recognize the reality of religion, not merely its symbolic value, and consider this when explaining how and why practitioners make choices about orthodoxy and orthopraxy.

7 SECULAR AND SPIRITUAL ROUTES TO KNOWLEDGE

Secular public education trains children to think via the official historical narratives of the Republic and integrates them into the urban-oriented, secular, modernist future. Though all children attend the required eight years of school, access to secondary and higher education is not universal or equal. As Henry J. Rutz and Erol M. Balkan argue in their study of the rise of the middle class in Istanbul, access to elite education creates and reproduces the class system.[1] In the Yuntdağ, until recently, villagers have not benefited from secular education. There are two reasons for this: secular public education came late to the region and villagers valued an Islamic education more highly.

During the period of my research, I saw how villagers began to learn the value of obtaining a secular education, especially for improving the lives of their children. And in realizing its value, they sought ways to integrate themselves into the urban-oriented Republic. But Islamic education and ideas about knowledge, learning, books, and reading all continue to be important. Paul Stirling, who wrote the first ethnographic study of a Turkish village, describes the same for a rural region in Central Anatolia in the 1950s. "Traditionally, the only purpose of learning was religious. Even now villagers say that the great benefit of being able to read is that it enables one to acquire religious knowledge."[2] Stirling's words made a great deal of sense as I puzzled out various misunderstandings. While I understood okumak in a secular sense—"to read" or "to study"—villagers meant to pray and to worship. I read books to learn a writer's perspective or to indulge in novels for enjoyment, while villagers read the Qur'an. They are not interested in multiple views of the world but in one view: God's. They also "read" when they pray. Prayer is understood as reciting texts, not the Christian Protestant conceptualization of prayer as a personal communication with God, like an interior conversation. When villagers pray, they are not describing their personal struggles to God but reciting prayers, performing movements, or intoning the Qur'an. Though prayer is not a conversation, individuals communicate personal concerns by increasing the numbers of *rakat*, each movement of the namaz. People might perform these movements with someone or something specific in mind.

Though the villagers do not all understand the meaning of the words they recite in prayer, since these are in Arabic, they use the word *bilmek*, to know, to indicate the ability to recite prayers and texts. Women in Kayalarca remark that women in Yeniyurt "know" more than they do, meaning they can read (intone the words of) the Qur'an. They also use bilmek to refer to the Yeniyurt women's ability to read Ottoman. Knowledge in this sense extends beyond knowing texts to spiritual power as well. Villagers describe people with spiritual power, such as unofficial imams, referred to as hocas, whom they visit to write healing muskas or amulets. They describe these men as "knowing a lot" (*pek biliyorlar*). Muhammed Zühdü, is described as having "known a lot." He was trained in Islamic textual knowledge and worked as an imam but his "knowing" includes his ability to turn into a pigeon each day and fly to Mecca to perform the morning namaz and then fly back to the village. In Islamic hagiographies, "birds . . . sometimes function as metaphors for the individual's soul."[3] Sarı Ismail Padişah, a disciple of Hacı Bektaş, for instance, turns into a falcon.[4] Knowledge, then, is understood by devout villagers, not only in terms of having the scholarly ability to read and understand, interpret and analyze, but as being connected to a richly embodied, miraculous, and historically inflected efficacy of praxis. In this way, villagers' discussions of bilmek blur the line between orthodoxy, correct doctrine, and orthopraxy, correct practice.

The word *kitap*, book, had weighty significance. Whereas I had many books, which were piled on a chair beside my bed, households all had one, the Qur'an, secured in a decorated bag, hung on a nail high in a room, or put on a high shelf. Sometimes villagers have more books, usually of a religious nature, crumbling texts in Ottoman preserved from the past or more recently published works. These books have spiritual power, not only information. Muskas, amulets, small triangular packets of Qur'anic text written by a hoca, sewn into cloth and attached to undergarments with pins or worn on the body under clothing on a string, are prayers for specific purposes—to promote fertility, to prevent headaches, to prevent nightmares, and so on. Papers covered in Qur'anic text, prayers for some purpose, dissolved in water and drunk, achieve the same end, but the text is ingested. These amulets demonstrate the power of Qur'anic texts and the quasi-magical effects of ingesting them, thereby incorporating them into the body. Elderly women, as I discussed in a previous chapter, known for their healing power, pray over the sick or those with some affliction and then blow on, over, and around the individual spreading the prayer and the efficacious power of the words with their breath. The efficacy of the Qur'an, then, is conveyed to people physically, through the media of water, breath, and sound, or it is conducted to the person through contact with the skin, such as muskas worn under one's clothing.

My orientation to books was quite different. Once an elderly woman visited me while I was ill. I was lying in bed, while she sat on the floor beside me. She picked up some of my books, piled haphazardly, and said, "You look at these and call that work?" She laughed when I told her, "Yes, that was what I did." I noticed that she did not use the word okumak (read) but merely *baka baka* (look), to describe what I did with books. She was trying to work out the differences in our orientation to learning, knowledge, and work, mine secular and hers spiritual. While I have a measure of respect for my books, though I write in them and leave them piled by my bed, the villagers easily dispensed with secular books, children's schoolbooks, by using pages to start fires in the winter. A young man, seeing a book I had been reading on my bus trip to Manisa, said somewhat accusingly, "I know what these books are, they are novels! I also read them to pass the time while in the military." My books never would merit the respect due the Qur'an, I realized, and even my attitude toward books demonstrated their disposable nature as physical objects.

Villagers undertake study to master Islamic texts to become a hoca, a learned person, an imam, or more often, someone who can intone the Qur'an with fluency. As I studied households and labor in Kayalarca, I learned that many of the men had been trained as imams. Two were employed as such. One was in the village and a second worked in a town near Manisa. I learned that until the recent past, parents had invested in their son's education with the expectation that he should become an imam. Though many had invested in an Islamic education for their sons, few were able to master the exams required to gain a position, unlike the many imams emerging from Yeniyurt village. But in Kayalarca, many men knew the basics and could read the Qur'an and prayers, such as the Mevlut poem. In short, even by the year 2000, villagers widely interpreted okumak, bilmek, and kitap in spiritual ways, just as Stirling found among villagers in the 1950s. Children, though, because they had the experience of a secular education and, through this, the ideological imprint of secularization policies, were differently oriented toward education and the potential for advancement in the urban-oriented nation.

ISLAMIC EDUCATION AND THE STATE DURING THE EARLY REPUBLIC

Public education spreads a secular worldview and state ideologies of modernity. As Sam Kaplan discusses in his book *The Pedagogical State*, one of the first laws of the new Republic, the Unification of Instruction in 1922, put all educational institutions under state control. In accord with secularization policies, it followed that medreses, or religious schools and seminaries, were closed. By 1938, Islam was removed from all curricula.[5] In the rural Yuntdağ, in contrast, there were no secular schools during the early republican era. Yeniyurt's medrese was closed, but this did not result in the immediate construction of a secular school.

The meaning of knowledge was challenged when the many informal imams and hocas working in the region were expected to cease preaching and instructing. Some had formal training, such as Muhammed Zühdü, who studied in a medrese in Bergama and Konya along with three other men in the region. Born in 1882, he would have been forty at the time the Republic was founded. These men would have posed a threat to the state control of Islam and the meaning of learning as secular. Many in the villages revere this hoca in part because his legacy maintains a link to this alternative way of thinking about spiritual knowledge. Visiting a house one day, I walked in as the father was watching an imam on television. I directed the discussion to the newly minted saint in Recepli, whose tomb I would soon visit. He said about Muhammed Zühdü: "He knew the most," honing his point by adding, "When this hoca was around, there was no television, so unlike now when one can sit at home and listen to hocas on television, at that time, they listened to this man. He could answer any question one might have." I asked if the hocas on television have more power, authority, and knowledge than the Recepli hoca. He said, very enthusiastically, "The Recepli hoca knew more than the hocas on TV!" Given the respect villagers had for these learned spiritual men, one can imagine the resistance they would have felt when all imams not officially recognized by the state were expected to cease their activities in the 1920s. Due to resistance in rural regions, imams and hocas went underground. In towns and cities tarikats, Islamic brotherhoods, also hid their activities.[6] In short, Islam could not so easily be removed from daily life in either rural or urban places. State policies challenged these learned men as well, as the more diffuse cultural sense of Islam spread across the land, embodied by individuals, and in village mosques and medreses. The villages and surrounding landscape were filled with sites of spiritual practice and knowledge: village mosques; saints' tombs; sacred mountaintops, wells and certain trees; a village medrese; and numerous hocas and imams. All these places would have become suspect in the state's attempts to reduce and control Islamic practice and contain it in mosques.

Secularization policies were intended to radically transform society as a speech delivered in Kastamonu on the Black Sea coast in 1925, by Mustafa Kemal, demonstrates. Atatürk famously declared, "'Gentlemen . . . the Republic of Turkey cannot be a country of Sheiks, dervishes, disciples, and followers. The most correct and truest path is the path of civilization.'"[7] It is not insignificant that Atatürk used the term *path*, with its close associations with Islam, to direct the nation to a new one. It follows that the early republican state attempted to fully replace one set of institutions, Islamic ones, with secular ones because Islam as an all-encompassing way of life was seen as uncivilized. This creates a conflict in rural Sunni regions, where people are devoted to the state and are respectful of authority but not necessarily respectful of the particulars of these policies or the secularist worldview that regards Islam as uncivilized. Though many older villagers express ambivalence about early state policies, such as putting the call to prayer in Turkish, even the elderly agree with laicism, the state control of Islam. This explains why villagers in this region did not resist but made activities covert. In fact, their strategy was wise. The state loosened these policies over time, until the present, when public Islamist movements openly operate and are tolerated by the government. Villagers support the notion of an authoritarian state that controls, commands, and forbids; they do not support a liberal, secular, multicultural, multisectarian world composed of atomized individuals who regard religion as a private matter of belief and not Islam as a way of life.

When I talked with a woman in her twenties, she mused on how things in the past were better than now. I asked her why and she replied, "In the past, everything was forbidden." Justifying laicism, an elderly man described how at the end of the Ottoman Empire, many sheiks emerged who taught "wrong things." "They were ignorant and they used people for their own benefit, filling their pockets with money. They had power. To clean their influence from religious practice, the state forbade the teaching of the Qur'an." He added that the Diyanet was founded in 1924, one year after the foundation of the Republic, and proudly recounted how the Diyanet was established by Atatürk in order to control and regulate religion. Though this particular man approved of the authoritarian control of Islam by the state, he did not extend his argument to the objectives of secularization, which public secular education by definition would achieve. In this way, loyalty to Atatürk's legacy and the state is retained in villager descriptions of the past, while the socially transformative goals of secularization policies are overlooked or not understood.

Villagers who do not have a secular education attribute secularization to communists who are godless—literally, without a book, *kitapsız*. Some older villagers argue that communists, not national leaders, tried to cleanse social and political life of Islamic practice. For instance, one village woman asserted that Atatürk never forbade the wearing of the headscarf; it was the communists who did this. "Atatürk," she asserted, "was a good Muslim." Atatürk never illegalized the "veil" but he discouraged it. Villagers thereby wrongly remember—or simply do not know because they did not attend school—the secularization policies of the Republic. They attribute these to leftist political groups and movements, which were discredited after the 1980 military coup. Thus, many unschooled villagers continue to live in a world in which an authoritarian laicist state takes over the legitimizing spiritual authority of the former Empire, and do not recognize or perhaps know the import of secularization itself.

Though the new state expected Islamic leaders to vanish, they did not immediately replace Islamic knowledge with secular knowledge by providing schools in rural areas. In cities and provincial towns, schools were built to create a new idea of knowledge and learning, one divided from Islam. Sensing that they had missed both the former world in which Islamic authority was uncontested and the new one in which secular learning provided opportunities, many elderly people regret their lack of exposure to both secular and Islamic education. These expressions of regret are particularly gendered. Boys were often taught to read the Qur'an in secret, but girls faced barriers to attending classes. Young men performing their military service were taught to read and write in modern Turkish. In this way military service ameliorated rural men's illiteracy. Obviously, rural women did not benefit. One elderly woman described how she knows neither the old nor the new alphabets. She attributed her lack of education, both spiritual and secular, to her difficult early life as an orphan. As a child, she lived in a neighboring village with her grandparents. There was a school, but she was not allowed to attend it. She recounted how her grandfather said girls did not need to go to school. Her daughter, who was sitting with us, added quickly and a bit defensively that going to school in that era was not required. Not only could this elderly woman not attend secular school, she could not have an Islamic education either. She described how she never learned to read the Qur'an because at that time, in the 1940s, it was forbidden to teach it. She added that the hocas still taught the Qur'an in secret but that the gendarme, the regional police, often broke up the classes. I asked how the gendarme would have known that the Qur'an was being taught in a particular village. She described how in a village everyone would know what everyone else was doing. Word would get out. This suggests that some villagers may have approved of the state control of Islam and informed the gendarme, or that through male conversation in the coffeehouses, word leaked out and passed from village to village. I asked if forbidding teaching the Qur'an was unique to the village where she lived. She and her daughter both said, with emphasis, that it was widespread throughout all the villages.

Another woman, Kezban, from Kayalarca and now elderly, was present when the gendarme came to break up the children's Qur'an classes. In my interview with her, she took time from spinning thread to describe how she had been small and studying the Qur'an with the hoca when the gendarme came. "They said it was forbidden to teach the Qur'an," she said, adding, "Who knows why it was forbidden, but it was forbidden. This was during Inönü's time." Inönü, Atatürk's close associate, succeeded him as president following Atatürk's death in 1938. Inönü is widely blamed for all harsh policies of the early republican period, while Atatürk is revered for creating the nation. For instance, after describing how the regional police broke up Qur'an classes, this woman quickly mentioned "the hocas, who were hanged"—a reference to an incident in Menemen, a small town near Manisa, in 1930.

The Menemen incident was a popular uprising led by a Nakşibendi sheik or, in Andrew Mango's account, a dervish (follower of a mystical order), who demanded the restoration of the caliphate and of shariat (Islamic law). An officer, Kubilay, appointed to investigate, was attacked by a mob and beheaded. His head was stuck on a pole for display and paraded in the town.[8] The uprising was quelled when the dervish died in detention and twenty-eight of the lynch mob, including the dervish's son, were hanged. I asked Kezban if she witnessed the event. She said no, but that she had heard about it because news of the event was discussed in the villages. The incident in Menemen occurred while Atatürk was president, but no one said this, instead they implied that the blame should be put on İnönü.

I noticed that many people made a slight slippage in critiquing events and policies under Atatürk by quickly referring to İnönü. By not making it clear who was actually in power at that time, I think my interlocutors expected to confuse me, leading me to believe that İnönü was to blame. In this way, Atatürk is insulated from critique. This is not surprising; after all, it is a crime to criticize Atatürk. After the Menemen incident, Atatürk "demanded that Menemen should be declared a *ville maudite* (accursed town) and razed to the ground and its inhabitants transported, that no mercy should be shown to religious fanatics, even women, that executions should not be delayed, and that opposition journalists should, at least, be frightened by being made to appear before the court martial."[9] Though I never heard a villager describe the aftermath of the event, or Atatürk's preferred means of managing the uprising, the incident is frequently cited when someone is making the case that the state has suppressed religion.

Elderly female villagers, because they have lived through a number of regimes, are aware of the effect of the transformation of state policies and how these relate to their lack of secular and spiritual literacy, the ability to read the Qur'an in Arabic. One elderly woman described how, while she could not read the Qur'an, her parents could. "The older people knew, but they learned under a different state." "When the state changed," her daughter added, "it became forbidden to teach the Qur'an." Another elderly woman, Ayşe nene, told me, "I can read neither the old nor the new script, I will burn in hell!" She believes that being able to read the Qur'an is not merely a good deed, as many say, but a requirement for entry into heaven. This belief makes her early experiences as a child, being barred from learning to read the Qur'an in Arabic and the Turkish language in Latin script, especially traumatic. Iftariye, now an elderly woman and mother of one of the two imams from Kayalarca, had been one of the few girls who studied the Qur'an. She and the imam's wife, who was sitting with us at the time of our conversation, added that though it was forbidden to teach the Qur'an, there were many who did so by gathering in houses. Similar classes were held in Yeniyurt.

State secularization policies forbade unofficial imams from teaching and preaching. As the stories from the elderly relate, children were affected by these

policies when the gendarme broke up classes. The effect of state power in relatively remote rural places, directed at children studying with local imams, would
have frightened many, and it is clear from the tone in which people describe
their memories that they still feel frightened and angry about these experiences
of state intrusion. Unless the gendarme were patrolling villages, it seems someone would have had to inform the gendarme of these activities, and that—in
a time without cars, paved roads, or telephones—this would have required an
investment in energy, walking or riding a horse to the gendarme station. State
policies thereby intruded on village solidarity. Resistance to these policies also
implies opposition to fellow villagers who accepted them.

While attending women's prayer gatherings, the intergenerational differences
in Islamic learning—the result of state policies—were evident. While many elderly women in Kayalarca dwell on their condition of illiteracy and ignorance,
and some are fearful that they will burn in hell, they pray regularly, fast, many
perform the annual sacrifice during Kurban, and they practice good deeds.
Some women have been able to make the hac (pilgrimage) to Mecca. They wear
diaphanous white cotton scarves atop their two or three other headscarves, ad-
vertising their status as pilgrims. But when women meet on Fridays to recite the
Yasin forty-one times, they have to "tespih çekiyor," say their prayer beads. Their
daughters learned to intone the Qur'an in the era after the 1950 election, when
the Democratic Party (DP) won. This party, which İnönü allowed to be formed
in 1946, opposed the Republican People's Party (CHP; Cumhuriyet Halk Partisi),
which represented Atatürk and policies of secularization, westernization, and
modernization. As Feroz Ahmad argues, with the election of the DP, "the center of political life shifted from the cities to the provinces largely untouched by
Kemalist reforms or modern secular culture."[10] Provincial elites and the masses
of rural people pushed for the relaxation of radical secularization policies and
the reversal of a number of reforms, including the recital of the call to prayer in
Turkish. The shift in state policies is evident when one observes how women of
the middle generation (now mothers and young grandmothers), who grew up
post-1950, after the beginning of multiparty democracy, command skills in intoning the Qur'an. And the effects of state policies after the 1980 coup is apparent
when noticing how these same mothers look admiringly at their daughters, who
demonstrate the importance, not only of learning to read the Qur'an in Arabic,
but of doing so with tarikats, which promote women's knowledge through female hocas. Elderly women who grew up under Atatürk's and then İnönü's strict
secularization policies finger their prayer beads. Though in Kayalarca the inter-

generational differences in spiritual learning among women are notable, more surprising is that in the atmosphere of the radical secularization policies of the 1930s, women in Yeniyurt not only learned to read the Qur'an in Arabic but also learned Ottoman. There, a kilometer away from Kayalarca, the "culture of Islamic learning" sustained not only resistance to the state but kept alive the Ottoman past and did so despite prejudice against girls' spiritual training.

THE DIYANET AND THE PRODUCTION OF OFFICIAL IMAMS

Clearly, the early republican state was interested in reshaping structures of Islamic authority from the Ottoman Empire by attempting to stop imams and hocas from teaching. Kayalarca's last unofficial imam was the father of the eldest man in the village, called Deveci, after his profession as camel driver. The Deveci's father had declared that davul and zurna music was a sin, an aspect of his effort to objectify and purify Islamic practice. This local-level decision transformed the nature of marriage rituals and spread a notion of correct piety in the region. It is this freewheeling individual power of local imams which state authorities wanted to control. But instead of devising a government system that would address spiritual needs, the Diyanet, founded in 1924, did not open Imam Hatip schools until 1950—a result of the DP winning the national election. There was a gap, then, when few imams had official training. After the 1950 election, when state policies toward secularization eased up, a new system for becoming an imam was put into place. One could study in a new Imam Hatip school or pass a government exam. Village men who had not studied at Imam Hatip schools began to gain official rank as imams via the Diyanet's system of exams. This means that many of the secretly taught young boys learned enough to pass the state exams and that unofficial imams were able to gain an official status. Though clearly defying the state's control of unofficial imams by allowing men to teach their children to read the Qur'an in secret, villagers in Yeniyurt chose to take state exams to become official imams once this became possible. In other words, they did not establish or become involved with tarikats, thereby creating an alternative to the state system, despite the troubles they experienced with state control. They were ready to conform to the state once policies protected Islam and regularized official knowledge.

One such man from Yeniyurt who became an imam in this era was Ali Hacı. Born in the 1930s, he could have studied in a state Imam Hatip school, but he was unable to because his father had died when he was eleven. Forced to remain in the village to help support his family, he studied the Qur'an with his uncle who was the imam in Yeniyurt. Having completed his elementary school education and studied independently, he passed the state exam and was appointed to be imam in Kayalarca though he continued to reside in Yeniyurt. He traveled back and forth between Kayalarca and Yeniyurt several times a day to deliver the call to prayer and lead prayers in Kayalarca's mosque. Like all imams, he led prayers for holidays and memorial events, and Mevluts for Kandil and other occasions; was present for rain prayers; performed the Islamic wedding called the *nikah*; buried the dead; and prayed for young men when they departed for military service. He also taught children how to perform the namaz, to be good Muslims, and the basics of reading the Qur'an in Arabic. Later in life he made the hac to Mecca and is called variously by the titles hoca and hacı.

Ali Hacı is well respected in the villages for his kind and gentle manner and his knowledge of Islamic learning. He is also known for having trained a number of *hafız* (one who has memorized the Qur'an), in Kayalarca and Yeniyurt. Though Ali Hacı trained many who became hafız, interestingly, he was not one himself. He teaches those who want to study, without charging a fee. Hafız study for two to three years. There are no female hafız in the area, but he teaches women to intone the Qur'an in Arabic and instructs them in religious matters. Of the many men who became hafız under his guidance some became official imams and others work as unofficial imams or hocas. Kayalarca's current official imam was one of Ali Hacı's students, who also became a hafız. In this way, Kayalarca's current imam keeps alive Yeniyurt's local legacy of Islamic training via Ali Hacı. Ali Hacı's son Orhan has achieved the rank of vaiz (a preacher, that is, someone qualified to write not only deliver sermons), higher than imam. Orhan was appointed to a mosque in Bamberg, Germany, via the DITIB (Diyanet İşleri Türk Islam Birliği, or Turkish Islamic Union for the Institution of Religion), the Diyanet's branch in Germany. Orhan, under his father's guidance, became a hafız when he was a boy. He pursued his studies at an Imam Hatip school in Manisa and later earned his degree from the Faculty of Theology at Istanbul University. He is also a hacı, many times over having made the pilgrimage to Mecca as part of his employment with the Diyanet.

Given the number of young men from Yeniyurt who have gained positions as imam, I was interested in why so few from Kayalarca have had as much success. I interviewed several in 2008. One man, then in his forties, described some of the obstacles he faced. Though a hafız and a student at an Imam Hatip school

for many years, he abandoned his studies because the state changed the requirements for attaining the position of imam while he was a student. Disappointed
that the requirements had been increased, he gave up. I interviewed another
young man who was studying at an Imam Hatip school. In his third year, he
seemed sheepish about the question of whether or not he would become an
imam. He said that he had not really thought about it. When I asked, "But people who go to this school become imams, don't they?" he replied, "Sometimes,
or they continue on to the university." He and his father, sitting with me in their
two-room house, pointed out that it has become considerably harder to become
an imam; a student must graduate from high school and finish the theological
faculty in a university or take a two-year course after high school. The young
man said that many used to want to become imams, but that now, as his father
also affirmed, many do not want to do so because the requirements are so ex-
acting. Though being an imam continues to be a respectable profession, many
want a quicker path to making money, a necessary step before marriage.

In Yeniyurt I talked to one of Ali Hacı's granddaughters, who is attending
an Imam Hatip school in Manisa. She seemed more confident about her future
after studying in an Imam Hatip school than did the young man in Kayalarca.
When I asked her if she had chosen the school herself and why, she said that
she had chosen it and she pointed out its benefits. By finishing high school at
an Imam Hatip school she would be able to get both an Islamic and a secular education. After receiving her diploma, she said, she could continue on to
the university. However, as she noted, the government frequently changes the
rules and creates obstacles that prevent graduates from Imam Hatip schools
from going on to universities.[11] Nevertheless, she felt something positive would
come of her efforts. Her goal was to become a public school religion teacher.
Religion classes are mandatory in all public schools and many young pious
women want this job because it gives them a respected profession allowing
them to maintain a pious life in public. One girl from Kayalarca attending a
secular high school in Manisa expressed the desire to become a religious class
teacher. She pointed out that though she would not be able to wear a headscarf,
because this would be impossible in a government building, she could, like her
own religion teacher, wear a wig instead.

Ali Hacı's granddaughter alluded to a source of frequent struggle in Turkey's
education system. Though Imam Hatip schools are public high schools, secularists often try to prevent Imam Hatip graduates from taking the entrance
exam for the university system. This exam, called the ÖSS (Öğrenci Seçme

[handwritten margin note: requirements to graduate from Iman Schools & go to uni or becomean iman keep changing) becoming harder — disuades many youth]

Sinavı, or Student Selection Exam), is a terrible burden for all young people in Turkey. Students can take the exam once a year. The results determine not only where you can attend but also the subject of your major. Students cannot change either where they will go to school or what they will major in unless they retake the exam. Many students spend years studying in private exam schools, which drill students to the exams, hoping that they can get a spot they want. Needless to say, the time and expense exceeds that of the typical village family, which would also have to find housing for their child in Manisa, where the exam schools are located.

For Imam Hatip graduates, there are even greater difficulties. Frequently and arbitrarily, they are barred from taking the exams on the grounds that these schools are less rigorous than secular high schools. The argument that Imam Hatip graduates are not qualified for taking the university exam is unconvincing given that if students are unprepared, they will not pass. Rather, it seems clear that secularists are worried that graduates from Imam Hatip schools will pass the university exams. The path for pious students to become doctors, lawyers, and businesspeople is then clear, and inevitably pious people will begin to work in publicly visible jobs. The fear is that if publicly pious people work in prestigious jobs, they will spread the visibility of piety, thereby deprivatizing Islam. This would be regarded as an attack on secularism, in which Islam is expected to be invisible or at least not visible among educated prosperous members of society. If Imam Hatip graduates are allowed into the exams, the educational system would create opportunities for everyone and transform the class system, reinforced by the current system of secular elite education.[12] For this reason, policies regarding the graduates of Imam Hatip schools are in a state of constant flux.[13] Students of these schools, then, live in a state of uncertainty about their futures. Some give up their education midway due to changes in state policy—such as the man in his forties.

SECULAR EDUCATION AND THE HUMILIATION OF ILLITERACY

It should be clear by now that there are distinct differences between Yeniyurt and Kayalarca, especially with regard to villagers' opportunities in education. Yeniyurt was and still is regarded as a center of Islamic learning. Many men there have become imams. But many men and women in Yeniyurt have also benefited from the secular education system. To understand why, we need to consider how villages get schools in the first place. All villages are connected to a city, which provides public services, such as the infrastructure for water, electricity, telephone, roads, and schools. By the mid-twentieth century, Kayalarca and Yeniyurt were both connected to Bergama, a market town to the north. To the south of Yeniyurt, villages were connected to Manisa. Before blaming Bergama for not helping villages develop, it is important to note that overall gains in infrastructure have been incremental. None of the villages in the Yuntdağ that I visited have a sewage system. Some still lack a water system, which brings running water to houses, but all have electricity and telephones, which villages obtained in the late 1970s and early 1980s. A key difference in a village's development was whether or not it had a school. Those connected to Manisa early on obtained an elementary school before those connected to Bergama. Koruköy, for instance, a village to the south of Yeniyurt, had a school in the 1950s. Villagers in Kayalarca were frustrated by Bergama's lax support, and they petitioned to be connected to Manisa.[14] After they won this petition, Yeniyurt followed suit. In 1967, Kayalarca obtained an elementary school. According to a survey of villages in Anatolia, by 1968, 88 percent of the villages in the sample had an elementary school.[15] It was not the case, then, that every village in Turkey had an elementary school. But, confusingly, Yeniyurt had an elementary school by the late 1950s, when the village was connected to Bergama. Why Yeniyurt had been able to get a public school at least a decade earlier is unclear. No one in either village could account for this discrepancy. It is possible that the state was replacing the (crumbling) medrese with another educational institution.

The lack of a school in Kayalarca, during a time when Yeniyurt had one, had been a source of anger and tension between the two villages. The Yeniyurt villagers would not allow children from Kayalarca to enroll in their school. Somewhat callously, villagers in Yeniyurt often say with regard to villagers in Kayalarca, making an implicit comparison to themselves: "There is no ignorance here." In Kayalarca, many who were children when the elementary school was established in 1967 did not receive the basic four years of education because they could not adjust to school and/or their parents did not think it was necessary. Many middle-aged people describe how difficult it was for them to try to learn in school when they were already in their teens.

Because men were given a second chance to learn to read and write during their military service, however, women were at a special disadvantage. One elderly woman in Kayalarca has often told me the story about how she went to school for one day in her life. I asked her what she learned and she said she learned the letter A, for Ayşe (her name), but that she quickly forgot it again. It is not uncommon to meet older women who suffered from illiteracy in other regions where they had a school because their parents would not permit them to attend. An elderly woman in the town of Tepeli described how she never learned to read because her parents said there was no point in educating girls. Seeing her obvious emotion, I asked if she was angry with her parents. She exclaimed, "Yes!" Looking me in the eye, she said, "There is nothing harder in life than illiteracy!" Though she was never sent to school, she managed to learn to read in Arabic and Turkish, "in the new and old scripts," that is, Ottoman. She also learned to intone the Qur'an in Arabic. She described how she studied her children's schoolbooks and, with great difficulty, taught herself. Many elderly women in villages tell similar stories. Their fathers dismissed their desire for an education as unnecessary, and only through their own efforts did they manage to achieve literacy. Like this woman in Tepeli, their interest in being educated related not only to understanding modern Turkish but also to learning Ottoman and Arabic. Thus, when older people discuss literacy they do not imagine that this should relate solely to modern Turkish. Sitting with an elderly woman in Kayalarca, I asked if she had been to school. She said, "The teachers wouldn't take us." She never learned to read in modern Turkish, nor did she learn to read the Qur'an—although her parents both could. Her mother, Havva, came from Yeniyurt and as a direct descendant of the imams from Of knew the Qur'an. My interviewee exclaimed, "I never learned to read!" and described how difficult it was. She explained that in Manisa people want to give to the elderly: "They say, 'Grandma, sign your name here.' But I don't know how and I have to tell them. They have me press my finger and leave my fingerprint instead."

The elderly and middle-aged dwell on the humiliating experiences of illiteracy, and the sense of being left out of the urban-oriented achievements of modernity, and Islamic knowledge. This sense of loss and frustration spurs older people to send their children to secular schools and Qur'an courses. The couple I lived with worked hard to send their son and daughter to school. They sent their son to trade school to become a marble worker after he finished the required five years of elementary education (the requirement has since changed). But he abandoned his training and flounders from job to job as an adult, relying on his parents' good will for help though he is married with children. His parents, who were hopeful for their daughter, sent her to a secular high school, followed by years of private exam prep classes. She obtained her high school diploma and passed the university exam, but because the spot she won was for a university far away from Manisa, her father refused to send her to the two-year hospitality program. Though willing to educate his daughter, he was not willing to have her live far away. The expenses for educating their children were very steep. Socially, the couple has endured the critiques of fellow villagers who jealously disapprove of all their apparently wasted efforts, unwilling or unable to make the same investments and sacrifices.

Though the elderly include both religious and secular education in their descriptions of their own educational experiences, middle-aged and younger villagers have begun to distinguish education in secular and religious terms. As they have begun to focus on the benefits of urban life, which includes a secular education, expectations for their children's futures have changed. This is partially the result of state policies. In 2000, the national mandatory educational requirement was raised from five to eight years. Other assistance has also been forthcoming from the government. To attend middle school previously, parents had to pay for the daily bus trip to a nearby town, a uniform, books, and incidental expenses. After 2000, when children were required to attend middle school, the state began covering transportation costs. The state also assists poor families with the cost of books, uniforms, and lunches. It is now financially possible to educate a child for eight years, but poor families tend to be reluctant to make the investment in their daughters. As one mother, a widow, said about her daughter, "If she were a boy, I would have registered her for school this year, but as a girl, I chose not to send her. She will weave carpets with her older sister." It is illegal not to send one's child to school but the fines are rarely enforced.

The state does not require children to receive a high school education. For this reason, all rural children face obstacles in attending high school because they have to pass entrance exams, need families to support them while attending, and have to find a place to live in Manisa for the duration. But girls face a further obstacle due to the headscarf issue. Women's bodies and comportment, both Islamist and secularist, are an overdetermined symbol of modernity. Reams have been written on the headscarf debate, and the topic is of intense interest because women's clothing has become a symbolic marker of how civilization is defined. Because secularism is understood as the privatization of religion, women in headscarves, visible and public symbols of piety, have been barred from entering government buildings, which are by definition public, including schools, courthouses, and parliament.[16] For students, the problem has been that secularization, modernization, and westernization policies prevent pious women from achieving an education and a position, unless they conform to state-mandated rules regarding female comportment. Pious women are thereby the objects and subjects of social control by the state, as well as their families. In this way, modernity as rendered in the Turkish case becomes an illiberal social engineering project often working against women's interests. Elite Islamists, as Jenny White describes, have worked to reconfigure ideas about modernity and civilization to argue that a truly democratic society allows women the right to wear headscarves.[17] In an interesting inversion of Atatürk's famous quote about Turkey needing to follow the path of civilization and not that of Islam, Erdoğan was quoted as saying in a 2010 article in *Hürriyet*, "Depriving young women from studying in universities due to their external appearance, belief, or family structure was a primitive and unprogressive approach."[18] Civilization is the ideological object of redefinition, now being used to expand public Islam, but not human rights, the freedom of religion, or public expression generally. The ban against women wearing headscarves in universities was lifted in 2010,[19] and more recently girls attending Imam Hatip schools and female students attending religion classes in secular schools are allowed to wear headscarves.[20]

The headscarf is viewed as a highly charged political symbol, which can be read from a number of angles. It demonstrates piety, local identity, and fashion sense. For some, it is a persistent demonstration of Turkey's inability to modernize and secularize, a symbol of patriarchal control, and for others, it is an expression of religious freedom and the right to make piety visible. In rural spaces where religion has never been privatized and therefore does not require deprivatization, rural women wear headscarves almost without exception. The bare head, in contrast, is a symbol of secular Kemalist modernity, marked as progressive and western. As Jenny White describes, the scarves signal class distinctions.[21] Headscarves come in a number of forms, from drab everyday, multicolored cheerful polyester, to stunning red or turquoise green silk turbans worn by fashionable young Islamist women in Istanbul. In villages, where there are fewer class distinctions, headscarves refer to local village styles and special occasions. Women wear a traditional and local form of head covering, such as a heavy black cotton scarf with a simple white decoration with heavy beaded oya (crochet edging), a modern Islamist form of head covering such as a large enveloping polyester scarf, or a fashionable headscarf, such as a sequined brightly colored scarf edged in fancy oya. Women wear different kinds of scarves, with different political and social import, for different occasions: a wedding in the city (Islamist scarf), a village holiday or ritual celebration (sparkling colorful cotton), or a bitter cold winter day (heavy black with beaded oya). An elderly woman might always wear a white cotton scarf or white cotton gauzy covering draped over two others, a sign of her pilgrimage to Mecca with the alın bez, a black decorated scarf wrapped around the forehead. While a young woman might wear a seemingly traditional cotton headscarf decorated with heavy beads and sequins during the cold wintry months in the village, this does not mean that she will not wear a large polyester Islamist-style head covering while attending a wedding in Manisa, and nothing at all while attending high school. Though it is obvious that people dress for occasions, the Islamist urban position dismisses rural women's cotton headscarves as traditional, unconscious of modern Islam. However, rural women are conscious of the political and social meaning of the different scarves, worn in relation to occasion and age, as well as fashion.

Though the term *başörtüsü*, head covering, is commonplace in ideological discussions about the headscarf, in rural areas, people talk about women as open (*açık*) or closed (*kapalı*). The difference lies not only in head covering but in overall attire and worldview, sexual access, and moral comportment. A woman who wears no headscarf is always açık, and her openness is expressed not only through headgear but in other clothing and makeup as well. Reading clothing, though, can be confusing. Kemalist women—those who either follow the principles of the republican secularist revolution or are employed by the government—are "open" in the sense that they do not wear headscarves or other Islamist clothing, but this does not mean that they can dress freely, on an individual level. Rather, they have to conform to the state-mandated policies of female emancipation, in which Kemalist women present themselves as sexually neutral.[22]

Rural women experience the pressure of needing to demonstrate a rural identity in the village, especially one that expresses the village's own identity, a more modern spin on Islam at urban events or more public and prestigious ones (like weddings). Covered rural women cover not only their hair but their ears, neck, and chest in big enveloping scarves. As one young woman explained, "As Hanafi, we believe that women should show their beauty by covering themselves and only showing their faces." In the village, they cover their bodies in baggy şalvar, which conceal the contours of the body, and shirts and vests, which cover their arms to their wrists. Village women increase their coverage when they go to the city by wearing a big manto, or raincoat. The manto covers their rural şalvar and themselves. Şalvar are a pointed symbol of a rural underclass. Women are embarrassed by the symbolic import of şalvar at the same time they are outraged that they should be made to feel this way. Many express the fear that if they do not conceal their rural identities in the city, they will be cheated or taken advantage of. At the same time that şalvar are a symbol of rurality, women love them and are loathe to replace them with a skirt, which they find cumbersome and awkward. Islamist clothing, in the sense of modernist urban devout attire worn in the city, is not merely a sign of piety but also a cloak for rurality. Many women wear it to cover up their class identity, not only as a sign of their greater piety. Though women cover their bodies very thoroughly, they leave their faces exposed. There are Islamic groups in Turkey in which women wear enveloping black *çarşaf* (literally "a sheet," a large black cloth worn over the head and around the body reaching to the ankles), which partially conceal their faces, especially mouths, and black gloves, to cover their hands. I have not seen women dressed in this manner in Manisa, but have in Istanbul where they are members of particular religious communities.[23] In rural Turkey and provincial cities, the sign of a truly conservative woman is not whether she wears a headscarf, because everyone does, but whether she wears stockings in the summer. Most rural women wear sandals in the summer and leave their feet bare, but the more conservative wear stockings.

Though in rural areas all women cover, there is the important exception of women who work for the state: schoolteachers and midwives. As I mentioned earlier, as civil servants these women do not merely choose not to cover but are barred from covering. In fact, they are also barred from dressing in revealing or provocative ways, as assessed by the government. Their clothing is symbolic of the Kemalist revolution as Islamists' women's clothing is symbolic of their public piety, and rural women's clothing of their local village identities. As the schoolteacher described, she can wear makeup but only in a modest manner, cannot expose herself in low-cut outfits, and cannot demonstrate any overt sign of Islamic identity by covering her head. Female civil employees are expected to be neither secularist, in the sense that they live as they might like, nor Islamist or visibly pious, but Kemalist. As a result, they straddle a middle line, trying to appear as modern as possible in a standardized manner, with pants that are neither tight nor too loose, shirts that neither reveal nor conceal. They have to conform to the state's expectations of correct female Kemalist comportment, a desexualized but recognizably female person.[24] And because they live as examples of state policies in rural places, they have to present themselves as if on duty every day. The schoolteacher, for instance, was disturbed by how I wore village clothing. She could not accept that this was "fun" and a way to engage with rural fashions and learn what it feels like to move about as a rural woman. The midwife was more relaxed because she had been in the region for decades. As well, she was past childbearing age when restrictions on women's movements and gossip about them is most intense. She wore simple rural-style headscarves to weddings to show her solidarity with the rural people she had served for decades. The schoolteacher, however, did not have the same freedom as a young woman. She always went out bareheaded and in pants. This difference did not bother villagers in the least. She had many friends, among the daring married young women, who liked to smoke and joke around with her.

During the decade of my research, 2000–2010, the headscarf issue was intensely debated because it affected girls who wanted to attend school. But this is not the only reason why parents are reluctant to send their children to school. The elementary school is not an issue because it is in the village, but sending a daughter to middle school requires allowing her to go to a town about thirty minutes away. Without the same degree of supervision and at an age increasingly sensitive to developing crushes and flirtations, parents fear exposing their daughters to the town and the mixed atmosphere of the classroom. In other words, the full import of *açıklık*, openness, would befall her. Despite a few exceptions, however, the majority of girls attended middle school. The real obstacle is high school, for all the reasons I have already discussed: the schools are in Manisa, an hour from the village, and they are expensive, not only because are there fees, books, uniforms, and traveling costs, but because the child would have to stay in the city. In addition, attending school means allowing a daughter to become or dabble with being open.

Zübeyde was the first girl from Kayalarca to earn her high school diploma. As Çevriye's daughter, president of the cooperative, one might assume that working in the women's cooperative made it possible for the mother to encourage her daughter to attend high school. To the contrary, it was her father who insisted that she receive an education.[25] He said, "I want my daughter to have a better life. I want her to be educated." In many ways Zübeyde has secured a more comfortable adult life than that experienced by her parents. Zübeyde described her high school as *sosyete*, meaning that it was of a higher class. She said there were many rich children attending. The term *zengin*, rich, is used to refer to people who are secular Kemalists, not only wealthy. In a show of bravado, Zübeyde remarked, "Everything was available: cigarettes, alcohol, drugs." She also claimed that they had *ot sigara*, marijuana, adding that she never tried these things but that she had begun to smoke tobacco while in high school.

Exposed to a different life in the city, she felt alienated from her former village friends. While living in the city she met a man from a different region and decided to marry him. Now upon her return for special holidays with her husband and baby to the village, she says she does not talk to people because they gossip. She complained, "they say I became a *hanım* [lady], but this is stupid since I speak the same way, dress the same as they do, eat the same foods. . . . What does this mean, I've become a hanım!?" Jealous of her advantages and the successful match, she remarked that the village men are not nice to her husband. In part, they focus on his high-society style of eating on a separate plate, rather than sharing a metal bowl. "He grew up eating from his own plate and he wants to do this in the village as well. People can't understand it." I said, "They've seen tourists doing this." In response she noted in exasperation, "They call us 'tourists' for these things, foreigners!"

Being the first girl to finish high school was both an accomplishment and a burden because it marked Zübeyde as different. Now that the path has been broken, however, other girls are following in her footsteps with less difficulty. Kayalarca's imam is dedicated to educating his daughters. Visiting him at one of the coffeehouses where he spent time each day smoking and chatting, I asked him what he wanted for his daughters. He said that he hoped they can pass the exams and enter the university after earning their high school diplomas. Without family in the city or enough money to buy an apartment, he said his elder daughter stayed at a dormitory in Manisa run by the Süleymancıs because there was no other place for her in Manisa. According to Yavuz, "As of 2003, they (the Süleymancı) run the most powerful dormitory networks in Turkey."[26] Interestingly, she attends a secular high school.

In my discussion with the imam's daughter, she remarked that her father had said that she and her sisters needed to get professions. She feels supported by her family in her efforts to get an education. In her bedroom, which she shared with her sister, she showed me photographs of her friends saved on her computer. I noted that many are "open" while some are "closed." I asked her about this and she said that in the school, of course, everyone is "open," meaning that she is attending a public high school where the state enforces the no-headscarf rule. But she added that some of her friends are "closed" when they leave the school. She said that she has thought a great deal about this question, whether to have an "open" or "closed" life, because she hopes to have a profession. She listed some options that she would consider, including lawyer, but she noted that these choices would be dependent on her father allowing her to become "open." She said if she has a profession, she would have to be "open" in the office and maybe she would be "open" generally, but naturally her father, who is an imam, wants her to be "closed."

Girls who attend school face many questions about the kind of physical comportment they choose, which has implications for the kind of profession they can have and, in fact, whether they will have a profession at all. Beyond political, the headscarf question is existential and personal. Though girls feel a degree of empowerment by being trusted to go to school in the city away from their parents, they also continue to rely on their fathers' permission in choosing not only a profession but whether they will develop a "closed" or "open" physical comportment in the future.

From 1998 to 2010, the villagers in Kayalarca slowly transformed their orientation toward education from seeing it as a spiritual practice to viewing it as a necessary step to gaining the benefits of citizenship. This means that many parents want their children to finish middle school, ideally complete high school, and possibly work toward the achievement of a university degree. The desire for higher education is often extended to girls. Many parents who are serious about their children's ability in obtaining an education move to Manisa. They recognize that the benefits of citizenship require migration or temporary settlement in the city. For the young, achieving a higher education is de facto assumed to be the preliminary step to moving to the city permanently. A move to the city helps individuals obtain the benefits of state resources through health care, education, access to markets, and an involvement with national ideologies and politics. Some who want these benefits but do not have an advanced degree have begun to treat their home village as a suburb. These people, typically but not always men, commute to work in factories. Kayalarca and Yeniyurt are slightly too far away to make a daily commute palatable, being over an hour in each direction, but there are many who tolerate the commute to keep housing costs down. No one pays rent in the villages. While employment in the city provides many benefits, for those who do not have an advanced education, the forms of employment available, usually factory work, make commuting seem a good solution to paying rent.

In Yeniyurt, with its longer history of disciplined Islamic scholarship and having a public school a decade before Kayalarca, villagers have been more successful in achieving higher degrees and obtaining jobs in the professions. Many live in Manisa and in other towns and cities in western Turkey, a few further afield, such as the one who works in Germany. Yet, the village remains a vital place, where Islamic scholarship as well as secular education is respected. But Yeniyurt's experience is exceptional, given the many, especially women, who suffered the humiliations of illiteracy.

Villagers experience a geographic and existential separation from the state. In part, this separation has benefits. There is less political pressure to conform to ideological dictates on secularism and Islam, and when villagers want greater benefits of citizenship, engagement in a monetized economy, and higher education, they can choose to have it. But this entails leaving the village. The state, in other words, has little interest in providing services for rural people, as villagers often complain. Rurality, thereby, not only marks villagers as different, it raises questions about their rights as citizens. The nation is imagined as urban; there is no room for alternatives. It is no surprise then that the cities are filled with migrants.

8 AN ENTREPRENEURIAL "NEO-TARIKAT" AND ISLAMIC EDUCATION

An alternative to secular education for villagers from Kayalarca, including studying at an Imam Hatip high school, is to study with what Olivier Roy refers to as a neo-tarikat, the Süleymancıs.[1] Villagers in Yeniyurt are against this group; no one has studied with them and they are not invited to the village to deliver sermons. Thus, my discussion of the role of this group in the Yuntdağ excludes Yeniyurt but includes Kayalarca and two other villages in the region, Mallı and Gambeşli.

Unlike other Islamist movements, such as the Nurcus and Gülenists, the Süleymancıs are active in rural places. They demonstrate through a broad geographic interest that they are not merely offering a counterhegemonic alternative to secular Kemalism, but are involved in a broader Islamic movement, which includes rural people. While Roy refers to this group as a neo-tarikat, villagers call it a tarikat, and members a community (cemaat). I describe the historical origin of the group and their Qur'an classes, from the perspective of rural people from the Yuntdağ or those connected to Yuntdağ villages, in Turkey and Germany. Unlike Ahmet Yükleyen, who studied this group in Holland and Germany, I did not have access to their daily workings but learned about them through people who had studied with them. I am interested in how they have influenced Islamic ritual and training in the Yuntdağ, though my inquiry led me to Germany.

By meeting needs in populations outside their community, the Süleymancıs expand upon the nature and shape of Sunni Islam and show an entrepreneurial impulse to provide interested members of the public with religious services and education. The fact that they provide services, such as sermons, and create institutions, such as Qur'an schools, challenges the legitimacy of the laic state by offering religious expertise outside the Diyanet's control. Though threatening to laicism, this neo-tarikat gestures toward the possibility of a different kind of secularism, which values religious freedom and religious pluralism. As I have mentioned, tarikats are illegal, but alternative spiritual groups are allowed to organize as associations (derneks) or foundations (vakıfs), as Silverstein says in his book on a Sufi group.[2] Organized as an association or foundation, these groups are legal, but they are organized under different ministries than the Diyanet. Yükleyen, for instance, describes that one dernek under which the Süleymancı community organized its Qur'an courses in Turkey in the 1990s was the Kuran Kursları ve Diğer Okullar Öğrencilerine Yardım Dernekleri Federasyonu (Federation of Associations for Supporting Qur'anic Courses and Other Schools' Students). This group was registered under the Ministry of Education.[3] Thus, under the legal cover of the dernek or vakıf, groups gain a legal standing and are allowed to function as religious organizations, despite being outside the control of the Diyanet. Somewhat counterintuitively, then, by being allowed to operate under a different branch of government, religious freedom or at least pluralism for Sunnis is introduced by sidestepping the Diyanet's control. This does not mean that all forms of religion are tolerated or that groups which do not cede to government control in some manner are legal.

Through the legal cover of religiously oriented civil society associations and foundations, the government shows how it establishes structures that reappropriate a form of religious pluralism, in a style reminiscent of the Ottoman era. This relatively new but limited pluralism reflects continuity with the Ottoman past, when tarikats operated legally and other religious groups, what are now called minorities, Christians and Jews, were able to exist within different legal frameworks and communities, called the millet system. Thus, these new Sunni associations can be interpreted as radical because they threaten to dismantle laicism. Appealing to many scholars, they seem fashionable rifts on a Neo-Ottoman religious worldview. They are a form of civil and public religion, a demonstration of how Sunni Islam is being deprivatized.

While the Ottoman era may be one source of inspiration for establishing legal shields under which alternative Sunni organizations are able to function, there is evidence that the United States is another. Jenny White quotes Recep Tayyip Erdoğan as saying "he favored a secular system 'like the American system' instead of Kemalist laicism."[4] American-style secularism means separating the state from religion. In the United States, the government is prevented from establishing religion. But it does define what is correctly religious in particular legal cases.[5] In Turkey, American-style secularism would require dismantling the Diyanet and laicism. It is not clear that the Turkish government is willing to go that far. Instead, Sunnis who make this argument imply that alternative Sunni groups should be able to organize and operate without fear of the state, but they are not arguing that all religious groups should have the freedom to operate without government intrusion. Certainly, the campaign to assimilate Alevi communities into acting like Sunnis, by building mosques, for instance, does not lend credence that there is a genuine interest in religious freedom.[6] In any case, the legal and social conditions within which Sunni neo-tarikats work are recent developments of the post-1980-coup era, when the state loosened up regulations regarding Sunni groups.

Neo-brotherhoods, according to Roy, build on traditional frameworks but include innovations. Usually founded by one sheik who writes books on his interpretations of the Qur'an and other Islamic texts, the sheik uses media, such as television and the Internet, to disseminate his message. He or his followers recruit individuals as members, rather than family-corporate groups, because these ties have been broken through migration.[7] "A neo-brotherhood targets an individual who no longer has roots in a primary community and lives in a purely non-spiritual environment."[8] Roy argues that the group helps to re-create the sense of community lost to the individual through migration. Through networks of members who see to every aspect of the recruit's life, including personal and professional connections and finding spouses, the individual is reintegrated into a collectivity. Thus, in terms of Roy's argument, neo-tarikats exist because migration and immigration is an alienating experience, causing a collapse in social networks and a disintegration of religious communities.

As my discussion will show, the Süleymancıs, which have upward of four million followers,[9] straddle traditional tarikat and neo-tarikat structures. They operate in relatively traditional Islamic contexts, such as the rural Yuntdağ, where kin groups are not dispersed; people do not feel a sense of alienation (or not in the same manner as immigrants and displaced people); and an Islamic way of life, worldview, and sense of time and relationship to eternity are meaningful aspects of everyday life. But at the same time, the group caters to immigrants who have been displaced, such as Turkish immigrants in Germany and the Netherlands and migrants from rural villages living in provincial towns, as well as in the megacity of Istanbul. They also utilize face-to-face contacts and media forms, especially the Web, to spread their viewpoint.

The Süleymancıs, because they are able to appeal to both kinds of population—a traditional, rural underclass of devout skeptics of the republican secularization project who value kinship and community, and alienated proto-Islamists who suffer from displacement and *gurbet* (exile) such as Turkish immigrants in Germany—the community is especially powerful. There is much that these two social groups have in common, often overlooked by researchers who perpetuate the categorization of rural Islam as essentially different from urban practice. Though immigrants are often regarded as displaced and disconnected, social and kin networks and common values link these two groups. Many Turkish immigrants, even in the second and third generations, bring spouses from Turkey, even first cousins from their parents' natal village. By connecting these groups and worldviews within one community, those who are seeking greater cosmopolitan connections, such as rural people, find satisfaction in being part of a global Islamic movement. Those who are nostalgically searching for the coherency of a pious community in a contemporary form find social and moral sustenance in the neo-tarikat or other religious associations or foundations. The broad appeal of these groups is not that they target those who suffer from alienation but that they appeal to devout people generally, regardless of where they live and what form of modernity they have experienced.

In Turkey, the group has several thousand Qur'an schools. In Germany, the organization referred to as the Islamic Cultural Center (Verband der Islamischen Kulturzentren in German, and Islam Kültür Derneği in Turkish) was founded in 1973 and has over three hundred member associations, some of which include Qur'an schools. Though the fact that the Süleymancıs are able to cater to many kinds of population would lead one to suspect that Roy's definition of them as a neo-tarikat is misplaced, the historical circumstances of their foundation and interaction with state institutions in the history of the Republic demonstrates that the term is useful for thinking about what the group wants to accomplish.

There are some terminological issues that need to be addressed before proceeding. In discussion among people who are not members, the group is referred to as the *Süleymancılar*, the Turkish plural of *Süleymancı*, those who are devotes of Süleyman. I have been using an English plural. The term *Süleymancılar* is regarded as pejorative among members who refer to themselves, as Yükleyen does,[10] as Süleymanlı, literally meaning those who are with

Süleyman, meaning they follow him. Clearly the English does not convey the sense that these two suffixes, -cı and –lı, imply in Turkish. Conducting a search on the Internet for Süleymancı or Süleymancılar tends to yield articles in Turkish which take a negative view of the group, but searching for "Süleyman Tunahan," the founder's name, does not. As of 2012, searching under "Süleymanlı" did not yield information on the group. Despite the fact that Süleymancıs is regarded as a negative term among members, I use it because this is the term my informants use. I never heard a villager use the term Süleymanlı.

AMBIVALENCE OF THE TERM *TARIKAT*

A second terminological issue is the term *tarikat*, which I have employed in the same loose manner as villagers do. As Banu Eligür argues, tarikats were associated in the Ottoman era with provincial and popular, mystical Islam in contrast to the urban, state-based *ulema* (Islamic legal scholars).[11] Bernard Lewis writes that tarikats "had established themselves in almost every town and village in Turkey. Through their close links with the guilds and corporations, they were able to dominate the professional and social, as well as religious life of the artisan and much of the merchant classes."[12] While the term does not seem always to have been negative in Ottoman Turkey, tarikats were criticized for corruption in the late Empire.[13] In republican Turkey, use of the term tarikat often implies clandestine, antistate activity. This is because tarikats were disbanded in 1925 as part of Atatürk's reforms. Tarikats provided the basis for an alternative political organization, led by local religiously legitimized leaders, that rivaled the state's power. The reasons for disbanding these groups, then, was mainly political, but some tarikats did support the transition to the Republic.[14]

In this era, religious groups are sensitive to the historical and political issues underlying the disbanding of tarikats, and for this reason members are quick to correct the use of the word tarikat in describing them. As Yükleyen says, "The Süleymanlı fear the persecution of the Turkish state which banned the traditional sufi orders, so they reject any claims of being a tarikat, or Sufi order."[15] Yükleyen defined the group as a cemaat, a community, with some aspects of the group's function relating to tarikats, in that there is a mystical component of the group relating to the founder's spiritual power and role as a final member in a chain of descent.[16] He thereby lends Roy's designation of them as a "neo-tarikat" further credence.[17] Other tarikat-like groups or communities, such as the followers of Fethullah Gülen, called Fethullahcılar or Gülenciler, pose the same question about the use of the term tarikat.[18] Jeremy Walton, an anthropologist who has studied the Gülenists in Istanbul, argues that members would not use the term "tarikat" to describe themselves because they view tarikats as oppressive institutions. Individuals who participate in the Gülen movement, in Walton's work, say they are free to leave if they like.[19] It is not clear that members of tarikats in the past could not leave. Perhaps because affiliation with these orders was closely interconnected with kinship, regional, and occupational identities, leaving was not a conceptual option.

In any case, the Gülenists depict tarikats as intolerant and authoritarian, and thereby distance themselves from these qualities by framing themselves as civil society organizations. Unlike the Süleymancıs, the Gülen movement, which emerged from the Nurcus or Nur movement in the 1980s, is a transnational, powerful, and wealthy organization. Berna Turam estimates the group to have six million followers.[20] They own newspapers, such as *Zaman*; the Turkish television channel Samanyolu, which also broadcasts to the Turkish population in Europe; and five hundred schools worldwide, including seven universities in Turkey. Therefore, due to their massive resources, conforming to state definitions reframes their activities and dissuades critics that they are clandestine, antistate, or politically radical in character. In fact, many believe they are embedded within state institutions, such as the police force.[21]

Villagers have ambivalent feelings about the term tarikat. In their usage, tarikat refers to a community that has a sense of commonality as a spiritual group, under the leadership of a man, living or not, whose philosophy, written or not, guides them in Islamic practice, connects them to an historic legacy and spiritual authority, but is also potentially against the state control of Islam and by extension the state itself. The Süleymancıs resemble villagers' notions of tarikats so completely that they do not hesitate to use this term when discussing them.

Though some villagers are involved with the group, others argue that tarikats are socially constricting and force people in their spiritual practice. One man who abandoned his studies to become an imam remarked that he did not like the "very religious" people in Turkey. He said, "Our religion is free [serbest], not forced. And these people, the extremely religious [aşırı dinciler], force people." He then cited as examples the Nurcus and the Süleymancıs. Another man from a different village where there is a Süleymancı Qur'an school, described how the Süleymancıs would not talk to people outside their community. Others described how they are very conservative and do not mix with or talk to others. Arife, a middle-aged mother of three, said in reference to her daughter, who now lives in Izmir, "If my daughter joined their group, then she would not even talk to me!" Arife said, "We are not conservative like that at all; we perform the namaz, fast, and have Kurban, but we don't belong to extreme conservative groups, like tarikats. We do what we need to do for God."

In talking to Zübeyde, who lives in a provincial town, I asked if she would have chosen someone to marry who was involved with a religious community. She replied, "No." Explaining, she said that if she had chosen someone involved with the Süleymancıs, for instance, they would have complained about what she wore, her head covering and other clothing, and they would have tried to get too involved in her life, trying to force her to do things. She said, "I don't think our religion is the way they claim it to be. It is not about forcing people. We live in a free society. People should be able to choose the kind of life they want and this includes how they are religious." Her position is that it is not only that religious groups prevent their members from leaving, but that they force members to participate in ways that are oppressive. From her standpoint, religion should be a personal form of expression, which is free from interference. From her viewpoint, the state's control of Islam via the Diyanet creates a climate in which individuals are protected from such intrusions and can choose forms of religious expression. Her perspective echoes that of Hakan Yavuz on the Süleymancı: "These networks helped create an impenetrable social capital, as it were, of trust in social networks but with very little room for free thought."[22] Some, then, trust laicism to create a climate within which spiritual practice is freely chosen and protected from the intrusion of religious communities, while others believe that state control prevents the free operation of Sunni groups.

I have been describing villager reactions to the term tarikat vis-à-vis their perception of republican concern with the integrity of the state, but there is a German angle to the question, which I now will explore. This detour to Germany will bring us back to Turkey and to a different understanding of how and why religious communities have become more visible in Turkey. Due to Turkey's long history of emigration to western Europe and the importance of tarikats or neo-tarikats as transnational communities, it will be useful to consider German state policies regarding Islamic groups. In Germany, state policies provide two legal structures for religious groups, the *Verein*, or organization, and the public law corporation.[23] Muslim organizations of all varieties, tarikats, Alevi, and the DITIB, the Diyanet's branch in Germany, all organize under the structure of Verein. Though legal, these groups are not recognized by the German state as being specifically religious. Like a dernek in Turkey, they can be formed for almost any civil society intent. There are no Islamic groups that have gained corporate status.[24]

The result is that Sunni Muslims who organize through the DITIB, the Diyanet's branch in Germany, describe being insulted that they have not been able to gain the status of a corporation, though many Christian churches and Jewish denominations have. Being on a par with all other Islamic groups troubles their perception that Sunni Islam constructed by the Turkish state is more authentic than the forms of Islam coming from tarikats, communities, and Alevi associations. On the other hand, because the German government makes no distinction, all groups are able to establish themselves and operate openly in a manner impossible in Turkey. True, the status of dernek enables many groups to exist in Turkey, but they constantly belabor the point that they are not tarikats. And many behave clandestinely because they are afraid they will be closed by the government for some infraction. Though allowed to organize in comparative freedom in Germany, in Turkey, these same groups instill a sense of anxiety and fear. On the one hand, there is fear of the group undermining state authority, and on the other, the group is afraid of the state. In Germany, though these groups are not regarded as legally religious, religious pluralism and something like religious freedom is possible.

While conducting research in Bamberg, I learned of how the German government makes many efforts to educate the public about different religious communities. The DITIB mosque participates in these state programs and has open days when they invite the public. Members were impressed that they were given a forum for expressing themselves and a way to connect with the non-Muslims living in the town. Though government policies attempt to create an open atmosphere and a sense of mutual understanding, there is a history of antagonism between the Turkish and German populations and among the different Turkish communities. This became evident to me when mosque members began to describe the history of the foundation of various mosques, Diyanet-oriented and Süleymancı, in particular. This history is recognized institutionally and the DITIB is attempting to ameliorate it. Orhan, a native of Yeniyurt and imam at the DITIB mosque in Bamberg, described how at one of the last national DITIB meetings for Turkish imams appointed in Germany, they were instructed to visit imams from other mosques and establish friendly relationships. This means that the Turkish state's organization, the DITIB, instructs its representatives to create friendly relationships with non-DITIB mosques, those which in Turkey would be illegal. Orhan described how he makes efforts to visit the Süleymancı mosque and said that although he had tried to be warm and friendly, the Süleymancıs were a bit cold and suspicious. Because these groups are anxious about each other in Turkey, though living in Germany, they bring the bad feelings and sense of suspicion to their relationships abroad. Interestingly, among all the Sunni organizations in Germany, the Süleymancıs were the first to reach out to Turkish immigrants.

Though lingering politics from Turkey and the history of difficulties within immigrant communities in Germany complicates the easy relationship between groups, there are also demonstrations by individuals that the existence of a pluralistic Turkish Sunni world is imaginable in Germany. In discussion with a female hoca of the Süleymancı community in Bamberg, Germany, I asked about the differences between the Süleymancıs and Gülenists. She remarked that they are indifferent, "Ne seviyoruz, ne sevmiyoruz [We neither love them nor not love them]." She explained that one might be able to understand one tarikat's theological explanations of Islam better than another and therefore one would feel a greater affinity for some explanations rather than others. She continued by saying that one might find the Diyanet's books on Islam easier to understand, while another might find Gülen's explanations good. She pointed out a key difference between the groups by explaining how the Süleymancıs work to train people in reading the Qur'an in Arabic but that Gülen explained the meaning of the Qur'an. Thus, different groups service different needs. She found both activities important to the expansion and maintenance of Islamic practice and belief, and distinguished what tasks they did well, thereby suggesting that both were necessary. To emphasize the unity of different communities, she said, "They all gather beneath God's banner." Rükiye, Orhan's wife, who was accompanying me, supported her by adding, "All Muslims are brothers." In other words, all Muslims are brothers and therefore one should not make distinctions between groups of Muslims. Rükiye argued that the fundamentals of Islam did not change, regardless of what community you belong to. She thereby suggested that Islam is one, but that there are different communities one can belong to which facilitate individual practice. Her perspective, as well as that of the female hoca from the Süleymancıs, references the umma, global community of Muslims not the Turkish state as the foundation of spiritual legitimacy. This perspective is not uncommon among some Muslims in Turkey, but in Turkey many argue that the government needs to control these groups.

Upon returning to the Yuntdağ from Germany, I happened one day to be talking in English to the Norwegian DOBAG dealer. I was walking up a hill with several villagers and the dealer. I mentioned that I had been to Bamberg and had visited imams from the Yuntdağ working at both the DITIB mosque and the Süleymancı mosque. The dealer, himself German, who has worked with the Kayalarca villagers for decades and who brings rug tourists from Europe to visit, was surprised because his understanding of the region did not include Islamic groups and their connections to Turkish immigrants in Germany. My friends accompanying me were straining to understand what I was saying, due to my use of English. When I used the word "tarikat," they began interrupting my conversation with the dealer and a parallel conversation in Turkish developed alongside the one I was having in English.

A young man whose wife studied with the Süleymancıs, and who had had a wedding with a sermon rather than music and dance, interjected in this conversation with the dealer, "Kimberly, there are no tarikats here."

I said, "I know, I was talking about Germany."

An older woman leapt into the Turkish conversation: "There might be tarikats and Süleymancıs in Germany but there are none here!"

"I know, but there are tarikats in Turkey, in Manisa, Tepeli, Istanbul . . . ," I clarified.

She replied, "Well, they are in cities!"

"Yes," I said, "but they are also in a neighboring village." She knew this, but persisted in saying that there are none here, and then I added, "Well, they have Qur'an courses in Mallı."

She said, "We send our children to these schools for God so that they might learn to read the Qur'an, but not because they are part of a tarikat."

In an attempt to defuse the term tarikat, I unsuccessfully added, "But this is what this tarikat does, they teach children to read the Qur'an."

The word "tarikat" had a lightning-like effect on her. She was anxious and eager to argue that tarikats did not exist in her village. Clearly, she was afraid that there would be consequences if I reported the existence of tarikats in the region. Later I asked her for some clarification, seeing that I had upset her and that clearly the term tarikat bothered her, but not the group's activities, teaching children to read the Qur'an in Arabic and delivering sermons for weddings, both of which she approved and admired. She explained, people "who gather together in a house should not, but those who gather in a mosque are okay." In her concern about appearing to support groups, which by definition challenge the state construction of Islam, she claimed that groups in themselves were okay, as long as they gathered in mosques rather than houses.

By mosques, she meant official ones, not secret ones. Her comment then indicated the importance of state-controlled Islam, as located in the state-run mosque. But her critique was based more on the location of where Islamic authority is generated rather than the activities. It is impossible for nonstate Islamic groups to use the state-run mosque. A consequence of her critique was that she implicitly argued that correct Islam is state Islam and also Islam associated with men, and that women should not act as spiritual leaders, since they avoid mosques except during the month of Ramazan. Knowing her well, I understood the emotional foundation of her argument, that she was protecting her village from defamation. But, I do not think she thought out the implications of using mosques rather than houses for worship. As a woman, she works hard to improve the efficacy of her spiritual practice by learning to read the Qur'an in Arabic and Ottoman texts, gathering with women in houses to read the Yasin on Fridays, sending her daughter to study with an unofficial hoca because she thought the official one was not as learned, and happily participating in women's gatherings which reflect Islamic traditions of the region. She never gathered with women in houses as a tarikat—we understood that well—but she was not against the activities these groups facilitated either. I did not mention it, but many of the activities she enjoyed would be critiqued by practitioners concerned with orthodoxy, both in the Diyanet and in tarikats. Because she was reluctant to enter the mosque since she saw it as a male-defined space, her argument shut her out of the very activities she argued were possible only when held in a mosque. We overlooked these inconsistencies, but the impossibility of being a rural woman in Turkey, actively engaged in Islam, was evident.

After my return from Germany, I wanted to visit the Bamberg Süleymancı imam's relatives. Çevriye agreed to accompany me. Afterward, we had a conversation about Islamic authority and the state.

Çevriye described the meeting to her husband, Mühettin: "They call this hoca a hoca but he isn't a real one. He doesn't work for the state." She described how the son openly explained the workings of the Süleymancıs.

Mühettin said, "They are probably afraid to discuss it, because it is against the state."

"No," Çevriye replied, "he fearlessly described how they studied with the Süleymancıs."

I commented: "They aren't really secret."

"If you ask me," added Mühettin, "I'd say they are wrong. They are against the state."

"They do one thing, they teach young people to read the Qur'an in Arabic," I said, and described how the hoca in Germany had shown me the books they taught and what they did. "They are not really approved by the state, but they do not do anything other than this, or so it seems."

Mühettin concluded that they are neither approved nor disapproved by the state. He argued that they occupy a position between being illegal and being unofficial. They are tolerated.

I remarked, because I wanted to explore the question with them of how the state regulates Islam versus how these groups operate with greater freedom in Europe, "In Germany, because everything is freer, they are very important."

Mühettin concluded: "That may be in Germany, but here they are not."

In my discussion with another middle-aged man, he remarked that he thought it better when the state took control of religion because when tarikats gain control, they teach "different" things. He noted the Nurcus and the Süleymancıs, saying that when these groups get power, "it leads to the creation of terrorist groups." In short, in Germany many Turkish Muslims have a positive experience of relative religious freedom, but in Turkey the fear persists that alternative groups undermine state authority. Nevertheless, the actual Islamic practices—the daily prayer, charitable activities, efforts to learn to read the Qur'an in Arabic, and so on—are not significantly different in rural Turkey and a town in Germany.

WHO ARE THE SÜLEYMANCIS?

The Süleymancıs are followers of Süleyman Hilmi Tunahan, an Ottoman legal scholar born in a village in the Balkans in 1888. He was part of the Nakşibendi Sufi order, of which Süleymancıs consider themselves to be descendants.[25] Tunahan has spiritual importance among followers. "Tunahan is accepted as the thirty-third and last segment of the Naqshibandiyya Sisile, the spiritual chain connecting sheiks of this order to [sic] Prophet Muhammed."[26] He is regarded as the last member of this chain because, according to followers, the Ottoman Empire is considered the last true Islamic state. This means that for members Süleyman Tunahan's teachings are an alternative doctrine to that created and disseminated by the Diyanet. And by claiming that the Ottoman Empire was the last Islamic state, other Islamic states are discredited. Furthermore, the Diyanet is understood as a product of secularism through the management of Islam within human institutions.

Though the stance of the Süleymancıs toward the republican state seems to be rigid, the Süleymancı community reframed itself in a manner acceptable after the development of a true multiparty democratic system in the 1950 election. Thereafter, in 1952, Tunahan was able to establish the first "official Qur'anic course" under the Diyanet.[27] This would have been one of the schools that Ali Hacı, Orhan's father, might have entered if he had not been a poor orphan. With the change in regime in 1950 and the official relaxation of secularization policies, the group softened its antirepublican stance. "As a result of the 1949 decision to open Qur'an seminaries and hire more preachers for state mosques, Tunahan trained and employed preachers for the Directorate of Religious Affairs."[28] Scholars do not typically note that the Süleymancıs educated imams in the official branch of government designed to construct Sunni Islam.[29] My rural interlocutors also seemed unaware of this early link between the group and the Diyanet. By the mid-1960s, the graduates of Imam Hatip schools were allowed to become Diyanet employees,[30] thereby creating a connection between the Süleymancıs and the Diyanet. By 1971, with the coup d'état, all religious schools were nationalized.[31] This means the Diyanet began to train imams itself, which disempowered the Süleymancıs' former position as both the source of imams and the employees for the Diyanet. The classes they ran became illegal, but the government tolerated them. As Eligür describes, "The DP (Democratic Party of the 50s) . . . turned a blind eye toward the Quran courses of the Islamic brotherhoods. For example, Süleymancıs facing legal measures were released by orders of some DP parliamentarians and of Prime Minister Adnan Menderes."[32] It is at this point that the group takes a quasi-clandestine attitude toward official Islam, created by the Diyanet.

By the early 1970s, the Süleymancıs expanded their focus by catering to the needs of Turkish immigrants in Europe. At that time, the Diyanet had not established any mosques or cultural centers for Turkish Muslims abroad. Clearly, the Süleymancıs felt they were in competition with the Diyanet, and by looking for followers abroad among immigrants, who as Roy argues are an alienated population ripe for an Islamist movement, they found a new foothold. Initially recruited as temporary guest workers, Turkish immigrants were not integrated into western European societies. In this era, many men went abroad to work, living in dormitories and sending most of their pay back to their families. After the labor program ended in the 1970s, families were able to unite through family reunification policies. It was at this juncture that the Süleymancıs began to offer services to Turkish immigrant populations. With families, these populations formed coherent communities. Due to state policies in Germany, which prevented Turks from obtaining German citizenship, immigrants clung to Turkey. Neither fully European from the perspective of Europeans nor accepted as authentically Turkish among Turks, they nevertheless retained Turkish citizenship. In Turkey these immigrants often return and are referred to as "Alamancılar," literally "those with Germany." Rather than necessarily either living in Germany or Turkey, they developed a transnational identity facilitated by businesses and media,[33] the importation of spouses,[34] and something like religious freedom abroad.[35] Many live part-time in both countries in order to get state benefits both ways. By building networks among Sunni Turkish immigrants, the Süleymancıs were able to funnel resources into building schools and dormitories in Turkey, bringing German-style or European-style Turkish Sunni Islam to Turkey.

As Yavuz argues, the 1980 military coup "enhanced the Süleymancı network, as the state regarded the Turkish-Islamic Synthesis as a new national identity."[36] Prime Minister Özal, elected in 1983 and himself a follower of Sheik Kotku, a member of the Nakşibendi order, developed a neoliberal stance toward both the economy and religion.[37] As Turam argues, "Islamism in Turkey developed in tune with, and along with, an expanding free market."[38] The development of an upwardly mobile Anatolian class of businessmen, mass rural-urban migration, and transnational migrants, all investing in Islamic groups, resulted in an expansion and flourishing of Sunni Islam in civil society. The relationship the Süleymancıs have to the state has changed with the transformation in regimes. And the state itself reshaped its orientation toward secularization policies and religiously oriented groups.

In the 1990s, Islamist political power mobilized in political parties: Refah, the AKP, Fazilet, and Saadet. The Süleymancıs are critical of Islamist movements that use Islam for political ends. And though the Süleymancıs have benefited from entrepreneurial opportunities and neoliberalism, they have worked against a burgeoning hedonistic and consumerist society. The Süleymancıs "prefer to live within a democratic and capitalist system but with an opportunity to build a set of inner walls within themselves against the corrupting influences of consumerism."[39] As Yavuz and others make clear, the Süleymancıs should not be confused with political Islamist groups such as the AKP, headed by Erdoğan; or Milli Görüş, a Turkish Sunni nationalist group founded by

Erbakan in Germany; or the Refah Party, of which Erbakan was also a founder (disbanded in the soft coup of 1997) in Turkey. Rather, as Yükleyen argues, the Süleymancıs are a Sufi group that seeks the exploration of the inner, esoteric experience of Islam. They train children to read the Qur'an in Arabic and educate male and female hocas. The Süleymancıs' focus has been on the expansion of members and followers, as well as the continuation of what Yavuz refers to as conservative, traditional religious education based on memorization, not analysis or commentary on Islamic texts.[40] Through this focus on traditional Islamic education, the Süleymancıs are a thriving transnational community, critical of political Islamists and neoliberalism but benefiting from both developments.

The relaxation of state policies toward religious groups created entrepreneurial opportunities. The Süleymancıs assess the needs of a given population and provide services tailored for that community, without discriminating against rural, urban, provincial, or Turkish national and transnational populations. In the villages, the Süleymancıs cater to the poor. They make special efforts to extend their services to rural areas, where parents are eager to have their children receive training in Islamic knowledge by providing low- to no-cost Qur'an schools. They recognize that women want Islamic services, such as sermons for women's ritual occasions. In towns, they run Qur'an schools—often with students from rural regions as students—lead collective readings of the Qur'an, give sermons, and provide low-cost child care for working mothers. In the cities, their boarding schools assist poor rural families by providing a safe and morally secure place where children can board while attending secular public high schools or Imam Hatip schools. As I have described, the imam's daughter boards at one of these dorms, although she attends a secular high school where the female students are uncovered. The group thereby demonstrates a relatively liberal attitude toward housing students and shows it is not isolating students or radicalizing them. Female migrants from villages seek out the Süleymancıs female hocas' guided readings of the Qur'an during the month of Ramazan. They pay a fee and give some small gifts in compensation, and are glad to have the chance to earn merit by reading the whole book.

Though many fear religious and political groups, the feeling of cultural loss caused by republican secularization policies, which the Süleymancıs address, is shared by many who are not members. As an imam in rural Turkey asked me rhetorically, "Imagine what it would be like if in the United States they changed to the Arabic script in one day? Everyone would instantly become illiterate." He described how his grandfather continued to use the Arabic script because this

is what he learned as a child. He added that the shift in script made one generation illiterate and this created many problems, including a gap between those
who knew the new script and those who knew the old script. He reflected on
the fact that he cannot read the old books, arguing further that the linguistic
divide between Ottoman and contemporary Turkish created a collective sense
of alienation from the past. Reflecting on the gap in the language, which divides
literature written in Ottoman from that in modern Turkish, he went further by
remarking on how little of this era has been described by historians. "This early
republican history has not been written about and we know little." He remarked
that changing the script used in Turkish to the Latin one made reading the
Qur'an difficult for people, because they first had to learn the Arabic script.
In both describing what useful services tarikats accomplish and delegitimiz-
ing their authority, he said that there were some, Said Nursi and Süleyman,
who taught people to read the Qur'an in Arabic. After these men died, those
who learned from them have continued to think of themselves as Nurcus or as
Süleymancıs, but all they did was to teach people to read the Qur'an in Arabic.
In other words, he did not find these groups especially radical. As he pointed
out, one can obtain the same services in Diyanet courses.

A sense of alienation from the past and cultural loss resulting from radical
secularization and modernization policies is palpable when talking with educated people, regardless of whether they are devout or not. Turkish informants,
professors, imams, and schoolteachers expressed a sense of loss about not having access to historical narratives. As the imam pointed out, most people cannot
even read the gravestones of their ancestors. This policy implicitly framed literacy in the new nation as a youthful skill because older people caught outside
the new script and new forms of literary expression, such as newspapers, would
have had difficulty in adapting. They then would be cut off from all written ma-
terials, and young people would never read any literature from the former era.
Thus, the change in script bifurcated all literate expressions of the population,
isolating both groups, those who knew Ottoman and those who knew modern
Turkish, from being able to communicate or understand each other. In the decades since, interest and curiosity about the early era of the Republic and those
who experienced these changes explains the contemporary enthusiasm for oral
history, as Leyla Neyzi's work demonstrates.[41]

The Süleymancıs fill the space of longing for knowledge of the past in two
ways. First, they present a logical solution for people who want to read the old
script by teaching them to read the Qur'an in Arabic. They thereby fulfill a

desire many have to achieve an Ottoman-style traditional Islamic education. Once having learned to read the Arabic script, learning Ottoman is possible. Second, they address lingering feelings of ambivalence toward early republican reforms through the formation of a community that critiques them and actively works to keep alive the script and style of scholarship from that era. The group then poses a question about the existence of the Republic and the legitimacy of the reforms on which the new society is founded.

THE SÜLEYMANCI QUR'AN SCHOOLS IN TURKEY AND GERMANY

While I was visiting Orhan, Ali Hacı's son, appointed to the DITIB mosque in Bamberg, he suggested that we visit the Süleymancı mosque with his wife, Rükiye. Having made arrangements, I arrived at the DITIB mosque on the appointed day and someone from the community drove us to the Süleymancı mosque. Rükiye let out a cry of recognition when we pulled into the courtyard; later, inside, she looked curiously over the top of the plastic stick-on window decals, which cover the windows in the women's section. We were next door to the kindergarten where she brought her daughter every day, but she had never noticed that the Süleymancı mosque and Qur'an school were next door to the kindergarten. The establishment blends in with the surrounding buildings in the neighborhood; only a small metal plaque on the gate indicates that this is not an ordinary apartment building.

Once inside, Orhan went to find the imam and sit with the men. Rükiye and I went to talk to the imam's wife. Cheerful and plump, Yasemin took us upstairs to meet the female Qur'an students. The large, three-floor building retained in its stairwell the feel of a prewar apartment building, with massive wooden railings and big windows, but all the rooms and halls on each floor had been completely redone. On the ground floor are a kitchen and a mosque, where the men meet and pray. On the second floor are a large mosque, a kitchen with long tables, and a few other rooms with sofas. On the third floor are a laundry, a few bedrooms, a couple of empty rooms without tables or chairs where students study, and a bathroom. What I mean to indicate in this description is that the rooms are used in the same manner as villagers use theirs, without designating particular rooms for special purposes (eating, sleeping, etc.). Many of the students came to the Qur'an school each day after they had attended public school, and they often stayed at the school during their summer vacations and holidays. The large mosque up-

stairs, lined in tiles from Turkey and wall-to-wall carpeting with bands indicating where people should line in rows to perform the namaz, resembles recently
constructed mosques throughout Turkey. These new mosques draw on Turkish
Islamic cultural motifs: wall-to-wall carpeting with big stripes rather than small
hand-woven carpets, big gleaming chandeliers instead of electrified oil lamps in
Ottoman mosques, and lots of machine-decorated tile work in blue, referencing
classic Iznik tiles. Yasemin explained they needed two mosques, the upstairs one
being bigger, because on holidays more people came for prayer.

Yasemin showed us every corner of the women's section. As we went from
room to room, we met about ten female students who were sitting together on
the floor studying. They looked at me shyly and demurely. I was not invited to
speak to them and they made no attempts to speak to me. I never interviewed
the imam, only his wife. Rükiye and I never had a chance to visit the downstairs' mosque, because men were sitting there. Due to their strict practice of
gender segregation, unlike the members of Orhan's DITIB mosque, there was
no chance I would be invited to attend one of the men's services. On another
occasion at the imam's apartment, I made a faux pas by sitting down in a room
where there were men. Rükiye gestured me out and whispered that "they,"
meaning members of the tarikat, "don't talk to women." We sat with the imam's
wife in a child's room. Surrounded by a crib, a changing table, and numerous
children's toys, the association of women with sequestered motherhood did not
escape me. Though the imam was surprised when I sat in his living room, he
opened up to me in the hallway, as we were putting on our shoes and coats to
leave. He wanted news and a sense of the cozy and hospitable atmosphere of
life in the villages—and I told him of some of my experiences over the decade
doing research among people in his home region. I noted, though, that the
structures of social interaction created by the tarikat did not make it possible
for him to re-create the pleasant atmosphere of village sociality in his apartment in Bamberg—which Çevriye and I later experienced when we visited his
mother and brother in his home village in the Yuntdağ.

Yasemin ushered us into one of the kitchens, where she set a table for us and
we ate together and talked. I asked questions about the structure of the organization. She explained that there are two full-time employees, aside from her
husband and herself. Describing the history of the institution, Yasemin said that
in the past, they rented spaces until they purchased the apartment building from
a company in the 1990s. There are 150 members, but she added that many more
come for events, such as a weekly lunch. Both mosques are involved in fund-

raising for their institutions. Like the DITIB mosque, each week the community cooks a lunch, which they sell. Women make *lahmacun* (a sort of Turkish pizza) on Fridays, which they sell to earn some income for the mosque. The DITIB mosque, Rükiye pointed out, makes meatballs for the same purpose. Yasemin said they earn about four hundred euros a week with lunch sales. Rükiye estimated that they also made about that amount with theirs. Given the closed atmosphere of both mosques, only members and friends in the community buy from them. Unlike the Süleymancı mosque, the DITIB mosque has a grocery store in one of the buildings, with proceeds going to the mosque. I ventured into the store and noticed that all the products were from Turkey, ranging from biscuits, tea, candy, and jam to frozen *halal* (Islamically obtained) meat, fish, and produce.

Both mosques create a cozy social atmosphere for all ages and genders, giving a sense of Turkey abroad. As Roy explains in *Globalized Islam*, they act as communities that cater to people who feel displaced. Imams' wives play a significant role in creating this social atmosphere. Unlike imams' wives in Turkey who do not play a role in the mosque, those in Germany teach the Qur'an to girls and women. Also, in Germany, the mosque provides a range of social services to its members. There are offices, schools, shops, apartments, social halls for everyone, and tearooms especially for men. The mosque, then, contains a collection of different rooms used for social purposes, for business, and prayer. Paradoxically, Turkish mosques in Germany function more like Ottoman külliyes (mosque complexes) than Turkish mosques in Turkey.

Despite the social atmosphere of these institutions, the Süleymanlıs structure their organization through a series of hierarchies, among the students, the believers, and within the mosque organizations. At the lowest level, which is that of my village interlocutors in Turkey and the students I met in Bamberg, students in Qur'an schools learn to intone the Qur'an. After the age of fourteen, they may be initiated into the group. If they continue their study, they are sent to Cologne to study Arabic. If they advance to the next stage, they study in Istanbul, reading classical texts in Hanafi law, the Qur'an, and Ismail Hakki Bursevi's work on the Qur'an, called Ruhul Beyan. If they complete this course, they earn a diploma, which makes them a hoca and potential leader of a mosque[42]—the Diyanet's equivalent of becoming an imam. It is notable that the Süleymancıs' program for advancement is transnational.

The imam's brother back in the Yuntdağ told a similar but more personal story of his brother's education in the community. After the brother had finished his required public school education, which at that time would have been five years, his father was musing on his son's future one day at the village coffee-house. It happened that a man, a member of the Süleymancıs, was there, who said that he could take the imam's son and continue his education in Manisa for free. The son went to live in a dormitory run by the community and to study with them. At the same time, he finished his high school diploma at a state public school. He took the ÖSS exam for entering the university and, because students in Turkey cannot choose the field of study for their major, he was placed in archaeology. Realizing that he did not want to be an archaeologist, he decided not to go, but studied for another year to repeat the ÖSS exam. Again, however, this second time he did not get a field he wanted. Because he had gotten qualifications through the Süleymancıs, he gave up on the secular school system. Soon thereafter, his marriage to Yasemin was arranged within the organization and he was sent to Germany. His wedding was held in Germany, which prevented his village family from attending. Çevriye, who accompanied me to meet the imam's family, was shocked by this detail. Village families are very involved in their children's marriages,[43] and a son's marriage is a cornerstone of a mother's life. That the group took over the role of his natal family is a significant demonstration that Roy is right about how these organizations reproduce kinship ties for members. What is surprising is that this happened for a young man who was neither a migrant nor an immigrant.

The brother explained that his brother was the first in the village to finish his studies with the Süleymancıs and the only one to be appointed to a mosque outside the country. Since his brother's success, several other villagers have become hocas with the tarikat. They, the brother described, have gone all over Turkey, to Istanbul, Uşak, and other places. He estimated that there are ten Süleymancı hocas from the village. He also described that there are many girls from there studying with the tarikat. He estimated that from this small village of about three hundred, there are thirty-five students studying with the tarikat, ten of whom are girls. He added that students do not have to pay to study, an obvious incentive for poor village families. As we sat in his mother's modest kitchen on floor cushions, drinking tea and eating bread and white cheese, the brother described how their village is very poor and the Süleymancıs help them.[44] Though some students become hocas with the Süleymancıs, he said, there are some who continue their schooling at Imam Hatip schools and become official imams or public school religion teachers.

More intriguing was the imam's wife's personal history. She was the child of a brief relationship between a Turkish immigrant and a German woman. It seemed she did not have a relationship with her mother, because her father took her after birth to raise her. She was sent to Turkey to attend school, including high school. Thereafter, she studied for a diploma in Istanbul with the Süleymancıs. After earning her diploma, she was sent back to Germany by the tarikat and worked in a number of Qur'an schools in various small German towns. During that time, her marriage was arranged within the tarikat.

It is not clear to which level Yasemin finished in Istanbul or how women's studies differ. But women trained by the Süleymancıs exist and are referred to as "hocas" by my rural informants. This means the community (of nonmembers) recognizes them as having spiritual knowledge. Through the Diyanet, girls can become public school religion teachers or vaiz, but there is no lower role of imam available to them. They therefore have to study harder than men who want to achieve the position of imam. The difference between women's opportunities in the neo-tarikat and in the Diyanet is due to the strict practice of gender segregation in the Süleymancı community. Because men and women do not mix and imams cannot teach girls and women, as do official imams who work with the Diyanet, there is a need for female hocas who can teach the Qur'an, deliver sermons, and lead Qur'anic readings to groups of women. Segregation provides women with more opportunities to study and lead within the group than they would experience if they followed the Diyanet's version of Sunni Islam.

Yasemin proudly pointed out that the Süleymancıs have schools all over the world, "like Gülen." At this school, in addition to female students, there are about twenty-two to twenty-five male students who come during vacations. Students who attend during the week pay fifty euros per month and those who board pay a hundred euros per month. She said that there is a sliding scale for payment, which can be reduced when students have siblings who also attend. She pointed out that this fee was meant to be a good deed, not necessarily amounting to the sum needed to cover expenses. In Turkey, as numerous informants described, the Süleymancıs accept reduced payments for the disadvantaged.

In terms of the activities at the school, they have five namaz per day. She described how they study the Qur'an in Arabic, beginning by learning words. They then move on to memorizing individual suras (verses). After this, they learn to read the Qur'an in a *tecvitli* style, with correct pronunciation in a special nasal tone. Rükiye, who has also dedicated her life to studying the Qur'an and other Islamic texts, interjected at this point, "From the cradle to the grave,

man and woman must study." When I asked Yasemin about whether they read
the Qur'an with the Turkish parallel text, she said that though one can read it
with the parallel text, there is something "secret" in the words, which can never
be fully understood. She added that learning to interpret the meaning of the
words would be a great *sevap* (meritorious act), but she said that only "God
knows" the full meaning. There is, therefore, according to the Süleymancıs, a
deep esoteric nature to the Qur'an, which cannot be ascertained by humans.
But the Süleymancıs believe that Sufi masters can interpret the Qur'an for
members. Yükleyen describes the discussions among male masters, explaining
the need for intermediaries: "The voltage at the place of electrical production
is high so there are regulators that convert it to the level of home use. Just like
this, divine light is so powerful that we need Sufi masters as intermediaries to
regulate it for individual usage."[45] In our discussion, Rükiye added that volumes
had been written on each sentence in the Qur'an, but the real meaning was still
not fully understood. The Süleymancı hoca and Rükiye both agreed that learning to recite the Qur'an was crucial. Understanding, however, may exceed that
of the ordinary practitioner. Neither mentioned the role of Sufi masters who
serve as intermediaries to interpretation. Again, Yükleyen, in his more intensive study of the group, goes into some detail on this matter: "They believe in
an inner meaning (*batini*) of the Quran, which is attained only by those who
have spiritual access. Reason does not play a role in finding Islamic truth and
knowledge. Instead, it is submission to a spiritual master that opens the path."[46]
Herein lies a crucial difference. A master who can interpret the truth is very
different from a state employee who leads prayer. Villagers readily describe
the imam as a memur, a civil servant, rather than a master. Though some may
argue that there *is* nothing radical about their practices, the spiritual orientation is quite different. The tarikat is functioning as such, with a strict order of
members, leaders, and teachers, who are connected to a spiritual chain of com-
manders with Tunahan at its origin.

THE EXPERIENCE OF ATTENDING QUR'AN SCHOOLS AMONG RURAL VILLAGERS

Though villagers debate the merit and legality of tarikats, many parents in
Kayalarca send their boys and girls to study with the Süleymancıs. Students attend boarding schools for at least a year, or, if they live within walking distance,
daily classes. Among the families actively engaged in sending their children to

study with the Süleymancıs, not surprisingly, discussions about tarikats were matter-of-fact. The fear and anxieties others in Kayalarca express did not dominate these conversations. Conveniently, there is a boys' Qur'an school in Mallı, an hour's walk away. About five boys from Kayalarca were attending the school there, though several others have in the past. On my visit to that village with a young couple from Kayalarca, we noted that their building on the edge of the village was noticeably different from the other village constructions, set apart from the settlement and with multiple stories. The husband had studied at that school instead of attending a secular high school.

You have met this couple a few times in various chapters. They were the ones who chose to have the sohbetli nişan (engagement party with a sermon) but a wedding with music and dance. And although Elif was devout, she was unschooled in confining her interest to orthodox spiritual practice. She had been one of the few women to visit the graveyard on Arife Günü at the end of Ramazan, and she was an enthusiastic participant at Yeniyurt's Sakal-ı Serif, though her husband disapproved. Elif never studied with a tarikat but she studied with the village imam during the summers, like most children in the village. Though she has some formal training in Islamic knowledge, she does not feel constrained about engaging in cultural Islamic practices or involving herself with the tarikat for her engagement rituals. On the other hand, her husband was educated by a tarikat but he was not so strict as to prohibit having a wedding with music and dance. They therefore combine a number of strains of involvement in Islam, a bricolage of practices and attitudes that I have highlighted throughout the text.

On our day-trip, we did not venture to the school itself because it was closed for break, but talked to the husband's friends and relatives who had studied there and who lived in the village. They described that there is no mosque inside the dormitory, unlike the one I saw in Germany. In Turkey such a mosque would be unofficial and therefore illegal, though as Cihan Tuğal mentions there are many, such those he mentions in a neighborhood in Istanbul.[47] When the husband studied in the school there had been thirty to forty students; five years later, in 2009, there were twenty-five. Students came from a number of villages in the region, including Kayalarca. A widow in Kayalarca with six children sent both her boys to study there. One was currently boarded there and studied both at the Qur'an school and at the public middle school. Her elder son studied for one and a half years, but she said he only studied long enough to learn to perform the namaz and read the Yasin. This school, then, is an important place for parents in the region to send their sons to learn the Qur'an. It has yet to lead to any boys or girls becoming hocas in the group. Financially disadvantaged families, like the widow with six children, benefit from the low to zero cost of boarding and educating their sons.

There are many other, similar Süleymancı Qur'an schools in the region. Visiting a woman my age, I learned that her son is attending a Süleymancı Qur'an school in Manisa, "where he can learn to read the Qur'an better." She said that he wants to go to an Imam Hatip school, after this year of preparation, and hopes to become an imam or public school religion teacher in the future. His mother remarked, "The money is good. Being a hoca is a good profession." I mention this detail because it shows that some villagers do not expect there to be an antagonistic relationship between the state and the Süleymancıs, and village parents continue to think that being an imam is a lucrative profession. She also neatly sidestepped any deeper reason to become an imam. For her, it is a job.

Among the female Süleymancı students in Kayalarca, there are about six who attended one-year programs in provincial towns near Manisa. One had recently married her first cousin, whose family had migrated to France. She left Turkey to be with him. Another, Semiha, had recently married in the village. She is quiet, thoughtful, and seems very young, compared to the quick-witted, sexy, and outgoing girls in her peer group in Kayalarca, who did not attend a Qur'an school or secular high school. She and her husband had a sohbetli nişan and the wedding party also was celebrated with a sermon. Semiha described why she had attended a Süleymancı Qur'an school. After finishing middle school, she had wanted to continue her studies by going to high school—which would have necessitated locating a place to live in the city. Though there are Süleymancı-run dormitories, her father would not let her consider staying in one in order to go to secular high school. "Burası köy yeri [This is a village]," he had said. What he meant was it would be inappropriate for her, as a girl, to go to high school, since she would have to go to Manisa. Clearly, her father was referencing the fact that she would have to appropriate an open lifestyle at a public secular school and she would be under less supervision if she lived in the city. Instead, her parents sent her to a Qur'an school in a provincial town near Manisa.

Semiha described how life at the school was organized in a quasi-monastic manner. In a typical day, they performed the first namaz, returned to bed, got up again, had breakfast, and then studied the Qur'an. By studying the Qur'an, she followed the same program as that at the school in Bamberg where students first learn to read words in Arabic and then learn phrases from the Qur'an. After lunch, they had *ilmihal* class (the Islamic equivalent of catechism), which included studying a book that described how to perform the namaz, and the Rubu-u Daire, a book on verses in the Qur'an and with general discussion of Islam. After finishing these lessons, they had time to play on swings and make popcorn. Afterward they had dinner. I asked her what she liked most, and after saying that she enjoyed playing and making popcorn, she revised her answer and said she liked reading the Qur'an. Indeed, she is frequently called upon by the members of the women's group, which meets on Fridays to read the Yasin forty-one times. As one of the only young women in the village who can competently read the Qur'an, she is much admired for her skill. She has become a model alternative to studying in a secular high school. Older villagers comment that girls who chose to study in secular high schools have all left the village to marry. Elderly villagers also often comment on and openly complain about these girls when they visit the village because they no longer dress in şalvar and a headscarf. Instead, they wear jeans and go around with their heads bare. In contrast, Semiha is an example of an Islamically educated young woman who remained in the village and married well and properly (meaning she did not elope). Through individuals like her, purified scholarly Islam will slowly make its mark on rural spirituality.

CONSIDERING THE IMPORTANCE OF ALTERNATIVE SUNNI COMMUNITIES

In the widening domain of Turkish Sunni Islamic transnational organizations, the Süleymancıs—a neo-tarikat, employing Roy's terminology—bridges the gap between groups that focus on the elite (like the Gülen movement), those catering to urbanists and migrants (like Milli Görüş in Germany), and those rooted in Anatolian piety, such as the recent saint Muhammed Zühdü. While each group has a unique history, all respond to the Ottoman Empire as a legitimizing foundation of Islamic authority. Despite the Republic's incorporation of Islam in the Diyanet, the post-1980-coup changes created a type of secularism in which public, alternative, and plural Sunni Islams became possible. The history of the Süleymancıs demonstrates its reaction to radical secularization policies of the early Republic. This history, with its traumatizing details, the conversion of the script, the intrusion of the state in Islamic training, the sense of historical loss, and the erosion of cultural memory, explains the

Süleymancıs' stance toward the state in Turkey today. Individuals in villages, provincial towns, and cities in Turkey, both among people who are critical and among those who participate in the group, regard the tarikat's implicit critique of Turkish laicism as self-evident. Some are fearful of the Süleymancıs' claim to legitimacy, which clearly operates outside the domain of the Diyanet, while others support the construction of a Turkish Sunni transnational view, which would allow for the operation of religious organizations outside the purview of the Diyanet, in which "all Muslims are brothers," leading to more open spiritual and religious groups.

An important aspect of the growth of Sunni Islamic communities in Turkey after the 1990s is money coming from abroad. As Turkish immigrants in Europe established themselves and began to make more income, they donated to religious organizations. As Eligür argues, "The Islamists directed the flow of the Islamic capital into Turkey to create an opportunity for Turkish Islamist bourgeoisie to become a wealthy, industrial class that would provide economic support for the movement."[48] It is notable that both the Süleymancı and DITIB Web sites in German have on their home pages bank accounts for donations. The DITIB's bank account includes one for donations for the construction of the mosque in Cologne—a controversial project, but one of symbolic significance in the literal construction of Turkish state Sunni Islam abroad. The Diyanet Web site (in Turkish) for Turkey, in contrast, has no such numbers, though the devout pay zekat and perform hayır (good deeds). In Turkey, the technological, media-based structure of donation is less established than are face-to-face donations. In Germany, finding information about making a donation via the Internet is part of the media landscape that people inhabit. The fuel for building an Islamist middle class has come, in part, from Turkey's relationship to European emigrants, building a population of people who feel alienated by both Turkey and Germany, but who also learn from Europe.

The continual interest that immigrants have in maintaining links to Turkey helps movements such as the Süleymancıs. Indeed, they were the first community to cater to the needs of Turkish immigrants abroad, establishing their organization in 1973. Guest workers, who mainly came from rural, devout backgrounds, wanted spiritual communities abroad, especially when they started bringing their spouses and children to join them. The Gastarbeiter, or guest-worker program, which brought Turkish men to Germany for short-term labor contracts, ended in 1973, but through family reunification policies of the German government, Turkish immigrant communities grew. As such, they were founded on families in neighborhoods, rather than on men living in dormitories.[49] The creation of family life necessitated devout religious communities, mosques, which provide services in education, community for the annual fast, a means to make the pilgrimage, a way to repatriate one's body after death, sermons, and a space for creating a Turkish social life. All of these services and activities create a moral atmosphere of Islamic piety among Turkish immigrants, mimicking the pious life they had back home, or wish they had had.

The public face of the Süleymancıs is somewhat confusing when considered from the vantage point of Web sites in Turkish and German, and buildings in Turkey and Germany. Although the Süleymancıs operate openly in Germany, their concealed habitus is evident; one can walk past a mosque and Qur'an school complex with no knowledge of its existence. In contrast, online they have a clear and understandable Web site in German. There are explanations of their goals, lists with addresses of their mosques and schools, and brochures on projects, some with funding from the German government. This Web site indicates that it is an interface with the German-speaking public. In Turkey, the Süleymancıs are very private. Though one can easily learn of their activities in cities like Istanbul and their dormitories in towns are impressive, there are no attempts to communicate more generally. When I attempted to visit one of their dormitories in a small town, I was told to leave. Clearly, they do not want to communicate with outsiders. This closed attitude protects them from curious and intrusive Turks. Upon my giving a lecture at a university in Istanbul on my research on this group in Germany, Turkish intellectuals scratched their heads, never having heard of the group. This is striking given the fact that German sociologists all actively know of and study the group. A further demonstration of their lack of interest in communicating with the Turkish-speaking secular public is their online presence composed of unofficial pages, not ones created by an organization to rival the Diyanet's Web site.

Nevertheless, the Süleymancıs are active in serving people and identifying their spiritual needs. In rural regions and provincial towns, the tarikat is well known and among a certain segment of the Istanbul population, which has roots in the Anatolian Sunni Islamic world, it is also well known. Reportedly, they meet once a week at the Eyüp mosque. Their services are welcome and they cater to the poor by reducing the costs of Qur'an courses for youth. From the rural poor, they find young people whose futures are limited. The imam's story demonstrates that young rural men are able to rise in rank as they study to become hocas who guide communities and they gain positions abroad becoming successful migrants. His story is notable given the anecdote about the disappointed village man who gave up his studies in an Imam Hatip school when the government changed the rules during his training. The Süleymancıs imam's wife's story demonstrates another sort of outreach, even more interesting, because it shows how in managing the offspring of Turkish immigrants of casual relationships, they create members who might be stigmatized elsewhere.

In short, the neo-tarikat demonstrates a shifting history, one of late accommodation to state secularism, followed by movement abroad. Snubbed by the state when the Diyanet took over Imam Hatip schools, they retreated. Seeing a new opening abroad, they ventured forth, looking for new constituencies. Creating transnational Turkish networks facilitated their operations in Turkey. Benefiting from the growth of public Islam and the flourishing of Sunni associations, they reframed themselves as an association. Their diffident stance toward political Islam and toward politics generally demonstrates the importance of their spiritual project, one they advance by teaching children to read the Qur'an in Arabic—a reference to the troubled legacy of radical secularization policies, remembered by rural Anatolians. The Süleymancıs pointedly keep separate from party politics in Turkey. Not participating in party politics, however, does not mean that the Süleymancıs are apolitical. The groups' multiple forms, differing agendas, and styles of self-representation, demonstrate their attentiveness to the contexts of power within which they work.

9 DEALING WITH THE SECULAR WORLD
A Trip to the Beach

Rural life in the Yuntdağ is deliberately constructed as devout, shielded from many of the political conflicts in cities, resulting from the collision of secular and Islamic worldviews. Villagers live in a space where Islam has never been privatized. Their experience of time is shaped through life rituals grounded in Islamic belief and practice.

Life in spaces of living Islam is richly rewarding but requires discipline and conformity to gendered forms of bodily comportment, which in turn respond to spiritually encoded physical behaviors for men and women. How people dress, talk, use public and private spaces, speak, and act are all visible, noticeable signs that individuals think and enact a normative Sunni worldview. The village is a place where people watch each other closely and assess their behaviors. The pressure to behave, especially for young people, whose actions are watched with pointed interest by older generations who assess their prospects in marriage based on moral grounds, can be intense.

Due to limited opportunities in rural life, in recent years more people are choosing to leave permanently, commute daily, or live temporarily in cities to earn money or get an education. They leave behind or take a break from the rural Islamic way of life. In this different urban space, they make choices about whether they will take up a secular lifestyle, become an urban Islamist, or live on the margins of urban spaces re-creating a rural-styled Islamic practice. The potential for leaving reinforces the protected nature of rural spaces, introducing the need for deliberate moral practice inflected with Islam. Thereby, villagers become engaged in a self-conscious Islam, one engaged in assessing the veracity and efficacy of pious practices, the meaning and purpose of cultural beliefs and rituals, and ultimately the content of rural orthodoxy.

A trip to the beach with Çevriye and Mühettin's extended family, including members who had migrated to Manisa and beyond, highlights some of the complexities of how people make choices about the kind of Islam they practice, as well as whether they select a secular or nonsecular worldview. This family is becoming increasingly typical: some remain in the village, some migrate to the city as young adults, bringing their children with them, and others combine marriage with migration to establish urban adult lives.

On a day in June 2009, having arrived from Istanbul by train the night before, I visited Zübeyde, Çevriye and Mühettin's daughter, who had recently married. She was living in a town between Istanbul and Manisa. During this period of my research, 2008–10, I often stopped to see her on my way to Kayalarca. I had met Zübeyde in 2000 when she was thirteen. At that time, in Kayalarca, I lived downstairs in her parents' house, occupying a storage room, but I would go upstairs to cook and eat with the family. Zübeyde and I became close over the year and half I did my fieldwork. I kept a lookout for her in the afternoons when she returned from middle school, in a town about thirty minutes away. After she had changed out of her school uniform, we would talk while walking around the village and the surrounding *yaban* (wild areas). Once she said exuberantly, as we sat on some boulders on a mountaintop, eating sweets we had bought at the village shop, "Adam gibiyiz! [We are like men!]." What she meant was that we were claiming the freedom to wander (*gezmek*) in the mountains without fear. This is what young men, those with delikanlı (wild blood), do. That night I was chastised by her parents, who told me we should never again visit the mountaintop "alone," by which they meant we required a married woman as a chaperone. I was learning what it meant to be a village "girl." Zübeyde knew what girlhood implied, which is why she took the chance to be with me and overstep the restrictions girls typically abide by—hence her announcement that we were "like men." I appreciated her spirit and sense of "resistance," but I later learned to see her mother's point of view, to the extent that she accused me of being "just like her mother."

Though curtailed from being able to walk freely in the village, Zübeyde's sense of possibility expanded when she went to study at a high school in Manisa. In the city, she lived with her brother, his young wife, and their new baby. I saw her off and on in the intervening years when she visited the village and on my short visits to Manisa. On her first visit home for an important holiday after beginning high school, I recall how we watched her stoop to kiss her grandmother's hand and press it to her forehead in greeting after descending from the bus. Our eyes welled up as we watched them cry. Clearly, the separation from her family and the village had been difficult, more so than she would have admitted.

After receiving her high school diploma, she studied at private exam preparation schools for the university exam while working. She held jobs in factories and later was employed by the accountant who kept the books for the carpet cooperative based in the village. These experiences of life in the city, fighting to hold her own in a context where she was constantly being pigeonholed as a villager, had made her wiser. She was tough. She had had to fight off men at her jobs and while walking in the city streets to school and work. Having experienced more freedom than a typical village woman who has migrated to the city—most cannot leave the apartment without permission—she had a more realistic understanding of the challenges of trying to survive as a village woman in an urban environment.

Though she finally passed the ÖSS exam to enter the university, the place she won was in a town far from Manisa. The course, in hotel hospitality, would have lasted only two years, but her parents balked at sending her away and into a field that involved meeting strangers and sitting at a desk at night. Disappointed, she gave up on trying to take the exam again and worked full-time in the city. In the meantime, she had a suitor from the village, a boy who lived across the way from her parents' house. But her parents disapproved of his family. His mother had a reputation for being mean to her daughters-in-law, and Zübeyde's parents refused to consent to the marriage proposal. Though Zübeyde had been allowed more independence than most girls, she conceded to her parents' wishes, knowing that the only way she could have married him was to elope. She remarked that her father had said that if she eloped it would kill him. Though stricken psychologically, as she said, she endured the breakup.

She had the good fortune to meet another man, while working in a factory in Manisa. He was a good match, though he was from a different region. After the families had made their inquiries and allowed the engagement to become official, she and her future husband were able to proceed with the wedding plans. Zübeyde described her wedding (I missed it because it was during the academic year) as having been very painful. This is not surprising, given that brides describe their weddings as the most difficult day of their lives, because they have to leave their natal families. Together, we watched the many hours of video footage with her mother in Zübeyde's comfortable new apartment. Zübeyde pointed out the moment when she had to separate from her family and all her kin and friends in her village and get in a car to go to the distant town. The video showed her tear-streaked face, puffy and exhausted, but it did not show the moment when she said she fainted. Brides are expected to cry during the last day of the three-day ritual but few actually faint.

By 2009, the young girl in her school uniform, watching television in the afternoons, halfheartedly studying for exams, and talking about boys, was now a young woman, with her own apartment, a husband, and a baby. She seemed very happy. During my frequent visits, I explored her town and met people as we attended weddings and circumcision parties. It seemed pleasant enough, but as Zübeyde critically remarked it was "neither a village nor a city." Having lived in both, she knew the warm, cozy but at times claustrophobic, gossip-ridden atmosphere of villages, where everyone knows everyone else. The city, in Zübeyde's experience, is filled with excitement and possibility, places to shop and hang out in public, tea gardens and bakeries, relatives and fellow villagers, and the hard dangers associated with disconnected people: thieves, cheats, and exploiters.

On that particular day in June 2009, it was early morning and I was sitting at her kitchen table, looking toward the edge of the town to where the half-completed apartment buildings gave way to fields and, in the far distance, mountains. I listened to the harsh noise of the town loudspeaker, as it interrupted my reverie with local announcements,[1] and I struggled to make out the meaning through the echo and din. Having woken early, I had wandered around the apartment searching for a lighter so I could light the stove to make tea. Finding none, I drank some cold tea left in the pot. I heard some noise in the next room, sounds that indicated that Zübeyde had gotten up. She stumbled into the kitchen holding a lit cigarette, evidence of a lighter, I thought. She stood jauntily with one foot on the balcony, the other in the kitchen, as she blew smoke out the apartment. I asked her for the lighter, remarking how my investigation had led me to every drawer and tabletop. She said, "It was in the bathroom, of course." She explained that she usually smoked in the bathroom to avoid harming the baby. Beginning a pot of fresh tea, our conversation wandered past the events of the last year, her new baby boy, a civil service exam she was hoping to pass so she could sell train tickets in the town train station, and what I was planning to do in her home village. A possible trip to the beach came up and she asked if I would like to come along. Why not, I thought, imagining this would be with her husband and son. We would go to the open market later that day to look for a bathing suit that would accommodate her postpregnancy body.

While having breakfast after Zübeyde had finished her cigarette, I asked Zübeyde about her life as a Muslim. She explained that she had studied the Qur'an with one of the unofficial imams working in the village. I asked why she had not attended the Qur'an classes given by the village imam, like most other children. She explained that her parents had mistrusted the imam's knowledge, though he had also studied with Ali Hacı and had become a hafız under his guidance. She added that she had learned enough to perform the namaz and some extra prayers, but that she was not very advanced. This early background in Islamic training, however, showed that her parents considered whom they thought she should study with, and that they were willing to send her to an unofficial imam. When I pointed this out, she mentioned that many people chose to send their children to this hoca, and that it was not because they were fanatics. She said, "Because the imam is from Karalarca, he does not get angry and report the other unofficial imams to the state for their work in teaching the Qur'an to children." I knew that these unofficial imams also taught women who wanted to learn to recite the Qur'an in Arabic. In short, employing an unofficial imam for guidance and instruction is regarded as an ordinary and apolitical decision.

I asked Zübeyde about her transition from her childhood in the village to Manisa, where she studied at a high school and later worked. I summarized for her what I recalled from her life as I had seen it. I said that after she had adjusted to her life in Manisa, she seemed to have discovered a new type of life, and had friends with many backgrounds, her best friend being an Alevi girl. I added that she had found a different life, by which I obliquely implied her seemingly secular lifestyle, and I gestured to the fact that she did not cover her head after moving to Manisa. Zübeyde argued that she had never covered because she was always in school as a child and that wearing a scarf in the village was not a religious expression but how one dressed in the village. She thereby interpreted her village headscarf, as do many scholars of contemporary Turkish politics and contemporary Islamists,[2] as a form of local and traditional dress, not one motivated by a purified or objectified understanding of Islam. I asked her if she considered herself a Muslim, seeing that she was discounting the times she wore a headscarf in the village as being an expression of piety: "How can you drink beer, not wear a headscarf, wear a bikini on the beach, and still see yourself as a Muslim?" She responded by saying that *ibadet* (worship) is in one place and that her life is in another. That is, they are separate. She described that though she did not practice all the daily prayers, she did keep the fast during the month of Ramazan. Reinforcing the fact that she was involved in pious events, she described how she and her mother-in-law had had a prayer service and a meal at her apartment with invited female guests to celebrate the birth of her son. And she pointed out that she and her husband participated in the Sacrifice holiday, Kurban Bayramı, with her in-laws and parents, by visiting and eating a share of the meat. She and her husband would "enter" (*girmek*, to enter, as everyone says) into the sacrifice when they had accumulated enough wealth.

Zübeyde's capacity to be a secular Muslim, who keeps worship in a private and personal space, was not unusual in her social group. She described how she had a similar conversation with some friends in Manisa, who had gone to Imam Hatip schools. These young men had become hafız, she said, pointing out that they "had reached a much higher place than myself" (in terms of religious education). She said, "I asked them the same question you are asking me, 'How can you be a Muslim, a hafız at that, and yet drink alcohol?' Their answer was the same as mine: 'Religious practice is in one place and drinking alcohol another.' They referred to themselves as 'modern hafız.'" She laughed when she said this because the juxtaposition of the revered status of being a hafız was comical when paired with the term *modern*. When her friends combined the two modes of being, hafızness and modernity, they made a deliberately comical, almost ironic statement, underscoring their playful attitude about piety and modernity.

In a serious tone, she then clarified: "I studied with both the unofficial and official imams during the summers." She added, "Of course, I cover up when I pray. I simply go outside like this." By "this" she indicated her bare head, and though she was wearing şalvar at that moment, she also referred to the pants and T-shirts she typically wears outside.

Though the headscarf has gotten a great deal of press, few write about şalvar, the typically rural garment worn by men and women in Anatolia. Formerly rural women often prefer to wear şalvar but they only do so while at home. To project a modern sensibility, Zübeyde, like many of her peers, wears tight pants and low-cut shirts while outside. I often noted that she would change from her şalvar to a more modern outfit when her husband came home from work. Her dressing practice was similar to my own in this part of Turkey, in that I wore şalvar in the village but wore jeans in cities. I often removed my headscarf upon arriving in Manisa, as older female villagers accompanying me put on an enveloping manto over their şalvar. We often noted the comical moment when I took off and they put on. These rural women were not covering because they were uncovered, they were concealing their rural-style clothing and cloaking themselves in the symbolically powerful Islamist manto, the rain-coat. They thereby treated the city in the same manner I did: as a place where one displayed a modern sensibility. The difference was that my modern sensibility is secular, while theirs is Islamic.

Zübeyde did not indulge in a rural Muslim or Islamist identity in private or public spaces by wearing either the cotton headscarf typical of rural women or the enveloping polyester one worn by Islamists. In other words, Zübeyde and I were performing the same kind of persona in public spaces by wearing "open" clothing outside, but we enjoyed the easy rural sensibility of wearing şalvar at home and in the domestic atmosphere of the villages. And we both put on şalvar and a headscarf while visiting people in the village to show respect for the villagers.

But I had noticed something unusual about how women dressed in her new town, where, unlike in Manisa, the politics of rurality seemed less intense. In this town, women—whether Islamists, former villagers, or secular-minded young people—often wear şalvar without a headscarf. Şalvar, thereby, are not identified as a part of a rural clothing style. They are considered comfortable, if not fashionable. Noticing this difference, and because I like wearing şalvar, I began wearing them around the town.

As a result of my clothing style, I had many interesting experiences. Elderly people came up to me to chat because they thought I was from the town, and state officials, like policemen and railroad station managers, somehow more able to identify my foreignness, were open-jawed in disbelief.[3] Zübeyde was not able to do the same as me, however. Her performance of a modern sensibility was important to her in-laws and husband because she is from a village. She needed to prove that she was not slipping into a rural (implying backward) style of dressing that would reveal her origins. At home alone, though, where she could relax, she wore şalvar.

While Zübeyde feels the need to maintain the bodily comportment of youthful secular modernity in public, her mother-in-law feels the need to maintain the comportment of a respected older mother in public, and the domestic status of quasi-urban sensibility and modern devout civilization at home. She does this in a number of ways. For one, she wears şalvar and covers her head. Unlike Zübeyde, her mother-in-law could justify her clothing style from a number of standpoints (if she were challenged about it): she originally is from a village; she lives in a town where wearing şalvar is not frowned upon (unlike in Manisa);

and as an older woman with two sons, one of whom is married and himself a father, she has a very stable social status, meaning she can wear what she wants. Additionally, she works every day in the fields with her husband, and şalvar are far better work clothes than pants. But more importantly, unlike her daughter-in-law, who lives a secular life, she does not live in the same secular world. She covers, prays every day, and performs the other essential expressions of being a Muslim—fasting, participating in the sacrifice during Kurban, giving to the poor, and being a believer. She also participates in Friday gatherings, like women in Manisa and now Kayalarca, reading the Yasin forty-one times. Not at odds with her piety, she keeps a self-consciously modern household where, unlike in villages, everyone eats at a table from their own plates using silverware.

Later, while Zübeyde and I looked through some of her photographs, I noticed two pictures of her drinking beer at a bar. I asked, half-jokingly, "Do you show these to your mother?" She said, "No! I hide these." I thought as much and recalled how her husband had rushed just as his mother-in-law was arriving to hide beer and other things they did not want found. She said that when her mother saw the photograph of her in a bikini at the beach, her mother had said, "Oh no, you will burn [in hell, not from a sunburn]!" Zübeyde said she had replied laughingly, "I don't think so!" Intentionally dampening my joke about the photograph, she explained that she drinks very little anyway, adding that she was breastfeeding now. Though this comment implied that she would not drink while breastfeeding, more importantly, it related to another conversation we had about aging and piety. As a mother, she had entered a new stage of life, and she implied that she would no longer be dabbling in the pleasures of youth.

Zübeyde regarded herself at that time, in her midtwenties, as being able to live a secular lifestyle, but she expected to transform her relationship to Islamic practice as she aged. She explained that though she did not cover her head now, this did not mean that she would not cover in the future. In fact, many young people, former villagers living in cities and towns, who lead a secular lifestyle, explained to me that they would increase their piety as they aged. They thereby imagine they will do what their parents and grandparents are doing, which is to become more pious and diligent about prayer and fasting later in life. The degree of change, though, is different. Their parents and grandparents in the village fast for having laughed in their youth, while those in the younger generation will have to make up for not having prayed, fasted, and having drunk alcohol in their youth.

I provide this brief prelude to the trip to the beach to communicate how Zübeyde, a former villager, the only girl in the history of the village to have earned a high school diploma, who had had radically different experiences from her mother and most other villagers and former village women, sees herself as a Muslim in a very different light from the majority of the people I have discussed in this book. Her different perspective can be explained in part by her education, which involved an engagement with the secular ideologies of the state. As Sam Kaplan discusses, the state employs public education as a tool for teaching children how to be secular, modern citizens.[4] In Zübeyde's case, and even in the case of her friends who attended Imam Hatip schools, the pedagogical project of the state seems to have succeeded in teaching them that a secular lifestyle divides worship from life and that one can enjoy the benefits of modernity and have a Turkish Sunni Islamic identity. They do not unequivocally embrace secularity, though, because they expect that as they age they will tailor their lives to fit the type of piety their parents and grandparents exhibit. In this way, engagement with being a secular Muslim, one who practices as the Diyanet allows them, is part of their imaginative life narrative, a period of time, not a permanent state of being.

While education seems the most obvious explanation for how Zübeyde learned to be a secular Muslim, her experiences in the city also explain her different perspective. While she lived in Manisa with her brother and his wife, two young people who were preoccupied with their early marital life, a baby, and the struggles of trying to find jobs and maintain an income, Zübeyde had a lot of freedom. As she explained, she was able to wander in the streets without the need for constant supervision. Most young women who live in the city with their parents, in a dormitory as a student, or as young wives in new apartments, do not have this liberty. I noted when I visited two, young, recently married women who had settled in the city that they were anxious about walking me to the bus station because they rarely were able to leave their apartments. Like these young married women, Zübeyde lost the freedom to wander when she married not because her husband would forbid it but because there was nowhere to go in this new town.

Manisa may seem a small provincial city, filled with a notably devout and conservative population in comparison to Istanbul—a global megalopolis of over twelve million—but to people who migrate to Manisa and even among those who are native to it, the place offers enjoyment and pleasure in public spaces. There are Ottoman mosque complexes, impressive and historical artifacts of the past, enormous open markets bustling with shoppers, parks, restaurants, and tea gardens filled with families and young people enjoying themselves. The neighborhood of Fatih in Istanbul most resembles Manisa's street ambiance. Fatih is notoriously religiously conservative but also filled with fun and enjoyment, if one imagines these spaces from the perspective of pious women who typically cannot leave their apartments. There are crowds window-shopping in the streets, and many people in the stores buying goods of ritual importance for marriage: formal Islamic-style gowns, wedding gold, kitchenware, elaborate bedroom sets, Islamic-style house decorations (gilded Qur'anic calligraphic panels for example), and goods for the aftermath of the wedding, such as sexy lingerie and baby equipment. Without a doubt Manisa's and Fatih's economies are based on marriage and family, and this lends for a particular orientation in the street, a sense that everyone is getting married, having children, and marrying off their children in style. These experiences are part of the expression of a devout population, moral economy, and vibrant capitalism.

Zübeyde had left behind this exciting public urban world to enter a small provincial town, which, as she critiqued in annoyance, had neither the charms of village life nor the pleasures of a city. In a place where people do not know each other with the same intimacy as the village and without anywhere to go to have fun in an anonymous atmosphere, the provincial town, in her eyes (and those of her young friends), was boring. A frequent refrain to these understandable critiques was her acknowledgment of a comfortable life in the town. Unlike most migrants in Manisa, she did not have to struggle to make a living. Her husband worked and she could stay at home and look after the baby. She had achieved what many would find an enviable life: a secular lifestyle in relative material comfort, without cares or worries, the only pitfall being a slightly boring town. The trip to the beach was central to her future plans for fun in the summer.

With the intention that I would join in on the trip to the beach later in the summer, I left Zübeyde in her town to visit her parents in the village. At that point, I began to understand what the trip was really about. The trip to the beach was not a frivolous occasion for fun and enjoyment but a collective gift to Çevriye's sister's son Yusuf, who would be beginning his military service. Unlike the manner in which Zübeyde had presented the trip to me, as a fun occasion, the event in the village and in Manisa was being framed as one laden with symbolic import. Yusuf lived in Manisa with his parents, who migrated there in the mid-1990s. All of Yusuf's older relatives were anxious about his welfare, and eager to give him something he wanted before making his sacrifice to the nation by becoming a soldier. Sitting with his mother in her apartment in Manisa, she explained how they had told him he could have whatever he wanted before he left for the military. He had said he wanted to go to the beach.

Finally, the day for our trip arrived. Çevriye and I made the hour-long trip to Manisa in the morning, using her husband's minivan. I parked the vehicle near Çevriye's son's apartment, from which we would depart with Çevriye's son, his wife, their ten-year-old daughter, Yusuf, his mother, his sister and her fiancé, Zübeyde, her husband, and their baby boy. But at this point in the story, where Çevriye and I were climbing the darkened staircase up to the apartment, the details of our journey were still not clear to me. I asked about it, while lugging bags of food and equipment for the voyage, but Çevriye's answers were ambiguous.

As we ate a midday meal of bread, cheese, tea, and sugar, Çevriye's son's wife clarified the plan. Zübeyde and her husband and baby boy would arrive in the following hours. We would stay in Manisa until about midnight, when we would all squeeze into two vehicles and make the two-hour trip to the beach. We would arrive around two o'clock at night and sleep in the cars until the park opened in the morning. Going at night was part of the adventure. Everyone was excited, but I should add that everyone did not come—Mühettin, Çevriye's husband, for example. The previous day, while preparing dinner, I asked him if he would come. He had exclaimed, standing in the doorway, "You couldn't pay me to go to a place like that!" I was taken aback and honestly was unsure why he felt so strongly about not going to the beach. But I began to realize that the trip to the beach was a pointedly symbolic event, one which demonstrated a youthful secular lifestyle, as well as a gift for a sacrifice. As talk of our impending trip circulated in the village, I heard more people mention how they disapproved of the practice, because men and women mix together, half-naked, at the beach. I recalled watching television with a group of girls and their mothers one evening years ago. A fashion program was on the air and women in skimpy bathing suits were walking a runway. The mothers were becoming heated about allowing their girls to see these pictures, and one exclaimed in disgust, "Pis hayvanlar! [Dirty animals!]," but no one changed the channel.

Though Mühettin was in a position to decline on the beach trip, the rest of the family was in a state of controlled hysteria because Yusuf might be stationed in the southeast, where the Kurdish uprising and ongoing civil war had martyred many soldiers. Over forty thousand people had died in the conflict, over more than twenty-five years. The potential danger that Yusuf faced increased his authority, and his feeling he had a right to say that he wanted to visit the beach before going to perform his military service. And yet a trip to the beach, a seemingly innocent event, was complicated by Islamic values of modesty.

At night in Çevriye's son's apartment, as I tried to sleep before our departure, I thought about this bundle of conflicts—Islamic modesty on the one hand versus a wish for fun at the beach before experiencing life-threatening danger on the other. In my dream state, I heard noises from outside the hot room where I lay: the doorbell and telephone ringing, sounds of people coming and going, and voices raised in laughter, noises of visitors eating until 3:30 A.M., when Çevriye's six-year-old granddaughter came into the room and announced, "We are leaving now!" I staggered to my feet and left the room. Çevriye was carrying the last things we needed, and said, "Hurry, we are leaving!" Once outside, the pace was slower. We had two cars, Mühettin's and Zübeyde's husband's, and a lot of stuff: kilims, blankets, carpets, plastic mats, a gas cooker, pots, pans, oil, tomatoes, eggplant, salt, bread, cookies, and other personal items, towels, clothes, bathing suits, and about twelve people. As we stood among the piles of things, the obvious problem of where to put them and the people loomed before us. Mühettin had warned Çevriye and me before we left that his minivan would fit five people. He reminded us that the traffic police would stop us if we overstuffed the car. But without Mühettin present, the configuration of the interior space of his beloved van was up to wilder interpretation.

The pace picked up, and through a series of frantic commands simultaneously uttered by Çevriye, her sister, Çevriye's son, and Zübeyde's husband, stuff was rearranged, young men squished into the back, and finally, amazingly, we all fit in. Our voices rang out in the dark and deserted streets, only stray dogs and street cats watching us. Then we were off, babies on laps and legs squeezed together. Çevriye's son sped down the highway, drifting between lanes as we drove on the empty highway to Izmir. Turning from the highway, we began driving on smaller roads, past Kuşadası and to the park. Passengers drifted between sleep and consciousness. Upon arrival we saw a huge line of cars filling the road, parked in the darkness. I understood then that our plan was not uncommon. It was chilly and people had established small beds for themselves on the sidewalk, lying on cardboard, plastic mats, covered in blankets and quilts, with pillows, all with the same designs and configuration as the things we had.

Since I could not sleep, I spent thirty minutes walking around by myself, skirting the sleeping people on the sidewalk. After a while I returned and found Çevriye sitting on a chair outside a closed restaurant. I could hear waves crashing on the shore, though I could not see the sea in the black night. She looked unhappy. She wanted to go into the forest and pee in the woods, since there was no bathroom. Now that I had arrived, I could accompany her into the woods. We meandered along the edge of the road and saw that there was a wire fence, preventing people from entering the woods, probably because lots of people would have liked to use it as a bathroom. Walking between the parked cars with sleeping people in them and around people laid out on the sidewalks, we passed the occasional man in shorts collecting empty beer bottles.

Çevriye remarked suddenly, "This place is filled with sin!"

I replied, "Sin? I don't see it," stepping over an empty beer bottle.

She said, "Sin! Don't you know what sin is?"

I said, "Yes, but where is the sin here?"

She listed the sins: "There is no ezan, no namaz. It is dirty. People drink alcohol. I would never have come here, except for my children! I agreed to look after the baby. Otherwise, I never would have come!"

Thinking about how Mühettin had stood his ground and refused to come, I asked, "Is this why Mühettin said, 'You couldn't pay me to go to a place like that?'"

"Of course," she said.

Çevriye's remarks and our allusion to Mühettin's forceful outburst the previous day led me to think about the problem of maintaining a pious life in public spaces, as we continued to pick our way among what I now saw through Çevriye's eyes as throngs of sinners lying on the sidewalk, packed in their cars, waiting to embark upon a day of pleasure in the dirt of their disordered lives. I thought about the many paths people were taking in this small group of people I knew. I considered how quite a few people who had left the village were testing out a secular lifestyle, while others were turning to Islamist organizations. Clearly, there was a lot more practiced flexibility than Çevriye's comments let on. Besides which, we were also at the beach. But it did seem even more evident from the perspective of the beach that the village is a place that is constructed as closed, protected, religious, and conservative. What I mean by "constructed" is that the village space is deliberately, self-consciously Islamic, even if some of the practices involve cultural memory. Yet, even in that carefully tended Islamic space, not everyone obeyed all the rules regarding Islamic moral behavior. Some young people had sex before marriage, the unlucky ones demonstrating the fact with their bellies. This happened to one young woman I knew in 2000. I marveled at how she would appear at village events, newly married, with her big belly showing. The women looked through her, as if she were not there. Her parents had cut off all contact. And as Zübeyde sought to set me straight on village life she point out that "men were drunk at Sehriye's wedding," though people claim there is no drinking in the village. It is not, in other words, that the village is a place where everyone is morally clean—as Çevriye implied in her critique of the people going to the beach—but it is a space believed to be distinct from the spaces outside the village. Those who try to maintain this space expect that people who leave it will fall into sin and will be more likely to suffer damnation. This is why parents often refuse to allow their daughters to attend high school and send them to Qur'an schools instead. They do not want their daughters to stray from the moral path of rural life. In addition to decisions about education, choosing a spouse shapes one's future. Parents direct children toward certain kinds of spouses, if not actually arranging marriages. Though taking a day-trip to the beach seems much less important than making a decision about migrating or marrying, older villagers treated the trip as if it were a step on the path to moral corruption.

I thought about this as we picked our way in the dim light through the crowd. Then the gates opened and we rushed to the cars and sped in with hundreds of others. We found a spot under a tree with a picnic table, and things seemed to be going well, as we transported our bags and sacks, kilims and blankets to the woods. I swam in the sea at around nine in the morning, when everyone else thought it too cold, and returned to find Çevriye having a conversation with her granddaughter, her son's daughter, who was saying that she wanted to be a policewoman when she grew up.[5] Çevriye replied, "You cannot be a policewoman." Sitting with them at the picnic table, I was reminded of a conversation that Zübeyde had with her parents when she was about fourteen. She also said she wanted to be a policewoman. I was surprised how her parents replied, "You can't!" I had asked Zübeyde why she had wanted to be a policewoman at that time and she replied that she wanted to carry a gun. At another point, she said she wanted to be a soldier. It seemed obvious to me that both Zübeyde and her niece expressed the wish to be someone who wields power. But in response to these yearnings, they are told pointedly and directly that they "cannot."

Sitting at the picnic table and drinking some lukewarm tea with Çevriye and her granddaughter, Zübeyde joined us and they all began to debate the merits of being a policewoman. I was reminded of an earlier conversation I had had with Zübeyde about her prospects for employment after she married. She had said that she had wanted a job, and a chance had opened up for her in a nearby city, which was easily accessible by train from her new town. But she had to ask her husband for permission to work, as all women in her social world do. Her husband flatly forbade it. She remarked, "Then I had my son," and kissing his rounded head as he sat in her lap, she said, "Now he is my job."

I was jolted back to the beach as I considered what seemed to be adding up at that moment to an obvious narrative of how women are prevented from fulfilling their desires. It is easy to dwell on girls and women being controlled through patriarchal authorities: fathers and husbands, and interpreting this as the outcome of being Muslim. I reminded myself that this interpretation skews the wider cultural construction of constraints before authority, which are prevalent in Turkish secular and Islamic societies. After all, we were at the beach for a young man who faced what everyone thought was a terrible constraint on his life, but also an essential duty, a condition he had to fulfill as a male citizen: soldierhood. While a young woman might want to be a soldier, she cannot because she is female; and while a young man might not want to be a soldier, he must because he is male. Both are rigid conditions against which girls and boys struggle, but I marveled how no one seemed to consider the possibility that women could become soldiers and that men might elect not to.

Aside from the obvious lack of individual choice is the relationship between duty and constraint. These are interlinked conditions, essential to consider when trying to understand individual lives. It is not liberty and individual freedom that constitute the self in Turkey, as Americans would like to imagine about themselves, but the ability to take on the responsibilities of these intertwined, constraining social positions, which delineate the contours of what it means to be a person. I noted how often villagers use the word *izin* (permission). Izin is required by workers from their bosses, women from their husbands, children from their fathers, and everyone from the state. When I first arrived in the village, an older man asked me very seriously if I had "izin" to be there. Somewhat confused, I wondered if he was referring to my visa, but after we talked I understood that he wanted to know if my father had granted me permission to be there. Undoubtedly, my answer would have dumbfounded him as I was not savvy enough to simply answer "yes" but instead, "Why would I need his permission to be here?" I now see that an unmarried woman could never leave her house, never mind her country, without permission from a man, her father or husband. The man asked further in genuine concern, "Does he know you are here?" Now I understand that he must have thought that I had run away without telling anyone, like eloping without a husband—the very thought of which is absurd.

While one is constrained by the kind of person one is (male/female, old/ young), actions are constrained by whether it is required (*mecbur*), such as performing one's military service or conditional (*şart*), such as getting married. Villagers, confused about who I was, would ask in these early months of research in 2000 if it was "mecbur" that I be there. I lamely would reply that I was doing a project for school and this was yes, mecbur. Existing inside this triangle of conditions, requirements, and the need for permission, shaped by age and gender, creates the person. While these three sides of the triangle channel possibility and action, they also connect the individual to others. One never drifts alone as an individual—that person is by definition no one—but is pushed and pulled and shaped by duties and constraints, facts of one's existence, to be connected to others. As Zübeyde had said to me once in exasperation, "We live together, connected, not like you, wandering."

Villagers explain that these structures, age and gender, which determine how and whether one can act, are defined by Islam. They are imagined to be the structures that define Muslim moral behavior, but these constraints are also deployed by the secular state to shape the role and meaning of citizenship. The secular state draws on an Islamic moral worldview in creating the conditions of citizenship, personhood in a modern nation-state, lending this condition meaning and weight. The implementation of a parallel cultural system defining individual action by the secular state may be seen as a contradiction, a paradox, a fact of civil religion, or a savvy deployment of cultural religious and secular worldviews, but it sacralizes duties to the state.

Though youth are under fierce pressure to fulfill their duties, as defined by their families, the state, and Islam, it is significant that young people also claim youth (*gençlik*) as an exceptional period of time when they can have fun. They relax Islamic practice and claim permission to suspend the requirements of piety, though they still cannot escape getting married or conducting their military service. The trip to the beach was an event designed to swap Islamic piety for fun, in advance payment for the sacrifice of required military service. Like Asef Bayat's discussion of young people in Egypt and Iran who claim youth as a period when they can experiment with "good and bad," using Islam to offset their bad behaviors, drinking alcohol, engaging in illicit relationships, and so on, the young people here also see this as a legitimate period for having fun.[6] This fun, though, is not lighthearted and carefree but calculated against the future costs of obligations to the state and God. Of course, those who practice Islam diligently would regard this youthful exceptionalism as a self-indulgent excuse—or worse, a sin. For these people, obligations to the state do not offset the duties demanded by Islam.

The park, then, was a civil space where people implemented this youthful sense of enjoyment and fun, one weighed down by potential spiritual and secular costs and obligations. Looking around, I began to think that the beach could be seen as a metaphor of Turkish society, much as Clifford Geertz read the cockfight as a story the Balinese tell about themselves.[7] Considering how the place was structured, it was not as unconsciously sinful as the villagers who refused to come claimed. This beach was neither a secularist nor an Islamist beach; it did not explicitly cater to either the lower middle classes nor the elite. Rather, it made accommodations to everyone: secular, Islamist, lower middle class, and elite. Though some of my companions looked at their neighbors with suspicion and some claimed that they were sure to be damned in the next life, and it seemed these critical glances were being returned, people still mixed. They put up with difference. Which is not to say that the place exhibited a democratic ethos. Class differences were evident in how the beach was socially organized. It had two sections. On the one side, one could sit on wooden chaise longues free of charge; on the other, there were rented plastic recliners. But rather than merely being about the ability to pay, the rented-chair region was occupied by people of a different social orientation, which was evident in that the women all wore conventional (from a western perspective) bathing suits and many were reading books. They presented themselves as secular Kemalist in their comportment. The majority of the revelers were in the free zone. There were chic young women in bikinis, women covered head to toe in Islamic bathing costumes, young men in shorts, gypsies in long dresses and flowing hair, and village women jumping into the water fully clothed in şalvar. The social difference in how the beach was being used was obvious, but no one mentioned it. In my party, Çevriye and her sister, both older women and mothers, who were giving this trip to Çevriye's sister's son Yusuf as his parting gift, remained on land and never ventured to the water. Both regarded the mixture of people in the sand and water as sinful. Çevriye was wearing şalvar and a headscarf, her sister a long skirt and headscarf. Çevriye had brought her overcoat, which would cover her şalvar, disguising her rural status, but it was too hot to endure. Her sister did not have her overcoat, since she had already achieved an urban Islamist position via her ankle-length skirt. Çevriye's daughter-in-law, who presents herself as an urban Islamist, was wearing a headscarf, long skirt, and long-sleeved shirt.

She entered the water fully clothed to play with her daughter. Zübeyde wore her modest one-piece because as she said, she no longer felt comfortable in her former bikini after having had a baby. Yusuf's sister was wearing a tiny bikini on her slight frame. Yusuf and all the men wore shorts and no top, unless they were concerned about sunburn. The configuration of bodies, in dress and out, demonstrated the gendered, geographic, devout, and class-specific accommodations individuals made to their enjoyment on the beach. Though the land divided the population by class, everyone mixed in the water. These class divisions dissolved, temporarily, just as youth suspend piety.

Though villagers disapproved and many refused to participate, those at the beach did not see their enjoyment in the water as disharmonious with their greater Islamic project. There were women in head-to-toe Islamic bathing costumes, and others fully clothed. These individuals represented an Islamist position, which makes accommodations for pleasure and consumption while maintaining public signs of devotion. Pious villagers do not accommodate a worldview, such as that exhibited by these urban Islamists, which allows for enjoyment, public piety, and obvious consumption. To them, pleasure and enjoyment require a suspension of deliberate self-control and a disregard for wasting what could otherwise be shared. Though many, like the people I have described here, experiment with lifestyles and worldviews, they do so after crossing the geographic borders of rural piety.

At a picnic table, happily coated in salt, my hair damp, and feeling a bit worn out from our adventure, I talked to Yusuf over tea. I asked him, half-jokingly, if he thought women should be soldiers, to which he said yes. His mother was sitting beside him and I asked her the same question. She looked shocked and laughed in discomfort at the absurdity of my question. Pulling herself together, she remarked: "Our sons become soldiers, our daughters brides." Her parallel construction of the life duties and sacrifices of men and women was clearly drawn. Indeed, as I described previously, villagers conceptualize marriage as a sacrifice for women and a necessary condition for adulthood, exactly how the military service is imaged for young men. Yusuf turned to Zübeyde and asked her whether she thought women should be soldiers. I already knew she did and she confirmed this in her enthusiastic response. He asked why and Zübeyde speculated that she liked the uniform. And she added, she wanted a gun. Thinking more, she said that she thought it would be interesting because soldiers get to go to different places and see things, an obvious commentary on her new married life in the small provincial town. Yusuf dismissed Zübeyde's desire to be a soldier as childish, focused only on the potential fun and excitement. It seemed to me that Zübeyde desired the power men have, and while she cannot be a man, having a gun might suffice. Yusuf, however, was preoccupied. He lowered his head as if the weight of his impending future duty had fallen on his shoulders. Though he did not elaborate, it seemed he thought it unfair that only men have to become soldiers.

A few days later, back in the village, I was sitting with Zübeyde's father when he happened to begin discussing the problem of modernity, as expressed through the body. He touched on the controversial subject of short-sleeved shirts, which many villagers believe are a sin. Mühettin pointed to his shirt and said, "I have never worn short sleeves, but now men and women go around with short sleeves." He expressed the opinion that people are becoming less devout and more relaxed because they wear short-sleeved shirts. He added in pointed reference to our trip that at the beach "people are going around 'open' and this is wrong." He conceded that his son, his wife, their daughter, Zübeyde and her husband, and Yusuf and his sister all liked going to the beach, but he added, "It was wrong for them to go open. They could have worn clothes, but they did not." I added that his granddaughter loved going to the beach, to which he replied morbidly, "Probably she will end up naked," meaning that she would not cover her head and would dress in an open, secular style.

I said, "I didn't know. We will have to see," and asked him if he thought Zübeyde should be "closed as well."

"Yes," he said.

"Maybe when she gets older she will close" I responded.

Mühettin concluded: "Maybe, but it is much harder to close when you have been open."

Mühettin's remarks underlined the demands and obligations of rural piety and the dangers of engaging with the secular world.

EPILOGUE

Asef Bayat urges us to think about nonmovements,[8] at a time when scholars feel an urgency to study movements. It is hard to overlook the obvious power and importance of Islamist movements, mobilization, political parties, and associations. Here, however, I have described people who do not belong to a movement but—through the incremental decisions about where to study or live, whom to love, how to dress and speak—collectively transform how society functions. Though they may not frame their decisions as individual choices but as forced options, required acts, or conditions which have to be met, individuals make selections which add up to change. But this is not entirely what I have tried to convey. Explaining religion as being about meeting social needs is reductive and functionalist. Here, I have taken care to describe the dimensions of Islamic practice as they are connected to sincere expressions of concern for individual salvation, collective reverence for the past, and/or a turn to an Islamist future. Seemingly mundane and ordinary questions about what to do with one's life relate, as I have argued throughout this book, to spiritual questions about life itself, its meaning, purpose, shape, and dimension. Thus, the issue of going to the beach, entering a presumptively secular space, reverberates with deep questions about one's life.

By studying nonmovements, one confronts the fact that people do not always agree with each other. And that people do not act consistently according to an ideological path which has no twists or turns. It is notable that the people in this rural region do not all agree with each other, even though their lives, when viewed from the outside, would seem homogenous and founded on assumptions about collective, pious, and traditional rural life. They disagree on many points: where to live, how to live, whom to love, and what to think about. Their search for answers to these questions leads them in different directions, some to remain in the region and others to migrate, some to search for a secular education and life and others an Islamist one. The multiplicity of personal directions is itself a surprise because rural life is assumed to be mired in blind tradition. Yet, there are trends which are contemporary: engagement with state religious power, involvement with neo-tarikats, interest in a secular worldview, feeling a reverence for local heritage, or being anxious about the role of the past in an Islamist future. As such, this book has explored evolving and transforming Sunni Islamic practice and social change. As many people pointed out to me, my questions were not about Islam; they were social questions. They were right: my research has not really been about doctrine, about orthodoxy qua orthodoxy, but about practice as it is negotiated among people, over time, in relation to different sources of power.

An overriding concern for many of the people I interviewed is how Muslims are represented and depicted by others. The concern with representation leads many to argue that rural Islam is not "really Islam at all." Those with rural roots will more gently gesture to the need for improvement in their relatives' practices, that they are on the road to true Islam, even if they could use some more

Knowing about it and honoring it

schooling. These people may feel embarrassed that I have revealed rural forms of practice rooted in cultural memory and the messiness of how people think about and rationalize their decisions about piety. For those who insist on the purity and uniformity of Islam, for those who demand that Islam should take the form certified by the government, or for those who demand that individuals act consistently without deviation from an ideological program, this book may be regarded as wrong or, worse, heretical. Ethnography is hubris, and designed to tease out the inconsistencies in our lives.

REFERENCE MATTER

NOTES

INTRODUCTION

1. I use the English plural *s* in pluralizing Turkish words rather than the Turkish plural *lEr*.

2. Female hocas in the Süleymancı community have ascended to this level through a specific course of training, much like male imams who were trained by the state. There are no female imams trained by the state.

3. Talal Asad, *Genealogies of Religion* (Baltimore: Johns Hopkins University Press, 1993), 35.

4. Jose Casanova, *Public Religions in the Modern World* (Chicago: University of Chicago Press, 1994), 55.

5. Reading Isaac Bashevis Singer, *In My Father's Court* (New York: Farrar, Straus and Giroux, 1966), helped me understand a world in which religion is not yet privatized.

6. Kristen Ghodsee, *Muslim Lives in Eastern Europe* (Princeton, NJ: Princeton University Press, 2010), 22.

7. Samuli Schielke, "Policing Ambiguity: Muslim Saints–Day Festivals and the Moral Geography of Public Space in Egypt," *American Ethnologist* 35, no. 4 (2008): 539–52.

8. Saba Mahmood, *Politics of Piety* (Princeton, NJ: Princeton University Press, 2005).

9. Amira Mittermaier, *Dreams That Matter: Egyptian Landscapes of the Imagination* (Berkeley: University of California Press, 2011).

10. Mandana Limbert, *In the Time of Oil: Piety, Memory, and Social Life in an Omani Town* (Stanford, CA: Stanford University Press, 2010).

11. Dorothea Schultz, "(Re)Turning to Proper Muslim Practice: Islamic Moral Renewal and Women's Conflicting Assertions of Sunni Identity in Urban Mali," *Africa Today* 54, no. 4 (2008): 21–43.

12. Berna Turam, *Between Islam and the State* (Stanford, CA: Stanford University Press, 2007).

13. Ahmet Yükleyen, *Localizing Islam in Europe* (Syracuse, NY: Syracuse University Press, 2012).

14. Asef Bayat, *Life as Politics: How Ordinary People Change the Middle East* (Stanford, CA: Stanford University Press, 2010), 172–73.

15. Olivier Roy, *Globalized Islam* (New York: Columbia University Press, 2004), 157; Dale F. Eickelman and James Piscatori, *Muslim Politics* (Princeton, NJ: Princeton University Press, 1996), 117–19.

16. Reinhold Loeffler, *Islam in Practice: Religious Belief in a Persian Village* (Albany: State University of New York Press Press, 1988).

17. Magnus Marsden, *Living Islam* (Cambridge: Cambridge University Press, 2005).

18. Erik Mueggler, *The Age of Wild Ghosts: Memory, Violence, and Place in Southwest China* (Berkeley: University of California Press, 2001).

19. Margaret Paxson, *Solovyovo: The Story of Memory in a Russian Village* (Washington, DC, and Bloomington: Woodrow Wilson Center Press and Indiana University Press, 2005).

20. I thank Anna Sun for sharing her manuscript on Confucianism in China at the Institute for Advanced Study. This work is forthcoming from Princeton University Press, 2013.

21. Works which consider this gray area ethnographically include: Cihan Tuğal, *Passive Revolution* (Stanford, CA: Stanford University Press, 2009); Catharina Raudvere, *The Book and the Roses* (Istanbul: Swedish Research Institute in Istanbul, 2002); Brian Silverstein, *Islam and Modernity in Turkey* (New York: Palgrave, 2011).

22. See the Muhammed Zühdü Web site, www.muhammedzuhdu.com/v1 (last accessed November 2, 2012).

23. See Sibel Bozdoğan, *Modernism and Nation Building* (Seattle: University of Washington Press, 2001); Zeynep Kezer, "Contesting Urban Space in Early Republican Ankara," *Journal of Architectural Education* 52, no. 1 (1998): 11–19.

24. Ottoman is distinctly different from modern Turkish, written in the Arabic alphabet and with different grammatical structures and vocabulary—I am unable to read it.

25. Reşat Kasaba, *A Moveable Empire: Ottoman Nomads, Migrants, and Refugees* (Seattle: University of Washington Press, 2009), 21.

26. Halil Inalcık, "The Yürüks: Their Origins, Expansion, and Economic Role," in *Oriental Carpet and Textile Studies*, vol. 2, edited by Robert Pinner and Walter B. Denny (London: Hali Publications, 1986), 43.

27. Kasaba, *Moveable Empire*.

28. Jeremy Walton, "Practices of Neo-Ottomanism: Making Space and Place Virtuous in Istanbul," in *Orienting Istanbul: Cultural Capital of Europe?* edited by Levent Soysal, Deniz Göktürk, and Ipek Türeli (London: Routledge, 2010); Raudvere, *Book and the Roses*, 12: 72.

29. Kimberly Hart, "The Decline of a Cooperative," in *Cross-Stitching Textile Economies with Value, Sanctity, and Transnationalism*, edited by Patricia A. McAnany and Walter Little (New York: AltaMira, 2011).

30. Damla Işik, "Woven Assemblages: Globalization, Gender, Labor, and Authenticity in Turkey's Carpet Industry" (Ph.D. diss., Department of Anthropology, University of Arizona, Tucson, 2007).

31. I will address terminological questions about *tarikat* later in the book.

32. Cihan Tuğal, *Passive Revolution* (Stanford, CA: Stanford University Press, 2009).

33. Yasin Navaro-Yashin, *Faces of the State: Secularism and Public Life in Turkey* (Princeton, NJ: Princeton University Press, 2002).

34. Jenny White, *Islamist Mobilization in Turkey: A Study in Vernacular Politics* (Seattle: University of Washington Press, 2002).

35. Nilüfer Göle, *The Forbidden Modern* (Ann Arbor: University of Michigan Press, 1996).

36. Esra Özyürek, *Nostalgia for the Modern: State Secularism and Everyday Politics in Turkey* (Durham, NC: Duke University Press, 2006).

37. Michael Meeker, *A Nation of Empire: The Ottoman Legacy of Turkish Modernity* (Berkeley: University of California Press, 2002).

CHAPTER 1: SECULAR TIME AND THE INDIVIDUAL

1. Erik Zürcher, *Turkey: A Modern History* (London: I. B. Tauris, 2004), 147–49.

2. Nazli Ökten, "An Endless Death and an Eternal Mourning," in *The Politics of Public Memory*, edited by Esra Özyürek (Syracuse, NY: Syracuse University Press, 2007), 98–99.

3. Catharina Raudvere, *The Book and the Roses* (Istanbul: Swedish Research Institute in Istanbul, 2002), 47.

4. Kemal Kirişci, "Migration and Turkey: The Dynamics of State, Society, and Politics," in *The Cambridge History of Turkey*, vol. 4, *Turkey in the Modern World*, edited by Reşat Kasaba (Cambridge: Cambridge University Press, 2008), 175–83.

5. Elizabeth Shakman Hurd, *The Politics of Secularism in International Politics* (Princeton, NJ: Princeton University Press, 2008), 54.

6. Joan Wallach Scott, *The Politics of the Veil* (Princeton, NJ: Princeton University Press, 2007), 15.

7. Jeremy Walton, "Practices of Neo-Ottomanism: Making Space and Place Virtuous in Istanbul," in *Orienting Istanbul: Cultural Capital of Europe?* edited by Levent Soysal, Deniz Göktürk, and Ipek Türeli (London: Routledge, 2010), 89.

8. Esra Özyürek, "The Politics of Public Memory," in *The Politics of Public Memory*, edited by Esra Özyurek (Syracuse, NY: Syracuse University Press, 2007), 116–31.

9. Marcy Brink-Danan, *Jewish Life in 21st-Century Turkey* (Bloomington: Indiana University Press, 2012).

10. Brian Silverstein, "Islam and Modernity in Turkey," *Anthropological Quarterly* 76, no. 3 (2003): 511.

11. See Erik Zürcher, *Turkey: A Modern History* (London: I. B. Tauris, 2004), 186–95, for a historical narrative of these reforms.

12. Gavin Brockett, *How Happy to Call Oneself a Turk: Provincial Newspapers and the Negotiation of a Muslim National Identity* (Austin: University of Texas Press, 2011), 2.

13. Banu Eligür, *The Mobilization of Political Islam in Turkey* (Cambridge: Cambridge University Press, 2010), 46–48.

14. Richard Pfaff, "Disengagement from Traditionalism in Turkey and Iran," *Western Political Quarterly* 16, no. 1 (1963): 96; Hakan Yavuz, "The Assassination of Collective Memory: The Case of Turkey," *Muslim World* 89, nos. 3–4 (1999): 202.

15. Eligür, *Mobilization of Political Islam in Turkey*, 50–51.

16. Martin Stokes, *The Republic of Love: Cultural Intimacy in Turkish Popular Music* (Chicago: University of Chicago Press, 2010), 24.

17. Cihan Tuğal, "The Appeal of Islamic Politics," *Sociological Quarterly* 47 (2006): 266.

18. Zeynep Kezer, "Familiar Things in Strange Places: Ankara's Ethnography Museum and the Legacy of Islam in Republican Turkey," *Perspectives on Vernacular Architecture* 8 (2000): 103.

19. Esra Özyürek, *Nostalgia for the Modern: State Secularism and Everyday Politics in Turkey* (Durham, NC: Duke University Press, 2006), 3–4.

20. Ayşe Kadioğlu, "Republican Epistemology and Islamic Discourses in Turkey in the 1990s," *Muslim World* 88, no. 1 (1998): 13.

21. S. M. Can Bilsel, "'Our Anatolia': Organicism and the Making of Humanist Culture in Turkey," *Muqarnas* 24 (2007): 234.

22. Katherine Pratt Ewing, *Stolen Honor: Stigmatizing Muslim Men in Berlin* (Stanford, CA: Stanford University Press, 2008), 27–51.

23. Ziya Gökalp, *Turkish Nationalism and Western Civilization*, translated by Niyazi Berkes (London: George Allen and Unwin, 1959).

24. Bilsel, "'Our Anatolia,'" 234.

25. Eligür, *Mobilization of Political Islam in Turkey*, 39.

26. Andrew Mango, *Atatürk: The Biography of the Founder of Modern Turkey* (New York: Overlook Press, 1999), 495–96.

27. Kirby Fay Berkes, "The Village Instiute Movement of Turkey" (Ph.D. diss., Columbia Teachers College, Columbia University, 1960), 330.

28. Asim Karaomerlioğlu, "The Village Institutes Experience in Turkey," *British Journal of Middle Eastern Studies* 25, no. 1 (1998): 47–73.

29. Zürcher, *Turkey*, 195.

30. Richard Tapper, ed., *Islam in Modern Turkey* (New York: I. B. Tauris, 1991), 10.

31. Sam Kaplan, *The Pedagogical State* (Stanford, CA: Stanford University Press, 2006), 76.

32. Hakan Yavuz, *Islamic Political Identity in Turkey* (Oxford: Oxford University Press, 2003), 73.

33. Bilsel, "'Our Anatolia,'" 235.

34. Sami Zubaida, "Turkish Islam and National Identity," *Middle East Report* 199 (April–June 1996): 11; Jenny White, "Islamic Chic," in *Istanbul: Between the Global and the Local*, edited by Çağlar Keyder (New York: Rowman and Littlefield Publishers, 1999), 79.

35. Ümit Çizre, "Ideology, Context, and Interest: The Turkish Military," in *The Cambridge History of Turkey*, vol. 4, *Turkey in the Modern World*, edited by Reşat Kasaba (Cambridge: Cambridge University Press, 2008), 314.

36. Yavuz, *Islamic Political Identity in Turkey*, 73.

37. Eligür, *Mobilization of Political Islam in Turkey*, 101.

38. Kaplan, *Pedagogical State*, 81.

39. See Leyla Neyzi, "Object or Subject? The Paradox of 'Youth' in Turkey," *International Journal of Middle East Studies* 33, no. 3 (2001): 418.

40. Ahmet Yükleyen, *Localizing Islam in Europe* (Syracuse, NY: Syracuse University Press, 2012), 69.

41. Talip Kucukcan, "Sacralization of the State and Secular Nationalism: Foundations of Civil Religion in Turkey," *George Washington International Law Review* 41, no. 4 (2010): 970.

42. Yükleyen, *Localizing Islam in Europe*, 97.

43. Bayat, *Life as Politics*, 243.

44. The *Mavi Marmara* is a boat owned by a Turkish human rights organization used to break the Israeli embargo of the Gaza Strip. The ship was attacked by Israeli military forces, though it was manned by civilians, in May 2010. Nine activists were killed. The event inspired passionate discussion about Israel and the United States in the villages.

CHAPTER 2: ISLAMIC TIME AND THE VILLAGE

1. Carol Greenhouse, *A Moment's Notice: Time Politics Across Cultures* (Ithaca, NY: Cornell University Press, 1996), 3.

2. Hakan Yavuz, "The Assassination of Collective Memory," *Muslim World* 89, nos. 3–4 (1999): 200.

3. Zeynep Gürsel, *Coffee Futures* (Watertown, MA: Documentary Educational Resources, 2009).

4. Esra Özyürek, *Nostalgia for the Modern: State Secularism and Everyday Politics in Turkey* (Durham, NC: Duke University Press, 2006).

5. Ibid., 61.

6. Samanyolu is financially and ideologically connected to Fethullah Gülen and Kanal 7 is affiliated with the former Refah Party, according to Kira Kosnick, *Migrant Media* (Bloomington, IN: Indiana University Press, 2007), 113.

7. It happens that I recorded this discussion while it happened and therefore decided to preserve the spoken language of the young girl in which she said "sins" as *künahlar* rather than with the correct Turkish, *günahlar*.

8. Asef Bayat, "Islamism and the Politics of Fun," *Public Culture* 19, no. 3 (2007): 433–59.

9. Ibid., 457.

10. Ibid., 436.

11. See Samuli Schielke, "Habitus of the Authentic, Order of the Rational: Contesting Saints' Festivals in Contemporary Egypt," *Critique: Critical Middle Eastern Studies* 12, no. 2 (2003): 155–72.

12. Saba Mahmood, *Politics of Piety* (Princeton, NJ: Princeton University Press), 143.

13. Ahmet Yükleyen, *Localizing Islam in Europe* (Syracuse, NY: Syracuse University Press, 2012), 26.

14. The Yasin, chapter 36 of the Qur'an, is regarded as its "heart," and is read often on such occasions as when people visit a saint's tomb, upon visiting the graves of relatives on Arife Günü, and by women during their prayer gatherings.

15. I thank Esra Özyürek for this insight.

16. Arnold Van Gennep, *The Rites of Passage* (Chicago: University of Chicago Press, 1960).

17. International Strategic Research Organization, "Turkish President Approves Laws on Paid Military Service and Match-Fixing Penalties," December 14, 2011, *Journal of Turkish Weekly*, www.turkishweekly.net/news/127959/turkish-president-approves-laws-on-paid-military-service-and-match-fixing-penalties.html (last accessed January 15, 2013).

18. The PKK, or Kurdistan Workers' Party, founded in 1977, is a neo–Marxist organization led by Abdullah Öcalan, currently in prison in Turkey. The organization has led a Kurdish uprising called at times a civil war in southeastern Turkey. Kurds associated with the PKK want to establish an independent Kurdistan. See Hamit Bozarslan, "Kurds and the Turkish State," in *The Cambridge History of Turkey*, vol. 4, *Turkey in the Modern World*, edited by Reşat Kasaba (Cambridge: Cambridge University Press, 2008), 333–56.

19. Murafa Üstünova and Kerime Üstünova, "Soldier Wedding in Kaynarca," *Journal of Folklore Research* 43, no. 2 (2006): 177.

20. Ibid., 184.

21. Yael Navaro-Yashin, *Faces of the State: Secularism and Public Life in Turkey* (Princeton, NJ: Princeton University Press, 2002), 119.

22. Robert Bellah, "Civil Religion in America," *Daedalus* 96, no. 1 (1967): 1–21; Talip Kucukcan, "Sacralization of the State and Secular Nationalism: Foundations of Civil Religion in Turkey," *George Washington International Law Review* 41, no. 4 (2010): 963–83.

23. Michael Herzfeld, "Performative Categories and Symbols of Passage in Rural Greece," *Journal of American Folklore* 94, no. 371 (1981): 48.

24. Zeynep Kezer, "Contesting Urban Space in Early Republican Ankara," *Journal of Architectural Education* 52, no. 1 (1998): 14.

25. Winnifred Fallers Sullivan, *The Impossibility of Religious Freedom* (Princeton, NJ: Princeton University Press, 2005), 94–95.

26. Ibid., 159.

CHAPTER 3: GOOD DEEDS AND THE MORAL ECONOMY

Adapted from Kimberly Hart, "Performing Piety and Islamic Modernity in a Turkish Village," *Ethnology* 46, no. 4 (2007): 289–304.

1. Şevket Pamuk, "Economic Change in Twentieth-Century Turkey," in *The Cambridge History of Turkey*, vol. 4, *Turkey in the Modern World*, edited by Reşat Kasaba (Cambridge: Cambridge University Press, 2008), 286–87.

2. Cihan Tuğal, "Islamism in Turkey: Beyond Instrument and Meaning," *Economy and Society* 31, no. 1 (2002): 98.

3. Laura Deeb, *An Enchanted Modern* (Princeton, NJ: Princeton University Press, 2006), 8.

4. See Reinhold Loeffler, *Islam in Practice: Religious Belief in a Persian Village* (Albany: State University of New York Press Press, 1988).

5. Jonathan Benthall, "Financial Worship: The Quranic Injunction to Almsgiving," *Journal of the Royal Anthropological Institute* 5, no. 1 (1999): 30.

6. John L. Esposito, *Islam: The Straight Path* (New York: Oxford University Press, 1991), 91.

7. Benthall, "Financial Worship," 29.

8. Bill Maurer, *Mutual Life, Limited* (Princeton, NJ: Princeton University Press, 2005), 107.

9. Katherine Bowie, "The Alchemy of Charity," *American Anthropologist* 100, no. 2 (1998): 476; Maurer, *Mutual Life, Limited*, 69.

10. Maurer, *Mutual Life, Limited*, 93.

11. Benthall, "Financial Worship," 30.

12. Maurer, *Mutual Life, Limited*, 93.

13. Nawawi, quoted in F. E. Peters, *A Reader on Classical Islam* (Princeton, NJ: Princeton University Press, 1994), 153–54.

14. Amy Singer, *Charity in Islamic Societies* (Cambridge: Cambridge University Press, 2008), 68.

15. Marcel Mauss, *The Gift*, translated by W. D. Halls (New York: W. W. Norton, 1990), 18.

16. Tuğal, "Islamism in Turkey," 103.

17. Günseli Berik, *Women Carpet Weavers in Rural Turkey* (Geneva: International Labour Office, 1987); T. B. Ehlers, *Silent Looms* (Austin: University of Texas Press, 2000); Jeffrey Cohen, *Cooperation and Community* (Austin: University of Texas Press, 1999).

18. Tuğal, "Islamism in Turkey," 91.

19. See Jenny White, *Money Makes Us Relatives* (Austin: University of Texas Press, 1994), 93–98.

20. It is far from the case that children do not help their parents in the villages. Many girls weave full-time and contribute to the household income pool until they marry and sons contribute some amount of their earnings when they work in cheese workshops. Adult married children continue to assist their parents economically and look after them in old age.

21. Reşat Kasaba, *A Moveable Empire: Ottoman Nomads, Migrants, and Refugees* (Seattle: University of Washington Press, 2009), for example, describes how nomads had animals and transported goods during the Ottoman era. Apparently, former nomads continued to work transporting goods by camel during the early decades of the republic.

22. Carol Delaney, *The Seed and the Soil* (Berkeley: University of California Press, 1991), 107; Loeffler, *Islam in Practice*, 15; Jenny White, *Islamist Mobilization in Turkey: A Study in Vernacular Politics* (Seattle: University of Washington Press, 2002), 20–21.

23. See, e.g., White, *Money Makes Us Relatives*, 74.

24. Kimberly Hart, "The Economy and Morality of Elopement in Rural Western Turkey," *Ethnologia Europaea* 40, no. 1 (2010): 58–76.

25. Ibid.

26. Suzan Ilcan, "Marriage Regulation and the Rhetoric of Alliance in Northwestern Turkey," *Ethnology* 33, no. 4 (1994): 280.

27. James C. Scott, *Weapons of the Weak* (New Haven, CT: Yale University Press, 1985), 171.

28. Benthall, "Financial Worship," 32.

29. Scott, *Weapons of the Weak*, 172.

30. Paul Stirling, *Turkish Village* (New York: John Wiley and Sons, 1966), 246–54.

31. Nilüfer Göle, *The Forbidden Modern* (Ann Arbor: University of Michigan Press, 1996), 52.

32. White, *Islamist Mobilization*, 198–99.

33. Suzan Ilcan, "Social Spaces and the Micropolitics of Differentiation: An Example from Northwestern Turkey," *Ethnology* 38, no. 3 (1999): 243–56.

34. White, *Islamist Mobilization*, 21.

35. Ibid., 68.

36. White, *Money Makes Us Relatives*, 95–98.

37. Loeffler, *Islam in Practice*, 15.

38. Ibid.

39. White, *Money Makes Us Relatives*, 93–96.

40. Loeffler, *Islam in Practice*, 15.

41. White, *Money Makes Us Relatives*, 72, 119–20.

42. Tuğal, "Islamism in Turkey," 99.

CHAPTER 4: CONSTRUCTING ISLAM

1. Kabir Tambar, "The Aesthetics of Public Visibility: Alevi Semah and the Paradoxes of Pluralism in Turkey," *Comparative Studies in Society and History* 52, no. 3 (2010): 652–79.

2. BBC, "Vatican and Muslims Condemn Swiss Minaret Ban," November 30, 2009, available at http://news.bbc.co.uk/go/pr/fr/-/2/hi/europe/8385893.stm (last accessed November 16, 2012).

3. Carolin Jenkner, "Go-Ahead for Germany's Biggest Mosque," *Der Spiegel International*, August 29, 2008.

4. Gerdien Jonker, "The Mevlana Mosque in Berlin-Kreuzberg: An Unsolved Conflict," *Journal of Ethnic and Migration Studies* 31, no. 6 (2005): 1067–81; Michael Kaczmarek, "The Mosque Controversy," September 27, 2007, available at www.eurotopics.net/en/home/presseschau/archiv/magazin/kultur-verteilerseite-neu/moscheebauten_2007_09/debatte_moscheebauten_2007_09/ Euro-Topics, owned by the Federal Agency for Civic Education (Bundeszentrale für politische Bildung) (last accessed January 5, 2013).

5. Clyde Haberman, "Putting 'Un-American' in Perspective," *New York Times*, March 21, 2011.

6. Sefa Şimşek, Zerrin Polvan, and Tayfun Yeşilşerit, "The Mosque as a Divisive Symbol in the Turkish Political Landscape," *Turkish Studies* 7, no. 3 (2006): 489–508.

7. Marc Baer, "The Great Fire of 1660 and the Islamization of Christian and Jewish Space in Istanbul," *International Journal of Middle East Studies* 36, no. 2 (2004): 159–81.

8. Zeynep Kezer, "Contesting Urban Space in Early Republican Ankara," *Journal of Architectural Education* 52, no. 1 (1998): 11–19; Kezer, "An Imaginable Community: The Material Culture of Nation-Building in Early Republican Turkey," *Society and Space* 27, no. 3 (2009): 508–30.

9. Amy Singer, *Charity in Islamic Societies* (Cambridge: Cambridge University Press, 2008), 93.

10. Ibid., 188.

11. Ibid., 189.

12. Ibid., 191.

13. Zeynep Kezer, "Familiar Things in Strange Places: Ankara's Ethnography Museum and the Legacy of Islam in Republican Turkey," *Perspectives on Vernacular Architecture* 8 (2000): 101–16.

14. Reha Günay, *A Guide to the Works of Sinan the Architect in Istanbul* (Istanbul: Yam Yayın, 2006), 76–96.

15. Nuran Kara Pilehvarian, Nur Urfalıoğlu, and Lütfi Yazıcıoğlu, *Fountains in Ottoman Istanbul* (Istanbul: Yapı Yayın, 2004).

16. Amy Singer, *Constructing Ottoman Beneficence* (Albany: State University of New York Press, 2002).

17. Anatolian News Agency, "Süleymaniye Library Holds Turkey's Treasure," *Hürriyet Daily News*, May 24, 2012.

18. Kezer, "Familiar Things in Strange Places," 110.

19. Singer, *Constructing Ottoman Beneficence*.

20. Ibid., 183.

21. Gülru Necipoğlu-Kafadar, "The Süleymaniye Complex in Istanbul: An Interpretation," *Muqarnas* 3 (1985): 92–117.

22. Andrew Mango, *Atatürk: The Biography of the Founder of Modern Turkey* (New York: Overlook Press, 1999), 411.

23. Necipoğlu-Kafadar, "Süleymaniye Complex."

24. Kandils are holy evenings in the Islamic calendar.

25. Saba Mahmood, *Politics of Piety* (Princeton, NJ: Princeton University Press, 2005).

26. According to the *Redhouse Türkce-Osmanlica-Ingilizce Dictionary* (17th printing, 1999), *maşatlik* means "a non-Muslim cemetery, especially a Jewish one."

27. Ilhan Başgöz, "Rain-Making Ceremonies in Turkey and Seasonal Festivals," *Journal of the American Oriental Society* 87, no. 3 (1967): 304–6.

28. Michael Meeker, *A Nation of Empire: The Ottoman Legacy of Turkish Modernity* (Berkeley: University of California Press, 2002), 199 n. 30.

29. Ibid., 108.

30. Ibid., xii.

31. Ibid., 57.

32. Ibid.

33. The *lu* in *Oflu* is a suffix meaning "with." Added to place names, it refers to a person's origin, such as "Amerikalı."

34. Meeker, *Nation of Empire*, 58.

35. Ibid.

36. *Muska*, also called *nuska* or *nusha*, is a triangular amulet made of a packet of cloth with a piece of paper with a Koranic verse selected to address some purpose tucked inside.

37. See Kimberly Hart, "Weaving Modernity, Commercializing Carpets: Collective Memory and Contested Tradition in Örselli Village," in *The Politics of Public Memory in Turkey*, edited by Esra Özyürek (Syracuse, NY: Syracuse University Press, 2007), 28.

38. Jeremy Walton, "Practices of Neo-Ottomanism: Making Space and Place Virtuous in Istanbul," in *Orienting Istanbul: Cultural Capital of Europe?* edited by Levent Soysal, Deniz Göktürk, and Ipek Türeli (London: Routledge, 2010), 94.

39. Zeynep Kezer, "Molding the Republican Generation: Children and the Didactic Uses of Urban Space in Early Republican Turkey," in *Designing Modern Childhoods: History, Space, and the Material Culture of Children*, edited by Marta Gutman and Ning de Coninck-Smith (New Brunswick, NJ: Rutgers University Press, 2008), 131.

40. Necipoğlu-Kafadar, "Süleymaniye Complex in Istanbul."

41. Sultan Camii, completed in 1522, was not built by Mimar Sinan.

42. An imam is a prayer leader and is not expected to compose sermons until reaching the rank of vaiz.

43. Because it was a funny news piece, this was reported in a number of places, including the BBC, "Istanbul's Tuneless Muezzins Get Voice Training," http://news.bbc.co.uk/2/hi/europe/8665977.stm (last accessed November 16, 2012).

CHAPTER 5: WOMEN'S TRADITIONS AND INNOVATIONS

1. Saba Mahmood, *Politics of Piety* (Princeton, NJ: Princeton University Press, 2005).

2. Laura Deeb, *An Enchanted Modern* (Princeton, NJ: Princeton University Press, 2006).

3. Tone Bringa, *Being Muslim the Bosnian Way: Identity and Community in a Central Bosnian Village* (Princeton, NJ: Princeton University Press, 1995).

4. See Esra Özyürek, ed., *The Politics of Public Memory in Turkey* (Syracuse, NY: Syracuse University Press, 2007), 3.

5. Ahmet Yükleyen, "Production of Mystical Islam in Europe: Religious Authorization in the Süleymanlı Sufi Community," *Contemporary Islam* 4 (2010): 269–88.

6. I asked a few times to make sure I understood the name of the dede but I cannot unravel what *oncak* means. It is possible I misheard and the word was *ocak*, meaning hearth, kiln, or oven.

7. Please recall my discussion of the mixing of national and sectarian identities generally in Turkey, such that Turks are imagined to be Muslims. Foreigners (*yabancı*, *gavur*), similarly, are regarded as Christians and Greeks, former inhabitants of western Anatolia who fled or were exchanged with Turkish populations after the War of Independence, unless specifically identified as Jews.

8. Ahmet Yükleyen, "Sufism and Islamic Groups in Contemporary Turkey," in *The Cambridge History of Turkey*, vol. 4, *Turkey in the Modern World*, edited by Reşat Kasaba (Cambridge: Cambridge University Press, 2008), 386.

9. David Shankland, *The Alevis in Turkey* (New York: Routledge, 2003), 104–6.

10. Irene Melikoff, "From God of Heaven to King of Men: Popular Islam Among Turkish tribes from Central Asia to Anatolia," *Religion, State, and Society* 24, nos. 2–3 (1996): 135.

11. See the Muhammed Zühdü Web site, www.muhammedzuhdu.com/v1/ (last accessed November 2, 2012).

12. Amira Mittermaier, *Dreams That Matter: Egyptian Landscapes of the Imagination* (Berkeley: University of California Press, 2011), 6.

13. Ilhan Başgöz, "Dream Motif in Turkish Folk Stories and Shamanistic Initiation," *Asian Folklore Studies* 26, no. 1 (1967): 5–6.

14. Ibid., 12.

15. The Diyanet posts rules at tombs it administers. These outline what one is forbidden to do, including light candles, wipe one's face, circumambulate the tomb, leave food, lie down on the tomb, and so on. The signs state in a ham-fisted manner that these practices "have been absolutely forbidden in our religion [dinimizce kesinlikle yasaklanmıştır]." It is notable that the wording indicates that they were forbidden in the past using a passive mode of the reported *miş* tense, indicating that the Diyanet did not witness the time when they were forbidden. In fact, it was the Diyanet that created these regulations.

16. Esra Özyürek, *Nostalgia for the Modern: State Secularism and Everyday Politics in Turkey* (Durham, NC: Duke University Press, 2006), 103.

17. Yael Navaro-Yashin, *Faces of the State: Secularism and Public Life in Turkey* (Princeton, NJ: Princeton University Press, 2002), 193–94.

18. Sibel Bozdoğan, *Modernism and Nation Building* (Seattle: University of Washington Press, 2001), 44.

19. The example Özyürek discusses is of a mountaintop in an Alevi village, which all the more effectively points to mystical power. Özyürek, *Nostalgia for the Modern*, 103–4.

20. Walter Denny, "Atatürk and Political Art in Turkey," *Turkish Studies Association Bulletin* 6, no. 2 (1982): 18.

21. Mary Elaine Hegland, "Flagellation and Fundamentalism: (Trans)forming Meaning, Identity, and Gender Through Pakistani Women's Rituals of Mourning," *American Ethnologist* 25, no. 2 (1998): 240–66.

22. A *mevlevihane* housed male initiates and members in the Mevlevi order.

23. Perween Hassan, "The Footprint of the Prophet," *Muqarnas* 10 (1993): 335–43.

24. F. E. Peters, *A Reader on Classical Islam* (Princeton, NJ: Princeton University Press, 1994), 169–70.

25. I am typically not invited into the mosque during the namaz but am during Mevluts.

26. Marco Schöller, *The Living and the Dead in Islam*, vol. 2 (Wiesbaden: Harrassowitz Verlag, 2004), 578.

27. Ibid., 22.

28. Ibid., 28.

29. Ibid., 36.

30. Asef Bayat, *Life as Politics: How Ordinary People Change the Middle East* (Stanford, CA: Stanford University Press, 2010), 14–15.

CHAPTER 6: RITUAL PURIFICATION
AND THE PERNICIOUS DANGER OF CULTURE

Adapted from Kimberly Hart, "The Orthodoxization of Ritual Practice in Western Anatolia," *American Ethnologist* 36, no. 4 (2005): 735–49.

1. Kristen Ghodsee, *Muslim Lives in Eastern Europe* (Princeton, NJ: Princeton University Press, 2010).

2. Ibid.

3. Cihan Tuğal, *Passive Revolution* (Stanford, CA: Stanford University Press, 2009).

4. Brian Silverstein, *Islam and Modernity in Turkey* (New York: Palgrave, 2011).

5. Amira Mittermaier, *Dreams That Matter: Egyptian Landscapes of the Imagination* (Berkeley: University of California Press, 2011).

6. Kai Kresse, "Muslim Politics in Postcolonial Kenya," *Journal of the Royal Anthropological Institute* 15, no. 1 (2009): S81.

7. Cihan Tuğal, "The Appeal of Islamic Politics," *Sociological Quarterly* 47 (2006): 257.

8. Ibid., 265–66.

9. Pierre Nora, "Between Memory and History: Les Lieux de Memoire," *Representations* 26 (1989): 7–24.

10. Brian Silverstein, "Disciplines of Presence in Modern Turkey: Discourse, Companionship, and the Mass Mediation of Islamic Practice," *Cultural Anthropology* 23, no. 1 (2008): 134–35.

11. Berna Turam, "The Politics of Engagement between Islam and the Secular State," *British Journal of Sociology* 55, no. 2 (2004): 259–81; Hakan Yavuz and John Esposito, *Turkish Islam and the Secular State: The Gülen Movement* (Syracuse, NY: Syracuse University Press, 2003).

12 Laura Deeb, *An Enchanted Modern* (Princeton, NJ: Princeton University Press, 2006), 8.

13. Talal Asad, *Genealogies of Religion* (Baltimore: Johns Hopkins University Press, 1993), 210.

14. Mandana Limbert, "The Sacred Date: Gifts of God in an Omani Town," *Ethnos* 73 (2008): 375.

15. June Anderson, *Return to Tradition* (Seattle: University of Washington Press, 1998), 65.

16. Tuğal, "Appeal of Islamic Politics," 258.

17. Asad, *Genealogies of Religion*, 210.

18. Martin Stokes, "Music, Fate, and State: Turkey's Arabesk Debate," *Middle East Report* 160 (1989): 29.

19. Martin Stokes, "Islam, the Turkish State, and Arabesk," *Popular Music* 11, no. 2 (1992): 214.

20. Nancy Tapper and Richard Tapper, "The Birth of the Prophet: Ritual and Gender in Turkish Islam," *Man* 22 (1987): 73.

21. Carol Delaney, *The Seed and the Soil* (Berkeley: University of California Press, 1991), 317–19; Julie Marcus, "Equal Rites and Women in Turkey," *Mankind* 17, no. 2 (1987): 120–28; Nazli Ökten, "An Endless Death and an Eternal Mourning," in *The Poli-*

tics of Public Memory in Turkey, edited by Esra Özyürek (Syracuse, NY: Syracuse University Press, 2007), 98–99; Tapper and Tapper, "Birth of the Prophet."

22. Tone Bringa, *Being Muslim the Bosnian Way: Identity and Community in a Central Bosnian Village* (Princeton, NJ: Princeton University Press, 1995), 169–71.

23. Tapper and Tapper, "Birth of the Prophet"; Bringa, *Being Muslim the Bosnian Way*; Marcus, "Equal Rites and Women in Turkey."

24. The upturned washbasin resembles the "frame drum" discussed by Doubleday, who argues that this type of drum is associated with women in the Mediterranean region since ancient times. The village women never mentioned that they once had actual drums. Veronica Doubleday, "The Frame Drum in the Middle East: Women, Musical Instruments, and Power," *Ethnomusicology* 43, no. 1 (1999): 101–34.

25. I thank Abbas Karakaya for this insight.

26. Asef Bayat, *Life as Politics: How Ordinary People Change the Middle East* (Stanford, CA: Stanford University Press, 2010), 139.

27. Rasmussen describes how youthful Tuareg (a Muslim population in Niger, West Africa) enjoy music and dance festivals but older people avoid them and instead turn to prayer. Many, she says, believe that the musical instruments young people play are inhabited by the devil. Susan Rasmussen, "Wedding of Calm and Wedding of Noise: Aging Performed and Aging Misquoted in Tuareg Rites of Passage," *Journal of Anthropological Research* 57, no. 3 (2001): 285–86.

28. Nancy Tapper and Richard Tapper, "'Thank God We're Secular!' Aspects of Fundamentalism in a Turkish Town," in *Studies in Religious Fundamentalism*, edited by Lionel Caplan (Albany: State University of New York Press Press, 1987), 59; Jenny White, *Islamist Mobilization in Turkey: A Study in Vernacular Politics* (Seattle, WA: University of Washington Press, 2002), 35.

29. Lara Deeb, "Piety Politics and the Role of a Transnational Feminist Analysis," *Journal of the Royal Anthropological Institute* 15, no. 1 (2009): S122.

30. Saba Mahmood, *Politics of Piety* (Princeton, NJ: Princeton University Press, 2005).

31. See the essays in Gaonkar's collected volume for examples of how scholars have assessed the meaning of modernity in nonwestern contexts. Dilip Parameshwar Gaonkar, ed., *Alternative Modernities* (Durham, NC: Duke University Press, 2001).

32. Nilüfer Göle, *The Forbidden Modern* (Ann Arbor: University of Michigan Press, 1996), 113.

33. Tuğal, "Appeal of Islamic Politics," 259.

34. Göle, *Forbidden Modern*, 113.

35. Lila Abu-Lughod, *Writing Women's Worlds: Bedouin Stories* (Berkeley: University of California Press, 1993), 9.

36. Michael Herzfeld, *Cultural Intimacy: Social Poetics in the Nation-State* (New York: Routledge, 1997), 1.

37. Mark Liechty, *Suitably Modern* (Princeton, NJ: Princeton University Press, 2003), 22.

38. Judith Butler, *Gender Trouble: Feminism and the Subversion of Identity* (New York: Routledge, 1990), 17.

39. James Carrier, "Occidentalism: The World Turned Upside Down," *American Ethnologist* 19, no. 2 (1992): 195–212.

40. Edward Said, *Orientalism* (New York: Vintage Books, 1978).

41. Renato Rosaldo, "Imperialist Nostalgia," *Representations* 26 (1989): 107–22.

42. Esra Özyürek, *Nostalgia for the Modern: State Secularism and Everyday Politics in Turkey* (Durham, NC: Duke University Press, 2006), 4–6.

43. Deeb, *Enchanted Modern*, 33.

44. Orhan Pamuk, *Istanbul: Memories and the City* (New York: Vintage International, 2004), 35.

45. Ibid.

46. Herzfeld, *Cultural Intimacy*, 3.

47. Hakan Yavuz, "The Assassination of Collective Memory: The Case of Turkey," *Muslim World* 89, nos. 3–4 (1999): 200.

48. Richard Pfaff, "Disengagement from Traditionalism in Turkey and Iran," *Western Political Quarterly* 16, no. 1 (1963): 95.

CHAPTER 7: SECULAR AND SPIRITUAL ROUTES TO KNOWLEDGE

1. Henry J. Rutz and Erol M. Balkan, *Reproducing Class: Education, Neoliberalism, and the Rise of the Middle Class in Istanbul* (New York: Berghahn, 2010).

2. Paul Stirling, *Turkish Village* (New York: John Wiley and Sons, 1966), 230.

3. John Renard, ed., *Tales of God's Friends* (Berkeley: University of California Press, 2009), 9.

4. Vernon James Schubel and Nurten Kiliç-Schubel, "Sari Islamail: The Beloved Disciple of Haci Betas Veli," in *Tales of God's Friends*, edited by John Renard (Berkeley: University of California Press, 2009), 147.

5. Sam Kaplan, *The Pedagogical State* (Stanford, CA: Stanford University Press, 2006), 42.

6. Feroz Ahmad, "Politics and Political Parties in Republican Turkey," in *The Cambridge History of Turkey*, vol. 4, *Turkey in the Modern World*, edited by Reşat Kasaba (Cambridge: Cambridge University Press, 2008), 229.

7. Quoted in ibid., 229.

8. Andrew Mango, *Atatürk: The Biography of the Founder of Modern Turkey* (New York: Overlook Press, 1999), 475.

9. Ibid., 476.

10. Ahmad, "Politics and Political Parties," 232.

11. Mona Hassan, "Women Preaching for the Secular State: Official Female Preachers (Bayan Vaizler) in Contemporary Turkey," *International Journal of Middle East Studies* 43, no. 3 (2011): 457.

12. Henry J. Rutz and Erol M. Balkan, *Reproducing Class*.

13. Kaplan, *Pedagogical State*, 45–46.

14. Bergama is no longer a regional center but connected to the province of Izmir. Manisa continues to be the center of its own province.

15. Ahmet Tugaç, "Indices of Modernization: Erenköy, a Case of Local Initiative," in *Turkey: Geographic and Social Perspectives*, edited by Erol Tümertekin, Peter Benedict, and Fatma Mansur (Leiden: Brill, 1974), 159.

16. Yael Navaro-Yashin, *Faces of the State: Secularism and Public Life in Turkey* (Princeton, NJ: Princeton University Press, 2002), 97; Esra Özyürek, *Nostalgia for the Modern: State Secularism and Everyday Politics in Turkey* (Durham, NC: Duke University Press, 2006), 165.

17. Jenny White, *Islamist Mobilization in Turkey: A Study in Vernacular Politics* (Seattle: University of Washington Press, 2002), 235.

18. Erisa Dautaj Şenerdem, "Headscarf Issue Needs Social Consensus, Turkish Expert Says," *Hürriyet Daily News*, October 24, 2010.

19. Jonathan Head, "Quiet End to Turkey's College Headscarf Ban," BBC, December 31, 2010, www.bbc.co.uk/news/world-europe-11880622 (last accessed January 2, 2013).

20. Daren Butler, "Turkey Lifts Headscarf Ban in Religious Schools," Reuters, November 28, 2012, www.reuters.com/article/2012/11/28/us-turkey-headscarf-idUSBRE8AR0JW20121128 (last accessed January 2, 2013).

21. White, *Islamist Mobilization*, 225.

22. Deniz Kandiyoti, "Emancipated by Unliberated? Reflections on the Turkish Case," *Feminist Studies* 13, no. 2 (1987): 328.

23. Catharina Raudvere, *The Book and the Roses* (Istanbul: Swedish Research Institute in Istanbul, 2002), 37.

24. Kaplan, *Pedagogical State*, 98; Esra Özyürek, *Nostalgia for the Modern: State Secularism and Everyday Politics in Turkey* (Durham, NC: Duke University Press, 2006), 45.

25. It is interesting to note that once, while discussing Çevriye's leadership role in the village, she noted that it was because her husband encouraged her and "gave her permission to work." All women need permission from their husbands or fathers to work. Her husband also described his supportive role, which helped Çevriye become a leader in the cooperative, but he did not emphasize how he had given her "permission."

26. Hakan Yavuz, *Islamic Political Identity in Turkey* (Oxford: Oxford University Press, 2003), 147.

CHAPTER 8: AN ENTREPRENEURIAL "NEO-TARIKAT" AND ISLAMIC EDUCATION

1. Olivier Roy, *Globalized Islam* (New York: Columbia University Press, 2004), 221.

2. Brian Silverstein, *Islam and Modernity in Turkey* (New York: Palgrave, 2011), 183.

3. Ahmet Yükleyen, *Localizing Islam in Europe* (Syracuse: Syracuse University Press, 2012), 65.

4. Jenny White, *Islamist Mobilization in Turkey: A Study in Vernacular Politics* (Seattle: University of Washington Press, 2002), 139.

5. Winnifred Fallers Sullivan, *The Impossibility of Religious Freedom* (Princeton, NJ: Princeton University Press, 2005).

6. Immigration and Refugee Board of Canada, "Treatment of Alevis by Society and Government Authorities; State Response to Mistreatment (2008–May 2012)," June 1, 2012, TUR104076.E, available at www.unhcr.org/refworld/docid/4fead9552.html (last accessed January 15, 2013).

7. Roy, *Globalized Islam*: 221–22.

8. Ibid., 222–23.

9. Ahmet Yükleyen, "Sufism and Islamic Groups in Contemporary Turkey," in *The Cambridge History of Turkey*, vol. 4, edited by Reşat Kasaba (Cambridge: Cambridge University Press, 2008), 384.

10. Ahmet Yükleyen, "Production of Mystical Islam in Europe: Religious Authorization in the Süleymanlı Sufi Community," *Contemporary Islam* 4 (2010): 269–88.

11. Banu Eligür, *The Mobilization of Political Islam in Turkey* (Cambridge: Cambridge University Press, 2010), 46.

12. Bernard Lewis, *The Emergence of Modern Turkey*, 2nd ed. (London: Oxford University Press, 1968), 407).

13. Brian Silverstein, "Sufism and Governmentality in the Late Ottoman Empire," *Comparative Studies of South Asia, Africa, and the Middle East* 29, no. 2 (2009): 171–85.

14. Eligür, *Mobilization of Political Islam in Turkey*, 47.

15. Yükleyen, "Production of Mystical Islam in Europe," 64.

16. Yükleyen, *Localizing Islam in Europe*, 383.

17. Roy, *Globalized Islam*, 222.

18. Roy refers to the Gülen movement as a neo-tarikat; ibid., 80.

19. Jeremy Walton, "Horizons and Histories of Liberal Piety: Civil Islam and Secularism in Contemporary Turkey" (Ph.D. diss., Department of Anthropology, University of Chicago, 2009), 113.

20. Berna Turam, *Between Islam and the State* (Stanford, CA: Stanford University Press, 2007), 12.

21. Fiachra Gibbons, "Turkey's Enlightenment Languishes, Like the Journalists in Its Prisons," *The Guardian*, March 13, 2012.

22. Hakan Yavuz, *Islamic Political Identity in Turkey* (Oxford: Oxford University Press, 2003), 148.

23. "Religious Communities and the State in Germany," Federal Ministry of the Interior, www.bmi.bund.de/EN/Themen/PolitikGesellschaft/KirchenReligion/StaatReligion/StaatReligion_node.html (last accessed November 16, 2012).

24. The government has granted most of the country's major religious communities "public law corporation" (PLC) status, the benefits of which include the ability to collect contributions in accordance with rules similar to tax laws, building and tax regulation privileges, and the right to offer denominational religious education in state schools. PLCs also receive funds from the country's "church tax"—between 8 and 9 percent of one's income tax that is paid to the officially recognized denomination of which an individual is a registered member. Traditions that lack a centrally organized national structure—most notably Islam—have had difficulty attaining PLC status and the benefits that come with it. Georgetown University, Berkley Center for Religion, Peace, and

World Affairs, http://berkleycenter.georgetown.edu/resources/countries/germany (last accessed November 16, 2012).

25. Yükleyen argues that the Süleymanlı are more correctly a religious community, *cemaat*, not a Sufi order. Nevertheless, their practices, as Yükleyen describes, involve engagement with mystical teachings from their founder. Yükleyen, *Localizing Islam in Europe*.

26. Yükleyen, "Production of Mystical Islam in Europe," 274.

27. Ibid., 275.

28. Yavuz, *Islamic Political Identity in Turkey*, 146.

29. Jonker writes about the early history of the Süleymancıs: "The founders of the Turkish Sufi lay communities kept their distance from these state theologians as a matter of course." Gerdien Jonker, "The Transformation of a Sufi Order into a Lay Community: The Süleymancı Movement in Germany and Beyond," in *European Muslims and the Secular State*, edited by Jocelyne Cesari and Sean McLoughlin (Burlington, VT: Ashgate Publishing, 2005), 172.

30. Yavuz, *Islamic Political Identity in Turkey*, 146.

31. Yükleyen, "Sufism and Islamic Groups," 384.

32. Eligür, *Mobilization of Political Islam in Turkey*, 57–58.

33. Kira Kosnick, *Migrant Media* (Bloomington: Indiana University Press, 2007).

34. Katherine Pratt Ewing, *Stolen Honor: Stigmatizing Muslim Men in Berlin* (Stanford, CA: Stanford University Press, 2008), 102.

35. Yükleyen, *Localizing Islam in Europe*, 27.

36. Yavuz, *Islamic Political Identity in Turkey*, 147.

37. Recall that Süleyman Tunahan studied with the Nakşibendi and branched off this group, when he founded his own.

38. Turam, *Between Islam and the State*, 49.

39. Yavuz, *Islamic Political Identity in Turkey*, 148.

40. Ibid.

41. See, for example, Leyla Neyzi, "Remembering to Forget: Sabbateanism, National Identity, and Subjectivity in Turkey," *Comparative Studies in Society and History* 44, no. 1 (2002): 137–58.

42. Yükleyen, "Production of Mystical Islam in Europe," 279.

43. Kimberly Hart, "Love by Arrangement: The Ambiguity of 'Spousal Choice' in a Turkish Village," *Journal of the Royal Anthropological Institute* 13 (2007): 345–62.

44. At the time we arrived to visit, the brother was working in the forests converting cut trees to charcoal. This had been a common occupation in the southern region of the Yuntdağ before the mountaintops were deforested about fifty years ago. As the former camel driver described, they took loads of charcoal to the cities by camel train and returned with goods to trade, such as salt, vegetables, and cloth.

45. Yükleyen, "Production of Mystical Islam in Europe," 277.

46. Ibid.

47. Cihan Tuğal, *Passive Revolution* (Stanford, CA: Stanford University Press, 2009), 1.

48. Eligür, *Mobilization of Political Islam in Turkey*, 131.

49. Barbara Wolbert, "The Visual Production of Location," *Visual Anthropology Review* 17, no. 1 (2001): 21–35.

CHAPTER 9: DEALING WITH THE SECULAR WORLD

1. Though many towns continue the practice, Kezer describes how in provincial towns in the early republic, because there were few radios, loudspeakers were connected to one radio, so that the whole town could hear national events being broadcast. Zeynep Kezer, "An Imaginable Community: The Material Culture of Nation-Building in Early Republican Turkey," *Society and Space* 27 (2009): 523–24.

2. Yeşim Arat, *Rethinking Islam and Democracy: Islamist Women in Turkish Politics* (Albany: State University of New York Press, 2005), 23; Nilüfer Göle, *The Forbidden Modern* (Ann Arbor: University of Michigan Press, 1996), 5.

3. This town has many return migrants from Germany, referred to as Alamancılar or Almancılar, so it is not that surprising that an elderly townsperson would not be astounded to see a woman who seems quasi–Turkish and quasi–foreign.

4. Sam Kaplan, *The Pedagogical State* (Stanford, CA: Stanford University Press, 2006).

5. In Turkish this would not be a gendered term, *polis*, but the implication of the conversation was that females cannot be police, though there are many policewomen in Turkey.

6. Asef Bayat, *Life as Politics: How Ordinary People Change the Middle East* (Stanford, CA: Stanford University Press, 2010), 210.

7. Clifford Geertz, *The Interpretations of Cultures* (New York: Basic Books, 1973), 448.

8. Bayat, *Life as Politics*, 210.

BIBLIOGRAPHY

Abramowitz, Morton. 1993. "Dateline Ankara: Turkey After Özal." *Foreign Policy* 91: 164–81.

Abu-Lughod, Lila. 1990. "The Romance of Resistance." *American Ethnologist* 17 (1): 41–55.

———. 1993. "Islam and the Gendered Discourses of Death." *International Journal of Middle East Studies* 25 (2): 187–205.

———. 1993. *Writing Women's Worlds: Bedouin Stories.* Berkeley: University of California Press.

Abu-Zahira, Nadia. 1988. "The Rain Rituals as Rites of Spiritual Passage." *International Journal of Middle East Studies* 20 (4): 507–29.

Adanalı, Ahmet Hadi. 2008. "The Presidency of Religious Affairs and the Principle of Secularism in Turkey." *Muslim World* 98 (April–July): 228–41.

Agrama, Hussein. 2010. "Secularism, Sovereignty, Indeterminacy: Is Egypt a Secular or Religious State?" *Comparative Studies in Society and History* 52 (3): 495–523.

Ahmad, Feroz. 2008. "Politics and Political Parties in Republican Turkey." In *The Cambridge History of Turkey*, vol. 4, *Turkey in the Modern World*, edited by Reşat Kasaba, 226–65. Cambridge: Cambridge University Press.

Akin, Erkan, and Ömer Karasapan. 1988. "Turkey's Tarikats." *Middle East Report* 153 (July–August): 16.

———. 1988. "The 'Turkish-Islamic Synthesis.'" *Middle East Report* 153 (July–August): 18.

Albertini, Tamara. 2003. "The Seductiveness of Certainty: The Destruction of Islam's Intellectual Legacy by the Fundamentalists." *Philosophy East and West* 53: 455–70.

Amad, Feroz. 1981. "Military Intervention and the Crisis in Turkey." *MERIP Reports* 93: 5–24.

———. 1984. "The Turkish Elections of 1983." *MERIP Reports* 122: 3–11.

———. 1988. "Islamic Reassertion in Turkey." *Third World Quarterly* 10 (2): 750–69.

Anatolian News Agency. "Süleymaniye Library Holds Turkey's Treasure." *Hürriyet Daily News*, May 24, 2012.

Anderson, June. 1998. *Return to Tradition.* Seattle: University of Washington Press.

Appadurai, Arjun. 1996. *Modernity at Large.* Minneapolis: University of Minnesota Press.

Arat, Yeşim. 1997. "The Project of Modernity and Women in Turkey." In *Rethinking Modernity and National Identity in Turkey*, edited by Reşat Kasaba and Sibel Bozdoğan, 95–112. Seattle: University of Washington Press.

———. 1998. "Feminists, Islamists, and Political Change in Turkey." *Political Psychology* 19 (1): 117–31.

———. 2005. *Rethinking Islam and Democracy: Islamist Women in Turkish Politics.* Albany: State University of New York Press.

Arberry, A. J., trans. 1996. *The Koran, Interpreted.* New York: Simon and Schuster.

Asad, Talal. 1993. *Genealogies of Religion.* Baltimore: Johns Hopkins University Press.

———. 2003. *Formations of the Secular: Christianity, Islam, Modernity.* Stanford, CA: Stanford University Press.

Ata, Ulvi. 2008. "The Educational Services of the PRA and Its Contribution to Religious Education in Turkey." *Muslim World* 98 (April–July): 302–12.

Atasoy, Yıldız. 2009. *Islam's Marriage with Neoliberalism: State Transformation in Turkey.* New York: Palgrave Macmillan.

Avcıoğlu, Nebahat. 2007. "Identity-as-Form: The Mosque in the West." *Cultural Analysis* 6: 91–112.

Aydın, Mehmet. 2008. "Diyanet's Global Vision." *Muslim World* 98 (April–July): 164–72.

Aydın, Mustafa. 2004. "Süleymancılık." In *Modern Türkiye'de Siyasi Düşünce: Islamcılık* (Social Thought in Modern Turkey: Islamism), edited by Yaşin Aktay, 308–22. Istanbul: Iletişim.

Baer, Marc. 2004. "The Double Bind of Race and Religion: The Conversion of the Dönme to Turkish Secular Nationalism." *Comparative Studies in Society and History* 46 (4): 682–708.

———. 2004. "The Great Fire of 1660 and the Islamization of Christian and Jewish Space in Istanbul." *International Journal of Middle East Studies* 36 (2): 159–81.

Bardakoğlu, Ali. 2008. "The Structure, Mission, and Social Function of the Presidency of Religious Affairs (PRA)." *Muslim World* 98 (April–July): 173–81.

Başgöz, Ilhan. 1967. "Dream Motif in Turkish Folk Stories and Shamanistic Initiation." *Asian Folklore Studies* 26 (1): 1–18.

———. 1967. "Rain-Making Ceremonies in Turkey and Seasonal Festivals." *Journal of the American Oriental Society* 87 (3): 304–6.

———. 1978. "Folklore Studies and Nationalism in Turkey." In *Folklore, Nationalism, and Politics*, edited by Felix Oinas, 123–37. Bloomington, IN: Slavica Publishers.

Bayat, Asef. 2005. "Islamism and Social Movement Theory." *Third World Quarterly* 26 (6): 891–908.

———. 2007. "Islamism and the Politics of Fun." *Public Culture* 19 (3): 433–59.

———. 2010. *Life as Politics: How Ordinary People Change the Middle East.* Stanford, CA: Stanford University Press.

BBC. 2009. "Vatican and Muslims Condemn Swiss Minaret Ban." BBC, November 30, http://news.bbc.co.uk/go/pr/fr/-/2/hi/europe/8385893.stm (last accessed November 16, 2012).

Bellah, Robert. 1967. "Civil Religion in America." *Daedalus* 96 (1): 1–21.

Beller-Hann, Ildiko, and Chris Hann. 2001. *Turkish Region.* Santa Fe: School of American Research Press.

Bent, Theodore. 1891. "The Yourouks of Asia Minor." *Journal of the Anthropological Institute of Great Britain and Ireland* 20: 269–76.

Benthall, Jonathan. 1999. "Financial Worship: The Quranic Injunction to Almsgiving." *Journal of the Royal Anthropological Institute* 5 (1): 27–42.

Benton, Cathy. 1996. "Many Contradictions: Women and Islamists in Turkey." *Muslim World* 86 (2): 106–29.

Berik, Günseli. 1987. *Women Carpet Weavers in Rural Turkey*. Geneva: International Labour Office.

Berkes, Kirby Fay. 1960. "The Village Institute Movement of Turkey: An Educational Mobilization for Social Change." Ph.D. diss., Columbia Teachers College, Columbia University.

Berkes, Niyazi. 1957. "Historical Background of Turkish Secularism." In *Islam and the West*, edited by Richard Frye, 41–68. The Hague: Mouton.

———. 1964. *The Development of Secularism in Turkey*. Montreal: McGill University Press.

———. 1974. "The Two Facets of the Kemalist Revolution." *Muslim World* 64: 292–307.

Bernal, Victoria. 1994. "Gender, Culture, and Capitalism: Women and the Remaking of Islamic 'Tradition' in a Sudanese Village." *Comparative Studies in Society and History* 36 (1): 36–67.

Bilefsky, Dan. 2009. "Frustrated with the West: Turks Revel in Empire Lost." *New York Times*, December 5, 2009.

Bilsel, S. M. Can. 2007. "'Our Anatolia': Organicism and the Making of Humanist Culture in Turkey." *Muqarnas* 24: 223–41.

Bonner, Michael, Mine Ener, and Amy Singer. 2003. *Poverty and Charity in Middle Eastern Contexts*. Albany: State University of New York Press.

Borneman, John. 1996. "Until Death Do Us Part: Marriage/Death in Anthropological Discourse." *American Ethnologist* 23 (2): 215–35.

Bowen, John. 1992. "On Scriptural Essentialism and Ritual Variation: Muslim Sacrifice in Sumatra and Morocco." *American Ethnologist* 19 (4): 656–71.

Bowie, Katherine. 1998. "The Alchemy of Charity." *American Anthropologist* 100 (2): 469–81.

Bozarslan, Hamit. "Kurds and the Turkish State." In *The Cambridge History of Turkey*, vol. 4, *Turkey in the Modern World*, edited by Reşat Kasaba, 333–56. Cambridge: Cambridge University Press.

Bozdoğan, Sibel. 2001. *Modernism and Nation Building*. Seattle: University of Washington Press.

———. 2007. "Reading Ottoman Architecture Through Modernist Lenses: Nationalist Historiography and the 'New' Architecture in the Early Republic." *Muqarnas* 24: 199–221.

Bozdoğan, Sibel, and Reşat Kasaba. 1997. *Rethinking Modernity and National Identity in Turkey*. Seattle: University of Washington Press.

Bringa, Tone. 1995. *Being Muslim the Bosnian Way: Identity and Community in a Central Bosnian Village*. Princeton, NJ: Princeton University Press.

Brink-Danan, Marcy. 2012. *Jewish Life in 21st-Century Turkey*. Bloomington: Indiana University Press.

Brockett, Gavin. 2011. *How Happy to Call Oneself a Turk: Provincial Newspapers and the Negotiation of a Muslim National Identity*. Austin: University of Texas Press.

Butler, Daren. 2012. "Turkey Lifts Headscarf Ban in Religious Schools." Reuters, November 28, www.reuters.com/article/2012/11/28/us-turkey-headscarf-idUSBRE8AR 0JW20121128 (last accessed January 2, 2013).

Butler, Judith. 1990. *Gender Trouble: Feminism and the Subversion of Identity*. New York: Routledge.

Çağatay, Neşet. 1968. "The Tradition of Mavlid Recitations in Islam Particularly in Turkey." *Studia Islamica* 28: 127–33.

Carrier, James. 1992. "Occidentalism: The World Turned Upside Down." *American Ethnologist* 19 (2): 195–212.

Casanova, Jose. 1994. *Public Religions in the Modern World*. Chicago: University of Chicago Press.

Cesari, Jocelyne, and Sean McLoughlin. 2005. *European Muslims and the Secular State*. Burlington, VT: Ashgate Publishers.

Çınar, Alev. 2001. "National History as a Contested Site: The Conquest of Istanbul and Islamist Negotiations of the Nation." *Comparative Studies in Society and History* 43 (2): 364–91.

Çizre, Ümit. 2008. "Ideology, Context, and Interest: The Turkish Military." In *The Cambridge History of Turkey*, vol. 4, *Turkey in the Modern World*, edited by Reşat Kasaba, 301–32. Cambridge: Cambridge University Press.

Cohen, Jeffrey 1999. *Cooperation and Community*. Austin: University of Texas Press.

Cook, Michael. 2003. *Forbidding Wrong in Islam*. Cambridge: Cambridge University Press.

Deeb, Lara. 2006. *An Enchanted Modern*. Princeton, NJ: Princeton University Press.

———. 2009. "Piety Politics and the Role of a Transnational Feminist Analysis." *Journal of the Royal Anthropological Institute* 15 (1): S112–S126.

Delaney, Carol. 1991. *The Seed and the Soil*. Berkeley: University of California Press.

Denny, Walter. 1982. "Atatürk and Political Art in Turkey." *Turkish Studies Association Bulletin* 6 (2): 17–23.

Dere, Ali. 2008. "The PRA of Turkey: The Emergence, Evolution and Perception of Its Religious Services Outside of Turkey." *Muslim World* 98 (April–July): 291–301.

Deringil, Selim. 1993. "The Invention of Tradition as Public Image in the Late Ottoman Empire, 1808–1908." *Society for Comparative Study of Society and History* 35 (1): 3–29.

Doubleday, Veronica. 1999. "The Frame Drum in the Middle East: Women, Musical Instruments, and Power." *Ethnomusicology* 43 (1): 101–34.

Dressler, Markus. 2008. "Religio-Secular Metamorphoses: The Re-making of Turkish Alevism." *Journal of the American Academy of Religion* 76 (2): 280–311.

Ehlers, Tracy Bachrach. 2000. *Silent Looms*. Austin: University of Texas Press.

Eickelman, Dale F., and James Piscatori. 1996. *Muslim Politics*. Princeton, NJ: Princeton University Press.

Eligür, Banu. 2010. *The Mobilization of Political Islam in Turkey*. Cambridge: Cambridge University Press.

Er, Izzet. 2008. "Religious Services of the PRA." *Muslim World* 98 (April–July): 271–81.

Erdem, Gazi. 2008. "Religious Services in Turkey: From the Office of the Şeyhülislam to the Diyanet." *Muslim World* 98 (April–July): 199–215.

Erşahin, Seyfettin. 2008. "The Ottoman Foundation of the Turkish Republic's Diyanet: Ziya Gökalp's Diyanet Ishlari Nazarati." *Muslim World* 98 (April–July): 182–98.

Esposito, John L. 1991. *Islam: The Straight Path*. New York: Oxford University Press.

Ewing, Katherine Pratt. 2008. *Stolen Honor: Stigmatizing Muslim Men in Berlin*. Stanford, CA: Stanford University Press.

Fader, Ayala. 2009. *Mitzvah Girls*. Princeton, NJ: Princeton University Press.

Gaonkar, Dilip Parameshwar, ed. 2001. *Alternative Modernities*. Durham, NC: Duke University Press.

Geertz, Clifford. *The Interpretation of Cultures*. New York: Basic Books, 1973.

Ghodsee, Kristen. 2010. *Muslim Lives in Eastern Europe*. Princeton, NJ: Princeton University Press.

Gibbons, Fiachra. 2012. "Turkey's Enlightenment Languishes, Like the Journalists in Its Prisons." *The Guardian*, March 13.

Giddens, Anthony. 1900. *The Consequences of Modernity*. Stanford, CA: Stanford University Press.

Gökalp, Ziya. 1959. *Turkish Nationalism and Western Civilization*. Translated by Niyazi Berkes. London: George Allen and Unwin.

Göle, Nilüfer. 1996. *The Forbidden Modern*. Ann Arbor: University of Michigan Press.

———. 1997. "Secularism and Islamism in Turkey: The Making of Elites and Counter Elites." *Middle East Journal* 51 (10): 46–58.

Görmez, Mehmet. 2008. "The Status of the Presidency of Religious Affairs in the Turkish Constitution and Its Execution." *Muslim World* 98 (April–July): 242–248.

Gözaydın, Iştar. 2006. "A Religious Administration to Secure Secularism." *Marburg Journal of Religion* 11 (1): 1–8.

———. 2008. "Diyanet and Politics." *Muslim World* 98 (April–July): 216–27.

Greenhouse, Carol. 1996. *A Moment's Notice: Time Politics Across Cultures*. Ithaca, NY: Cornell University Press.

Gulalp, Haldun. 1995. "Islamist Party Poised for National Power in Turkey." *Middle East Report* 194–95: 54–56.

Günay, Reha. 2006. *A Guide to the Works of Sinan the Architect in Istanbul*. Istanbul: Yam Yayın.

Gürsel, Zeynep. *Coffee Futures*. Watertown, MA: Documentary Educational Resources, 2009.

Haberman, Clyde. 2011. "Putting 'Un-American' in Perspective." *New York Times*, March 21, 2011.

Hann, Chris. 2000. "Problem with the (De)Privatization of Religion." *Anthropology Today* 16 (6): 14–20.

Hart, Kimberly. 1999. "Images and Aftermaths: The Use and Contextualization of

Atatürk Imagery in Political Debates in Turkey." *PoLar: Political and Legal Anthropology Review* 22 (1): 66–84.

———. 2007. "Weaving Modernity, Commercializing Carpets: Collective Memory and Contested Tradition in Örselli Village." In *The Politics of Public Memory in Turkey*, edited by Esra Özyürek, 16–39. Syracuse, NY: Syracuse University Press.

———. 2007. "Love by Arrangement: The Ambiguity of 'Spousal Choice' in a Turkish Village." *Journal of the Royal Anthropological Institute* 13: 345–62.

———. 2009. "Conflicts and Conundrums in a Women's Cooperative in Western Turkey." *Hagar* 9 (1): 25–42.

———. 2010. "The Economy and Morality of Elopement in Rural Western Turkey." *Ethnologia Europaea* 40 (1): 58–76.

———. 2011. "The Decline of a Cooperative." In *Cross-Stitching Textile Economies with Value, Sanctity, and Transnationalism*, edited by Patricia A. McAnany and Walter Little, 245–62. New York: AltaMira.

———. 2011. "Modernist Desires Among Recent Migrants in Western Turkey." *Nordic Journal of Migration Research* 2 (2): 34–41.

Hassan, Mona. 2011. "Reshaping Religious Authority in Contemporary Turkey: State-Sponsored Female Preachers." In *Women, Leadership, and Mosques: Changes in Contemporary Islamic Authority*, edited by Hilary Kalmbach and Masooda Bano, 85–103. Leiden: Brill.

———. 2011. "Women at the Intersection of Contemporary Turkish Politics, Religion, and Education: The Unexpected Path to Becoming a State-Sponsored Female Preacher." *Comparative Islamic Studies* 5 (1): 111–30.

———. 2011. "Women Preaching for the Secular State: Official Female Preachers (Bayan Vaizler) in Contemporary Turkey." *International Journal of Middle East Studies* 43 (3): 451–73.

Hassan, Perween. 1993. "The Footprint of the Prophet." *Muqarnas* 10: 335–43.

Head, Jonathan. 2010. "Quiet End to Turkey's College Headscarf Ban." BBC, December 31, www.bbc.co.uk/news/world-europe-11880622 (last accessed January 2, 2013).

Hegland, Mary Elaine. 1995. "Shi'a Women of Northwest Pakistan and Agency Through Practice: Ritual, Resistance, and Resilience." *PoLar: Political and Legal Anthropology Review* 18 (2): 65–79.

———. 1998. "Flagellation and Fundamentalism: (Trans)forming Meaning, Identity, and Gender Through Pakistani Women's Rituals of Mourning." *American Ethnologist* 25 (2): 240–66.

Helvacıoğlu, Banu. 1996. "'Allahu Ekber,' We Are Turks: Yearning for a Different Homecoming at the Periphery of Europe." *Third World Quarterly* 17 (3): 503–23.

Herzfeld, Michael. 1981. "Performative Categories and Symbols of Passage in Rural Greece." *Journal of American Folklore* 94 (371): 44–57.

———. 1985. *The Poetics of Manhood*. Princeton, NJ: Princeton University Press.

———. 1997. *Cultural Intimacy: Social Poetics in the Nation-State*. New York: Routledge.

Hobsbawn, Eric, and Terence Ranger, eds. 1983. *The Invention of Tradition*. Cambridge: Cambridge University Press.

Holy, Ladislav. 1988. "Gender and Ritual in an Islamic Society: The Berti of Darfur." *Man*, n.s., 23 (3): 469–87.

Ilcan, Suzan 1994. "Marriage Regulation and the Rhetoric of Alliance in Northwestern Turkey." *Ethnology* 33 (4): 273–96.

———. 1994. "Peasant Struggles and Social Change: Migration, Households, and Gender in a Rural Turkish Society." *International Migration Review* 28 (3): 554–77.

———. 1999. "Social Spaces and the Micropolitics of Differentiation: An Example from Northwestern Turkey." *Ethnology* 38 (3): 243–56.

Immigration and Refugee Board of Canada. 2012. "Treatment of Alevis by Society and Government Authorities; State Response to Mistreatment (2008–May 2012)," June 1, TUR104076.E, www.unhcr.org/refworld/docid/4fead9552.html (last accessed January 15, 2013).

Inalcık, Halil. 1986. "The Yürüks: Their Origins, Expansion, and Economic Role." In *Oriental Carpet and Textile Studies*, vol. 2, edited by Robert Pinner and Walter B. Denny, 39–65. London: Hali Publications.

International Strategic Research Organization. 2011. "Turkish President Approves Laws on Paid Military Service and Match-Fixing Penalties." *Journal of Turkish Weekly*, December 14, www.turkishweekly.net/news/127959/turkish-president-approves-laws-on-paid-military-service-and-match-fixing-penalties.html (last accessed January 15, 2013).

Işik, Damla. 2007. "Woven Assemblages: Globalization, Gender, Labor, and Authenticity in Turkey's Carpet Industry." Ph.D. diss., Department of Anthropology, University of Arizona, Tucson.

———. 2008. "On Sabir and Agency." *International Feminist Journal of Politics* 10 (4): 518–41.

Jacobson, Abigail. 2011. *From Empire to Empire*. Syracuse, NY: Syracuse University Press.

Jenkner, Carolin. "Go-Ahead for Germany's Biggest Mosque." *Der Spiegel International*, August 29, 2008.

Jonker, Gerdien. 2005. "The Mevlana Mosque in Berlin-Kreuzberg: An Unsolved Conflict." *Journal of Ethnic and Migration Studies* 31 (6): 1067–81.

———. 2005. "The Transformation of a Sufi Order into a Lay Community: The Süleymancı Movement in Germany and Beyond." In *European Muslims and the Secular State*, edited by Jocelyne Cesari and Sean McLoughlin, 113–28. Burlington, VT: Ashgate Publishing.

Kaczmarek, Michael. 2007. "The Mosque Controversy." Euro-Topics, owned by the Federal Agency for Civic Education (Bundeszentrale für politische Bildung), September 27, www.eurotopics.net/en/home/presseschau/archiv/magazin/kultur-verteilerseite-neu/moscheebauten_2007_09/debatte_moscheebauten_2007_09 (last accessed January 5, 2013).

Kadioğlu, Ayşe. 1994. "Women's Subordination in Turkey: Is Islam Really the Villain?" *Middle East Journal* 48 (4): 645–60.

———. 1996. "The Paradox of Turkish Nationalism and the Construction of Official Identity." *Middle Eastern Studies* 32 (2): 177–94.

———. 1998. "Republican Epistemology and Islamic Discourses in Turkey in the 1990s." *Muslim World* 88 (1): 1–21.

———. 2005. "Civil Society, Islam, and Democracy in Turkey: A Study of Three Islamic Non-Governmental Organizations." *Muslim World* 95: 23–41.

———. 2010. "The Pathologies of Turkish Republican Laicism." *Philosophy and Social Criticism* 36 (3–4): 489–504.

Kandiyoti, Deniz. 1974. "Some Social-Psychological Dimensions of Social Change in a Turkish Village." *British Journal of Sociology* 25 (1): 47–62.

———. 1987. "Emancipated by Unliberated? Reflections on the Turkish Case." *Feminist Studies* 13 (2): 317–38.

———. 1988. "Bargaining with Patriarchy." *Gender and Society* 2 (3): 274–90.

Kaplan, Sam. 2002. "Din-u Devlet All Over Again? The Politics of Military Secularism and Religious Militarism in Turkey Following the 1980 Coup." *International Journal of Middle East Studies* 34 (1): 113–27.

———. 2005. "Religious Nationalism: A Textbook Case from Turkey." *Comparative Studies of South Asia, Africa, and the Middle East* 25 (3): 665–76.

———. 2006. *The Pedagogical State*. Stanford, CA: Stanford University Press.

Kara Pilehvarian, Nuran, Nur Urfalıoğlu, and Lütfi Yazıcıoğlu. 2004. *Fountains in Ottoman Istanbul*. Istanbul: Yapı Yayın.

Karaman, Fikret. 2008. "The Status and Function of the PRA in the Turkish Republic." *Muslim World* 98 (April–July): 282–90.

Karaomerlioğlu, Asim. 1998. "The People's Houses and the Cult of the Peasant in Turkey." *Middle Eastern Studies* 34 (4): 67–91.

———. 1998. "The Village Institutes Experience in Turkey." *British Journal of Middle Eastern Studies* 25 (1): 47–73.

Karpat, Kemal. 1976. *The Gecekondu: Rural Migration and Urbanization*. Cambridge: Cambridge University Press.

Kasaba, Reşat, ed. 2008. *The Cambridge History of Turkey*, vol. 4, *Turkey in the Modern World*. Cambridge: Cambridge University Press.

———. 2009. *A Moveable Empire: Ottoman Nomads, Migrants, and Refugees*. Seattle: University of Washington Press.

Kemal, Ahmet. 1984. "Military Rule and the Future of Democracy in Turkey." *MERIP Reports* 122: 12–15.

Kezer, Zeynep. 1998. "Contesting Urban Space in Early Republican Ankara." *Journal of Architectural Education* 52 (1): 11–19.

———. 2000. "Familiar Things in Strange Places: Ankara's Ethnography Museum and the Legacy of Islam in Republican Turkey." *Perspectives on Vernacular Architecture* 8: 101–16.

———. 2008. "Molding the Republican Generation: Children and the Didactic Uses of Urban Space in Early Republican Turkey." In *Designing Modern Childhoods: History, Space, and the Material Culture of Children*, edited by Marta Gutman and Ning de Coninck-Smith, 128–51. New Brunswick, NJ: Rutgers University Press.

———. 2009. "An Imaginable Community: The Material Culture of Nation-Building in Early Republican Turkey." *Society and Space* 27 (3): 508–30.

Kirişci, Kemal. 2008. "Migration and Turkey: The Dynamics of State, Society, and Politics." In *The Cambridge History of Turkey*, vol. 4, *Turkey in the Modern World*, edited by Reşat Kasaba, 175–98. Cambridge: Cambridge University Press.

Kosnick, Kira. 2007. *Migrant Media*. Bloomington: Indiana University Press.

Kresse, Kai. 2009. "Muslim Politics in Postcolonial Kenya." *Journal of the Royal Anthropological Institute* 15 (1): S76–S94.

Krstic, Tijana. 2009. "Illuminated by the Light of Islam and the Glory of the Ottoman Sultanate: Self-Narratives of Conversion to Islam in the Age of Confessionalism." *Comparative Studies* 51 (1): 35–63.

Kuban, Doğan. 1987. "The Style of Sinan's Domed Structures." *Muqarnas* 4: 72–97.

Kucukcan, Talip. 2010. "Sacralization of the State and Secular Nationalism: Foundations of Civil Religion in Turkey." *George Washington International Law Review* 41 (4): 963–83.

Kurkcu, Ertuğrul. 1996. "The Crisis of the Turkish State." *Middle East Report* 199: 2–7.

Kuru, Ahmet. 2009. *Secularism and State Policies Toward Religion*. Cambridge: Cambridge University Press.

Kutlu, Sönmez. 2008. "The Presidency of Religious Affairs' Relationship with Religious Groups (Sects/Sufi Orders) in Turkey." *Muslim World* 98 (April–July): 249–63.

Laborde, Cecile. 2006. "Female Autonomy, Education, and the Hijab." *Critical Review of International Social and Political Philosophy* 9 (3): 351–77.

Lewis, Bernard. 1968. *The Emergence of Modern Turkey*. 2nd ed. London: Oxford University Press.

Liechty, Mark. 2003. *Suitably Modern*. Princeton, NJ: Princeton University Press.

Limbert, Mandana. 2008. "The Sacred Date: Gifts of God in an Omani Town." *Ethnos* 73: 361–76.

———. 2010. *In the Time of Oil: Piety, Memory, and Social Life in an Omani Town*. Stanford, CA: Stanford University Press.

Loeffler, Reinhold. 1988. *Islam in Practice: Religious Belief in a Persian Village*. Albany: State University of New York Press.

Mahmood, Saba. 2001. "Feminist Theory, Embodiment, and the Docile Agent: Some Reflections on the Egyptian Islamic Revival." *Cultural Anthropology* 16: 202–36.

———. 2001. "Rehearsed Spontaneity and the Conventionality of Ritual: Disciplines of Salat." *American Ethnologist* 28 (4): 827–53.

———. 2005. *Politics of Piety*. Princeton, NJ: Princeton University Press.

Mandel, Ruth. 2008. *Cosmopolitan Anxieties: Turkish Challenges to Citizenship and Belonging in Germany*. Durham, NC: Duke University Press.

Mango, Andrew. 1999. *Atatürk: The Biography of the Founder of Modern Turkey*. New York: Overlook Press.

Marcus, Julie. 1987. "Equal Rites and Women in Turkey." *Mankind* 17 (2): 120–28.

Mardin, Şerif. 1971. "Ideology and Religion in the Turkish Revolution." *International Journal of Middle East Studies* 2: 197–211.

———. 1982. "Turkey: Islam and Westernization." In *Religions and Societies: Asia and the Middle East*, edited by Carlo Caldarola, 171–98. New York: Mouton Publishers.

———. 1983. "Religion and Politics in Modern Turkey." In *Islam in the Political Process*, edited by James Piscatori, 138–59. Cambridge: Cambridge University Press.

———. 2006. *Religion, Society, and Modernity in Turkey*. Syracuse, NY: Syracuse University Press.

Margulies, Ronnie, and Ergin Yıldızoğlu. 1988. "The Political Uses of Islam in Turkey." *Middle East Journal* 153: 12–17, 50.

Marsden, Magnus. 2005. *Living Islam*. Cambridge: Cambridge University Press.

———. 2007. "Women, Politics, and Islamism in Northern Pakistan." *Modern Asian Studies* 422–23: 405–29.

Mas, Ruth. 2006. "Compelling the Muslim Subject: Memory as Post-Colonial Violence and the Public Performativity of 'Secular and Cultural Islam.'" *Muslim World* 96: 585–616.

Maurer, Bill 2005. *Mutual Life, Limited*. Princeton, NJ: Princeton University Press.

Mauss, Marcel. 1990. *The Gift*. Translated by W. D. Halls. New York: W. W. Norton.

Meeker, Michael. 2002. *A Nation of Empire: The Ottoman Legacy of Turkish Modernity*. Berkeley: University of California Press.

Melikoff, Irene. 1996. "From God of Heaven to King of Men: Popular Islam Among Turkish tribes from Central Asia to Anatolia." *Religion, State, and Society* 24 (2–3): 133–38.

Mepham, John. 1987. "Turkey: Reading the Small Print." *Middle East Report* 149: 19–25.

Mittermaier, Amira. 2011. *Dreams That Matter: Egyptian Landscapes of the Imagination*. Berkeley: University of California Press.

Mueggler, Erik. 2001. *The Age of Wild Ghosts: Memory, Violence, and Place in Southwest China*. Berkeley: University of California Press.

Navaro-Yashin, Yael. 2002. *Faces of the State: Secularism and Public Life in Turkey*. Princeton, NJ: Princeton University Press.

Necipoğlu-Kafadar, Gülru. 1985. "The Süleymaniye Complex in Istanbul: An Interpretation." *Muqarnas* 3: 92–117.

———. [*As* Necipoğlu, Gülru.] 2007. "Creation of a National Genius: Sinan and the Historiography of 'Classical' Ottoman Architecture." *Muqarnas* 24: 142–83.

Nelson, Cynthia. 1974. "Public and Private Politics: Women in the Middle Eastern World." *American Ethnologist* 1 (3): 551–63.

Neyzi, Leyla. 2001. "Object or Subject? The Paradox of 'Youth' in Turkey." *International Journal of Middle East Studies* 33 (3): 411–32.

———. 2002. "Remembering to Forget: Sabbateanism, National Identity, and Subjectivity in Turkey." *Comparative Studies in Society and History* 44 (1): 137–58.

———. 2003. "Trauma, Narrative, and Silence: The Military Journal of a Jewish 'Soldier' in Turkey During the Greco-Turkish War." *Turcica* 35: 291–313.

Nora, Pierre. 1989. "Between Memory and History: Les Lieux de Memoire." *Representations* 26: 7–24.

Öktem, Niyazi. 2002. "Religion in Turkey." *Brigham Young University Law Review* 2: 371–403.

Ökten, Nazli. 2007. "An Endless Death and an Eternal Mourning." In *The Politics of Public Memory in Turkey*, edited by Esra Özyürek, 95–113. Syracuse, NY: Syracuse University Press.

Okumuş, Ejder. 2008. "Turkey-Religiosity and the PRA." *Muslim World* 98 (April–July): 345–62.

Olson, Emelie. 1985. "Muslim Identity and Secularism in Contemporary Turkey: 'The Headscarf Dispute.'" *Anthropological Quarterly* 58 (4): 161–71.

———. 1994. "The Use of Religious Symbol Systems and Ritual in Turkey: Women's Activities at Muslim Saints' Shrines." *Muslim World* 84 (2–3): 202–16.

Öncü, Ayşe. 1995. "Packaging Islam: Cultural Politics on the Landscape of Turkish Commercial Television." *Public Culture* 8: 51–71.

Ousterhout, Robert. 1995. "Ethnic Identity and Cultural Appropriation in Early Ottoman Architecture." *Muqarnas* 12: 48–62.

Özçakmak, Şükran, and Gürkan Akgüneş. 2006. "Gerçek sahibi tarikatlar" (The Real Owners Are Tarikats). *Milliyet*, September 13, 2006.

Öztürkmen, Arzu. 1994. "The Role of People's Houses in the Making of National Culture in Turkey." *New Perspectives on Turkey* 11: 159–81.

Özyürek, Esra. 2006. *Nostalgia for the Modern: State Secularism and Everyday Politics in Turkey*. Durham, NC: Duke University Press.

———. 2007. "The Politics of Public Memory." In *The Politics of Public Memory in Turkey*, edited by Esra Özyürek, 114–37. Syracuse, NY: Syracuse University Press.

———, ed. 2007. *The Politics of Public Memory in Turkey*. Syracuse, NY: Syracuse University Press.

———. 2009. "Convert Alert." *Comparative Studies in Society and History* 51 (1): 91–116.

Pak, Soon-Yong. 2004. "Articulating the Boundary Between Secularism and Islamism: The Imam-Hatib Schools of Turkey." *Anthropology and Education Quarterly* 35 (3): 324–44.

———. 2004. "Cultural Politics and Vocational Religious Education: The Case of Turkey." *Comparative Education* 40 (3): 321–41.

Pamuk, Orhan. 2004. *Istanbul: Memories and the City*. New York: Vintage International.

Pamuk, Şevket. 2008. "Economic Change in Twentieth-Century Turkey." In *The Cambridge History of Turkey*, vol. 4, *Turkey in the Modern World*, edited by Reşat Kasaba, 266–300. Cambridge: Cambridge University Press.

Parla, Ayşe. 2001. "The 'Honor' of the State: Virginity Examinations in Turkey." *Feminist Studies* 27 (1): 65–88.

Parla, Taha, and Andrew Davison. 2008. "Secularism and Laicism in Turkey." In *Secularisms*, edited by Janet Jakobsen and Ann Pellegrini, 58–75. Durham, NC: Duke University Press.

Paxson, Margaret. 2005. *Solovyovo: The Story of Memory in a Russian Village*. Washington, DC, and Bloomington: Woodrow Wilson Center Press and Indiana University Press.

Peters, F. E. 1994. *A Reader on Classical Islam*. Princeton, NJ: Princeton University Press.

Pfaff, Richard. 1963. "Disengagement from Traditionalism in Turkey and Iran." *Western Political Quarterly* 16 (1): 79–98.

Pigg, Stacey. 1992. "Inventing Social Categories Through Place: Social Representation and Development in Nepal." *Comparative Studies in Society and History* 34 (3): 491–513.

———. 1996. "The Credible and the Credulous: The Question of 'Villagers' Beliefs' in Nepal." *Cultural Anthropology* 11 (2): 160–201.

Rasmussen, Susan. 2001. "Wedding of Calm and Wedding of Noise: Aging Performed and Aging Misquoted in Tuareg Rites of Passage." *Journal of Anthropological Research* 57 (3): 277–303.

Raudvere, Catharina. 2002. *The Book and the Roses*. Istanbul: Swedish Research Institute in Istanbul.

Reed, Howard. 1953. "A New Force at Work in Democratic Turkey." *Middle East Journal* 7 (1): 33–44.

———. 1954. "Revival of Islam in Secular Turkey." *Middle East Journal* 8 (3): 33–44.

———. 1955. "Turkey's New Imam-Hatip Schools." *Die Welt des Islams*, n.s., 4 (2–3): 150–63.

Renard, John, ed. 2009. *Tales of God's Friends*. Berkeley: University of California Press.

Rosaldo, Renato. 1989. "Imperialist Nostalgia." *Representations* 26: 107–22.

Roy, Olivier. 2004. *Globalized Islam*. New York: Columbia University Press.

Rudnyckyj, Daromir. 2009. "Market Islam in Indonesia." *Journal of the Royal Anthropological Institute* 15 (1): S183–S201.

———. 2009. "Spiritual Economies: Islam and Neoliberalism in Contemporary Indonesia." *Cultural Anthropology* 24 (1): 104–41.

Rutz, Henry. 1991. "The Rise and Demise of Imam-Hatib Schools: Discourses of Islamic Belonging and Denial in the Construction of Turkish Civic Culture." *PoLar: Political and Legal Anthropology Review* 22 (2): 93–103.

Rutz, Henry J., and Erol M. Balkan. 2010. *Reproducing Class: Education, Neoliberalism, and the Rise of the Middle Class in Istanbul*. New York: Berghahn.

Said, Edward. 1978. *Orientalism*. New York: Vintage Books.

Sakkalioğlu, Ümit Cizre. 1996. "Parameters and Strategies of Islam-State Interaction in Republican Turkey." *International Journal of Middle East Studies* 28 (2): 231–51.

———. 1997. "The Anatomy of the Turkish Military's Political Autonomy." *Comparative Politics* 29 (2): 151–66.

Salt, Jeremy. 1995. "Nationalism and the Rise of Muslim Sentiment in Turkey." *Middle Eastern Studies* 31 (1): 13–27.

Salvatore, Armando. 2004. "Making Public Space: Opportunities and Limits of Collective Action Among Muslims in Europe." *Journal of Ethnic and Migration Studies* 30 (5): 1013–31.

———. 2005. "The Euro-Islamic Roots of Secularity: A Difficult Equation." *Asian Journal of Social Science* 33 (3): 412–37.

———. 2009. "Secular Formations and Public Spheres in a Transcultural Perspective." *Journal of Intercultural Studies* 30 (3): 285–301.

Schein, Louisa. 1999. "Performing Modernity." *Cultural Anthropology* 14 (3): 361–95.

Schielke, Samuli. 2003. "Habitus of the Authentic, Order of the Rational: Contesting

Saints' Festivals in Contemporary Egypt." *Critique: Critical Middle Eastern Studies* 12 (2): 155–72.

——. 2008. "Boredom and Despair in Rural Egypt." *Contemporary Islam* 2: 251–70.

——. 2008. "Policing Ambiguity: Muslim Saints—Day Festivals and the Moral Geography of Public Space in Egypt." *American Ethnologist* 35 (4): 539–52.

——. 2009. "Being Good in Ramadan: Ambivalence, Fragmentation, and the Moral Self in the Lives of Young Egyptians." *Journal of the Royal Anthropological Institute* 15 (1): S24–S40.

Schimmel, Annemarie. 1992. *Islam: An Introduction*. New York: State University of New York Press.

Schöller, Marco. 2004. *The Living and the Dead in Islam*. Vol. 2. Wiesbaden: Harrassowitz Verlag.

Schubel, Vernon James, and Nurten Kiliç-Schubel. 2009. "Sari Islamail: The Beloved Disciple of Haci Betas Veli." In *Tales of God's Friends*, edited by John Renard, 145–49. Berkeley: University of California Press.

Schultz, Dorothea. 2008. "(Re)Turning to Proper Muslim Practice: Islamic Moral Renewal and Women's Conflicting Assertions of Sunni Identity in Urban Mali." *Africa Today* 54 (4): 21–43.

Scott, James C. 1985. *Weapons of the Weak*. New Haven, CT: Yale University Press.

Scott, Joan Wallach. 2007. *The Politics of the Veil*. Princeton, NJ: Princeton University Press.

Şenerdem, Erisa Dautaj. "Headscarf Issue Needs Social Consensus, Turkish Expert Says." *Hürriyet Daily News*. October 24, 2010.

Shahrani, Nazif. 2002. *The Kirghiz and Wakhi of Afghanistan*. Seattle: University of Washington Press.

Shakman Hurd, Elizabeth. 2008. *The Politics of Secularism in International Relations*. Princeton, NJ: Princeton University Press.

Shankland, David. 1999. "Integrating the Rural: Gellner and the Study of Anatolia." *Middle Eastern Studies* 35 (2): 132–49.

——. 2003. *The Alevis in Turkey*. New York: Routledge.

Shively, Kim. 2008. "Taming Islam: Studying Religion in Secular Turkey." *Anthropological Quarterly* 81 (3): 683–711.

Silverstein, Brian. 2003. "Islam and Modernity in Turkey." *Anthropological Quarterly* 76 (3): 497–517.

——. 2005. "Islamist Critique in Modern Turkey: Hermeneutics, Tradition, Genealogy." *Comparative Studies in Society and History* 47 (1): 134–60.

——. 2008. "Disciplines of Presence in Modern Turkey: Discourse, Companionship, and the Mass Mediation of Islamic Practice." *Cultural Anthropology* 23 (1): 118–53.

——. 2009. "Sufism and Governmentality in the Late Ottoman Empire." *Comparative Studies of South Asia, Africa, and the Middle East* 29 (2): 171–85.

——. 2011. *Islam and Modernity in Turkey*. New York: Palgrave.

Şimşek, Sefa, Zerrin Polvan, and Tayfun Yeşilşerit. 2006. "The Mosque as a Divisive Symbol in the Turkish Political Landscape." *Turkish Studies* 7 (3): 489–508.

Singer, Amy. 2002. *Constructing Ottoman Beneficence*. Albany: State University of New York Press.

———. 2008. *Charity in Islamic Societies*. Cambridge: Cambridge University Press.

Singer, Isaac Bashevis. 1966. *In My Father's Court*. New York: Farrar, Straus and Giroux.

Sirman, Nükhet. 1990. "State, Village, and Gender in Western Turkey." In *Turkish State, Turkish Society*, edited by Andrew Finkel and Nükhet Sirman, 21–51. New York: Routledge.

Slyomovics, Susan. 1998. *The Object of Memory*. Philadelphia: University of Pennsylvania Press.

Stirling, Paul. 1958. "Religious Change in Republican Turkey." *Middle East Journal* 12 (4): 395–408.

———. 1966. *Turkish Village*. New York: John Wiley and Sons.

Stokes, Martin. 1989. "Music, Fate, and State: Turkey's Arabesk Debate." *Middle East Report* 160: 27–30.

———. 1992. "Islam, the Turkish State, and Arabesk." *Popular Music* 11 (2): 213–27.

———. 2010. *The Republic of Love: Cultural Intimacy in Turkish Popular Music*. Chicago: University of Chicago Press.

Stone, Frank. 1974. "Rural Revitalization and the Village Institutes in Turkey: Sponsors and Critics." *Comparative Education Review* 18 (3): 419–29.

Sullivan, Winnifred Fallers. 2005. *The Impossibility of Religious Freedom*. Princeton, NJ: Princeton University Press.

———. 2011. *Prison Religion*. Princeton, NJ: Princeton University Press.

Swedenburg, Ted. 1990. "The Palestinian Peasant as National Signifier." *Anthropological Quarterly* 63 (1): 18–30.

Tambar, Kabir. 2010. "The Aesthetics of Public Visibility: Alevi Semah and the Paradoxes of Pluralism in Turkey." *Comparative Studies in Society and History* 52 (3): 652–79.

Tapper, Nancy. 1985. "Changing Wedding Rituals in a Turkish Town." *Journal of Turkish Studies* 9: 305–13.

———. 1990–91. "'Traditional' and 'Modern' Wedding Rituals in a Turkish Town." *International Journal of Turkish Studies* 5 (1–2): 135–54.

Tapper, Nancy, and Richard Tapper. 1987. "The Birth of the Prophet: Ritual and Gender in Turkish Islam." *Man* 22: 69–92.

———. 1987. "'Thank God We're Secular!' Aspects of Fundamentalism in a Turkish Town." In *Studies in Religious Fundamentalism*, edited by Lionel Caplan, 51–78. Albany: State University of New York Press.

Tapper, Richard, ed. 1991. *Islam in Modern Turkey*. New York: I. B. Tauris.

Taş, Kemaleddin. 2008. "The Social Status of the PRA in Turkey and Its Overall Assessment: Common Public Opinion." *Muslim World* 98 (April–July): 363–69.

Toprak, Binnaz. 1984. "Politicisation of Islam in a Secular State: The National Salvation Party in Turkey." In *From Nationalism to Revolutionary Islam*, edited by Said Amir Arjomand, 119–33. London: Macmillan.

Torab, Azam. 1996. "Piety as Gendered Agency." *Journal of the Royal Anthropological Institute* 2 (2): 235–52.

Trepanier, Nicolas. 2001. "Les Ordres: Tarikat et politique dans la Turquie republicaine." *Religiologiques* 23: 277–92.

Tugaç, Ahmet. 1974. "Indices of Modernization: Erenköy, a Case of Local Initiative." In *Turkey: Geographic and Social Perspectives*, edited by Erol Tümertekin, Peter Benedict, and Fatma Mansur, 156–78. Leiden: Brill.

Tuğal, Cihan. 2002. *Faces of the State: Secularism and Public Life in Turkey*. Princeton, NJ: Princeton University Press.

———. 2002. "Islamism in Turkey: Beyond Instrument and Meaning." *Economy and Society* 31 (1): 85–111.

———. 2006. "The Appeal of Islamic Politics." *Sociological Quarterly* 47: 245–73.

———. 2009. *Passive Revolution: Absorbing the Islamic Challenge*. Stanford, CA: Stanford University Press.

———. 2009. "Transforming Everyday Life: Islamism and Social Movement Theory." *Theory and Society* 38: 423–58.

Turam, Berna. 2004. "The Politics of Engagement between Islam and the Secular State." *British Journal of Sociology* 55 (2): 259–81.

———. 2007. *Between Islam and the State*. Stanford, CA: Stanford University Press.

Turan, Ömer. 2008. "The Turkish Diyanet Foundation." *Muslim World* 98 (April–July): 370–84.

Üstünova, Murafa, and Kerime Üstünova. 2006. "Soldier Wedding in Kaynarca." *Journal of Folklore Research* 43 (2): 175–85.

Van Gennep, Arnold. 1960. *The Rites of Passage*. Chicago: University of Chicago Press.

Vexliard, Alexandre, and Kemal Aytaç. 1964. "The 'Village Institutes' in Turkey." *Comparative Education Review* 8 (1): 41–47.

Wallerstein, Emmanuel. 1984. "The Development of the Concept of Development." *Sociological Theory* 2: 102–16.

Walton, Jeremy. 2009. "Horizons and Histories of Liberal Piety: Civil Islam and Secularism in Contemporary Turkey." Ph.D. diss., Department of Anthropology, University of Chicago.

———. 2010. "Practices of Neo-Ottomanism: Making Space and Place Virtuous in Istanbul." In *Orienting Istanbul: Cultural Capital of Europe?* edited by Levent Soysal, Deniz Göktürk, and Ipek Türeli, 88–103. London: Routledge.

Werbner, Pnina. 2003. *Pilgrims of Love*. Bloomington, IN: Indiana University Press.

White, Jenny. 1994. *Money Makes Us Relatives*. Austin: University of Texas Press.

———. 1999. "Islamic Chic." In *Istanbul: Between the Global and the Local*, edited by Çağlar Keyder, 77–91. New York: Rowman and Littlefield Publishers.

———. 2002. *Islamist Mobilization in Turkey: A Study in Vernacular Politics*. Seattle: University of Washington Press.

———. 2005. "The End of Islamism? Turkey's Muslimhood Model." In *Remaking Muslim Politics*, edited by Robert Hefner, 87–111. Princeton, NJ: Princeton University Press.

———. 2008. "Islam and Politics in Contemporary Turkey." In *The Cambridge History of Turkey*, vol. 4., *Turkey in the Modern World*, edited by Reşat Kasaba, 357–80. Cambridge: Cambridge University Press.

———. 2010. "Fear and Loathing in the Turkish National Imagination." *New Perspectives on Turkey* 19 (42) (Spring): 215–36.

Wolbert, Barbara. 2001. "The Visual Production of Location." *Visual Anthropology Review* 17 (1): 21–35.

Yalman, Nur. 1973. "Some Observations on Secularism in Islam: The Cultural Revolution in Turkey." *Daedalus* 102 (1): 139–68.

Yalpat, Altan. 1984. "Turkey's Economy Under the Generals." *MERIP Reports* 122: 16–24.

Yavuz, Hakan. 1999. "The Assassination of Collective Memory: The Case of Turkey." *Muslim World* 89 (3–4): 193–207.

———. 1999. "Toward an Islamic Liberalism? The Nurcu Movement and Fethullah Gülen." *Middle East Journal* 53 (4): 584–605.

———. 2000. "Cleansing Islam from the Public Sphere." *Journal of International Affairs* 54 (1): 21–42.

———. 2003. *Islamic Political Identity in Turkey.* Oxford: Oxford University Press.

———. 2004. "Is There a Turkish Islam? The Emergence of Convergence and Consensus." *Journal of Muslim Minority Affairs* 24 (2): 213–32.

Yavuz, Hakan, and John Esposito. 2003. *Turkish Islam and the Secular State: The Gülen Movement.* Syracuse, NY: Syracuse University Press.

Yılmaz, Ihsan. 2003. "Non-Recognition of Post-Modern Turkish Socio-Legal Reality and the Predicament of Women." *British Journal of Middle Eastern Studies* 30 (1): 25–41.

———. 2005. "State, Law, Civil Society, and Islam in Contemporary Turkey." *Muslim World* 95: 385–411.

Yükleyen, Ahmet. 2008. "Sufism and Islamic Groups in Contemporary Turkey." In *The Cambridge History of Turkey*, vol. 4, *Turkey in the Modern World*, edited by Reşat Kasaba, 381–87. Cambridge: Cambridge University Press.

———. 2009. "Localizing Islam in Europe: Religious Activism Among Turkish Islamic Organizations in the Netherlands." *Journal of Muslim Minority Affairs* 29 (3): 291–309.

———. 2010. "Production of Mystical Islam in Europe: Religious Authorization in the Süleymanlı Sufi Community." *Contemporary Islam* 4: 269–88.

———. 2012. *Localizing Islam in Europe.* Syracuse, NY: Syracuse University Press.

Zubaida, Sami 1996. "Turkish Islam and National Identity." *Middle East Report* 199 (April–June): 10–15.

Zürcher, Erik 1992. "The Ottoman Legacy of the Turkish Republic." *Die Welt des Islams* 32 (2): 237–53.

———. 2004. *Turkey: A Modern History.* London: I. B. Tauris.

INDEX

Page numbers in italics refer to illustrations.

modernization: alternative modernities, 168; attempts to modernize villages, 36–37; cultural Islamic traditions threaten, 152; differing paths to, 17; in early Republican reforms, 32–33, 36; elites associated with, 79; feeling of cultural loss as result of, 210; good deeds critique economic modernity, 76, 88–89; as illiberal social engineering project, 188; Islamic modernity, 76, 108, 136, 140; Islamist modernity, 107, 168–69; Kemalist support for, 8, 40, 188; modern *hafız*, 228; modernity as telos of progressive secular time, 43–44; modernity expressed through the body, 241; modernity seen as western, 44; modern self, 44; Ottoman Empire contrasted with, 170; pious modernity, 76–77, 89; progressive constructions of modernity, 168; Republican People's Party supports, 180; secular, modern citizens as goal of public education, 109, 172, 175, 231; secular education and modernism, 172; as urban in design, 15–16; used to create certain kind of person, 23; village accepts state construction of, 153; women's bodies as symbol of, 187

mosques, 90–113; classical Ottoman, 94–95, 110; in Cologne, 90, 220; DITIB, 202–3, 204, 212, 213; Diyanet as responsible for, 90, 94; groups seen as legitimated by meeting in, 204–5; for immigrants, 221; *külliye* (mosque complexes) pared down to, 91–94; as male domain, 61, 94, 96, 114, 115, 120, 161; Mevluts in, 125, 161, 167; minarets, 90, 108, 110; *namaz* in, 96, 115, 120; Neo-Ottoman, 91, 95; olive oil donations to, 84; political aspect of, 95; from prayer houses to, 97–99, 111; Sakal-ı Şerif (hair of the Prophet) at, 129–31; seen as symptom of re-Islamicization, 91; state control of, 29, 112; state suspicion of, 176; Süleymaniye in Istanbul, 93, 110; in towns, 2; in United States, 90–91; village, 90, 96, 98–99, 104–12, 142; in western Europe, 90; women avoid, 15, 62, 96–97, 107, 114, 115, 129–30; women's sections, 96, 99, 131, 161; in Yuntdağ region, 95–97

mountaintops: holy men associated with, 11, 120–21; nationalist use of, 121–22; pre-Islamic spiritual significance of, 122; state suspicion of, 176

mourning rituals, 68–73, 137

Mueggler, Erik, 8
Muhammediye, 122–23, 124, 155
Muhammed Zühdü, 11, 120–21, 126, 127, 173, 175, 205–6, 219, 224
Muradiye, mosque complex, 110
music: in Alevi ritual, 27; arabesk in, 32; at circumcision rituals, 66; *davul*, 156–60, 166, 167, 181; at engagement parties, 163; Islamists see as sinful, 12; as *mubah*, 157; replaced in wedding rituals, 152–53, 155, 156–60, 165–67, 181; *zurna*, 156–60, 166, 167, 181
muskas (amulets), 104, 173–74, 255n36

Nakşibendi order, 93, 206
namaz (prayer), 48–56; accumulating, 52–53, 54–56; missed, 54; in the mosque, 96, 115, 120; for soldier's departure, 67; at Süleymancı Qur'an schools, 215; what people feel when they perform, 53; by women, 96–97
naming of a baby, as a life course ritual, 56
Navaro-Yashin, Yael, 23, 68, 122
Necipoğlu-Kafadar, Gülru, 94–96
Neo-Ottomanism: as legitimizing foundation for new forms of Islam, 19, 108; *mehter* bands, 166, 167; mosque architecture, 91, 95, 108, 111; as response to western modernity, 44
neo-tarikats. See Islamic brotherhoods (*tarikats*; neo-tarikats)
Neyzi, Leyla, 210
nonmovements, 140, 241–42
Nurcus, 31, 41, 195, 200, 206, 210
Nursi, Said, 210

Öcalan, Abdullah, 252n18
Of, 101–5, 124, 128, *144*, 152, 160, 186
olive oil, 83–89
orthodoxy: blurring line with orthopraxy, 173; debates over, 2, 6; essentializing, 169–70; ethnographic approach to, 5; as in flux, 156; mosque architecture affected by, 90; orthodoxization, 154; reality of religion and choices about, 171; on Sakal-ı Şerif (hair of the Prophet), 128; as skewed toward men's needs, 15, 124; urban and rural questioning of, 151; villagers' concern with standards of, 87, 169
orthopraxy: anxieties about, 5; blurring

rain prayers (*yağmur duası*), 51, 95, 99, 114, 115
Rasmussen, Susan, 259n27
Refah Party, 40, 42, 208, 209, 251n6
religious authority: competing claims to, 1–24;
    location as factor in, 205; rural women seek
    outside the mosque, 168; of women, 58
religious holidays, 46
Republic, the, 25–32; establishment of, 26;
    Islamic education and the state during early,
    175–81; as secular, 26; as urban-oriented, 172.
    See also Atatürk (Mustafa Kemal)
Republican People's Party. *See* Cumhuriyet
    Halk Partisi
ritual washing (*aptes*), 48, 129
Roy, Olivier, 8, 195, 197, 198, 199, 207, 213, 214, 219
Rubu-u Daire, 219
rural Islam. *See* villagers
Ruhul Beyan (Bursevi), 213
Rutz, Henry J., 172

Saadet Party, 40, 208
sadaka (justice), 77–78
Said, Edward, 170
saints (holy men): differing attitudes toward
    venerating, 136; Mevlana, 126–27; on moun-
    taintops, 11, 120–21; Muhammed Zühdü,
    11, 120–21, 126, 127, 173, 175, 219; prayers to,
    95; tombs of, 30, 120, 121, 122, 126, 137, 154,
    176, 257n15; women and veneration of, 126;
    women's prayer service to Süleyman Hoca,
    117–27, *147*, 160
Sakal-ı Şerif (hair of the Prophet), 6, 19, 99,
    104, 108, 127–34
sala (prayer for the dead), 68–69
şalvar (baggy trousers), 1, 189, 190, 219, 228–30,
    239
Schielke, Samuli, 7
schoolteachers, 190–91
Schultz, Dorothea, 7
Scott, James C., 84
script, change of, 209–10, 219
secular education, 184–94; aim of, 172; com-
    munists associated with, 177; headscarves
    in public schools, 183, 187–91, 192–93; in
    Imam Hatip schools, 11, 183; Islamic schools
    replaced with, 30; religion classes in, 183;
    secular, modern citizens as goal of pub-
    lic education, 109, 172, 175, 231; villagers'
    divergent attitudes toward, 242; villagers on
    value of, 172

secularization: activists wish to return to con-
    dition prior to, 6; after election of 1950, 32,
    181; Atatürk in, 30, 74; calendars as secular,
    46; and care for the dead, 73; contradic-
    tory views of, 30; after coup of 1980, 9, 219;
    cultural Islamic traditions threaten, 152;
    debate over, 15; different leaders enforce
    or relax, 49; differing paths to, 17; in early
    Republican reforms, 32–33, 36, 128; Erdoğan
    on American secularism, 196–97; feeling
    of cultural loss as result of, 209–10; under
    İnönü, 10; and Islamic education in early
    Republic, 175–81; Kemalist support for, 8,
    40, 171; *külliye* functions curtailed in, 94;
    laicism distinguished from secularism, 28;
    leftism associated with, 177; mosques and,
    91; Neo-Ottomanism versus, 19; opposition
    to, 26, 32, 180; Ottoman Empire contrasted
    with, 170; purifying movements as secu-
    larist, 154; Republican People's Party sup-
    ports, 180; rural and provincial Anatolians
    oppose, 32; secular, modern citizens as goal
    of public education, 109, 172, 175, 231; secu-
    lar Muslims, 223–41; secular self, 44; secular
    time constructed in, 43; state-sponsored,
    3, 7, 9; Süleymancı community emerges in
    reaction to, 31, 219–20; as urban, 14–16, 231;
    used to create certain kind of person, 23;
    village accepts state construction of mod-
    ernization, 153; villagers' involvement in
    secularism, 7. *See also* laicism
Şeker Bayramı, holiday, *143*
sermons (*sohbets*): at engagement parties,
    164–65; replacing music and dance in wed-
    dings with, 152–53, 155, 163, 165–66
shamans, 121
Shankland, David, 119
Shi'a Islam, 29, 137, 154
short-sleeved shirts, subject of, 241
Silverstein, Brian, 152, 196
sin: accumulating *namaz* (prayer) to offset,
    52–53; alcohol use as, 159; the beach associ-
    ated with, 235; cultural Islamic traditions
    seen as, 22; *davul* music as, 160; elderly
    concern about accumulated, 49–50, 51;
    fun seen as leading to, 12, 65; good deeds
    weighed against, 164; short-sleeved shirts
    seen as, 241; throwing bread on ground as,
    118; women's fear of, 117
Singer, Amy, 78, 92, 93, 94

vaiz (religious leader), 100, 104, 164, 182, 215, 256n42

Vakıflar Bankası (Vakif Bank), 92

vakıfs. *See* Islamic foundations (*vakıfs*)

Van Gennep, Arnold, 66

Verband der Islamischen Kulturzentren. *See* Islamic Cultural Center (Islam Kültür Derneği)

Village Institutes (Köy Institütleri), 36, 39

villagers, 32–38; as agents of spiritual, economic, and infrastructural transformation, 168–69; anxiety over religious practices, 4–5, 30; attempts to modernize villages, 36–37; attitudes toward tarikats, 200; on being alone, 71; being a villager as existential question, 16; children sent to Süleymancı Qur'an schools, 216–19; constructed as closed, protected, religious, and conservative, 235–36; disagreements among, 242; drawbacks of village life, 16; as drawn to cities, 37; everyone knows everyone else, 226; family involvement in children's marriages, 214; features of state control in villages, 111–13; geographic stereotypes of, 171; headscarves required in villages, 38, 227, 229; in historical framework of Republic, 170; increasing involvement in urban life, 162; interviewed in this study, 13; Islamic associations, 3, 9; on Islamic education's value, 172–73; Islamic folk ritual enjoyed by, 51; Islamic time and the village, 43–73; in Islamist movements, 7, 8, 124, 153, 167–68; isolation of women absent among, 85–86; *izin* (permission) required for, 5, 237; marginalization of, 33, 38, 169; men run villages, 34; migration of, 7, 32, 33–34, 35, 38, 74, 124, 162, 193, 223–24; mixed religious practices of, 3, 14, 22, 164, 168, 217; mosque construction supported by, 90; Ottoman words used by, 123; pressure to conform among, 223; public and private elided by, 85; purifying movements compared with debates of, 151; as racialized ideological motif, 35–36, 41; rurality as politically charged category, 34; on rural life as more moral than urban life, 75; rural versus urban Islam, 8, 124, 151, 152, 169, 198, 223, 242–43; on secular education's value, 172; secularization, modernization, and westernization ignore, 16; in secular

world, 223–41; seen as underclass, 6, 8; settle in Manisa, 7, 14, 23, 124, 162, 193; social egalitarianism among, 16, 79; soldier's departure marked in, 67; the state has little interest in providing services for, 194; Süleymancı community as active in rural areas, 195, 209, 220, 221–22; as suspicious of fun, 50–51; as traditionally pious, 6; villages as bounded social spaces, 37–38; women's dress, 189–90

Wahabis, 152

Walton, Jeremy, 28, 30, 200

wedding ritual (*düğün*): circumcision ritual compared with, 63, 66; guests cluster according to kin or village, 130; Mevluts at, 160; music and dance replaced, 152–53, 155, 156–60, 165–67, 181; of Zübeyde, 225–26

westernization: cultural Islamic traditions threaten, 152; in early Republican reforms, 32–33, 36; Intellectuals' Hearth (Aydınlar Ocağı) on, 40; Kemalist support for, 8, 40; modernity seen as western, 44; nationalist defensive response to, 44; Ottoman Empire contrasted with, 170; Republican People's Party supports, 180; secular time constructed in, 43; as urban in design, 15–16; used to create certain kind of person, 23; village accepts state construction of modernization, 153; western self, 44

White, Jenny, 23, 80, 86, 187, 196–97

women: barriers to education for, 177–78, 185–93; cannot name a baby, 56; in carpet-weaving cooperative, 14, 18, 20, 75, 81, 85, 88, 124, 154, 162, 225; clothing for village, 38, 59, 189–90; cultural Islamic traditions led by, 6, 97; daily routine of, 46–47; dancing by, 65, 153, 157, 158; do not participate in slaughtering animals, 63–64; elderly make pilgrimage to Mecca, 116; female hocas from the Süleymancı community, 4, 11–12, 58, 115, 164, 203, 205, 206, 209, 215, 247n2; female-led Mevluts, 124–25; folk Islam associated with, 167; freedom of movement in villages, 16; Friday gatherings (Cuma Toplantısı), 134–36, *148*, 163; gender constraints on, 237–38, 240; girls achieve education, marry outside village, and assume secular lifestyle, 12; girls become women through marriage, 63, 67; *hafız*, 182; healing by, 117; in hetero-